DATE DUE			

Production and Inventory Management
in the
Technological Age

PAUL DEIS

Production and Inventory Management in the Technological Age

PRENTICE-HALL, INC. Englewood Cliffs, N.J. 07632

Library of Congress Cataloging in Publication Data

DEIS, PAUL.
  Production and inventory management in the technological age.

  Bibliography: p.
  Includes index.
  1. Production management.   I. Title.
TS155.D46 1983   658.5   82-23189
ISBN 0-13-724336-7

658.5
D36 P
128578
apn.1984

Printed in the United States of America

10 9 8 7 6 5 4 3 2 1

Editorial/production supervision
and interior design by Tom Aloisi
Cover design by 20/20 Services Inc.
Manufacturing buyer: Anthony Caruso

ISBN 0-13-724336-7

Prentice-Hall International, Inc., *London*
Prentice-Hall of Australia Pty. Limited, *Sydney*
Prentice-Hall Canada, Inc., *Toronto*
Editora Prentice-Hall do Brasil, Ltda., *Rio de Janeiro*
Prentice-Hall of India Private Limited, *New Delhi*
Prentice-Hall of Japan, Inc., *Tokyo*
Prentice-Hall of Southeast Asia Pte. Ltd., *Singapore*
Whitehall Books Limited, *Wellington, New Zealand*

To Richard, Jodi, Michele, Kathy, and Henry

Contents

3

MASTER PLANNING—SALES AND PRODUCTION, 24

4

PRODUCT STRUCTURES, 57

5

MANUFACTURING OPERATIONS AND WORK CENTER MANAGEMENT, 78

6

INVENTORY, 94

7

EXECUTING THE BUSINESS PLAN—MATERIAL, 120

9

MEASURING PERFORMANCE—
CLOSING ALL THE LOOPS, 216

12

KEY COMPUTER FACTORS, 281

13

THE PRESENT IS
THE FUTURE, 305

Preface

As this book goes to press, the United States is still in the grip of the worst recession since the Depression. Major manufacturing industries are especially hard hit. Unlike other recessions, however, a significant portion of this recession seems to be caused by the accumulated effects of poor management over many years in much of the manufacturing sector of the economy.

This effort is, of course, addressed to that sector. I felt a book was needed that stressed a broad grasp of the issues involved in truly effective manufacturing management, rather than a narrow technical proficiency in what I believe to be only part of the subject matter. This, then, became my objective in writing this book—to attempt to achieve true insight in the reader as to the essential interrelatedness of the three major factors that seem to be consistently found in the most successful manufacturing companies.

These three factors are as follows: development of a highly productive, participative social culture within the company, real excellence at the basics of good business management, and the effective use of formal systems (which these days includes advanced computer systems). Many companies seem to be trying to be successful by working at only one or two of these areas. In writing this book, my intention has been to stimulate interest, serious thought, discussion, and further investigation of these three major areas on the part of the reader. Above all, I hope managers blame outside factors less frequently for their lack of success when there is so much to be done at home.

I want to emphasize, above all, that there is little in this book that is original. I have only brought together the ideas of many others that are found in daily successful use in many companies. What originality there is perhaps lies in the presentation and the attempt to show the essential interrelatedness of basic good management, advanced computer technology, and the way people are treated in a company.

It is important to note what was not attempted here. I felt that technical completeness or proficiency at solving certain types of problems would just beg the entire question. (Moreover, no one person could write this book in the 80s, and even if it were possible, the end result would be a book that no one could lift.) These approaches have been in use for years and have demonstrably failed to produce a generation of red-hot manufacturing managers that can compete in a worldwide economy.

Recent signs and trends in manufacturing management are encouraging; many people in the field are starting to take a hard look at their operations and ask difficult questions. Interest in how the Japanese make things so well is growing rapidly. I prefer to believe that we are in the beginnings of a renewal, a renaissance, in manufacturing. It is to those people who want to be, or already are, a part of this process that I have directed my thoughts, words, and drawings in this book.

October, 1982   *Paul Deis, Marina Del Rey, California*

Acknowledgments

In any book such as this, where many powerful insights came to me from so many sources over a long period of time, a complete list of those who helped is impossible, or at least impractical. However, there is a handful of individuals whose support proved invaluable in actually completing the book. There is a second group of people who participated more indirectly in that their insights came to life in my mind, then matured and grew.

Of special note is Richard Watson, former editor of *Systems User Magazine,* my partner and closest friend, whose strong support, editing skill, and personal and technical wisdom helped turn a manuscript into a book. Bill Scott, master Manufacturing Engineer and P&IC instructor for many years, helped me get started with his encouragement, reviewed parts of the manuscript, and made useful suggestions.

My associates on the Board of Directors of the Los Angeles Chapter of APICS (The American Production and Inventory Control Society) who were especially helpful included Bob Williams, Paul Funk, Alan Farr, and Professor Bob DeVoe of California State University, Long Beach.

Reaching a little further back into the past, Ken Young, Harris White, and Ron Gardner were my best guides in the art, science, and systems of production management. Barbara Rahe Lindsey was most important in helping me learn how to deal with the vast intricacies of computers and manufacturing systems software. I must have learned something, because instead of the usual credit to the typist/slave who typed and retyped the manuscript, I can only give credit to the word processing system I used to write the bulk of the manuscript. Lonely perhaps, but incredibly efficient.

Production and Inventory Management in the Technological Age

Introduction

People who spend their energies developing and implementing business information systems are, by and large, visionaries. As a result, these efforts have their share of failures and some outstanding successes. Isaac Newton, the early English physicist, once said in a letter to a contemporary: "If I have seen farther than you, it has been by standing on the shoulders of giants." A similar statement could be made about the people who pioneered the systems discussed in this book.

Twenty years ago, production and inventory control was a largely clerical, statistically oriented, rather minor technical field in the spectrum of business management. Even manufacturing executives regarded it as a rather low-level skill area, if they recognized it at all. It was not a very exciting activity.

All this has changed. The development of computers of almost unbelievable power has provided systems designers and managers with a set of tools that could not have been previously imagined. Whole new concepts of how a business can be run became possible. Manufacturing businesses are generally the most complex form of business in existence and the most basic to a nation's economy. The computer, coupled with the visions of committed managers and imaginative system designers, has been used to develop a set of exciting, startlingly powerful concepts for managing these kinds of businesses.

From a relatively fragmented beginning, these concepts have been forged into a cohesive, integrated framework suitable for managing virtually any inventory-oriented business, especially manufacturing. Properly implemented, the results in many companies have bordered on astonishing.

Whereas there is a great deal in the published literature about the various aspects and pieces of this integrated framework, there is little that shows how the pieces fit together, or conveys the sense of excitement many in the field feel for these systems.

This book attempts to convey this sense of excitement and vision to readers in management, in more technical positions in the field, and to business students. By showing how all the parts of a fully integrated system fit together to form a comprehensive basis for managing the business, it is hoped that readers will take a set of concepts with them that they can use to understand and better manage the specific businesses and systems which they encounter.

Since the field of manufacturing planning and control systems is in fact rather complex and technical, in order to present it in a book of reasonable length, some of the more involved technical details in each subject area have been omitted. In any case, these details often vary widely from one industry and system to the next. As a result, to get value from the book, readers do not need to have an extensive background in either computer systems or inventory control.

The news media often seem to have a greater appetite for bad news than for good. Hence it is not surprising that some of the outstanding results achieved with these systems have gone largely unpublicized. Some of the results include:

- Dramatic reductions in inventory investment while sales show huge increases and inventory unit costs are climbing
- Cutting in-plant processing time from four months to four weeks
- Virtual elimination of customer back orders while reducing finished-goods inventory levels
- Substantial increases in profit margins while holding selling prices constant, even though material and labor costs increase

One of the primary economic indicators for years has been the inventory-to-sales ratio, which is used as a "leading" indicator for economic up- and downturns. Even though the kind of system discussed in this book is far from being the norm, the progress that has been made in inventory control thus far has been enough to cause many economists to alter their interpretation of this indicator. Inventories, in the aggregate, no longer suffer from over- and understocked conditions to the extent that has been the norm for decades.

Looking to the future, there seems little question that these advanced, integrated systems will eventually become the norm for business. Of course, new concepts will be developed in time that will enhance those presented here, and additional levels of sophistication will be reached to make these systems somewhat easier to manage on a day-to-day basis. Whatever develops in the future, however, it seems clear that the advances will be built on the conceptual foundations discussed in the following chapters.

1

The
New Environment

As the sun rose on the 1980s, manufacturers and distributors were faced with a new environment in which to operate. Gone were the days where companies that had dominated a particular market could pretty much count on things continuing that way. A variety of new problems now confront the management of these companies that will simply not go away. This book acknowledges the existence of these problems and focuses on the way well-managed companies of the present and probably the majority of those in the future will need to operate in order to survive.

Until fairly recently, management has experienced a world in which computers were only for the giant companies that could afford them, and where raw materials and purchased parts were in relatively plentiful supply at reasonable, predictable prices. Labor costs, especially skilled labor, was more a matter of how much one had to pay in a particular part of the country rather than whether labor could be had at all. Until the early 1970s, the availability of capital was not a pressing problem, since even fairly small companies could raise capital through the public equity market, and failing that, could usually raise debt capital either through the commercial paper market or through banks. The primary source of interference in management plans for its personnel were unions, and even there, a measure of predictability was obtained. In most parts of the country, labor could be counted on to turn in a relatively productive day's work.

Product life cycles were longer than those experienced at present, and the products themselves were somehow simpler to design, make, and sell. The time, investment, and risk required for new products were also less. The investment in inventory that was required was always seen to be a problem for control, but generally was dealt with by relatively crude techniques of estimates, guesses, and simply physically controlling it once it was in-house. Although outwardly sophisticated and complex, many companies have been managed for years by what may be referred to as the "holler and bellow" school of management: management by pressure on key executives. This is the "I don't care how you get it done, just do it" style of management.

This relatively informal way of doing business has been declining for some time under the pressure of greatly increased costs of doing business, more government regulation, skyrocketing material costs, labor difficulties, increased product complexity, capital shortages, the energy crisis, and related factors that have become part of our everyday business life. As is usually the case, some companies are far ahead of others in the development of more effective ways of managing in this environment. These companies are, in general, either more farsighted than their competitors, or are in the position of being more exposed to these problems than other companies. Some of them have simply had to get smarter or not continue to do business. Virtually all of these techniques involve a more formal method of operating a business, more integration of company activities, and team approaches to management (as opposed to relatively autonomous departments).

Thus the new environment is spawning an entirely new approach to managing business. In some industries, these techniques are already common, whereas in others they are still unknown. It seems only a matter of time before they become commonplace in every industry. For this reason this book will not address the traditional methods of managing inventory and production. The traditional, informal manual methods are becoming obsolete.

The key to this entire climate of change is, of course, the computer. Two major developments in this area have brought about this revolution in how companies are managed in inventory-oriented businesses. The first, well known, is the incredible drop in hardware costs. It is now cost effective (profitable, in other words) for even the smallest business to use computer systems to manage all its records. Often overlooked is that even though small computers are cheap, the internal workings are often even more complex than the larger computers of only a few years ago. Yet on the outside, to the operator of the system, they are made to appear simpler and easy to use.

Of even greater importance as far as this book is concerned is the convergence of thinking in the software development area. The American Production and Inventory Control Society (APICS) has for many years been at the forefront of efforts to develop a variety of powerful concepts, which when translated into programs, will yield a comprehensive, formal business system that can be used without modification in a startling variety of businesses. Many brilliant minds at a number of companies, working in conjunction with their counterparts at the larger computer companies, have developed these systems through a whole series of false starts, occasional outstanding successes, inadequate concepts, and the like, to produce a systems approach that permits (and requires) an entirely new way of managing a business.

As the reasons for the lack of success of otherwise proven systems have become better understood, it has become apparent that the systems themselves are no longer the reason for the lack of success. The most common single cause now is failure of top management to understand how a business must be managed with the new tools, and to bring about the policy and management changes required to allow these systems to function fully. This lack of success does not mean that these systems were failures. The point of view here is that these systems and the management tools they embody are such a radical change from anything experienced in the past that a high percentage of "failures" should be expected.

A similar, much simpler example can be found in the introduction of numerically controlled machinery. These pieces of equipment have been around for a long time, yet years were required before manufacturing began to understand fully how best to use them. Other examples can be found in other areas. Successful businessmen are by nature conservative survivors, like bankers. This is how they stay in business for many years, come what may. Yet at the same time, innovation in some areas is a necessity to maintain the progress of the business, and if management does not foster innovation in its own company, sooner or later someone in another company will.

We believe that examples of this "future shock" abound in industry after industry, as management tries to cope with the often enormous, frustrating pressures from government, the capital markets, and foreign competition, not to mention advanced technology. Who would have thought 10 or 15 years ago that the major competitors in the watchmaking industry would be coming from companies that were not even in the watch business at the time?

Planning and Control

The fundamental point of the new business environment is planning and control to a level that could hardly be conceived in most companies only a few years ago. To survive, companies that do the best job of understanding their markets, plan for meeting those needs the most effectively, and carry those plans out with well-managed, well-controlled activities are those that will be successful in every industry. Those companies that attempt to meet the competition with hunches instead of market research, with estimates and guesses in place of solid forecasts, and that try to continue to expedite their goals into reality will be having a progressively harder time of things as the future continues to become the present.

This book is a conceptual guideline for managing in the new environment with the new tools. Planning and control are, of necessity, a company-wide exercise. The point of view of top management is one that must be maintained at all times, since to do otherwise will fragment the goals of top management into opposing factions within the key departments. To function with maximum effectiveness, managers of a company must function as an interrelated team, with a common set of information, ground rules, improved communication, and common goals. An understanding of how each company function affects and is dependent on others is vital to achieving this level of effectiveness.

Planning assumes many guises. It is important to remember that there are many levels and types of plans within a single company. The more they all use an integrated set of data for their starting point, the better. The more clearly the interrelationships among various plans are understood, the better. The more frequently plans are updated and compared with actual results, the better. The more that reasons for discrepancies between planned and actual results are explored, understood, and factored into the revised plan, the better.

Any experienced top management executive will probably observe that these truisms are easy to say, but hard to do. That is certainly true. For manufacturing management particularly, the level of detail required to plan much of anything has always been so overwhelming that without computer systems, it was just not practical. With the new systems, however, this is no longer true. Detailed planning, forecasting of sales, calculations of requirements for resources, and countless other previously difficult tasks become not only achievable, but practical. And once they become practical, it is only a matter of time before they become standard techniques everywhere.

Computer Systems Assumed

Once one realizes the incredible efficiency of properly designed computer systems, it becomes immediately apparent that if part of a business can be handled better by computer systems, it is likely that a lot more of it can be similarly better handled. Much of the thinking in this area is dominated by assumptions that were developed during the period when the computer was difficult to use, expensive, and something that had to be applied very carefully to be cost effective. This, too, is an assumption that is disappearing. In the early days, one had to prepare data carefully to be input into the computer, correct computer errors, and so on. Only certain information could profitably be kept in the computer system. Even the task of entering data was very labor intensive.

The newer systems, however, extended the function of the computer into the person actually doing the job, as a technique to assist that person in the physical execution of the task. When one compares, for example, entering a sales order into an earlier computerized system, where the order was written up on a form, then sent to the data processing department for input and processing, with the technique of having an interactive terminal used by an order desk clerk to prepare the order itself, the difference becomes immediately apparent.

In the earlier case, the desk clerk must make all decisions and locate all information for the order manually, whereas in the later case, the computer actually provides all information needed to make the correct customer service decisions and actually prepare the order. At the end of the cycle, usually totaling one or two minutes, the order has not only been entered into the system, but all relevant decisions have been made in the process and supplied to the customer as required.

Frequently heard is the argument that this kind of approach costs a lot of money. But what is the alternative? The alternative is people—now very expensive, even for a clerk. Many companies now find that a clerk costs $20,000 per year to have in the business. The only way to increase significantly the productivity of such personnel is through this type of use of computer systems.

To reiterate, even for the smallest business, a computer system can prove to be a profitable investment. Let us turn it around and look at it another way. In a competitive situation, a company making extensive use of a computer system will simply have a lower cost of doing business. Can one afford, then, *not* to use a computer? Probably not, as a general rule. Of course, this position should be hedged somewhat by pointing out that the usual rule involving a capital investment versus a short-term expense must be considered. If one is planning on being in business only a short time, a computer may not pay off. Overall, however, the extensive use of computer systems throughout a manufacturing and distribution business is assumed. Virtually every concept in this book will involve the use of a computer system, either to maintain records or to develop management decision information from computer-maintained records.

Integrated Information

Integrated information, in a company context, means that all company functions use the same set of data for their information needs: in other words, base their decisions on the same set of records. This approach eliminates many, many conflicts that are traditional in many companies between accounting and engineering, material control and purchasing, the shop and marketing, and so on. One of the oldest battles concerns product structure information (bills of material). In many companies, one set of bill of material information was kept by accounting for costing purposes, another by design engineering for drawing records, and still another for manufacturing engineering for use in making the product, and sometimes still another by inventory control for planning material requirements.

Under an integrated business information concept, there is only one "real" set of bill of material records, used for all purposes. Again, this decision has only a little to do with the software itself. It has mostly to do with a top management decision to manage the company this way. Since this approach has time and again proven itself to be more effective than the fragmented one, it is assumed that this approach is the one to use, and the fragmented method will not be discussed.

The integrated approach becomes even clearer if one looks at the relationship between marketing and production. If marketing and production are not working to a commonly agreed sales/production plan, they will be at war. And this kind of disagreement, particularly on an ongoing basis, becomes quite expensive, although management will never get a regular report entitled "This Month's Cost of Departmental Disagreements."

The New Environment

One can begin to get a glimpse of how the future (and present) is shaping up at this point. The optimally managed manufacturing and distribution business, using the tools now available, will find that several assumptions are inherent in its management. One can list them as follows:

1. The company is managed primarily by formal systems, with specific, stated rules, criteria for decisions, and explicit procedures.
2. All work is done to the business plan rather than to the urgencies of the moment. If there is a problem, it is because the plan was not smart enough, and it is in the planning that the problem must be fixed. The day-to-day reality is governed by the plan, which was decided on quite some time in advance.
3. All company departments utilize the same data base. There is only one set of part numbers, cost figures, engineering information, schedules, and requirements. All management information is ultimately derived from this common data base; all decisions are reflected by information available in the data base.
4. Computers are cheap; people and material are expensive. Therefore, if the productivity of resources can be increased by using a computer, one is used.
5. One of the primary business needs is for flexibility—the ability to react quickly to change in spite of long lead times and rapidly changing market factors. Any computer technique is used that enables this response time to be shortened.
6. Those individuals who are the strongest managers in the company are those who understand how to work with a formal system, understand the company's computer systems, and most of all, understand how to work in a team with managers in other departments.

These assumptions are reflected throughout this book. The systems techniques described in the following pages have at their foundation the assumption that the business in general is managed in this way. The reason for this is simple. A formal system—and that is what these computer application systems are—simply cannot be made to work in an environment where management does not work within its own system, using instead the more traditional, informal techniques that preceded the development of these methods of managing a manufacturing and/or distribution business.

It should be pointed out that in the past, a great many company managers have supported the purchase of a computer system because they thought it could be simply brought in and somehow grafted onto the company's previous way of doing business. The belief that discrepancies between planned and actual could somehow be "forced" into existence by applying pressure to key people will die a slow, agonizing death, taking with it the companies in which these beliefs are the strongest. This is not to say that the pressure to perform inside a company can somehow be eliminated. It certainly cannot be. It definitely can be directed into more productive channels, however. And with the tools these systems provide, that is exactly what can and should happen.

CHAPTER 1 QUESTIONS

1. How have the availability and cost of the primary inputs to manufacturing changed in recent times?
2. How do informal and formal systems fit into the new manufacturing environment?
3. What is the most common reason manufacturing systems projects fall short of their expectations?
4. How do computers fit into the new methods of business?
5. Describe what "integrated information" means.
6. List the operating assumptions found in the optimally managed manufacturing and distribution business.

2

Key Concepts

Business Structure and Functions

The purpose of a business, it is often said, is to make a profit for those who have invested their money in the enterprise. However, as a business grows in size and the shareholders participate less and less directly in the profitability of the company, another definition is needed. The function of profits in this case is more to ensure the long-term survival of the company. Overall wealth accumulated by a company, then, can be said to be its prime goal, since this wealth (its assets) is the means by which it attains all other goals.

A successful, ongoing business accumulates this wealth by fulfilling the needs of its customers over a long period of time. For a manufacturing or distribution business, this may mean a continual evolution in the company's product offerings in response to a continued change in customers' needs. Staying in touch with these needs and actually getting products in customers' hands involves a considerable effort in the marketing and selling areas. The essential element for the long run includes staying in touch with and responding to changes in customers' needs. Mere selling of existing product lines can be successful only in the short run, and has been responsible for many a company's demise. Their products became obsolete.

To meet these needs, as defined by the marketing effort, a company must actually obtain the products, either by buying them from someone else and reselling them, or by buying other products and performing operations on them to add value—in other words, manufacturing them. Forming a link between the marketing and manufacturing efforts is the development of new products.

For a smaller business, with an easier-to-follow market and fewer, less complex products, keeping track of the variables involved in this process is somewhat more straightforward than in a larger firm. As a company grows in size and complexity, its staff also increases in size and complexity. Each department or division begins to operate relatively independently. The management philosophy in many firms today is derived from that of Alfred Sloan of General Motors. Sloan organized GM into independent divisions which competed with each other, fostering an aggressive, competitive, do-the-other-guys-in atmosphere. That this philosophy has been successful for many years is an understatement.

In recent years, however, newer management techniques have developed that take advantage of technologies not previously available. More has also been learned about what motivates people. The new technology is in the form of complex, highly integrated computer systems. The people skills that work best with these management tools are in the form of a more cooperative, teamwork environment in which management works together to achieve companywide goals. The Japanese have provided some stunning examples of the effectiveness of this approach when it is properly carried out.

Figure 2–1 illustrates what may be referred to as the structural hierarchy of a manufacturing business. At the preeminent, top position is the satisfaction of customer needs. To continue fulfilling customer needs in the long run, financial goals must be met. As a result, everything the company does must, ideally, contribute to these financial goals. The translation of the identified needs of the market, through the product development, production, and sales cycles, is the mechanism by which a company ensures its long-term existence and success.

In a manufacturing business, this process involves a tremendous amount of information, flowing from the market planning and engineering areas through the production planning, manufacturing activities, purchasing, and cost control parts of the business. State-of-the-art manufacturing systems allow more efficient communication of this flow of information between the various parts of the business, while allowing a great many smaller decisions to be made automatically.

The flow of information may be visualized as planning information start-

FIGURE 2-1
Business structure
hierarchy.

ing at the "top" of the hierarchy and flowing downward as more detailed plans are developed throughout the organization. The decision to offer a certain product, for example, in turn produces a sales forecast for how many are expected to be sold. This, in turn, leads to a planned production schedule, itself used to calculate the dependent demand for manufactured subassemblies, and finally, plans for purchasing material and plant equipment.

The control side of the picture runs more or less in reverse of the plan, flowing upward in the hierarchy. Monitoring purchased parts deliveries, for example, improves the chances of being able to meet production schedules for subassemblies. If the production and costs of these variables are kept according to plan, meeting final assembly production schedules and therefore sales forecast goals becomes possible.

This same planning and control logic applies to both the short and the long range. An integrated, state-of-the-art system can provide invaluable assistance to management in identifying areas of risk, potential barriers to accomplishing the goals, and in general shortening the response time to changes in the business environment. It is in this context that the systems concepts discussed in the following chapters should be placed. These concepts have the effect of pulling the entire business together in a more tightly knit, smoothly interrelated unit, enabling it to perform in ways that previously would have been impossible.

Systems—Formal and Informal

There are about five or six common definitions of the word *system*. Referred to here is the notion that a business information system is the logic, both stated and unstated, by which information is handled and the activities of the business are carried out using that information. The idea of interrelationships is central. Excluded are other types of systems, such as philosophical systems, although these, too, have logic and interrelationships.

Figure 2–2 illustrates what we refer to as the systems continuum. Information and management activities inside a business use a complex mix of formal and informal systems. The continuum shows the distinction between formal and informal as extremes. No company has a total management system that is

Informal	Formal
←	→
Personal	Impersonal
Very Flexible	Less Flexible
Low Predictability	High Predictability
Low Reliability	High Reliability
Many Individual Decisions	Premade Decisions (Criteria)
Autonomous, Independent, Single Person or Department	Highly Integrated Company-Wide

FIGURE 2–2
Systems continuum.

completely formal (as it appears that some government bureaucracies do), and many companies are managed in a completely informal way, with only their checking account comprising a formal system.

It is important to note at this point that computer-based systems are considerably toward the formal end of the continuum, depending on how much of the company's information is managed and maintained with a computer. It is this transition that causes much grief in companies starting their first large-scale manufacturing system implementation, and is responsible for many of the partial successes. The systems we discuss in this book reach far into the operations of the company; the company must be managed with them, not around them.

Informal systems are characterized, then, by their personal nature, many points of decision and discretion, flexibility, lack of structure, and a high degree of independence from other systems. They are also somewhat low in reliability since usually a particular individual is involved, or at least a single department which may or may not do things the same way twice. This gives rise, in turn, to a certain lack of predictability. The information produced by informal systems is analogous to a picture that is poorly focused or taken from a distance. It may be adequate for our purposes, but it is still less sharp than a picture developed by more detailed, precise methods.

Manual systems: These tend toward the informal for a variety of reasons:

- It is impractical to develop the high degree of integration required for more formal systems.
- Control is much more difficult; it is hard to ensure that everyone involved with the system's different parts always handles the information in a manner that is consistent with the overall functioning of the system. Government bureaucracies frequently are attempts to produce highly formal systems with completely manual methods. We all know what that is like, and the results.
- Formalizing a manual system is very labor intensive (i.e., expensive).
- There is often a belief among managers that the flexibility provided by informal systems is essential to the operation of a business. Those who have succeeded using formal systems would disagree.

Computer systems: While Chapter 12 discusses programs and software in more detail, several aspects are important to note here. Computer-based systems are more formal for the following reasons:

- The explicit nature of computer programs and records forces some rigidity into the system. One cannot write one's dog's name in the space for "On-Hand Balance" and expect a computer program to do anything with it.
- Because many files are all together in the computer system, a much higher degree of integration of information and function is possible. The development of more and more powerful computer systems parallels the development of truly company-wide formal systems. Until recently, even computer systems

could not conveniently handle a large number of sizable files at the same time, so integrating related information was cumbersome at best. This is no longer true. It is now possible to have virtually all of a company's information in a single data base accessible by all programs at the same time.

- Much greater control over how information is handled is possible in a computer program than in a manual procedure. The procedure shows how we would like to have it done; the program may be set up to make it possible for people to do their jobs only in certain specified ways. They must do them right to do them at all. This is how banks have handled the increasing avalanche of checks without real problems being experienced by customers.

A simple example will illustrate some of these basic differences. Figure 2-3 contrasts the manual and computer system approach to maintaining inventory and related purchase order records. The steps in the manual system are as follows. The inventory control clerk stocks parts and records them on cards in a file and requests purchasing to buy those that appear to be getting low (usually). The buyer closes purchases and sends copies of each purchase order to inventory (eventually). Key points:

- The purchase order file and inventory records are independent and related very loosely.
- Each person (buyer and inventory control clerk) operates with a high degree of independence.
- Frequent back-and-forth communication is needed to "close the gap."
- It takes some time for communication to pass and reaction to changes to be handled.
- There is a lot of flexibility in how purchased items are ordered and the inventory records maintained (if they are accurately maintained at all).

In the computerized system, the flow is somewhat more logical and stricter. It can be described as a series of steps:

1. Inventory control clerk enters receipts and issues to inventory records.
2. Computer reviews all inventory records periodically and lists those that are needed for the buyer.
3. Buyer prepares purchase orders in the computer, which automatically updates each related inventory record with the quantity ordered.
4. Inventory control clerk reviews a stock status report to ensure that all needed items are on order and in the quantity required, in effect cross-checking the buyer.

The key points of computerized flow are:

- The computer provides all back-and-forth communication between inventory control and buyer.

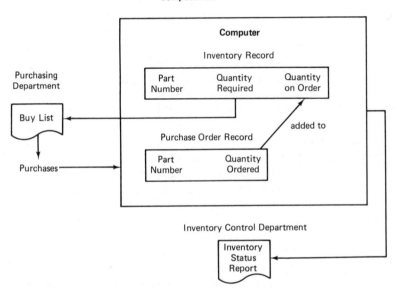

FIGURE 2-3   Manual and computerized systems contrasted.

- The computer programs, or system, controls how records are kept and the purchase order is produced.
- Communication between the two functions is virtually instantaneous and accurate.
- The system is more predictable, has a higher reliability (the programs always work the same way, until modified), and is less flexible than the manual system.
- We now have an overall system that integrates these two related functions.
- The computer system is clearly more formal than the manual method, according to all the criteria on the systems continuum.

A point of view often heard is that a manual system is really no system at all (assuming that it meets the informal system criteria), in that it is merely a collection of loosely related activities. To some extent this may be true, especially if the informal system offers very little control of the company's activities. However, since very effective, yet truly informal systems are often found, they may be regarded as simply another way of organizing a business's information and activities.

Records

Having introduced records by using them in an example, the concept can be examined more closely. Put simply, a *record* is a set of related pieces of information, or data. Unrelated, each piece of information is just data, and by itself, of little use. It is the relationship that makes information from data.

A record, then, is information about something. That something is frequently defined by saying that one of the pieces of data in the record is the *primary,* or identifying data. This can be a part number, account number at a bank, or a customer number. A name can be the primary data, but experience has shown numbers to be shorter and easier to use, and such a system avoids duplications of similar items. All other data belonging to the record may be termed *secondary.* Such data describe something about the primary data. A customer's address is secondary to his or her unique identifying number.

For example, take a checking account. The account number is primary. It identifies the account uniquely. The account name (which can be changed without altering the account record itself) and all other related information about the account, such as its balance, total deposits, and total checks, is secondary. Each secondary piece of data says something about that account and that account only.

A record on a form or in a card file on one's desk has spaces of a certain size for each entry. So does the record in a computer file. The only difference is that the assumed size of the entries must be made explicit in the computer file. For instance, the space for part number on the card file might be 1 inch long. If one writes really small, one can squeeze an 82-digit part number in that small space. In the computer, one must say exactly the maximum number of characters and spaces that will be allowed for the part number.

As a result, designing records for a computer system is different only in that one must be more precise. Otherwise, it is essentially the same process from a conceptual standpoint. One still defines what primary pieces of information will be kept on file and what pieces of secondary data are needed to describe the primary data adequately.

The key point to grasp here is that the idea is the same whether done in a manual or in a computer form. The physical form of the record, on paper or electronically coded, is the main difference.

Record interrelationships: How does one decide where each piece of data belongs in various records? First, what is the primary piece(s) of data? For instance, in the previous example, suppose that one also had a savings account. It would have its own account number and related secondary data.

Next, suppose that one wanted to be able to know the related checking account number and to find it immediately. The easiest way would be to add a piece of secondary data to the savings account record called "Related Checking Account Number" and put the checking account number there.

Thus one can see now that the same piece of data, the checking account number, is primary in one record and secondary in the other. In an inventory system, an identifying part number is primary for the inventory record and secondary for the purchase order. It is a part number on the purchase order and partly describes the purchase order, which has its own primary identifying number. Refer to Figure 2-4 to help visualize these relationships.

The alert reader will probably ask why the quantity is ordered in both records in this example. There are usually two reasons:

1. The same data actually are two different pieces of data, one describing something about the part number's status, the other something about the purchase order's makeup. There could be more than one purchase order for the same part number, in which case the quantity of that part ordered on all purchase orders would be added into one total for the part number record.

2. For speed and ease of reference. We only have to look in one place to know the on-order status of that part number, rather than shuffling through all possible purchase orders to locate the few with the part number we are interested in.

A brief review: A record is a set of related data, which together form a set of information about something identified by its primary data. One can add secondary pieces of data to describe the primary data further and/or to refer easily to related records. Virtually all information systems are built around

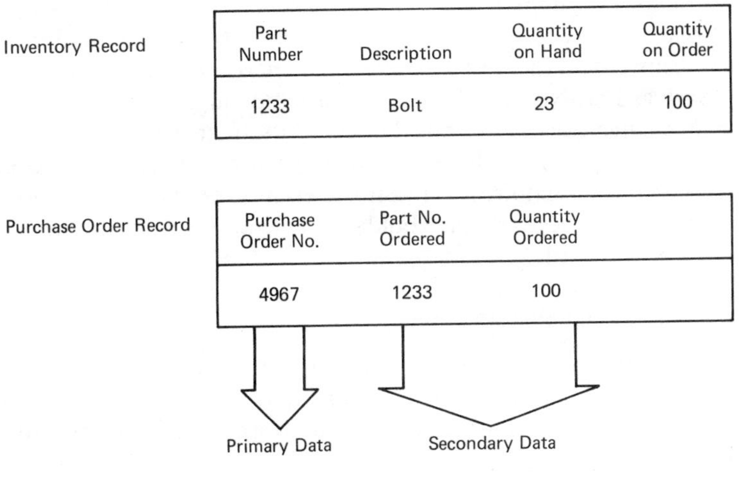

Inventory Record	Part Number	Description	Quantity on Hand	Quantity on Order
	1233	Bolt	23	100

Purchase Order Record	Purchase Order No.	Part No. Ordered	Quantity Ordered
	4967	1233	100

Primary Data   Secondary Data

FIGURE 2-4   Record data.

these concepts of records and data. How records can be combined to form higher levels of information or knowledge about a process or event will be discussed a little later.

Data Bases

The term *data base* has become quite a buzz word lately. It is used to mean a variety of things involving various kinds of technology. Generally, it refers to a whole set of related records or files. Thus all our inventory records together can be termed a file; and similarly for the purchase order records. Together, one could say that both files form the inventory data base. The data base could be enlarged by including other files.

More commonly, the term *data base* is used to describe a set of files, or record types as they are sometimes called, managed by a piece of special-purpose software called a *data base management system* (DBMS). In the earlier days of electronic data processing, having a large number of files or very large records was difficult, so a variety of tricky techniques were developed to cope with this problem. Most of these made the terms "record" and "file" much less clear, especially to nonprogrammers. This terminology is still very much with us and is one of those things that makes talking with a programmer difficult at times.

State-of-the-art systems, however, are easier to understand in the terms defined here. For these purposes, a file is considered to be a collection of records having an identical arrangement of types of data in the same physical sequence in the records. For example, the inventory file would consist only of those records formatted so that the first 15 characters are the part number, the second 30 are the description, and so on.

Since computer systems are more formal systems, every function and record must be explicitly defined and spelled out. This gives rise to a wide variety of permanent, semipermanent, and transient records within a system.

Permanent records are records used to control a system and its various optional features and functions. *Semipermanent records* are those that change slowly, such as Part Number records. Information in the record (its secondary data) may change constantly, but the record itself stays in the file for a long time. *Transient records* are those that carry specific event-related information, such as today's transactions for inventory receipts, or in a manual system, the written list of items received that would subsequently be posted to the more permanent inventory cards.

Procedural and System Logic

One of the supposedly mysterious things about computers are *programs,* or *software,* as they are called. Here, a program may be considered to be a sequential list of instructions for what to do with information in the records in the system.

These instructions are, conceptually, no different from a written procedure for a clerk to follow. We will use as an example posting a list of inventory receipts to an inventory card file. Either manually or in a computer, the procedure probably would go something like this:

1. Use two records, the inventory receipts list and the inventory master record.
2. Start at the top of the inventory record list (first record).
3. Find the inventory master record with the same part number.
4. Add the quantity received on the inventory received record to the quantity on hand on the corresponding inventory master record.
5. Return the inventory master record to the file.
6. Take the next line (record) on the inventory receipts list and start at step 3.
7. When all lines (records) on the inventory receipts list have been posted, finish by stamping the list "posted."
8. Return the inventory receipts list and the inventory master record file to their regular storage places.

The only difference between this procedure for a clerk and for a program, both doing the same thing using a computer, is that the clerk is smart and can think for himself; one can assume that he knows something about the task other than what is in the procedure. So one does not have to tell him absolutely everything. The computer, however, is a rather stupid brute, so the program must cover absolutely everything one intends for it to do, with no assumptions allowed.

Other than the smart–dumb distinction, computer programs and systems are designed in essentially the same way as a set of forms and procedures for a manual system. It is vital that the reader remember this throughout the book. Some of these systems become very complex. They all were, however, designed in this fashion, just with more detail and complexity.

System logic is the overall flow of information between many interrelated procedures or programs. Ideally, the logic of a system (and the information it manages) mirrors reality. This is done so that the information can be processed in place of the physical reality.

Because a computer is so fast, it can maintain a much more detailed picture of reality than is practical manually. Often, a first response to a new system is: "Who needs all that detail?" Here, however, the much higher level of detail in the pictures of reality that are constructed with a computer system brings several important consequences:

1. If the details are accurate, the "picture" is much sharper, in better focus (i.e., it is more accurate).
2. Since more detail brings higher volumes of data, it becomes harder to keep all of it accurate and it is more difficult to manage it.

3. Since the picture of reality produced by a highly detailed system is more precise, one usually notices at first that a lot of the details are apparently wrong. In most cases, these things were there all along, but there was no way of perceiving them.

Information Pyramids

Since, as we saw above, a computer system can keep far more detailed information about a business than we would ever attempt manually, we now find that we can get the same high-level management summary information as we could manually, but now it can be based on a far more accurate, more detailed picture of reality.

As a result, management decisions based on information developed this way are likely to be far better than those based on averages, hunches, incompatible data, or other shortcuts required by manual methods.

In the illustration in Figure 2–5, the report titled "Sales by Product Group" will tell a sales manager a lot more than will a stack of invoices. If all

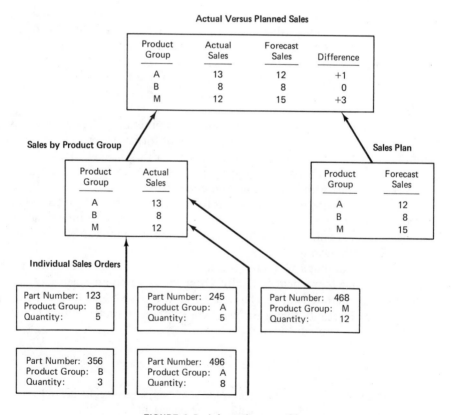

FIGURE 2-5   Information pyramid.

the invoices are accurate, the summary report will also be accurate. By the same token, so will the "Actual Versus Planned Sales Report" that the marketing director would want to see.

This concept of building up higher-level summaries, or lists of only certain records that form exceptions to a set of criteria, all drawn from a mass of data accurately collected at a very detailed level, is an extremely powerful, exciting concept that is at the core of state-of-the-art systems. It will appear repeatedly throughout this book.

Navigation of ships and airplanes has followed a similar line of development. Early systems of navigation merely provided the captain with a general direction, which had to be corrected frequently. Later, as more elaborate systems were developed that provided a much more detailed, precise picture of where the ship was and of the earth, it became possible to head straight for the destination along the planned course, with fewer, smaller corrections enroute.

Closed-Loop Systems and Subsystems

To continue the analogy, the most accurate navigation systems are those that included virtually continuous comparison of planned versus actual course. And so it is with the systems considered here. The more points in the system where planned results can be compared with actual results, and the more frequently this can be done, the smoother and straighter the business course will be. Because it is so critical, Chapter 9 is devoted entirely to this area.

Everyone has attended talks where the speaker drew loops or circles on the blackboard or chart. All too often, the topic is left hanging at this point. An explicit *closed loop* comprises planned events of a specific type that are compared to information collected about the actual events that constitute a closed loop. The more detailed the plan, the more precisely a course can be charted and the more opportunities there are to detect off-course conditions and do something about them.

With only a vague plan, a detailed report of actual events is rather useless (and boring, besides), because there is little one can do with it. Early computer systems were strong on the actual side of reporting events, and weak on the planning side. This is no longer true. State-of-the-art systems allow the development of an amazingly detailed plan of action, thereby providing many opportunities for comparison and, consequently, control.

These comparisons must involve like terms. If the sales plan is only in dollars, and the company sells Kahaziwoggles, dollarizing the week's sales of 84 different-sized Kahaziwoggles to compare with the sales "plan" provides one with no information that can be used as a basis for corrective action, other than to horse-whip the sales staff if it is too low. The most effective comparison would be with a plan specifying how many of each size of Kahaziwoggle were to be sold that week. Then, and only then, is there a solid basis for action, which is what running a business is about.

APICS Terminology

The American Production and Inventory Control Society (APICS) has worked steadily for years to standardize terms used in manufacturing planning and control systems. These terms grew out of a welter of industry-specific, regional, and personal-use terms. For some time, a 30-page dictionary of these terms has been published by APICS. In this book, every effort has been made to be consistent with these terms. Any deviations are to enhance the reader's grasp of concept by reducing the technical level of a term.

Communication is always enhanced by a common language. In the environment of manufacturing, there is almost more complexity than a single human being can comprehend. And the computer systems used to plan and control manufacturing are easily the most complex business computer systems in existence. If terminology is not clear and consistent, it can become very discouraging to attempt true understanding.

Supply and Demand Types

Demand may be defined as the expressed need for something—a requirement. The need may come from a variety of sources, inside or outside the company. A demand for an item may be unfilled (if it was out of stock on that day). So demand is distinct from what is actually sold or produced. It is what was wanted.

There are two basic types of demand, independent and dependent. *Independent demand* is that which is unrelated to demand for other items. Examples of independent demand include demand for finished goods, parts needed for destructive testing, and replacement parts sold for servicing a finished good.

Dependent demand is that which is directly related to or derived from the demand for other items. Planning systems calculate these demands from those of other items.

Any given part may be subject to more than one type of demand. An example would be a subassembly of a finished product. The subassembly would have a dependent demand derived from that of the finished product. Additional independent demand might come from its sale as a repair part for the finished product.

Sources of *supply* are several. A needed item may be purchased from a vendor (i.e., from outside the company). The item may be purchased and then have work done to modify and/or add value to it. Or the raw material might be purchased in some form and the complete manufacturing process performed on it to produce the product needed to sell.

Normally, most manufacturing consists of a complex mix of these three basic types of obtaining a way of supplying the demands for different items. The manufacture of any item involves a very complex process of purchasing items from a company, which in turn buys the parts or raw material from some other company, which in turn buys them in bulk from a refiner or smelter, and so on.

Information to and from these sources of supply are critical to a manufacturing or distribution company's success. The systems used to plan and control the company's activities must therefore include much information about outside sources of supply.

Internal sources of supply refers to intermediate steps in the manufacturing process. Usually, the demand is dependent and calculated from the demands for other parts. Of course, at the finished-goods level, the demand is independent and the source of supply usually internal.

This flow of requirements from a company's marketplace in the form of independent demand on items the company sells, through its product structures in the form of dependent demand to the company's suppliers, places virtually every manufacturing and distribution business at some point in a complex network of interrelated demands. The company is itself dependent on fulfilling the demands of its market for survival, and since it is also a customer for the vendor, the vendor in turn is partly dependent on one's own company's success. Variations in the flow anywhere in this network will have effects on a company's ability to achieve its goals. State-of-the-art planning and control systems allow a much greater level of control of these variables, and certainly a faster response time to changes.

CHAPTER 2 QUESTIONS

1. What is the most important goal for a company to ensure its long-run survival?
2. Describe the differences between the opposite ends of the formal/informal system continuum.
3. Where do computer-based systems fall on the continuum? Why?
4. Where do manual systems fall on the continuum? Why?
5. Define and explain the following:

   a. records
   b. primary data
   c. secondary data
   d. record interrelationship
   e. permanent, semipermanent, and transient records

6. What is a data base?
7. What is a computer program and what does it do with information it is given?
8. Describe how the computer can sharpen our picture of reality.
9. Summarize the information pyramid concept.
10. What is the identifying characteristic of a closed-loop system?
11. What is APICS? What has been one of its most important contributions?
12. Describe the difference between independent and dependent demand.
13. What are the sources of supply for a company?

3

Master Planning—
Sales and Production

This chapter discusses the four parts of the master planning process: from *strategic planning* through *researching the market;* and from *developing forecasts of independent demand* (sales) through *developing a master production schedule* to drive the detail planning system.

STRATEGIC PLANNING—THE FOUNDATION OF ALL PLANNING

In any purposeful activity, results are usually in direct proportion to the clarity of intention. The more clearly one can define one's objectives, the greater understanding one has of how to accomplish them. This alone yields a greater likelihood that goals will, in fact, be achieved. Strategic planning is the business version of this process. Although a full discussion of this critical management activity (that goes unmentioned too often) is beyond the scope of this book, some discussion is helpful. Attempting to perform detailed internal planning without a clear direction for the organization as a whole is an exercise in folly. Strategic planning charts the company direction. Sales forecasting builds on the broader foundation of a good strategic plan.

Although an obvious requirement for a large multinational company, strategic planning is also applicable to smaller companies operating in rather narrow markets. Most companies sell more than one product, and whether their accounting system shows it or not, the products have varying profitability and varying life cycles. Every product goes through what is commonly identified as the five phases of the product life cycle: introduction, growth, maturity, decline, and termination. A key part of developing a strategic plan is to understand where in this cycle each of the company's products are, and the approximate length of the overall life cycle. Thus, if most of a company's products are in a growth phase of their life cycles, a company strategy geared to growth is consistent and will produce better results than one geared to holding costs down, which would be appropriate to a company having most of its products in the mature or declining phase. Similarly, if a life-cycle analysis discloses that most of the company's products are in the mature phase, it would behoove management to develop a strategy geared to controlling marketing and distribution costs and to developing and introducing new products.

These facts seem rather obvious, yet the reader should ask himself how many companies that he has been connected with actually perform anything like this kind of analysis of the demand for their products. Realizing that the answer is that all too few companies actually do strategic planning, it is little wonder that many firms are almost literally driving off the economic cliff without realizing it until it is too late.

Having established that strategic planning to at least some extent is a good management practice, some specifics of the process are in order. Basically, the process involves the six steps discussed in the following paragraphs.

Goal Setting

After the events of the 1960s and 1970s, most business managers are quite aware of the numerous influences on their companies. Various interest groups have claims on a company's resources: the government, creditors, customers, and the community, in addition to the more obvious claims of employees, management, and suppliers. When company management formulates goals in each of these areas, it provides a concrete base for building more detailed strategies and policies, ones that do not conflict with each other.

Although it is appropriate for companies to review and alter their goal statements periodically, it should be obvious that, compared to strategies and policies, goal setting is slower to change and thus provides a stable base for the company.

General Environmental Factors

Understanding environmental factors that impinge on a business provides another solid basis for planning business activities. A business can take advantage of the varying currents in technical, social, political, and economic conditions. Depending on how management views the impact of these factors on the company's business, one type of detailed strategy, or another, will be appropriate. In a period of rising interest rates, for instance, a marketing strategy that depends on the ready availability of financing would not be a wise move.

The factors in a company's external environment normally interrelate in various ways. Political decisions, for example, obviously affect powerfully both social and economic factors. When the Occupational Safety and Health Administration (OSHA) became a political reality, for example, many businesses were affected profoundly. Those that were farsighted enough to see the effects these changes would have were affected the least. In the energy business, some utilities have preferred to continue to fight government decisions (and other political realities), making it more difficult and costly to burn low-grade oil in their generating facilities. Many of these companies compounded matters by not planning for pollution control equipment until it became an enormous expense and appeared like a disaster to management.

On the other hand, management at Public Service Company of New Mexico, for example, saw the handwriting in the statute books, if not on the walls. They implemented policies to be at the forefront of clean generating facilities and went to the expense and trouble of purchasing their own mammoth coal fields, to ensure fuel supplies well into the future. As a result, the customers of this utility experience a stability in their rates and supply that are only fond memories for the customers of some northeastern companies. This business outcome can be attributed directly to management that was relatively farsighted and realistic in assessing the probable impact of political developments on the environment in which the company would have to function.

A related factor that forms a general factor in a company's environment is the state of technology. By technology, one usually thinks of scientific discoveries or engineering developments. Actually, for a company, technology includes a much larger body of knowledge, including production processes, methods, various techniques for how to assemble things, and so on. Welding, for example, has a technology that falls into two broad categories. One is the equipment itself, ranging from hand-held torches to giant automatic machines. The other is the experience-developed body of knowledge relating to how best to use the equipment, what kind of materials make the best welds with certain metal alloys, and so on. Obviously, these two classes of information feed on each other. If a company uses welding extensively in its production processes, the state of this technology is very much a factor in evaluating the company's relative position in the industry.

Specific Environmental Factors

One method of moving environmental analysis from the general to the specific is to ask and answer a number of specific, detailed questions. Whereas an analysis of environmental factors concerns all or most industries, becoming specific helps identify and focus the company's purposes within the industry. The objective is to understand opportunities for and threats to the industry, and to identify requirements for success within the industry.

The first step is to define exactly what business a company is in. This sounds easy; "We're in the business of making power-steering pumps for 1947 Studebakers." The now classical example of errors in this step is the railroads.

The railroads saw themselves as being in the business of operating a collection of equipment rather than as satisfying their customers' transportation needs. In light of the continual change that affects most industries, "defining what business you are in" should be closely examined by every manufacturing and distribution company, probably every year, if not more often. This will prove crucial in deciding what products and services to introduce in the future to replace ones that are becoming obsolete.

Coupled with this definition is developing a detailed understanding of the source of demand for the company's products and whether it is direct or derived demand. Consumer items are an example of direct demand, whereas the demand for oil field drilling equipment is dependent on the number of new drilling rigs being started or upgraded. New rigs are in turn dependent on the amount of exploratory capital being committed, which is in turn dependent on the demand for petroleum products.

Once the source of demand for the company's products is well understood, each product can be examined to determine where in its life cycle it is (see Figure 3-1). Different management actions are appropriate for each stage. Each product goes through a cycle, which may last anywhere from a few months in the case of fad consumer items, to many years for some durable goods. The product is introduced, accompanied by much market research,

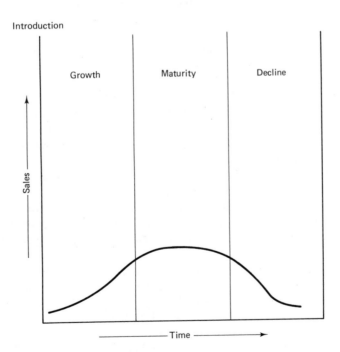

FIGURE 3-1   Product life-cycles.

development effort, and sales promotion. It then goes through a period of growth, during which most users of the product are found; efforts to streamline production are typical during this phase. Once the product reaches a mature stage, production ceases to be the priority problem and emphasis shifts to marketing and distribution.

Products in the mature stage are often referred to as "cash cows," in that they are established, seem to sell with little management emphasis, and consistently produce revenue and profits for the company. Earlier stages often consume capital, and certainly the introductory stage for a product incurs more expenses than it creates profit.

The final stage for a product's life cycle is its decline. During this period the market will seem to be drying up, competitors are beginning to make inroads, and new alternatives are being chosen by customers. The primary managerial emphasis during this period is controlling costs. Promotion campaigns during a product's declining stage are usually a waste of money and serve only to decrease profitability. If a company does not have new products in earlier life-cycle stages, and most of its products are in declining life-cycle stages, the company as a whole will be in a declining stage. Effective internal management, cost control, and dynamic marketing of products that are rapidly becoming obsolete can only serve to cushion the impact as the company goes out of business.

In a sense, staying closely connected with the source of demand for the company's products and continually introducing new items to satisfy that demand is the leading edge of planning, forecasting sales, and planning production. Failure to do this step successfully renders much of otherwise good management relatively ineffective.

Once products are identified that will satisfy the market's demand, the next step is to ensure that all required inputs are available to develop and produce them. Also, the question of industry capacity may be a major factor, especially if it is a capital-intensive production process with a lot of fixed costs. Even if the company has the necessary capital to increase its own capacity, and can secure the necessary labor and raw material inputs, entering a market or increasing market share in an industry experiencing an overcapacity situation will be much more difficult. The pet food industry, for example, has been in an overcapacity situation for some years. It is also a capital-intensive business. As a result, the wholesale market for these products has been characterized by price cutting. Consequently, entry into the market by new firms is very difficult.

During the 1980s many firms have experienced and will continue to experience problems with the supply of raw materials. These problems include extreme price instability, limited supply, poor quality, and long lead times. Material planning systems described in subsequent chapters can help develop detailed plans for overcoming some of these problems by specifying quantities and required dates much further in advance than was practical in the past. Conversely, with these systems, if supply problems are encountered, their effect can be reduced somewhat by allowing management to shift emphasis to products that have different raw materials.

Labor supply may also be a problem. If sufficient, appropriately skilled labor is available, but at prohibitive prices, or is not available at all, or if it is accompanied by union difficulties, production plans will be difficult to meet. Litton Industries, for example, attempted to develop a very large shipbuilding business in Mississippi during the early 1970s. Many observers considered the effort rather disastrous. Shipbuilding requires a large amount of highly skilled labor. There was plenty of cheap labor in Mississippi, but little of it was skilled. Even typists were being imported from the West Coast on temporary assignment to handle engineering documentation. Although other parts of Litton's plans were workable, this single factor turned out to be a serious constraint on the company's ability to meet its production and profit goals.

Even if the company is able to secure easy access to raw materials and good labor supplies, it must have ample capital to develop and produce its products at the production level needed to be competitive. Even if the industry is not capital intensive (one requiring large fixed-cost facilities), rapid growth of the company's business will require substantial increases in working capital just to finance the cash flow between the time labor and materials must be purchased and when customers actually pay. Many otherwise successful firms have failed just when success was being achieved because they became unable to pay their bills, due to lack of sufficient working capital. If a company's total production lead time is two months, for example, and its customers typically pay within 30 days, it will require enough capital to cover two to three months' expenses, even if there is no finished-goods inventory.

Thus, if a company's annual expenses are $1,200,000 with sales of 1.5 million, it will need working capital of about $200,000 to $300,000 just to cover its cash flow. If sales double to 3 million, the working-capital requirement increases to $400,000 to $600,000. So if the company needs its retained earnings to purchase productivity equipment, or goes through a period of low profitability, it will be constrained by insufficient working capital, even if sales growth is quite successful and production is well managed.

Closely related to requirements for the inputs of labor, raw materials, and capital is the question of industry organization and competition. Is the industry relatively monopolistic, or is it characterized by easy entry with many competitors? Is the basis for competition price or customer service, or some other basis? Is product design a basis for making one company's products different from another's? In the oil field drilling equipment industry, for example, each company tends to produce products that are rather different from its competitors, so there is little head-on competition, even though in principle many companies have the required production and engineering capabilities. As a result, the industry tends to be highly profitable for most companies. In addition, customer service is extremely important, so when combined with product design, price becomes a less important factor.

One of the factors in analyzing an industry, and a company's place in it, is the question of whether the company's products are sold as a commodity or whether a high degree of customer service is involved. A company selling bulk chemicals, or sand and gravel, for instance, is really just providing a material and the customer can probably easily purchase the material from any number of suppliers. Consequently, price and cost of transportation are prime factors in the buying decision. On the other hand, for companies providing a high level of customer service, such as the oil field equipment suppliers mentioned earlier, the service often becomes an integral part of the customer's business, and the company is selling something more than just the basic product.

Purchasers of computers often overlook this, as do buyers of equipment. What looks like a better price may in fact stem from a slower level of customer service from the computer vendor. Like the buyer of a complicated tool used in the oil field drilling process, the buyer of a computer must develop a symbiotic relationship with his supplier to assure full success. Generally, the more highly engineered the product, or the more integral its use to the success of the buyer, the more service becomes an important factor in the purchasing decision. Correctly evaluating the level of customer service required in the marketplace will substantially improve pricing and marketing strategy.

Identifying Company Strengths and Weaknesses

Once the environment that a company operates in is reasonably well understood, the strategic process is not complete until the company's relative strengths and weaknesses are analyzed in comparison to what is required for success within the industry and in comparison to its competitors. An effective strategy seeks to minimize the effect of areas of weakness and to build on areas of strength. Although some companies may be fairly strong in most areas, the normal case is that some degree of lopsidedness exists.

Probably the most important single factor is management. Does the company have a lot of depth; that is, are there a number of capable management people who are loyal to the company? Are provisions for succession well thought out, or are all the key decisions made by one or two people? Is there a middle management capable of controlling the company's day-to-day operations? Is the span of control large, with many individuals reporting to one or two key people, or are operational responsibilities assigned to many people, with a small group reporting to each manager? Finally, is the cultural climate within the company—the relationships between managers, staff, and line people—conducive to success, or are there morale problems, turnover, and a lack of individual development? Companies able to manage high internal growth rates are almost always very strong in this area. They do an excellent job of growing new management from within and creating team spirit, and respect exists for individual contributions.

In the financial area, one may ask whether the company is debt-free, with substantial liquid assets, profitable operations, and good budgeting and cost controls; or is the balance sheet heavy with short-term debt nearly offsetting assets? Depending on the answers to these questions, the company can adopt a strategy designed to use its substantial cash to develop many new products, to take on projects with high risk, or it may be forced to look for lower-profit, lower-risk projects and product lines that will enable the company to survive and work its way out of the heavy debt position. If a company is in a precarious financial situation, it usually simply cannot afford to take much in the way of risks, since only a mild failure may push it into bankruptcy.

Many companies that have not had particularly good management or an especially strong balance sheet have nevertheless gone on to achieve significant success because they possessed great strength in the operational side. Product engineering may be far ahead of its competitors, so that customers literally seek the company's product out and tolerate higher prices and long lead times. Or the manufacturing operation may be exceptionally well managed, with a large staff of skilled workers and advanced production equipment. Japanese companies, for instance, have in many cases made their enormous strength in managing production into an integral part of their overall strategy. The company's ability to consistently produce high-quality products on schedule and within short lead times is itself a major factor in the company's competitiveness in worldwide markets.

Finally, the outcome of this analysis of company strengths and weaknesses will not only affect strategic planning, but may also lead to committing funds to bolster especially weak areas. A company that is young and has grown rapidly frequently has outgrown its management, which has become increasingly stretched and overloaded. Once this becomes understood, management many elect to spend money improving itself in this area at the expense, say, of spending more money on research and development (R&D) or purchasing capital equipment.

Developing a Strategy

Generally, strategies can be characterized as designed to facilitate growth or to promote stability. Occasionally, if a company has gone through a period of reversals, retrenchment may be an appropriate strategy. Growth may be through acquisition (externally oriented) or by increasing sales of existing or new products (internally oriented). Other variations are to expand vertically or horizontally.

Figure 3–2 illustrates various options available for growth strategies. The key point here is that any growth strategy will use at least one of these alternatives as its base. The selection of which one will, of course, be a rather complex decision, based on the results of the analyses that were previously discussed. For example, a growth strategy based on acquiring other firms will require at least a reasonable degree of financial strength, coupled with the availability of an appropriate firm in the external environment to merge with or buy. Expanding in a forward, vertical fashion will require significant manage-

	Internal	External
Vertical Forward	Build own retail outlets or distribution centers	Acquire or merge competing retail outlets or distribution centers
Vertical Backward	Develop own raw materials or component suppliers	Acquire or merge raw material or component supplier
Horizontal	Develop products that will use existing distribution, marketing, or production facilities	Acquire or merge competing producers
Diversification	Develop products that fit corporate image	Acquire or merge firms that fit the company's personality

FIGURE 3-2   Growth strategy matrix (for manufacturer). (Source: From Bates, Donald L., and David L. Eldridge, *Strategy and Policy: Analysis, Formulation, and Implementation.* © 1980 Wm. C. Brown Company Publishers, Dubuque, Iowa. Reprinted by permission.)

ment expertise in the new type of business. Each alternative strategy must be evaluated in light of the appropriate environmental factors, both general and specific. In many companies, management selects a strategy almost by default, with little formal analysis or data. Often, a strategy is merely assumed (i.e., that more sales of existing products will satisfy all objectives). This situation usually produces a set of mismatched factors, where the requirements for the strategy do not fully fit the strategy itself. Internal growth, for example, will require changes in management style and depth. If these changes are not forthcoming, the company will become strangled by management bottlenecks and will have difficulty achieving its goals.

The purpose of this discussion is to point up the necessity for having a strategy and the consequences of not doing such an analysis or of doing it poorly. It is important to understand that a poor strategy does not manifest itself clearly with flashing red lights or a report entitled "Bad Strategy." Companies in this predicament instead experience an ongoing series of difficulties: short-term crises, problems in many areas of the business, and failure to meet schedules, forecasts, and profit objectives. In each case, management that has failed to formulate an effective strategy will spend its energies trying to cope with each problem as though it were unrelated to others.

If an effective strategy is formulated, a reasonably accurate longer-range sales forecast can be developed and maintained. With a good-quality sales forecast, effective production planning can be done, and with that, the full benefit of the more detailed planning systems described elsewhere in this book can be obtained. If these things are not well thought out, the result is inaccurate forecasts, constant significant changes to the production schedule, and frequent short-run crises, all of which substantially blunt the effectiveness of computer-based planning systems. Constant changes to the master schedule, for example, within the lead times for procurement of raw materials and in plant production times, leads to confusion, shop over- and underloading, material overages and shortages, and other problems for which these systems can only partially compensate.

It can hardly be emphasized enough that the lead time for important managerial decisions is invariably longer than one would think. Companies that have achieved large success, particularly in world markets, almost without exception do a superior job of detailed planning and strategy formulation well in advance of the time at which specific actions must occur. The result is a daily operational reality where virtually all events are planned in advance and are merely being carried out in the current period. This method of business management leads to a smooth operation, with fine tuning of the organization, its processes, people, and equipment, which can be accomplished in no other way.

Implementing the Strategy

A full discussion of strategy implementation is beyond the scope of this book. A brief review of highlights will be helpful, however. The essential step is to assemble a mechanism to cause the strategy to develop into reality. That mechanism, sometimes called a means–end chain, is mostly through the organizational structure of the company, wherein specific parts of execution of the strategy become part of the responsibility of individual managers. The actual production plan, for instance, will be the responsibility of both the marketing and manufacturing management groups. Procuring production facilities and equipment will be the responsibility of manufacturing and production engineering groups. If the strategy requires the development of a new field service capability, the job description and management objectives of the customer service manager may change radically. If an acquisition is involved, financial management becomes a key part of carrying out this strategy.

Above all, a strategy is still a plan for action, and little will be accomplished with the plan unless it is carried out effectively. And like all plans, short-term operating results need to be compared frequently with the plan. And the strategy is simply the broadest, longest-term plan of action for the company, the one upon which all other more short-term, specific plans must be based. Advanced, state-of-the-art computerized planning systems can substantially improve the quality and increase the level of details and internal consistency of detailed plans. Computer systems may even assist greatly in strategy formulation, but in the end, strategies must be formulated by creative, imaginative management thinking. It is a distinctly human process. The computer can provide data, execute decision criteria specified by people, but in the final analysis, only human beings can decide and act. How well this is done will determine how effective all other actions will be in achieving the company's goals and objectives.

MARKET RESEARCH

An integral part of the effective strategy is a detailed understanding of the market in which the company's products are to be sold. Good market research will substantially improve the accuracy of sales forecasts and therefore of production plans. There is also an information loop back to the strategic planning process to ensure that markets are of the size and nature assumed by the strategy. Since marketing research is also a rather complex subject, the discussion here will be confined to those data used to substantiate both strategic plans and product sales forecasts.

Market research for new products is somewhat different than that for well-established products. An idea for a new product may come from a variety of sources, such as field service people, salesmen, or more indirect studies of potential market segments. It may be an offshoot of an existing product, or the outcome of laboratory-oriented research. In any case, the key question is to establish a reasonably accurate estimate of the potential size and price for the product before significant amounts of capital are committed to its development, production, and sales efforts. Possible competition is an important factor, often overlooked.

The kinds of data available for a market research project are either primary or secondary. Collecting primary data consists of asking, in a systematic way, potential buyers of the product about their interest in it. Thus salespeople who are in frequent contact with buyers of similar products may be a good source of primary data, although not particularly systematic. For all practical purposes, secondary data comprise all other types of data. Examples of secondary data sources include:

- Internal company records
- Trade, professional, and business association records and publications
- Government agencies, such as the Departments of Labor, Commerce, and Agriculture, as well as various state and local agencies
- Private market research firms, such as A.C. Nielsen and Company
- Advertising (through various media)
- Nonprofit foundations
- University research organizations
- Libraries

As an example, a preliminary study using secondary data sources may be done to determine the potential size of the market for a new product. The Bureau of Labor Statistics may be consulted to identify the size and income level of potential buying populations. If the results are promising, a more detailed analysis might be contracted to a private market research firm, which may have more specific data to draw upon. Finally, if the outcome still looks encouraging, a carefully designed set of interviews of potential customers, based on a statistical sample, might be performed.

For existing products, information should be gathered specifically to support sales forecasts and to determine where each class of products is in its life cycle. The methods may not be nearly as elaborate as for a new-product proposal. For an ongoing business, offering a range of products from nearly obsolete products to new product introductions, a mixture of methods will probably be appropriate, geared, of course, to the amount of capital at risk. One of the risks of using mechanical methods of sales forecasting is that these usually rely on projections of various kinds of historical data. This approach tends to put management in touch with the product's life-cycle phase only in an indirect fashion, even if these projections are performed at the part number level. Supplementing such forecasts with market research data provides a more solid basis for decisions, such as whether to commit more capital to productivity equipment, promotion campaigns, or to adopt cost-cutting programs if a product is still selling but is nearing the end of its life cycle. Too frequently, demand for a product (which has sold well for years) will suddenly drop after the introduction of a competitor's new product. Historical projections provide little help in this case.

A company in a very narrow industry, which sells to a limited number of industrial buyers, for instance, really needs continuous feedback from its primary sources, such as field service, sales, and sales support staffs. New products are often test marketed in this environment by making several prototypes, selling them, and checking the results very closely before committing to full-scale production. For consumer items or other types of products where the number of customers is quite large, test marketing is especially valuable.

To reiterate then within the context of this book, the objective of market research is to produce supplementary data that improve the quality, accuracy, and reliability of product-level sales forecasts. A solid understanding of which products can be sold, to whom, at what quantities, and at what price provides feedback to the strategic planning process. The company can then go on and develop a complete business plan of action so that the projected demands of the forecasts can actually be met.

FORECASTING INDEPENDENT DEMAND

Independent demand is that which comes from outside the company, that is—what customers will buy. Parts and materials used in the production of the items customers buy are subject to dependent, or calculated, demand. If independent demand is known, exact quantities and required dates for subassemblies, component parts, and raw materials can be calculated through the bill of materials and lead times. Early inventory systems (statistical inventory control) simply treated all items as independent demand items. This approach is, put simply, ineffective and obsolete, and need not be discussed further.

Some excellent texts have been written entirely on the subject of forecasting. Many emphasize elaborate statistical techniques and require massive amounts of data or frequent revision to produce precision forecasts. This turns out to be inappropriate for day-to-day reality of manufacturing. Statistical emphasis obscures several points. First, it is top management's key responsibility to lead the business. That leading includes the planning processes described above. An integral part of this plan is an accurate statement of expected sales. Second, many companies exhibit excessive concern with the short run. This leads to a reactive posture in the marketplace, instead of a proactive one. Third, the most effective way to deal with forecasts is to reduce the need for absolute accuracy. If lead times are reduced, operations made flexible, and cooperative arrangements made with suppliers, long–range forecast accuracy becomes less important. Finally, and probably most important, the best source of accuracy in forecasting comes not from historical data, but from an intimate understanding of, and constant communication with, the firm's marketplace and all the factors that affect it.

It is surprising how many manufacturing and distribution companies do almost nothing in the way of exploring and increasing their understanding of why their customers buy. Often, sales forecasts are generated entirely by the sales force, which is under pressure to produce a picture of what they think management would like to see. Further, these "guesstimates" are compounded by not clearly assigning responsibility for accuracy of forecasting to anyone in particular. As a result, because material planners have to have *some* type of advance knowledge, they end up "doing the forecast." This is the end of the line, so to speak, and probably the worst place to do forecasting, because material planners usually have only historical data, and almost no contact or understanding of the marketplace.

The first point to emphasize, then, is that accurate forecasts can best be produced by the department most in touch with the marketplace—marketing, with top management involvement. If clear responsibility is assigned to those individuals with the best tools, then an ongoing effort to improve the quality of forecasts will bear fruit. Of course, the planning process must include a definite loop with manufacturing planning to ensure that what is forecasted can actually be produced. If not, the forecast must be altered, as well as sales planning.

Dollars-Only Forecasts

Forecasts that are only in terms of dollars are really useful only for cash planning, unless management seriously believes that sales of products are completely stable. Not even banks are in the business of selling dollars, so unless the forecast is made on the basis of quantities of items, or classes of items (which may then be dollarized by extending with selling prices), the forecast is not useful for planning manufacturing. A forecast that consists only of statements that so many dollars of products will be sold is worse than no plan at all. It serves only to delude management into thinking that they have a plan, when in fact the situation is completely out of control. The reason for this is simple. No deductions can be made from a dollar-only forecast about what kinds of materials, personnel, or plant facilities will be needed. Very few companies have a simple product line, made from readily available, cheap materials, coupled with unlimited plant capacity and an infinitely variable labor force. Therefore, practically all companies must plan their sales and production in units, or admit to themselves that their "plan" is a mere fiction.

Planning Horizons

It is axiomatic that forecasts are always wrong, and the farther out the forecast, the "wronger" it is. It is also true that forecasts are more accurate for families or groups of products than for individual items. The key question to deciding how far out to plan, and to what level of detail, is how much time is required to implement a change, or to respond to a change in market conditions. Generally, plant capacity is the resource with the longest lead time, although raising capital can also take a long time.

Figure 3–3 illustrates some characteristics of planning horizons and the relationship between forecast definition and time span for plant and equipment, products, and cash. As components of a long-range plan near the present, generalized statements must be translated into increasingly more specific requirements. And as the plan becomes more detailed, it must also become more "frozen," because changes become increasingly disruptive. Failure to recognize these relationships produces a climate of continual upheaval, confusion, and chaos as the production schedule is whipsawed around in attempts to respond to changes beyond the company's actual ability to do so.

Hal Mather suggests a "zones of planning" concept that provides more detailed insight. Figure 3–4 illustrates the relationships between planning zones.

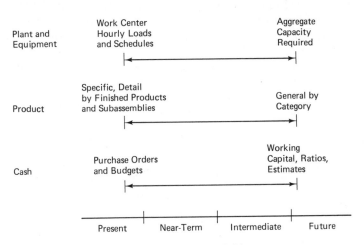

FIGURE 3-3   Forecast definition.

	Zone 1	Zone 2	Zone 3
Master Schedule Definition	Finished Products or Subassemblies	Product Line or Family Totals	Gross Totals by Plant or Product Category
System Data Necessary	Finished Product or Subassembly Bills of Material Detailed Routings and Processing Information	Typical Product or Family Bills of Material Bills of Labor or Resource Profiles	Average Ratios of Labor and Material Consumption
Information Generated	Subassembly or Finishing Schedules Allocation of Components to Specific Customer Orders Short-Lead-Time Item Procurement or Manufacture Direct Labor Assignments and Short Range Capacity Needs	Long-Lead-Time Material or Parts Schedules Gross Direct Labor Needs	Raw Material and Feedstock Schedules Plant and Machinery Needs
Zone Lengths and Buckets	Weeks	Months	Quarters

FIGURE 3-4   Zones of planning. (From "Too Much Precision, Not Enough Accuracy," by Hal Mather in 1979 APICS Conference Proceedings.)

Weekly planning (zone one) is by work order, including detailed item-specific bills of material and shop routings, with assigned start and completion dates. Moving out into the future, summary-type family bills of material and labor are used to produce monthly (zone two) plans, while even more summary-oriented, gross reporting types of information are used to produce quarterly plans (zone three).

Figure 3–5 illustrates the appropriate sources of information for prepar-

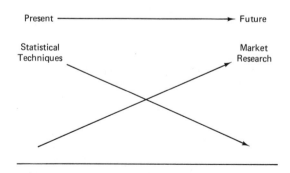

FIGURE 3-5
Forecast sources.

ing forecasts within each of these three zones. The closer to the present a forecast is, the more likely it is to resemble the immediate past. The converse is true of the distant future, when only indirect methods, such as extrinsic techniques, tying demand to economic indicators, for example, and market research will enable a meaningful forecast to be prepared.

Effect of Lead Times on Planning Horizons

No discussion of planning is complete without including lead times. Every company that manufactures products uses a certain number of weeks as its "standard production lead time." This number may be anything from several weeks up to six months. Yet in every case, when an emergency arises, product can be turned out (heavily expedited) in a much shorter period—often in only a few days. It has become more widely recognized that this phenomenon exists because the actual hours required to build a product are only a fraction of its total lead time. The remainder consists of queue, or waiting time. Effective queue controls are discussed in Chapter 8. It is mentioned here because of the effect of queue time on forecasting and forward planning.

Zone one in Hal Mather's scheme can be defined as the current period (within the plant or standard lead time). The longer this period, the more difficult it is to produce accurate forecasts. This in turn makes it more difficult to plan the current period. A determined effort by management to reduce and control lead times substantially not only reduces work-in-process inventory, but produces its biggest payoff by greatly simplifying forecasting and planning.

For example, in one company that manufactured printed circuit boards, before a queue-time reduction program, the standard order lead time was four months. Forecasts were made beyond that time frame. As a result, the in-plant schedules were beset by constant changes to orders and priorities. The queue control reduction program shrank the order lead time to four weeks. Raw material lead times essentially started at that point, instead of four months out. In fact, the company instituted a policy of not even accepting firm orders from its customers any farther in advance than this four-week period.

The effect cutting queue time has on developing an accurate forecast is startling. Forecasters in the example above are now querying their marketplace for estimates only two to three months out, instead of guessing the market demand six months or more in advance.

A similar result can be obtained through concentrated efforts with critical, long-lead-time suppliers. If production plans are dependent on raw materials that must be ordered months in advance, forecasting must be done this far out, in addition to the in-plant lead time. For instance, if a company must place its orders for specific castings with the foundry three months in advance, and the in-plant production time is four weeks, the *minimum* detailed forecasting period is 16 weeks, since firm orders for castings must be placed that far in advance.

If an agreement can be made with the foundry to commit to a certain dollar volume of business, in exchange for the right to specify which part numbers are cast just before the molds are poured, part number specific leads time can be shrunk dramatically, often to only one or two weeks. The effect on forecasting is similarly dramatic, because this action alone reduces the minimum detailed forecasting period to just six weeks, down from 16. Adding an in-plant queue reduction program, the minimum detailed forecasting period might shrink to as little as three or four weeks. Stated in terms of the zones of planning concept, zone one would span only three or four weeks instead of 16. Planning the remaining two zones would also become much simpler and therefore more accurate because the whole process has been condensed into a shorter period.

These and other actions can be taken to reduce the *need* for forecast accuracy, so the company can live with the inherent problem of inaccurate forecasts. By reducing the time required to respond to changes in the market-place, the need to plan in detail is also reduced. This means that intermediate- and long-range planning can remain effective even in fairly general terms.

In any case, the critical juncture of planning is when intermediate-term forecasts must be translated into ordering material, scheduling personnel, and scheduling workloads in the plant. At this point, the system must generate, one way or another, an end item part number specific forecast. This forecast can be turned into a master production schedule, which in turn is used by a material and capacity planning system to order specific quantities of purchased parts and perform detailed work center loading in the plant.

Forecasting Units

The ideal detailed forecast is part number specific at the end item level. However, in many companies this technique is just not workable, for a variety of reasons. The number of products may be very large or may consist of thousands of possible configurations. Or, all but a very few component parts or raw materials may be very easy to get or manufacture. In these cases, other approaches are needed. The main idea here is to forecast only those variables in the production equation that are critical to the company's ability to produce on schedule and meet customer demands for specific quantities and items when those demands arrive.

If the number of products is large, forecast accuracy can be improved by combining like parts into classes, categories, or family groupings. A screw and bolt manufacturer, for example, may have thousands of different items in its catalog. By grouping these items into families having common elements such as type of application (e.g., aircraft production), by material used, production equipment required, or by engineering characteristics (e.g., hex-head, slotted, etc.), a much smaller number of things have to be forecasted. And since the fluctuations around an average tend to be averaged out when a number of specific items are combined, the resulting summary forecast for the group becomes more accurate.

In other situations, where the number of end item configurations is great, but where they are assembled at the last minute for specific customer orders, it is appropriate to forecast by subassembly. The order entry system can capture demand data for specific configurations, which can be turned into demand for subassemblies, with the resulting data being used for the forecast. An example of a product with numerous possible end item configurations is connectors used in the electronics industry to connect various functional units. Figure 3-6 illustrates a somewhat simplified example. Attempting to accurately forecast demand for each of the 840 possible combinations is clearly a hopeless task. Similarly, using the end items to base a master schedule upon would be similarly impractical. In this case, some of the subassemblies have materials with long procurement times and complex machining to be performed.

Each connector consists of one of each of the four types of subassemblies. The connector can be assembled quickly from stocks of subassemblies and shipped as specific customer orders are received. Thus there is no need to plan at the end item level. By dropping down one level in the product structure, and forecasting at the subassembly level, only 22 different part numbers need to be forecast. These, in turn, can be adjusted to meet material and capacity limitations and then used as the master production schedule, which in turn will drive the material and capacity planning system. Finally, since the demand for many different end items is averaged together, the forecast for each of the 22 part numbers can be made much more accurately.

Another variation on this theme is that where the product consists of a relatively small number of component parts, most of which can be purchased or made on short notice, but which has one or two parts that take forever to get. This becomes clearer where these long-lead-time items are used in more than one end time. Figure 3-7 shows an example of a group of components used in more than one end item. All have relatively short lead times except components D and G. Following the logic discussed previously, the minimum detailed forecasting period would be D's seven weeks' lead time, plus whatever the in-plant lead time is. By shifting the forecasting effort to just parts D and G, a detailed forecast need not be prepared until part E's two-week lead time plus the in-plant time is approached. Accuracy will be gained in two ways: by reduc-

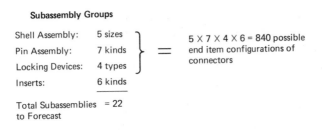

Subassembly Groups

Shell Assembly:	5 sizes	
Pin Assembly:	7 kinds	$5 \times 7 \times 4 \times 6 = 840$ possible end item configurations of connectors
Locking Devices:	4 types	
Inserts:	6 kinds	

Total Subassemblies = 22
to Forecast

FIGURE 3-6   Connector end-item configurations.

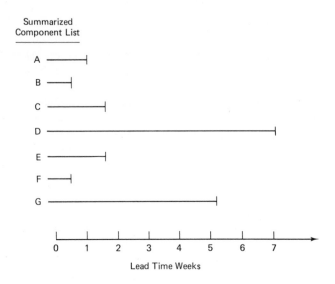

FIGURE 3-7   Key components in product structure.

ing the number of parts needing longer forecasts, and by shortening the period for detailed forecasting for the rest.

Forecasting Techniques

Over the years many different statistical techniques have been developed and used for forecasting demand for products. Many of these were developed during the period of "scientific" or statistical inventory control, where forecasting techniques were applied not only to independent demand items but to dependent items as well. These techniques fall into two groupings, extrinsic methods and intrinsic ones.

Extrinsic forecasting techniques build a data base of historical data connecting the demand for the company's products to some outside factor, such as the demand for another product, or some economic indicator. As such, for purposes of this discussion, extrinsic methods may be regarded as being part of strategic planning and relate to the market research effort. In most cases, the results are rather general and not specific enough to use to develop a detailed demand forecast. Exceptions would be in industries such as airplane subcontractors, where the actual demand for these extremely long lead time products is known precisely well in advance.

Like all forecasting techniques, extrinsic methods use standard statistical analysis techniques, such as regression analysis, various methods of developing correlations, and so on.

Of more interest here are *intrinsic* methods, those that use historical data collected internally by the company as a base for projecting future demand. The reader should notice that the term "demand" is used here instead of "sales." Although forecasts based on past shipments are common, so are the errors this practice causes. The demand for an item frequently occurs in a different time frame and quantity than actual shipments. The use of sales data perpetually masks this important distinction, building into the forecast all of the past problems with back orders, lost sales because the item was not available, cancellations, and the like. The goal of planning, after all, is to produce items that will be available at the times and in the quantities that customers want.

All intrinsic methods assume that the future will resemble the past and use a historical data base as its starting point. Obviously, the more complete and accurate the historical data are, the greater the possibility of producing an accurate forecast. Performing sophisticated techniques on an inadequate data base is somewhat like carrying an average of several rough estimates out to seven decimal places. Interesting, but useless.

Another useful guideline in developing a forecasting system is to employ the 80/20 rule. Reserve the most sophisticated, elaborate methods for the highest-volume items. Using simple models for the bulk of a company's products simplifies the entire process and makes it more understandable to the nontechnician.

There are four basic steps to forecasting with any intrinsic method, including:

1. Establishing the historical data base of demand, not sales, including quantities for each forecasting period (weeks, months, or quarters)
2. Selecting the forecast model that best fits past data (i.e., that would have produced accurate forecasts had it been used in the past)
3. Using that model to project future demand
4. Periodically updating the forecast and historical data with actual results (i.e., maintaining the forecast)

It should also be borne in mind that since forecasting is a statistical process, the assumption of a certain amount of error is built in. Therefore, any given forecasted quantity should be for a range that reflects the size of error due to the process itself. For instance, if a forecasting calculation yields a quantity of 100 units in period 3, and past forecasts have resulted in a mean average deviation, or error, of 9 units, then the forecast should be stated as 100 units plus or minus 9, or a range of 91 to 109.

It should be pointed out that this use of the mean average deviation, or MAD, is only an example. Other methods of developing a forecast range or variation figure may yield perfectly acceptable results. The key point here is that the results of the forecast calculation should not be interpreted in specific, literal terms.

Since not all products that are sold by many companies serve the same market, it may be appropriate to use different models for different items. In fact, in a state-of-the-art computer-based forecasting system, these forecast errors will be automatically tracked and a tracking signal calculated which tends to indicate the adequacy of the forecasting model used.

A full discussion of the many types of intrinsic forecasting models used is beyond the scope of this book. In any case, the thrust of this chapter is that accuracy in forecasting and in planning lies not in selecting the appropriate statistical model, but in understanding the marketplace and in doing everything possible to reduce the need for forecast accuracy. If no model can be found that is practical and can produce reasonably accurate forecasts for more than three months out, it is futile to run detailed planning out to 12 months. Ideally, the further out the forecast, the more summarized and general it becomes.

James I. Morgan and Robert E. Thiele, Jr., in the *Production and Inventory Control Handbook* (ed. James H. Green, McGraw-Hill, New York, 1970) discuss about 20 different forecasting models, including various types of moving averages, exponential smoothing techniques, and curve-fitting and regression models. The interested reader is invited to study this or a similar source if a full review of available models is desired. The discussion here will be limited to a single model, termed the constant model with trend and seasonal variation. The type of demand curve produced by each of the three methods included in this model are illustrated in Figure 3–8. This model was selected because it is in wide use, is implemented in many state-of-the-art computer-based systems, and illustrates the more common problems in developing a statistical forecast. Also, if there is no trend or seasonal variation, these values, in effect, just go to zero. They also illustrate the judgmental factor, in that smoothing constants are used

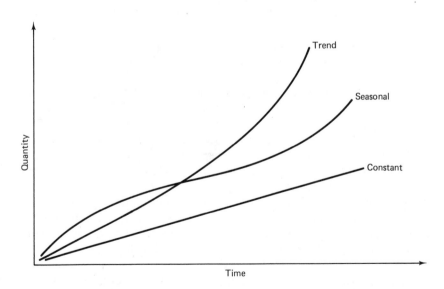

FIGURE 3-8   **Cumulative demand with three types of forecasting methods.**

in several places. The selection of the appropriate values for these constants is a matter of experience that comes only after working with a specific forecast through numerous cycles.

Figure 3–9 illustrates the steps required to calculate each of the values that compose the final equation that actually results in a forecasted quantity. The Greek letters alpha (α) and gamma (γ) are used to denote the smoothing constants. Their values may be anywhere between 0 and 1, although alpha is commonly between 0.1 and 0.2, and gamma is half of the value of alpha. The old single smoothed average is:

$$
\begin{array}{ll}
 & \text{previous forecasted quantity} \\
- & \text{quantities added for seasonal variation} \\
= & \text{old single smoothed average (SSAVG)}
\end{array}
$$

SSAVG is the starting point for subsequent computation.

A seasonal factor is a number applied to either increase or decrease the forecast to account for the season. Because the seasonal factor is used as a multiplier in the equations (shown in Figure 3–9), it is expressed in relation to 1.

1. Calculate untrended unseasoned Single Smoothed Average (SSAVG)	α = alpha or weighting factor $\dfrac{\text{New}}{\text{SSAVG}} = \dfrac{\text{Old}}{\text{SSAVG}} + \alpha \left(\begin{array}{c}\text{new} \\ \text{actual} \\ \text{demand}\end{array} - \begin{array}{c} \\ \text{old} \\ \text{SSAVG}\end{array} \right)$
2. Calculate trend (or rate of change)	γ = gamma or trend smoothing constant $\text{New trend} = \dfrac{\text{old}}{\text{trend}} + \gamma \left(\begin{array}{c}\text{new difference} \\ \text{in SSA's}\end{array} - \begin{array}{c}\text{old} \\ \text{trend}\end{array} \right)$
3. Calculate Seasonal Factors (SF)	(a seasonal factor of 10% = 1.1 here) $\dfrac{\text{New}}{\text{SF}} = \dfrac{\text{old}}{\text{SF}} + 2\alpha \left(\dfrac{\text{new actual demand}}{\text{new SSAVG}} - \dfrac{\text{old}}{\text{SF}} \right)$
4. Adjust period Seasonal Factor so the average of all remains equal to 1	n = the period number $\begin{array}{c}\text{Adjusted seasonal factor} \\ \text{for period } n\end{array} = \dfrac{\begin{array}{c}\text{Current unadjusted} \\ \text{seasonal factor for} \\ \text{period } n\end{array}}{\begin{array}{c}\text{current average of} \\ \text{all seasonal factors}\end{array}}$
5. Calculate forecasted demand for future periods	$\begin{array}{c}\text{Forecasted demand} \\ \text{for period } n\end{array} = \begin{array}{c}\text{new} \\ \text{SSAVG}\end{array} + n \left(\begin{array}{c}\text{new} \\ \text{trend}\end{array} \right) \left(\begin{array}{c}\text{adjusted} \\ \text{SF for} \\ \text{period } n\end{array} \right)$

FIGURE 3-9   Constant model with trend and seasonal variations.

If no seasonal variation is expected, the seasonal factor is 1; a minus 10% seasonal variation results in a 0.9 seasonal factor; a 1.2 seasonal factor denotes a 20% increase. The seasonal factor is not intended to change the total forecast but to adjust the distribution of demand within the total planning horizon. Therefore, the average of all the seasonal factors used must be 1. Otherwise, one would end up with a set of factors that did nothing other than increase or decrease the forecast.

Trend is the rate at which the demand is changing. It is assumed to be constant for each successive period in the forecasting process. Thus, if the new single smoothed, untrended average quantity is 50 units, and the trend is that demand has been increasing by 10 units per period, then the first forecasted period would have a quantity of 60, the second of 70, the third 80, and so on. Of course, there can also be downward or negative trends as well.

It is important to understand forecasting. Required data to calculate a new forecast using this model include the following:

- The old untrended, unseasonalized, single smoothed average from the last forecast
- The value of new actual demand
- Assigned values of the constants, alpha and gamma
- The old seasonal factors for each period from the last forecast
- The trend calculated from the last forecast

With these data one can calculate a forecasted quantity for any number of periods out into the future. However, it should be remembered that the further out one goes, the greater the likelihood that the calculated values for trends and seasonality will be proved wrong when the future period is actually experienced.

To calculate a complete forecast for an item, the following steps are performed, as summarized in Figure 3-9:

1. Calculate the new, untrended, unseasonalized, single smoothed average from the old average, the new actual demand for the most recent period, and the smoothing constant alpha.
2. Calculate the rate of change or trend between the new and old untrended, unseasonalized, single smoothed averages with the old trend value and the trend smoothing constant gamma.
3. Calculate the amount of variation due to seasonal fluctuation in demand using the old seasonal factor for that period, new actual demand for the most recent period, and the new untrended, unseasonalized, single smoothed average (obtained from step 1).
4. Adjust the seasonal factors for all periods being forecasted. This calculation is repeated for each period, calculating a new "current average of all factors."

5. Use the results of the previous four steps to calculate the demand for each period in succession for however many periods are to be forecasted. The number of periods is represented by the value n in the equations; n would equal 1 for the first period, 2 for the second, 3 for the third, and so on.

Figure 3-10 contains an example of a four-period forecast created using the model just discussed. The reader is invited to create several examples of his own using the formulas in Figure 3-9 to increase his understanding of this process.

Regarding the seasonal factors, two things should be noted. First, only the factors for the first period are recalculated. Each seasonal factor (one for each period for the year) is updated with a new seasonal, unadjusted factor calculation only once each year. Second, adjusting the seasonal factors is an iterative process, each of the four factors being adjusted one at a time, with the result being carried forward into the next cycle of calculations.

Note that the new seasonal factors, unadjusted, have an average greater than 1 after the first one has been recalculated. After the adjustment calculations, the entire set has been reduced slightly to bring its average back to a value of 1.

The results of these calculations are presented at the bottom of the illustration with the quantity added or subtracted to the overage due to the effects of both trend and seasonal variations. For a given forecasted item, or a particular period, the effect of either of these variables could be zero. Thus any

Data Input	Value	Calculated Data	Value
• Old Untrended, Unseasonalized Single Smoothed Average	50	• New Untrended, Unseasonalized Single Smoothed Average	52
• New Actual Demand	60	• New Trend	+4.7
• Alpha Constant	0.2	• New Seasonal Factors, Unadjusted	1.06
• Gamma Constant	0.1		0.90
• Old Trend	+5.0		1.00
			1.10
• Old Seasonal Factors	1.0	• Adjusted New Seasonal Factors	1.04
(4 periods only)	0.9		0.88
	1.0		0.99
	1.1		1.09

New Forecast

Period	1	2	3	4
Average	52	52	52	52
Due to Trend	+9.7	+9.4	+14.1	+18.8
Due to Seasonal Variations	+2.3	−7.4	−0.7	+ 6.4
Total Forecasted Quantity	59	54	65	77

FIGURE 3-10   Example forecast.

combinations of these variations can be used with this model to produce a forecasted quantity.

MASTER PRODUCTION SCHEDULING

The master production schedule is a company's statement of its production plan in terms of its end item part numbers, the planned quantity to be made, and the period in which the production is to be completed. In companies where a vast number of end item configurations are possible, master scheduling is best done at the subassembly level using modular bills of material (see Figure 3-11). It is important to distinguish between the master schedule and a complete production schedule, which includes all subassembly production as well as end items. Since in a state-of-the-art system, production schedules for subassemblies and components (dependent demand) are calculated from those of the end items (independent demand items), they are not considered to be part of the master schedule.

The purpose of the master production schedule is to drive the rest of the planning system, including both material and capacity. It is a statement of how the company plans to meet the independent demand for products as stated in the forecast. Since it drives the dependent demand calculations, the planning

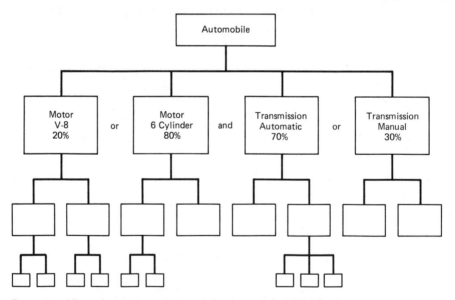

Every automobile requires a motor and a transmission. In a modular bill for planning purposes, the quantities used are entered as being less than 1. In this example the quantity for V-8 motors would be 0.2.

FIGURE 3-11   Modular bills of material.

horizon of the master schedule must include the longest procurement lead time plus the longest in-plant lead time product, at the very minimum. The more the master schedule can be frozen within this time period, the easier it gets to make the rest of the system perform properly. Significant changes introduced within this planning horizon must, by definition, cause overages or shortages at lower levels in the planning process. The lead time for each event, after all, is the time required to react to changes in the event.

Another purpose of the master production schedule is to convert the demand statement of the forecast into a statement of what actually will (or can) be built, given the production realities of the particular company. These realities include:

- Capacity limitations in key work centers
- Economic methods of production
- Material availability of required purchased items
- The company's goals and policies regarding stocking finished items

In most companies, it is neither possible nor desirable to follow every uptick and downtick of independent demand. Production of certain items may be feasible only on an infrequent basis. Conversely, a level rate of production may be preferable in other cases. Further, little is accomplished by scheduling more production of an item than can actually be made, due to a limit in a key work center. (A key work center for master scheduling purposes is one where a relatively inflexible limit exists that is close to the average production rate.) If one of the items required for production is in limited supply, scheduling more than this amount will only cause inventory buildup of all other items in the product's structure. Finally, since finished-goods inventory has many disadvantages, including high costs and tying up parts that could be used in the production of items in short supply, the company may have definite limits on the finished inventory of each item stocked.

The master production schedule, then, is where all the limiting factors on a company's ability to meet independent demand get resolved into a statement of what actually can be produced, not what management wishes it could make, or what the customers would like the company to make. Figure 3–12 shows the primary interfaces with other company and system functions.

Information regarding these limiting factors is obtained in several ways. Production economics are reflected as lot sizing rules in the system, and are established (properly) from cost studies by industrial engineering. Stocking limits for finished goods may be obvious in the case of an airplane manufacturer (none) or simply stated as safety stock levels calculated from past experience of forecast deviations. Management willingness to invest capital in finished goods may serve as an arbitrary limit by itself.

For information regarding capacity and material availability limitations, a state-of-the-art system will use greatly shortened versions of the bills of

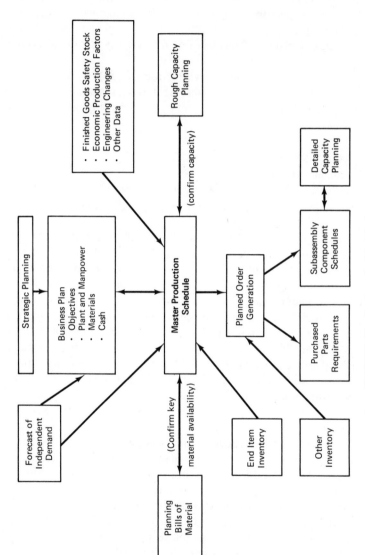

FIGURE 3–12   Master schedule interfaces.

material and routings to analyze the effect of master schedule changes. This is done to avoid running the changes through the entire planning system. Supplementary information concerning the effects of unforeseen machine breakdowns, material delivery problems, unplanned scrap, and the like will also be obtained and should be reflected in changes to the master production schedule.

Probably the most common error concerning master production scheduling and planning is that companies make it too simple to take the forecast and make it the master production schedule. It cannot be emphasized enough that the forecast must be uncoupled from the master scheduling process. A vast array of difficulties, confusion, unnecessary inventory, shortages, and the like follow from using an unrealistic master schedule to drive the material and capacity planning system. A closely related error is to make changes to the schedule within the time required to absorb the change.

Since the master schedule is the company's key part of the whole production planning process, it must be frequently updated, preferably at least weekly, as errors in the forecast, production problems, material shortages, and so on, come to light in the nearer of the plan. An example of a master production schedule (MPS) for an end item is shown in Figure 3–13. Illustrated are several important points:

- The forecast varies from week to week, and shows an error in the current period (week 1).
- The scheduled orders reflect the economic production quantity of 120 units, and so are placed only at intervals, rather than simply following the forecast.
- In the near term, the forecast becomes, in effect, actual demand.
- There is no such thing as a past due forecast.
- The safety stock quantity of 80 units serves not as a minimum, but as a buffer zone to cushion the variables.

Current On-Hand Quantity   =   0
Economic Production Quantity = 120
Safety Stock   = 80

Week

	Past Due	1	2	3	4	5	6	7	8
Forecast		40	40	40	35	30	25	40	40
Actual Demand	5	50	35	20	5		2		
MPS Orders		120		120				120	
Projected Available		65	25	105	70	40	15	95	55

FIGURE 3-13   Master production schedule example.

- Setting a master schedule quantity (MPS order) is clearly a matter of human judgment. The order in period seven, for example, might be moved into period six, since the projected available is only 15 and the period is further out into the future, and therefore subject to greater error.
- It is clearly necessary to update the schedule frequently.

A variety of computer techniques are available to aid the master scheduling process. The actual interface between forecast and schedule should be maintained in the system. One technique is to maintain the forecast as though it were just another set of "higher-level" requirements, similar to the requirements records in the planned order generation system, or material requirements planning system, discussed in Chapter 7. Another technique is to have the results of forecast calculations loaded into records that have a space, or a bucket for each planning period, usually a week. Thus the master schedule moves across this set of buckets like a train going down tracks. The forecast can be updated at different intervals from the master schedule without causing problems. Each weekly bucket in the example (week 1, 2, etc.) in a live system would have an actual date assigned to it, and these dates would be different between the forecast record and the master schedule. Figure 3-14 illustrates this. To simplify determining the availability of materials and the capacity of key work centers, many systems maintain product structure records that are used only by the master production scheduling system. The logic is the same as in the full-blown material requirements planning and capacity requirements planning systems described in Chapters 7 and 8, but only a few records are used, comparatively speaking.

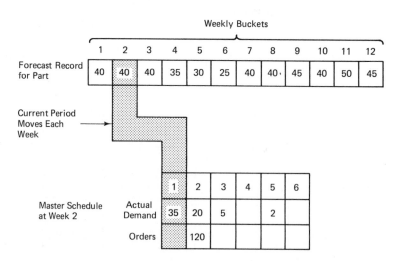

FIGURE 3-14   Forecast—master schedule interface.

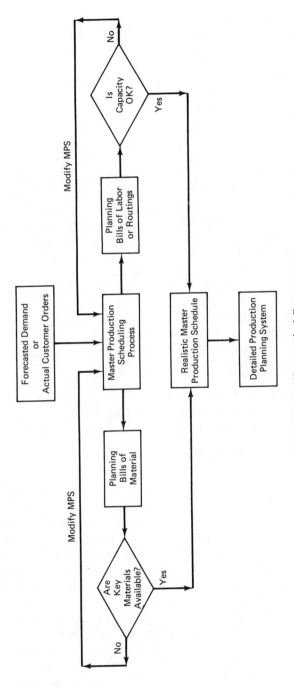

FIGURE 3-15 Master scheduling process.

Various ways of arranging product structure records into modular bills of material, super bills, and so on are discussed in Chapter 4. These models can be used to construct special-purpose planning bills of material that contain only key material items. The master scheduling system then takes its end items, or pseudo end items and does a simple, single-level requirements explosion to determine if the key raw materials needed to produce the end item or a group of items will be available in the same period. Similarly, a bill of labor can be constructed, using bill of material logic to calculate labor requirements for the entire master schedule in a single-level explosion process.

If the production process includes numerous work centers, but has only a few where bottlenecks typically occur, an abbreviated routing can be constructed for each end item, or for groups of end items (using a pseudo part number assigned to represent a whole group of end items using a similar production process). This abbreviated routing can be quickly exploded in a simple process by the computer to determine whether these key work centers will be overloaded. Conceptually speaking, the most accurate method of managing a master schedule is to have the master schedule orders drive the detailed planning systems for material and capacity, generate the entire subassembly and purchasing schedules, then examine where misfits or over- and underscheduling has occurred, modify the master schedule order, and replan. In the real world of production where thousands of parts, planned orders, and work centers may be involved, this process is just not practical. Hence a greatly abbreviated method, using a very simplified model of the production and material process, allows the master scheduler to make intelligent, well-founded decisions as to what can actually be produced. Figure 3–15 illustrates this process, using both planning bills of material to confirm/deny material availability and planning bills of labor or routings to check capacity availability.

The Realistic Master Production Schedule

There seems to be an endless debate among American manufacturing executives about how best to respond to the situation where a customer's order will not be delivered exactly when he wants. This is closely related to the question about infinite versus finite capacity planning. For many years, the prevailing opinion seemed to be that one accepted orders with the desired delivery date on it, then loaded these into the planning system, which dutifully produced a schedule with large variations in it, especially in the current period, which really contains all the past due orders.

This gives rise to a situation where everyone pretends that an order that is shown as due in 60 days is still on schedule, while the current period is actually spent working entirely on orders that were due some time in the past. Those due to be started this week actually don't get started for several weeks after their starting dates are past due. Normally accompanying this phenomenon are gross overstatements of lead times, the idea being that, this way, everything required for the item's production will be available at the scheduled start date just in case it should actually be started on that date, even though no one can remember such an instance.

Several things are true of this situation. The only time it is truly known for sure when a particular customer's order will be shipped is when it is in the final stages of production. At all other times, due dates are just an expression of what someone would *like* to have happen. Since orders do not run quickly through the shop, some being stopped to allow those with higher priorities to be completed, work in process is typically quite large. Inventories of raw materials and components are typically enlarged, since these items were purchased and delivered considerably in advance of when they actually will be used. Some customers have more power over the production schedule than others, so purchased materials needed for these orders often are subjected to special treatment, air freight, special handling, and the like. These actions cost significant amounts of money and therefore increase production costs.

People who work in these kinds of manufacturing companies often display a strong need for heroics, the need to solve or avert a crisis, seldom recognizing that the crisis is of their own making. Also common is a belief that success in production is attained by pressure, that if the production staff is not continually under intense pressure to meet deadlines, to hustle all the time, and generally hurry things along, it will become lethargic and unproductive.

Companies that consistently produce good-quality products, within budget, and on time have long since learned that these beliefs are simply not true. When an unrealistic production schedule is used, the situation is simply out of control, perhaps not completely, but certainly more out of control than where a realistic production schedule that is actually being met is the case. Pressure to perform according to discipline and order that is part of a formal system is one thing. Pressure to hurry is another.

A company that keeps its word to its customers, even if it is going to be late at times, invariably has a higher credibility than one that is unpredictable. The systems and concepts of managing a manufacturing business discussed in this and other chapters assume that company management grasps this fundamental point. These systems assume fairly strict discipline and cannot be made to work successfully without it. When the human organization exists that can fully use the methods and information systems that constitute the management state of the art for manufacturing and distribution businesses, the results are truly astonishing at times. Besides the improved business results, these companies are simply better places to work, not being as hard on their personnel.

This chapter has focused on the importance of knowing one's market well, doing the best possible job of forward planning to minimize surprises in the short run. The better job a company does of this forward planning process, including strategic planning, forecasting, market research, and master production scheduling, the easier the detailed planning process becomes and the more productive the entire company becomes.

CHAPTER 3 QUESTIONS

1. Why should a company do strategic planning?

2. What is the first step in the strategic planning process?

3. Describe several general environmental factors a company might face.

4. Why is defining the company's business so important?

5. What are the stages of a product's life cycle, and what are the characteristics of each stage?

6. How does competition in an industry relate to the commodity/customer service continuum?

7. What are some of the common consequences of not developing a cohesive strategy?

8. What is a means-end chain?

9. List several reasons for doing market research.

10. Distinguish between primary and secondary market research data and give examples of each.

11. What company department is in the best position to produce accurate sales forecasts? Why?

12. Why should dependent demand items *not* be forecasted?

13. What are some of the inherent shortcomings of highly statistical forecasting?

14. Describe the relationship between planning horizons and the level of planning detail used.

15. How does the kind of information sources differ for each of the zones of planning?

16. How do padded or excessively long in-plant or supplier lead times complicate the forecasting process?

17. Distinguish between extrinsic and intrinsic forecasting.

18. What is the main assumption of all intrinsic forecasting methods?

19. Why must the average of all seasonal factors in a set be 1.0?

20. Define and explain "forecast trend."

21. How are seasonal factors updated to reflect actual experiences?

22. Explain the difference between a forecast and the master production schedule.

23. Why should the forecast *not* be used to drive the rest of the planning system?

24. What are some of the predictable, common results from using an unrealistic master production schedule?

25. Describe the primary function of a master production schedule.

26. What are the key limiting factors that must be resolved informally in an effective master production schedule?

27. Describe the primary interface between the master production schedule and other company functions.

4

Product Structures

The Concept of a Part

In a simple inventory control environment, consisting of parts that are received, held, and issued, having a unique, unambiguous identifier for each item (the part number) is a straightforward, clear-cut way of keeping track of each item. In many companies, run under manual methods, identification of items is often blurred by having a single identifier that really covers a class of items. An example could be doors stocked and sold by a building products distributor. The catalog might identify a particular style of door as being a "C-23" door, with a note that all doors come in three heights and two widths and in right- and left-hand models. The staff writing up orders simply writes all the information down and the stock picker selects the appropriate door, which is not a problem because the stock picker can measure and examine the doors.

The computer system is not able to measure the actual stock, however, so some other method must be used. In actuality, the "C-23" door is really 12 different items (three heights times two widths times two models). If any information system, computerized or not, is to keep track of each of these items, each item must have a unique identifier. In other words, all items represented by the unique identifying part number must be completely interchangeable. In the engineer's terms, they must have the same form, fit, and function. Any modification of an item (e.g., painting) that makes it somehow different from others of the same type and prevents the complete interchangeability rule from applying requires that the different item be identified by assigning a separate identifier.

This seemingly simple principle can become somewhat involved in a highly engineered, complex production environment. Similar products from two different vendors may not be entirely interchangeable, requiring a different assembly procedure, or one may produce a different-quality level in the end product. In the area of manufactured parts, or subassemblies, deciding what to designate as a unique item depends on a variety of factors. The most important criterion is whether the item is to be stocked in the warehouse. If it is, then the same rule of interchangeability applies, which requires a unique identifier.

There is an enduring debate in many companies about what is referred to as the part numbering system. One camp desires the part number to tell a little story about the part, describing it in some fashion. These coded part numbers, and that is what they are, may include codes for anything from the end product the part belongs to, to the alloy it is made of, to the product group it is part of in the sales catalog. All coded part numbering systems (also termed significant systems) have one thing in common. Sooner or later the system usually becomes inadequate and must be changed. In other words, the coded scheme fails. This type of number is also quite long in most cases.

Companies having huge numbers of parts to identify faced this issue long ago. Descriptive information belongs in separate data fields, where it can be identified and similar parts grouped for various purposes. Chapter 6 discusses these codes in detail. The part number itself in these systems is simply a sequentially assigned four-, five-, or six-digit number that, in itself, stands for nothing in particular. It merely identifies a particular part. This means that the size of the part number is determined entirely by how many parts there are to be identified. As the number of parts to track increases, another digit is added. Sometimes an additional, calculated digit is added as a "check" digit, which serves to determine if the part number itself is a valid number.

Eliminating alphabetic characters from the part number also means less confusion between letters and numbers (i.e., more accuracy in writing or keying the part number). Most computer terminals have a 10-key numeric pad. An all-numeric part number is far easier to enter on this pad than is one with several alphabetic characters in it. Accuracy also increases simply because the number is short.

If descriptive information is structured according to the key-noun concept, a computer can list all parts according to description and the result will have all similar parts groups together. An example would be a 16-mm cadmium bolt, which would be described as a "bolt, cadmium, 16 mm."

For items that need to be identified in the production process, but which are seldom, if ever, stocked, it may be desirable to assign what the product structure refers to as a "phantom part number." This type of identifier is for a part that has only a transient existence during a production cycle; that is, it is immediately consumed in the production of a next-higher-level assembly.

Relationship Pairs

The records in a product structure system are, in essence, pairs of part numbers, which show that one is a component part of the other. The part that the component goes into is termed its parent part. Figure 4-1 shows a typical manufactured product, a projector, presented in simplified form. The company purchases already completed bases, arms, cases, bulbs, and mirrors from outside sources and assembles the projector. The projector parts list shows all the parts, arranged like an outline, so that the reader can see that the mirror, for example,

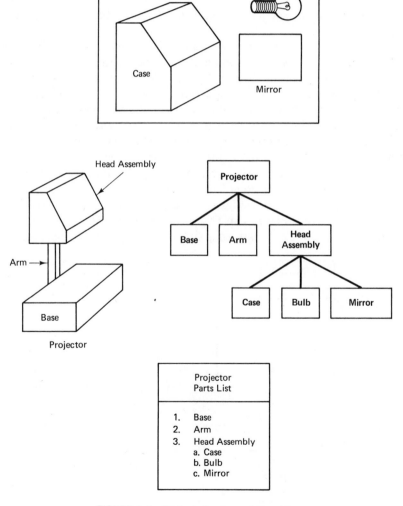

FIGURE 4-1   Product structure relationship.

Parent Part	Component Part
Projector	Base
Projector	Arm
Projector	Head Assembly
Head Assembly	Case
Head Assembly	Bulb
Head Assembly	Mirror

FIGURE 4-2   Product structure records for projector.

on the diagram represent parent-component relationships between pairs of parts.

The corresponding product structures in a computer file for the items in the projector would be shown as in Figure 4-2. Notice that there is one record for each line in the diagram. This technique of recording only the relationships between pairs of parts allows a product of complexity to have all its relationships described only once in the entire file, regardless of how many times it is used or how many products it is used in. If the head assembly, for example, were used in more than one type of projector, the head assembly's relationships are still described only once in the product structure file.

To illustrate how this works, refer to Figure 4-3, which shows the product structures of two different completed projectors which use the same head assembly. When these relationships are entered into the product structure file, they will be as shown in Figure 4-4. To generate a complete list of all parts going into the "projector, plain," the system simply looks up all records with a parent

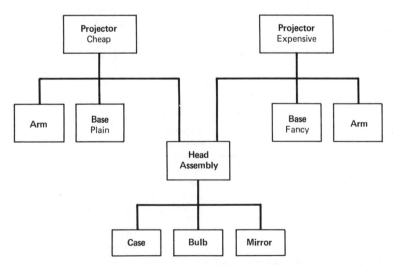

FIGURE 4-3   Product structures for two projectors using a common head assembly.

Parent Part	Component Part
Projector, Cheap	Arm
Projector, Cheap	Base — Plain
Projector, Cheap	Head Assembly
Projector, Expensive	Arm
Projector, Expensive	Base — Fancy
Projector, Expensive	Head Assembly
Head Assembly	Case
Head Assembly	Bulb
Head Assembly	Mirror

FIGURE 4-4
Product structure file records for two projectors.

part of "projector, cheap" and when it gets to the Head Assembly, it looks up those with a parent part of "head assembly" and lists the results. Figure 4-5 shows complete parts lists for both projectors, generated using this technique.

From this base of logical relationships to describe the relationships between parts in an assembly, or between chemicals in a solution-type product, it is fairly simple to add other, related pieces of secondary data to each product structure record, such as the quantity used, engineering effectivity dates, lead time adjustment, and so on. If additional information about each part is needed, such as description, cost, or on-hand balance, this can be obtained by looking up the corresponding Inventory Record.

To accomplish these kinds of tasks efficiently, computer software uses a technique referred to as "pointers" to go directly from one logically related record to the next to produce a "chain" of records comprising an entire set. This also makes the computer less dependent on the physical arrangements of records in its files.

In an integrated system, the pieces of data called "parent part" and "component part" in the example are supplemented by data showing the record location in the Inventory file for each part. This also makes it logically mandatory that each part referred to in a product structure exist also in the inventory and part master file, as it is often called. The technique of pointers is used throughout an integrated system to relate different pieces of logically connected information, such as the list of operations required to manufacture a part or the tooling used in a certain step.

Bills of Material

The examples used to illustrate how product structure relationships are managed in a computer system are instances of one use of product structure information. A parts list is usually called a *bill of material*. Each level of assembly is

Parts List Projector, Cheap	Parts List Projector, Expensive
1. Arm	1. Arm
2. Base — Plain	2. Base — Fancy
3. Head Assembly	3. Head Assembly
a. Case	a. Case
b. Bulb	b. Bulb
c. Mirror	c. Mirror

FIGURE 4-5
Parts list for two projectors.

referred to as an *indenture level,* with numbers assigned to each level, usually starting at the "zero" level at the end product stage. A bill of material listing for the projector would be as shown in Figure 4–6. If the same part is used repeatedly throughout a product's structure, it is sometimes desirable to list the product structure in summarized form, where the quantity used is the total of all usages for the part throughout the entire structure. This list is referred to as a *summarized bill of material.*

In the normal situation, the indenture levels of a product structure will correspond to levels of manufacture. Each level represents a separate set of manufacturing processes, with a work order issued to complete each. A product is completed, by starting at the lowest assembly level in a product's structure, completing it, with the completed item becoming a component in the next higher assembly's production, and so on until the final assembly stage is reached and the item is ready to be sold and shipped. Seen in this light, it is clear that the purpose of the product structure is to provide information for how the product is actually built (i.e., to drive the material planning and scheduling system). A closely related function is one of control of the design itself, so that what the designers intended the product to be in fact turns out to be the case when it is completed.

Bills of material and related lists may be said to be views of the product structure looking "downward." A single-level bill of material is simply the complete list of components going into one assembly, regardless of its level in the overall structure. A complete list of all parts for a product, from the completed item down to all purchased parts and raw materials, is simply a complete listing showing all assembly stages.

Where-Used Lists

For a variety of reasons, it is vital in the day-to-day operation of a manufacturing business to be able to view the product structure from the bottom up. For example, a particular purchased raw material may be used in a wide variety of

Indented Bill of Material		
Parent Part: Projector		
Level	Component Part	Quantity Used
0	Projector	1
1	Base	1
1	Arm	1
1	Head Assembly	1
2	Case	1
2	Bulb	1
2	Mirror	1

FIGURE 4-6   Indented bill of material for projector.

```
┌─────────────────────────────────────────────────────────────┐
│                                                             │
│                   Indented Where-Used List                  │
│                                                             │
│                 Component Part:  Bulb                       │
│                                                             │
│   Level            Next Higher Assembly         Quantity Used│
│                                                             │
│    2               Bulb                              1       │
│     1              Head Assembly                     1       │
│       0            Projector — Cheap                        │
│       0            Projector — Expensive                    │
│                                                             │
└─────────────────────────────────────────────────────────────┘
```

FIGURE 4-7   Indented where-used list for bulb.

parts throughout a company's entire product line. If the raw material becomes unavailable, or is to be changed, management needs to know all the uses of the material (i.e., where it is used). By means of the same pointer technique mentioned earlier, the product structure can be followed in reverse of the way the bill of material list presents it. The arm in the projector example would appear on a where-used list, showing that it was a purchased item used on both projectors. Carrying this concept further to include the indenture concept, an indented where-used list can be generated that goes all the way to the top of the product structure, as shown in Figure 4-7 for the part called "bulb."

As-Designed versus As-Built

Product structures have historically been viewed from the perspective of how each person used the information. The design engineer viewed the product from the standpoint of how to conceive and draw the product. The manufacturing engineer took the designer's drawings and prepared the material lists for use on the shop floor, which fit the way the company had to manufacture the product with the equipment and techniques available to it. Other functions adopted similar approaches, including material planners, cost accountants, marketing managers, and so on. Each was looking at the same product from a different point of view, much like the old parable of the blind men and the elephant. To say that this gave rise to intense differences of opinion between different departments in a company is to make a gross understatement, especially in companies making complex products.

As the power of integrated, computerized information systems have become more and more apparent to management, the advantages of developing ways of looking at the product that met every department's needs, yet used the same set of information as a source, became clearer. After all, the whole reason an engineer designs a product and provides information about the product is so that other people can use it to make it. And what point is there really in costing a product other than the way it is actually made, once the capability of doing so becomes available? The purpose of an integrated computer system is, among others, to communicate information rapidly to everyone who needs it. The effectiveness of such a system is obviously diminished considerably if the information must be "translated" by the recipient before it becomes useful.

For these reasons, and many others, companies that make the most effective use of their computer resources have, one way or the other, resolved this issue in favor of the use of a single set of product structure records, all used by every department. In this case, there is only one "official" product structure, even though other arrangements of the product structure may be made for special purposes, such as master scheduling. Finally, in some companies, this process has led to an entirely different way of designing products and drawing them. A computer-aided design system, for instance, can develop parts lists that can be fed directly into the product structure file and used by all other departments immediately. Under this approach, as soon as design engineering begins even considering probable changes to a product's structure, the information potentially becomes available to material planning so that existing inventory can be used up and not replaced by the time the new parts are to be used.

Drawing Control Systems

In most companies the practice of relying on actual drawings of the design will continue for some years. Although parts lists were historically written on the drawing itself by the engineer, this practice is now widely recognized as obsolete, with the parts list being maintained in the product structure file. In companies making highly engineered, complex products, the drawing process itself can become quite complex, and control of the drawings is critical. Consequently, drawing structure control systems have been developed, using a logical relationship system, pointers, where-used capabilities, and the like, all similar to the product structure logic. In addition, there may be sets of pointers defining logical relationships between each drawing and its associated parts as shown in the product structure file and in the part master file.

The Integrated Method

A variety of techniques have been developed to enable a company to use a single integrated data base to define its products. These techniques fall into several basic areas according to the purpose for which the product structure data is to be used. It must be pointed out here that the subject of structuring products is in actuality quite complex and a full discussion would comprise an entirely separate book. In fact, several have been written. The discussion here will survey only the most important, commonly used techniques. Most of the special cases are found in companies making either products of extreme complexity or where a relatively small number of components can be assembled into a numerically large number of possible combinations, such as connectors for electronic devices. The major areas where the techniques discussed below apply are to resolve design and manufacturing differences, the use of optional items, material planning and scheduling factors, and product costing.

Phantom part numbers: Many manufactured products contain subassemblies or parts that although identified on drawings as discrete items, and which may be stocked for service requirements, are normally consumed immediately in the manufacturing process. An example would be an item that is assembled on a feeder or branch assembly line going directly into the main assembly line. Figure 4–8 shows such an example. Product A contains subassembly C. A separate, discrete identity for C is needed, but to use the standard product structure for A to develop material plans and issue work orders would lead to the generation of two work orders.

The work order scheduling system will assume that work order 2 is to be completed first, completions of part C reported to inventory stock, and subsequently be issued to work order 1 in order that part A can be produced. If part C is designated as a phantom part, its identity in the product structure is preserved, and it remains an item in the inventory file that is otherwise no different from any other inventory item. The difference is that the work order generation logic will be changed to treat C and its components as being part of the assembly for part A. The result would be the revised work order 1 shown at the

Product Structure

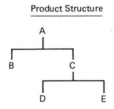

Work Orders

Work Order Number: 1
Parent Part: A
Components
    B
    C

And

Work Order Number: 2
Parent Part: C
Components:
    D
    E

If Part C Is Phantom:

Work Order Number: 1
Parent Part: A
Components:
    B
    C
    D
    E

FIGURE 4–8
Phantom part
numbers.

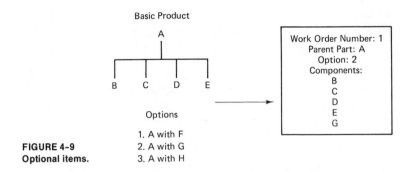

Basic Product

A

B   C   D   E

Options

1. A with F
2. A with G
3. A with H

Work Order Number: 1
Parent Part: A
Option: 2
Components:
B
C
D
E
G

FIGURE 4-9
Optional items.

bottom of the illustration. In all other respects, the relationship of part C in the product structure remains unchanged.

Optional items: This technique involves creating a standard product structure for the item, less all its possible options. It assumes that the options are not major reconfigurations of the item, but are relatively minor changes, such as the choice of a plastic or metal container for an otherwise identical product. The option to be included with the standard item is specified by choosing an option number. The option number has the effect of adding the product structure of the optional part to that of the standard, but for that work order only, leaving the basic product structure intact. Figure 4-9 illustrates this process. The product structure of part A is shown with optional extra parts F, G, and H. Each has an option number. A work order is generated for part A, selecting option 2, part A, with optional part G included. The system included part G with the components for part A. Optional parts F, G, and H could, of course, be complete subassemblies, each with its own list of components. In this case, the components of the optional part would be included.

Superbills and pseudo part numbers: If the use of optional items is to avoid excluding all the options from the planning process, another method is used to plan the options separately from the main item, which is driven by the master schedule. For part A in the previous example, the master schedule will state that so many units of A will be built each planning period (week, day, or month). Since the basic product does not include the options, dependent demand for the parts used in the options will not be derivable from the independent demand for part A, since they are not connected directly in the product structure. Accordingly, a special-purpose product structure must be assembled, where all optional items for part A are grouped, as though they were components of the pseudo part number.

Figure 4-10 shows examples of superbills. Two ways of relating part A and its options are shown. The first would allow the normal quantities for each part as used whenever they are included in part A to be preserved and would require that part A-1, a "pseudo" part number, be master scheduled separately

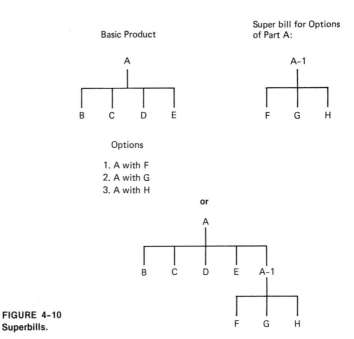

FIGURE 4-10
Superbills.

from part A. Another approach is to include the pseudo part in the product structure of part A, with the quantities used of each option reflecting a percentage of the frequency with which each option is expected to be used with part A. Thus, if either part F, G, or H must always be used with part A, their quantities used would be decimal quantities (e.g., 0.45 part F for each part A ordered) and their total would add up to 1 (equaling 100%). If the option is not mandatory, the total percentages for each option would not add up to 100%.

Lead Time Offsets

In many types of products, the actual assembly process taking place to complete a single work order may cover a considerable period of time. Not all components may be needed at the start date of the work order. In fact, certain expensive items may not be required until the very end of the production cycle. In normal cases, the work order planning system will assume that all components of a parent part are needed on the start date of the work order. If a quantity of items is to be assembled together over a relatively short period, this assumption holds. To allow for those cases where one or more components are needed either very much earlier or later than all the rest, a lead time offset can be included in a product structure record. This will have the effect of causing the material planning system to show that the part is needed earlier or later than the other components.

Figure 4-11 illustrates an example of lead time offsetting. Part A is composed of parts B, C, and D. Part D, however, is not needed until the last three

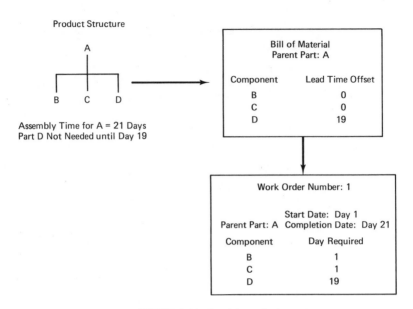

FIGURE 4-11   Lead-time offsets.

days of the production cycle. This fact is reflected in the product structure record for component D, as illustrated by the bill of material list for part A, where component part D is shown as having a lead time offset of 19 days. When the work order generation cycle creates a work order from the product structure records for part A, the lead time offset is added to the start date determined by the requirement for part A (required date minus the assembly time of 21 days). Thus component parts B and C are shown as being required on the start date of the work order (day 1) and component part D is shown as not required until day 19. When the work order is started (presumably on day 1), the cost of parts B and C will become part of work-in-process inventory, whereas part D will not until 19 days later. If part D is an assembly, to be made on its own work order, the system will not schedule D's completion date until day 19.

Product Costing

One of the most important uses of product structure data is in the development of product costs. If the product structure data itself is the source, the type of costing is the development of what the product is supposed to cost (i.e., its standard cost) assuming that standard production rates are used and that a planned purchase price for procured items is obtained. Labor and other production costs are obtained for each assembly from the operations or routing system, as discussed in Chapter 5. In this step, the cost of each operation is calculated, using labor, machine, and overhead costs associated with each work center the product passes through during its production cycle. The result of these calculations are placed in appropriate data fields in the part master file record for each assembly.

The next step in the building up of product costs is to start at the bottom, or purchased part level of each product, and accumulate the costs of each assembly upward through the product structure, following the where-used chain in the product structure file. This process is termed an implosion, or cost buildup. There are several methods of handling the different cost elements. These and other financial aspects are discussed in detail in Chapter 10. Figure 4-12 illustrates a hypothetical product, part A, together with its product structure. The condition of the records for each part before the cost buildup is performed are shown in the Part Master File. Material cost is known only for the purchased parts B, D, and F. The manufacturing cost (labor and overhead are considered together here to simplify the example) for the assemblies, parts E, C, and A, has already been calculated from the operations required to assemble each part using the production rates in the operations routing and hourly costs for labor and overhead in the work center file.

The next step is shown in Figure 4-13 after the cost buildup process has been completed. Note that the sources of cost for each assembly are kept separate, according to whether a cost element came from a component part at that level, or from a lower level. Thus the material cost of part C consists of the purchased cost of part D ($2.00) and the purchased cost of part F, carried up through assembly part E. The total cost of assembly part C is $13.21, the sum of

Product Structure

Part Master File

Part Number	Material Cost	Manufactured Cost*
A	——	5.36
B	3.00	——
C	——	4.65
D	2.00	——
E	——	3.12
F	4.00	——

FIGURE 4-12
Product costing before buildup.

*Obtained from manufacturing operations and work centers

Indented Product Cost

| | | Material Cost | Manufactured Cost | | | | Total Cost | |
| | | This Level | From Lower Levels | This Level | From Lower Levels | | This Level | From Lower Levels |
Level	Part Number	This Level	From Lower Levels	This Level	From Lower Levels		This Level	From Lower Levels
0	A	3.00	6.00	5.36	7.21		8.36	13.21
1	B	3.00	—	—	—		3.00	—
1	C	2.00	4.00	4.65	2.56		6.65	6.56
2	D	2.00	—	—	—		2.00	—
2	E	—	4.00	2.56	—		6.56	—
3	F	4.00	—	—	—		4.00	—

Total Cost of Part Number A, All Levels

Material: $ 9.00
Manufacturing: $12.57
Total: $21.57

FIGURE 4-13   Product costing after buildup.

$6.65 and $6.56. The reader is invited to study this example with a calculator to improve understanding.

An exercise such as the preceding, simple as it is, can nevertheless give one an appreciation of the power of the computer. Developing standard costs in a company having 5000 different part numbers, including perhaps 2000 different subassemblies and 500 end products is a truly formidable task without a computer and accurate product structure. It is easy to understand why a wide variety of shortcut methods are found in companies not yet using this approach. The advantages are clear. Standard costs are modular and essentially independent at any level in the product structure. Developing selling prices for service parts and subassemblies becomes simple. Standards can be easily recalculated using an inflation factor for existing purchase or manufacturing costs in a simulation run. The biggest advantage is that the same data are used by the actual production work order to compare planned versus actual part usages and labor time, each of which can easily be costed out. This fact alone gives management a powerful tool for tracking down and acting on cost variations.

Management Considerations

Since the product structure information, together with the information for each part and the operations required for each assembly, are in fact the information core of a manufacturing company, assigning management responsibility for its control is a major issue. In companies where management has not fully understood the significance of this fact, actual control of the data in the computer files has often been relegated to a rather low level individual, or worse still, scattered among a variety of poorly communicating departments with no one person having overall responsibility. That the result is a poorly focused picture of the company's reality is not surprising. The system costs the same or more to operate, yet serves as a dull, ineffective tool for managing the company.

Part of the reason for this difficulty is the notion that the company's staff takes actions, designs products, makes decisions, and so on, independently of the system, and then someone is supposed to tell the system later. Unfortunately, the world of manufacturing often changes so fast that the system never catches up. Enlightened management, on the other hand, arranges for a single, key manager, usually in the design or manufacturing engineering function to assume overall responsibility for all data in these files, and then sees to it that the company operates such that the computer system is itself the source of company information. Only if a system *must* be relied on will it become in fact reli*able*.

As more and more of the information used to manage a company is transferred to an increasingly integrated set of computer files, the operation of the company becomes, of necessity, more integrated and less fragmented and departmentalized. Each department tends more and more to be using the same source of information as other departments, even though it may be viewed differently. A highly integrated system brings an increasingly formal method to the business, requiring more discipline than in an informal system. Management must shift from relying on specific individuals to cause events to happen to one of relying on the system and its procedures to ensure that the business is properly run. The centrality to all parts of the business of this kind of integrated system requires that management assign a key manager for overall responsibility and to ensure that appropriate supporting procedures are implemented and used so that serious errors do not creep into the data base and cause substantial damage to the business as a whole.

Engineering Change Control

Even in companies that are making products not commonly thought to be engineered nevertheless have an engineering function. Since products are usually in a continual state of development and change, the control and management of these changes becomes central to the management of an integrated system. The critical factor in managing engineering change is one of communication of the potential or actual change to all parts of the business that need to know in order to perform their jobs effectively.

The two primary methods of handling engineering changes are by date and by serial number of the end product. A variation of the latter is according to a certain lot, in companies where batch processing is used. Engineering changes affect five primary areas in a manufacturing company:

- Changes to specific parts used in the product, such as a change in a purchased raw material or part, substituting one for another.
- Changes in the structure of parts, where logical relationships in the product structure are altered. A certain subassembly may be added, deleted, or changed in how it is assembled, for example.
- Changes in the operations or manufacturing steps used to produce the product. The product may be routed to a new, more efficient work center for production, but otherwise remains unchanged.
- Changes in work centers used to manufacture products. A new machine might be installed which would significantly alter the production rates and therefore production schedule lead times and costs.
- Tooling may be changed. A new cutting tool, die, or mold may be introduced to replace a now obsolete one.

In many cases, these changes are closely interrelated, especially where a new or radically redesigned product is being introduced. Their impact on the various departments in a manufacturing company can be substantial, especially if there is a significant time lag between the time the change is approved and the affected department learns of it. Communication mixups or time lags can and do cause lost production, excess inventory, scheduling inefficiencies, and costing problems. Obviously, not all of these changes would originate in a design engineering department alone.

When engineering development of a product and its subsequent shift into a manufacturing mode are examined, it becomes clear that there is considerable overlap in time between the development and production modes. Figure 4–14 illustrates the different steps in each phase and the typical extent to which they overlap. Clearly, if the production phase was not even started until the completion of the development phase, a great deal of time and consequently sales in a competitive market place would be lost. As products become more complex and lead times longer, this becomes more and more important in managing a business in a competitive environment.

The decision as to when to introduce an engineering change to an existing product or its effectivity date is usually based on four factors:

- *Immediate change.* Used in cases where the impact on inventory is considered not to be a factor. Product safety may be involved.
- *Availability of the new part, raw material, or tooling.* The new product cannot be produced until the required factor for the change is available for use.
- *Stock depletion.* It may be desirable to use up existing raw material or component inventory before shifting to the new one. A number of different part numbers may be affected simultaneously.
- *Serial number of the end product.* This method is used where the product change must be identified with a particular customer's order or when engineering information is maintained by serial number.

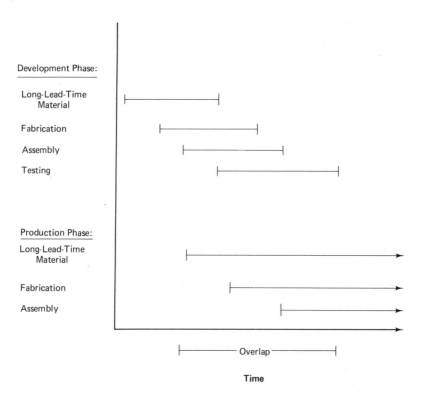

FIGURE 4-14   Development/production interface.

The first three factors result in a decision to implement the change by a certain date. The last factor depends solely on how many units are completed, and is independent, per se, of dates. By examining the master production schedule, a date can usually be assigned, however. Figure 4–15 illustrates an example of engineering change effectivity by dates. The assembly is part number 135, and today's date is 3/5/XX. The current product structure diagram for part 135 is shown on the left, and the revised version, after the change, is on the right. The bill of material list for part 135 shows that component parts 250 and 260 began to be used in the production of part 135 as of 1/10/XX. On 4/10/XX, the new item, part 270 will become effective in the production of part 135, changing its product structure on that date.

Serial number effectivity is considerably more complex than date effectivity. First, the specific subassembly where the change occurs must be identified, according to the end product serial number into which it will eventually be assembled. The net result of serial number effectivity is that the identity of the serial number of the end product must be carried all the way down the entire product structure.

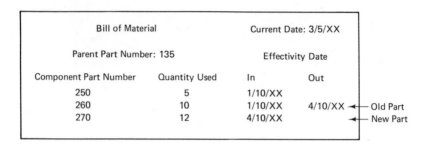

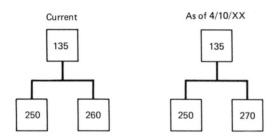

FIGURE 4-15   Engineering change effectivity.

Material Planning Impact

In the previous example, the change in part numbers used on part 135 from 260 to 270 means that any existing inventory of part 260 that the company may still own is now useless as far as part 135's production is concerned, unless it can be consumed before 4/10/XX. After that date, it really is useless and may eventually be sold as scrap. It also means that if sufficient quantities of part 270 are not available by 4/10/XX, the production of part 135 must be stopped. Of course, this is a literal interpretation of the dates which is seldom actually done.

However, within the material planning system, since the product structure changes on 4/10/XX, planned work orders generated by the system will contain part 270 after that date. If the lead time for obtaining part 270 is longer than from the current date to 4/10/XX, the system will show a past due condition for the procurement of part 270 (or the starting of a work order to make it). If management regards the change as vital, current production schedules will be disrupted so that part 270 can be started now, or expensive expediting charges will be incurred to try and get the part delivered before 4/10/XX.

This simple example of product change illustrates a number of important points about manufacturing, especially in an integrated, formal system environment:

- If people who are responsible for designating when changes are to be implemented in products do not understand the lead times or production and purchasing reality, considerable confusion and disruption can easily occur. Imagine the mess that results if the example had involved changes to many parts and lead times were long.

- If material planning knows about pending engineering changes in sufficient time to initiate action within the normal lead times, the changes can be easily accommodated by normal system logic.

- If the effectivity date change concerns a product introduction, and the effort is related to promotion or other marketing efforts, the inability to meet the change date will cause disruption of that effort as well.

- By using the system itself as the source of engineering information, creating new part numbers as the potential need for them is conceived instead of writing them on drawings first, then entering them into the system after approved, all other affected system functions know about the potential change at the earliest possible time.

- The responsibility of management in this situation is to assign responsibilities within the company so that one function does not disrupt the operation of another, in the manner of a two-headed horse.

Impact on Production

Even if an engineering change has no impact on the material planning function, which is seldom the case, it is still possible for it to affect the plant significantly. This can occur in two ways: scheduling of work orders by modifying the planned shop load, and by changing the ability of the plant to make the part.

The first effect occurs if engineering changes the operations used to make the part, directs that different work centers be used, or specifies that different production rates might apply. Even though the engineer is changing the standard for making the part, when the change is effective, all work orders after that change date must use the new operation routing. If the change is made too soon, production will already have been scheduled for those work centers and they may already be loaded with other work. The result is that a change to the process standard caused a disruption of the production schedule.

In the second case, if a work center change is planned, normally the production staff will be aware of it and may have initiated the change. However, if the change involves the use of a different article of tooling, such as a different cutting tool, the production rate may be changed, or the tool may not be available in sufficient numbers to produce the desired amount of the part. If this change is introduced with insufficient lead time, or without ensuring that the tool is actually available, production will suffer. This type of engineering change may also affect scheduling because it might call for the use of a tool that is already scheduled to be used in the production of a different part.

These two types of production effects stemming from engineering changes are only a general sample. In fact, the effects are often quite complex and difficult to trace. In many companies, engineering changes have never been introduced with sufficient lead time. As a result, production schedule disruptions are a normal part of everyday existence, with expediting of one part delaying the production of a previously planned one. In this situation, the usual result is that all production tends to run somewhat behind what the schedule calls for, deliveries run late, there is a lot of expediting for parts and tools, hurried changes of work orders on short notice, and so on. The basic root of all of this type of problem is inadequate communication and planning. The communication problem stems from the use of relatively informal systems that require much interdepartmental communication and translation of information by recipients so that they can do their part.

While the complete manufacturing data base can be said to consist of product structure, part information, operation routings, tooling, and work center information, the product structure is usually the most complex, most subject to change, and the most difficult to manage. Accurate and current product structure records in an integrated planning and control system are a virtually absolute requirement. Where top management understands this and takes intelligent action to ensure that the company's well-being is not endangered by serious communication mixups by delegating responsibility to the right manager, together with good control procedures, the results can and are often pleasantly surprising (and profitable).

CHAPTER 4 QUESTIONS

1. Define the concept of a part.
2. How does the product structure record connect the parent and component parts?
3. If the same subassembly is used in six different end items, how many times will the parent-component relationships within the subassembly be defined in the product structure records?
4. Describe briefly how bills of material and where-used lists are produced from the same sets of records.
5. What are some of the arguments for using only one set of product structure records in a company?
6. How does a phantom part number work and what are its purposes?
7. Define an "optional item."
8. When would one use a super-bill and why?
9. What are some of the benefits of using lead time offsetting where appropriate?
10. In product costing, where are labor costs developed?
11. Why are cost buildups started at the lowest level?
12. Why does cost building logic require keeping cost calculations separate from level to level?
13. It is often said that a manufacturing company's product structure records are its most important data file. Why?

14. What are the five primary areas in a company affected by engineering changes?

15. What are the fundamental factors in deciding upon the timing of an engineering change effectivity date?

16. Briefly describe its impact on the material planning process and upon production of engineering changes.

5

Manufacturing Operations and Work Center Management

This chapter discusses the conceptual factors involved in structuring work to be performed in a manufacturing facility. Although these concepts were originated in the piece parts production industries, minor alterations in the way they are utilized renders them equally applicable in the process or continuous production industries. One factor that has slowed the recognition of this fact has been that different types of industries usually have their own jargon, which emphasizes the differences between concepts instead of the similarities.

The usefulness of these concepts is in their flexibility as tools to develop production standards, plan work, and collect information about the accuracy of those plans as well as the actual costs of production. The focus is in two areas, defining the steps involved in the work itself, or product to be made, and in the productive centers or facilities in the plant used to perform that work.

Work Centers

The key identifier of a work center designates a physical facility in the plant, such as a molding machine, turret lathe, or assembly group. Depending on the business, the work center may be any of the following:

- A group of people performing a similar or closely interrelated set of tasks or products
- A group of similar machines, or a single machine, which may or may not have a dedicated labor force to operate them

- An entire set of machines, functioning together to perform a closely related set of processes on one or more products

There are some trade-offs involved in deciding how much detail a plant's resources should be defined. As a plant is broken down into more and more uniquely defined work centers (i.e., each machine assigned a unique identifier), the resulting picture of the plant that a planning system develops becomes potentially more complete as it becomes more detailed. The drawback is that scheduling work through a larger number of work centers adds substantially to the complexity of scheduling the work. And since there are more work centers, the amount of data that must be input to keep the picture of the plant in focus also increases substantially, including information such as quantity completed, completed operations, and start dates.

Other methods used to organize productive resources into work centers can include the following:

- By groups of similar machines, physically located together and with a range of slightly varying capacities and capabilities. (This is the "traditional" approach, based on the machine shop model for a plant.)
- Arranging otherwise dissimilar machines according to the product, so that they resemble an assembly line, where a number of operations are performed in closely timed sequences.
- According to cost of operations of the machines, such as those with high or low setup costs, to reduce the problem of small work orders being scheduled into work centers with high setup costs.
- An actual production assembly line, or flow line, can be considered to be a single work center having a single capacity, in that the entire sequence is run as a unit, or not at all.

As a result of this dilemma, the actual work centers that are defined in any plant are a compromise between the extremes of a very high amount of detail, and so few that the resulting picture is too vague to be of any use. If the number of work centers are too few, a critical, pacing operation may be buried in with orders for which a capacity constraint does not exist, comparatively speaking. Also, since work centers are a logical place to gather actual performance and cost information, the resulting data may be too general to enable management to pinpoint problems and apply corrective action.

The primary data that identify a work center merely designate it. The secondary data describe features of the work center that are important for the system's purposes. These secondary data fall into several areas:

- *Capacity information:* including available hours, planned and actual efficiency achieved, number of workers and machines, expected downtime, and shifts available.

- *Product costing:* including labor rates, machine operation costs, overhead rates (usually based on an hourly machine or labor rate), and planned and actual "earned hours."
- *Maintenance:* including downtime, costs of maintaining equipment, parts used, reliability statistics, and historical data.
- *Cost of operating the work center:* including utility costs; expendable supplies, such as lubricating oil (not normally "charged" to a particular work order) and, some types of scrap; factors for allocating overhead costs; overtime costs; and planned versus actual labor rates.

For scheduling purposes, a work center may include a number of identical machines or work groups which permit the parallel processing of work (i.e., the same work order's parts may be run simultaneously on more than one machine). The work centers may be defined such that one or more is an alternate, or backup for another, causing the scheduling system to load work onto the primary work center first, then load up the alternates with the overload. Chapter 8 discusses the process of loading work onto the work centers in detail, as this is one of the most important functions of work center data. For planning purposes, an outside vendor to which overloads can be subcontracted can be defined as an alternate work center. If such work is always subcontracted out, such as plating, then defining the vendor as a work center will enable the scheduling system to determine in advance how much work will be sent to this vendor with a given production schedule.

In the past, overhead costs have been typically developed by adding up the total expected fixed and semifixed costs for operating the entire facility for a given time period, normally a year. The operating plan will usually specify an expected number of total labor or machine hours to be worked during the period. The total operating costs are then divided by expected hours to yield an hourly overhead rate. Each "direct" hour worked is charged with an "indirect" hour of overhead to absorb into the product the cost of running the plant.

If a more precise method is desired, the overhead costs can be spread among different work centers by percentage factors that reflect the square footage of the work center, differences in the costs of machines, or amount of other overhead factors required to operate it (such as supervision), to obtain a work center specific overhead rate. The work center is a logical place to accumulate a wide variety of historical data that is useful to management in making investment decisions about the comparative profitability of different pieces of equipment or manufacturing approaches.

To summarize, the work center is a physically identifiable, unique department or subdepartment in a plant through which parts or material flow and have certain operations performed on them which add value to the product. There are standard labor and overhead rates associated with the work center, as well as specific data about capacity, production efficiencies, and costs.

Shift	Shift Hours	Number of Machines	Number of Men	Daily Available Machine Hours	Daily Available Labor Hours
1	8	4	3	32	24
2	8	4	3	32	24
3	4	4	1	16	4
				—	—
				80	52

Work Center Efficiency = 90%

Effective Capacity:	72 Hours	46.8 Hours

FIGURE 5-1   Work center capacity.

Work Center Capacity

In most companies, capacity can be defined in terms of work center machine and labor hours that are available. This type of capacity forms a foundation on which detailed capacity planning is based. Figure 5-1 illustrates the computation of available hours, or capacity for a work center. The efficiency rate experienced is assumed to be 90%, reflecting an average of minor downtime for the machines and breaks, and other indirect losses of time for the workers. Even though the available machine hours total 72 hours, the real constraint in the work center is labor, which is less at 46.8 hours available.

Attempting to schedule more than 46.8 hours of work each day into this work center will mean that its capacity is exceeded even if the load is less than 72 hours. This example assumes that the machines do not run themselves. If the machines are largely automatic, production rates may be specified as being two separate figures, one for machine and one for labor.

This example illustrates the common fact that in most companies, the constraint to production is labor, not machines. Up to certain limits, capacity can be increased simply by working overtime or adding another shift. However, if a machine is run 24 hours a day, and is not very dependent on labor to keep it running, the only way to increase capacity is to add another machine.

Work center capacity, then, can be defined in terms of available hours, which can be "used up" by loading work into the center. The extent to which these hours are used up depends on the production rates for different operations used in the production of various parts. For this reason, calculating a detailed capacity depends on the routings, discussed below, and the product mix stated in the master schedule.

Operation Routings

The traditional shop document in multiple-work-station manufacturing for many years has been a work order that describes the steps involved in the part's production. Starting with the raw material or component parts, placed in boxes or on pallets, the work order moves through the shop from one work center to the next to complete the various steps required to finish the part or parts. These steps are usually called routings, routers, operation sequences, or operation routings. The work order document itself is often referred to as a router, or shop traveler. It contains all the information necessary to make the part, including references to required tooling, drawings to refer to, quality specifications that apply to the various steps, as well as the raw material and component parts to be withdrawn from the warehouse. The steps themselves may include almost any operation, such as molding, turning, stamping, heat treating, assembling, and packaging. The descriptions for each step may be brief or include extensive narrative information.

State-of-the-art planning and control systems simply structure this information so that it can be efficiently used by a computer system. The work center information has already been discussed above. The central concept for routings is that of identifying measurable, discrete, uniquely identifiable steps in the overall process. Each step, or operation, is identified with a specific work center and specifies the expected standard production rate for that part when the specified step is performed in that work center. All of the steps identified taken together constitute the routing for a specific part number.

Figure 5-2 illustrates an example of individual operation routing steps for a turned wood product, such as a shelf bracket or shelf pole. The complete set of operations together is the routing for part 123, which is illustrated on drawing number A-1200. The operation numbers are assigned with intervals so that a future revision to the routing can be made without having to renumber all the subsequent steps after the new step is inserted. A complete routing for many products may involve dozens of steps or even hundreds.

The work center each step is to be performed in is identified. *Setup time* refers to the length of time required to get ready to perform the task, such as positioning the saw blade, setting up a template for the lathe, or loading the correct packaging material onto the packaging machine. The *production rate* refers to the expected number of pieces per hour that can be produced once the machine is set up. Some operations require little or no setup time, while in extreme cases several days may be required.

In the example above, there are four operation records, as seen from the computer system viewpoint. There may also be alternate routings that would be

Part Number: 123   Drawing Number: A-1200

Operation Number	Work Center Number	Operation Description	Setup Time (Hours)	Production Rate (Pieces/Hour)
10	C	Cut Raw Stock	0.10	350
20	F	Turn to Shape	0.15	175
30	A	Sand	0.00	225
40	G	Package	0.50	800

FIGURE 5-2   Operation routings.

used in an overload situation, or a given, assigned work center may have an alternate, which may involve a different production or efficiency rate. From a scheduling point of view, it is also apparent that the critical operation, the one that will limit the overall production rate for the part is the second, operation number 20, turning to shape.

Relating the routing to the product structure for the entire product, there will be a separate routing for each level of assembly in the product structure in most cases. The exception is where phantom product structure records are used to identify parts that have an identity, but are normally not stocked, flowing immediately into a higher-level assembly. Thus part 123 might be assembled with other parts into a packaged kit consisting of the bracket, shelf, screws, and so on. There would be a separate routing for this step, with part 123 and whatever else the completed kit included being called out as components in the product structure, and the corresponding routing instructions telling how to package the kit.

In order to use the routings for scheduling, additional information is needed concerning how long it takes to move the material from one work center to another and how long it is expected to wait before the next operation commences. Therefore, a complete operation routing record includes the time planned for these factors. A standard move time of, say, eight hours might be assumed. The length of time the partly completed parts would wait at the next work center before the operation is started might be assumed to be two days. This waiting time is usually referred to as Queue Time, which may have both before and after operation times. Chapter 8 discusses scheduling logic in detail.

Relationships between Work Center and Operation Records

In order to schedule and load a set of work centers, records describing each work center are linked to those for operations. Figure 5–3 illustrates these relationships. At the left are records for two work centers, A, a 10-inch saw, and B, a belt sander. Each has an associated efficiency rate and hourly cost of operating. On the right are three records selected from the operation routings for two parts, parts 123 and 456. Each operation record specifies a production rate, in terms of pieces per hour, and a certain work center in which the task is to be performed.

If another work center were to be used, a different production rate would be expected. In the hypothetical plant in this example, there might also be another type of saw available, but without an automatic feeding mechanism. In this case, the production rate for cutting part 123 to size might only be 230 pieces per hour.

To illustrate how these pieces of data are interrelated, assume that an order quantity, or lot size of 500 pieces of part 123, are to be cut to size. The time required to run these pieces through work center A, and the cost are calculated as follows:

Work Center Record

Work Center Number	Description	Efficiency Rate	Hourly Cost
A	10-Inch Saw	0.75	43.00
B	Belt Sander	0.80	36.00

Operation Record

Operation Number	Part Number	Work Center Number	Operation Description	Production Rate (Per Hour)
1	123	A	Cut to Size	350
2	123	B	Sand	225
5	456	A	Trim Ends	170

FIGURE 5-3   Work center and operation records.

Order quantity = 500

Standard production rate = 350 pieces per hour

Work center efficiency = 0.75 (75%)

1. Effective hourly production rate in work center A = Standard production rate × Work center efficiency, or

$$350 \times 0.75 = 262.5 \text{ pieces per hour}$$

2. Time required to run 500 pieces = Number of pieces × Effective production rate for work center, or

$$\frac{500}{262.5} = 1.9 \text{ hours}$$

3. Cost to produce 500 pieces = Hours required × Hourly cost rate, or

$$1.9 \text{ hours} \times \$43.00 \text{ per hour} = \$81.90 \text{ to make 500 pieces}$$

4. Cost per piece = Cost of order quantity ÷ number of pieces in order, or

$$\frac{\$81.90}{500} = \$0.163 \text{ per piece}$$

The reader may ask why the effective production rate of 262.5 pieces per hour is not used in the operation record instead of the standard of 350. There are several reasons for this. When industrial engineering establishes a standard rate for each operation involved in the manufacture of an item, the rate is determined in most cases either from experience with similar parts, or by an actual measurement of how many pieces an average operator can produce.

The actual output experienced during day-to-day operations is always less than this rate, reflecting individual operator variations, how well the work center is supervised, equipment maintenance, and the like. The work center efficiency rate is an average experienced over many different runs of a variety of parts through the work center and reflects the overall management of the work center. Distinguishing between an achievable production rate and an actual, net production rate is very important for planning purposes and for management of the work center.

As an example, suppose that the production schedule for part 123 had assumed the standard production rate of 350 pieces per hour. The result would be a production schedule that would always be getting further and further behind, since it was based on an unrealistic assumption. Assume further that the cost for the product was based on the assumption of 350 pieces per hour.

The cost per piece would then be calculated at $0.122 per piece, only 75% of the actual cost of $0.163. If the selling price for the product was based on these erroneous assumptions, it could very easily lead to a situation where the product is being produced at a loss.

It is tempting at this point to say that if the work center produced at 100% efficiency, the cost would in fact be $0.122 each. Unless there is some type of gross mismanagement that can be corrected in the work center, it is important to note that the real production rate will reflect what the company actually will experience in terms of output and cost. Profit planning is best placed on a determination of what is actual, not what perhaps could be. Arranging information in the fashion described above allows management to distinguish between the theoretical and what is actually being experienced, but without losing sight of how much room for improvement might be achieved.

If work orders for each part existed, they would be scheduled and loaded into the work centers using similar logic. The operation illustrated in Figure 5–3 would be loaded into the work center by following the arrows pointing to the appropriate work center. The example work order for 500 of part 123 being completed in work center A illustrates how a work center load is developed. In that example an order quantity of 500 pieces constitutes a load on work center A of 1.9 hours. If the work center was not already fully loaded, the work could be done on the day scheduled. On the other hand, if a full load of work was already scheduled, the additional load of 1.9 hours would exceed the work center's capacity and would have to be rescheduled.

Since the work center and operations records are linked, it is possible to turn the information around to generate a work center where-used list, as shown in Figure 5–4. This list shows all parts that flow through each work center and the operations that are performed on each in that work center. In the example, parts 123 and 456 flow through work center A to use the saw for two slightly different purposes.

The main value of this information is for both industrial engineering and management of the work center. Knowing what operation routing steps have been planned for a particular work center enables any errors in engineering to be caught by identifying operations that cannot actually or efficiently be performed by that work center.

The foreman in charge of that work center can determine what kinds of work tasks the planning system will schedule into his center. The engineer can

Work Center Number	Description	Part Number	Operation Number	Operation Description
A	10-Inch Saw	123	1	Cut to Size
		456	5	Trim Ends
B	Belt Sander	123	2	Sand

FIGURE 5-4
Work center
where-used list.

determine whether he has designed operation routings for products that all use the same few work centers, or whether he has spread the work through the shop more evenly. Management can use the information to examine the suitability of existing facilities to produce efficiently the types of products being made.

The work center where-used list is an excellent example of information that is virtually impossible to obtain manually, but relatively simple for a computer to produce. In a plant where hundreds of different routings exist, the work center loads will vary according to the production schedule and product mix. Compiling a list by work center would take weeks of clerical work, and in fact, is never done except in the simplest of plants. This is one of the many reasons that scheduling in a multiple work center plant is so difficult, if not impossible, to do.

The reality of scheduling in most companies is that work orders are launched into work in process, where some of the operations are performed and the parts become semicompleted. At various steps in the processing cycle, the semifinished parts just wait. Expediters identify the work orders that are behind schedule and move them through ahead of other work orders that are not yet behind schedule. As a result, printed schedules are usually not even close to realistic. The total lead time for a product to be manufactured may be given as six weeks, even though adding up all the standard run times from the operation routings may yield a time of only four days. The time parts spend waiting is usually 80% or more of the total production lead time.

To this add the fact that the production rates of each work center and each operation varies considerably and the result is a large number of variables each of which is somewhat dependent on the others. These differences are buffered, in effect, by allowing work to accumulate ahead of each work center. These individual piles of work increase and decrease over time, with the result that the work center is able to work at a fairly steady rate.

It is the size of these piles of work that largely determine the size of work in process. As product complexities increase, and the number of variables to consider in the scheduling process increase similarly, work in process tends to increase disproportionately, reflecting the increased difficulty in scheduling. Chapter 8 examines various methods for controlling these piles, or queues of work, as a method for controlling work in process investment.

Tooling

Another important variable in many companies' scheduling and production reality is that of tooling. These items are specifically designed parts that are attached to general-purpose machines to enable them to perform a very specific task. Examples would include molds, cutting tools, dies, templates, fitting gauges, and the like. They are a required part of the production of an item. Without the tool's availability, the part cannot be produced, even if there is available capacity and the required material is at hand in sufficient quantity.

Operation Routing Records

Part Number	Operation Number	Tool Number Required
123	10	B12
456	30	C15
678	40	B12

Tool Master Records

Tool Number	Description
B12	Cutting Tool
C15	Fitting Gauge

FIGURE 5–5
Tooling
relationships.

Since tooling items are so specific, in most companies they are assigned unique, identifying numbers of their own. Operation routing records refer to the tool number to be used on a specific step, which is in turn linked to the tooling master record, containing a complete description of the tool, plus other information related to the tool's life, its cost, how many sets of the tool exist, and so on. A given item of tooling may be used on a number of operations for making various parts.

Figure 5–5 illustrates the relationship between tooling records and operation routing records as they are structured in a computer system. Tool B12 is used in two different operation records, each representing a step in the production of two different parts. Since the relationships work both ways, a tooling where-used list can be generated as shown in Figure 5–6. Both sets of information are useful.

Since tooling is part of the production process, any document produced, such as a work order that shows the operation routings, should also show the tool items required to perform each step. For scheduling purposes, lack of a required tool is just as limiting as an unavailable machine. Consequently, the scheduling process should include a tool scheduling subsystem. The author is not aware of any standard manufacturing system package now available that schedules tooling or even checks a tool's availability before scheduling work into a work center. However, one way or the other, this critical step still has to be done if production is to stay on schedule.

An example would be a plastic molding operation where only one mold is

Tool Number	Tool Description	Part Number	Operation Number
B12	Cutting Tool	123	10
		678	40
C15	Fitting Gauge	456	30

FIGURE 5–6
Tooling
where-used list.

made (they are quite expensive) for each type of product to be molded. Since each part is run on only one molding machine at a time (no parallel production of the same part on two machines simultaneously), this might not appear to be a problem. Since the scheduling system assumes that the tooling is always available when needed, if the mold is out for repair at the time a work order calling for it is scheduled, the production schedule will be disrupted when the work center tries to run the part. Furthermore, since molded parts are usually at a lower level in the product structure, all higher assemblies through end products will not be producible until the mold becomes available again. This illustrates how the ramifications can be widespread from a seemingly simple schedule delay.

Manufacturing Information Relationships

In this chapter and in Chapter 4, five basic records have been identified as carrying the bulk of information pertaining to the manufacturing information base. Each record can have any number of pieces of secondary data to describe further the part of reality identified by the primary data. Figure 5-7 illustrates these basic relationships. Part records form the building blocks of the entire system, forming the collection point for engineering, inventory, costing, and other data.

These building blocks are defined into sets of relationships by the product structure records that correspond with the way the product goes together. The operation routing records describe how the product is to be made, while the work center and tooling records describe the resources available to manufacture the various items produced by the company.

These five types of records form the basis for all planning, scheduling, and costing and engineering control in the company. They are relatively permanent records, in that they change only as the product, manufacturing methods,

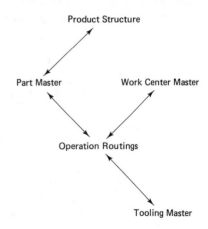

FIGURE 5-7   Manufacturing information relationships.

or resources themselves are changed. Other records generated from them, such as open work order records, are very dynamic, event-oriented records. Any number of work orders can be produced for a given part, and will always use the same set of part, product structure, and operation routing records as its basis, merely copying these records and adding dates to make the various parts of the records event oriented.

It is a matter of judgment as to how detailed these records should be, or in other words, how much information should be "put into the computer" and how much left to manual, filing cabinet methods. In general, the more other company functions need a piece of data, the more it should be included in the formal, computer system. Also, the more complete the information is in the system, the more accurate a picture of reality it can form, thereby increasing its usefulness to the company.

Even in cases where relatively small amounts of information are to be maintained, the power of a computer to organize, access, reorganize, and maintain information is such that if the cost is compared to that of a manual records system, the cost of a computerized method is usually much less, especially in the long run.

Much of this type of expansion of usefulness can be achieved by merely adding to the secondary data in a primary record. Figure 5-8 contains an example of an expanded record for work centers. In addition to the usual information needed for scheduling and product costing, one can add any number of pieces of data to accumulate various statistics, such as cumulative downtime, actual production hours, maintenance costs, and the like. All of these can enhance the value of a system and make it more useful in actually managing the company. These statistics can be analyzed according to a set of criteria, summarized via the information pyramid technique, and only exceptional conditions reported to management.

The other parts of a total company system discussed in subsequent chapters all use this manufacturing information base as their starting point. Additional records, such as drawing records, may be added to enhance the basic five records to accomplish their purpose. Text or narrative records may be added to

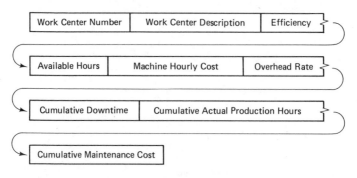

FIGURE 5-8   Expanded work center record.

carry descriptive data. The material planning part of the system will use a master production schedule, the inventory information in the part master records, and the product structure records to develop a complete, detailed manufacturing schedule and purchasing plan.

This plan, in turn, is taken by the capacity management part of the system and combined with the operation routing, work center, and tooling records to perform the tasks associated with capacity requirements calculations, capacity planning, short-range operation scheduling, and work center loading tasks.

The material and capacity planning functions use as their time-related base a set of work order records, both planned (unreleased to the shop) and released (currently part of work in process and in the shop). These records, in turn, form the basis for all planned versus actual material usages, scrap, labor and machine efficiencies, and work order (actual product) costing. Completed and closed work orders in turn form the basis for various history data records and are input into various cumulative data fields in the part, work center, and other records.

The development of all types of standard costs use the same five records as their source of data. The hourly rates in the work center master, when applied to the production rates in the operation routing records, yield the standard manufacturing cost to produce each assembly, subassembly, and component part. Building these costs up through the product structure and adding the purchased material costs from the part master records yields an accurate, builtup product standard cost for the various accounting functions.

In summary, it is evident that these different pieces of information are in fact highly integrated in reality. Traditional methods of doing things developed partly in response to the impossibility of doing business on a large scale while continuing to have all departments share the same information, records, and files. The power of the computer makes it possible to develop a realistic picture of the reality that exists in the company and to use the information in the manner in which it naturally occurs in the real world.

Managerial Considerations

As the next generation of managers takes its place, together with computers of unprecedented power and low cost, a new set of managerial skills will become a premium. Those managers who can effectively utilize the incredible power of computer systems to run their companies at levels of efficiency and effectiveness not achievable (or even imaginable) in the past will find that their companies have a substantial advantage in a competitive marketplace.

Connected with this are problems of organization within the company. The traditional, departmentalized, individual manager fiefdoms that still exist in many companies will tend to give way to more integrated ways of operating the business, in order to take full advantage of the power of highly integrated information systems.

For example, in the case of the information relationships, just discussed, between the five basic manufacturing records, who would be responsible for the overall integrity of the records under the traditional method of assigning responsibilities to managers? In the traditional method, manufacturing information responsibilities might be broken down as follows:

- *Design engineering:* as designed part numbers, product structures, some engineering change data
- *Manufacturing engineering:* as manufactured part numbers, product structure changes, operation routings, work center, and tooling data
- *Industrial engineering:* production rates, some input for work center efficiencies, labor rates, and some input to operation routings.
- *Production control:* ordering rules, lead times, inventory status, and some part numbers
- *Accounting:* labor costs, purchased material costs, standard costs, work center efficiency data, and planned versus actual costing

The only manager that these different departments have in common is the president of the company. All of these different pieces of information are needed, and must be accurate and timely if the company is to function at an optimum level, especially if the advantages of integrated systems are to be used. In many companies, there is a departmental pecking order, with real social barriers to communication prevalent. In extreme cases, people from one department do not even have their coffee breaks with people from other departments.

One of the first lessons that was learned in the development of large-scale computer systems was that duplicating the previous, manual method of record keeping caused real problems. These problems were there all along but were more difficult to see. With each department maintaining its own set of records, an endless series of duplication, communicating, and translation of what basically is the same information occurs. Placing these duplicated systems in a computer file merely allowed the same old mistakes to occur at a higher speed.

At the same time, management began to be aware of the limitation of having department managers and supervisors provide reports of their own activities. This allowed to go on a lot of covering up and blaming of others for shortcomings. With formal, highly integrated systems, management becomes less dependent on this reporting mechanism, since an integrated system, by its nature, includes the opportunity for many cross-checks.

As a result, some companies began to develop more integrated methods of managing their people, using different methods of assigning responsibilities, and developing a more teamwork-oriented climate. These changes facilitate the more effective use of computerized, integrated systems. It is not an accident that many of these companies have made startling accomplishments in their various markets.

As the growth in computer cost effectiveness and power continues, coupled with the increasing complexity and cost of doing business, these companies will have an even greater advantage than in the past. Those that emulate them in their methods will improve their chances of success in a challenging world.

CHAPTER 5 QUESTIONS

1. Define several methods of describing and organizing productive resources into work centers.
2. List some of the secondary data which are usually used to describe a work center.
3. Can an outside processing vendor be described as a work center? What would be the purpose of describing it in this way?
4. What is capacity? What happens when it is exceeded?
5. What is the purpose of operation routings, and how are they used?
6. Why is it desirable to distinguish between setup time and the production rate in a routing?
7. Describe when alternate routings would be used.
8. How do routings relate to product structure records?
9. What is move time and wait time?
10. Why is an effective production rate used to plan and cost instead of the engineering standard?
11. How is the work center efficiency rate different from the effective production rate?
12. Why does a plant become more difficult to run when the production rates in routings (or work center efficiency rates) are significantly inaccurate?
13. What is a work center where-used list and how is it generated? Is it practical to produce this list manually?
14. How does tooling relate to operations routings?
15. Name and describe the five basic manufacturing records, and explain how they relate to systems associated with other company functions.
16. There are five areas of responsibility for the data in these five records. Name each area of responsibility and the data associated with it.

6

Inventory

The Financial View

The most important aspect of understanding inventory is to realize that it may be a major financial investment for the company, often the only major capital investment required to operate the business. In recent times, and for the imaginable future, two powerful economic forces exert a consistent, strong pressure on this investment for virtually every inventory-intensive business. They are:

1. Continually rising cost of acquiring the inventory, driven by a variety of inflationary forces such as transportation costs, energy costs, and relative scarcity of raw materials, to name but a few.

2. Increasing cost of capital, both of debt financing and equity. Awareness of the impact of capital decisions is usually limited to top management, but is present, nonetheless. Smaller firms now must often grow solely through retained earnings, since obtaining public sources of equity capital is far more difficult than in the past. As interest rates hover in the range 15 to 20% it becomes increasingly difficult to justify either investing the company's cash assets in inventory, when higher returns are often available elsewhere at a lower risk, or to even continue in business at a lower rate of return.

From an accounting point of view, inventory is really items purchased as part of the cost of goods sold. It is a business expense. If each purchased item were sold the day it was received, there would be no capital investment required for inventory, regardless of the volume of business.

Since it is rare that a business can be arranged this way, items must be bought and held for some period of time before they are sold, either in themselves or as part of a finished good. It is this holding of inventory, then, that causes the need for capital investment. The length of time that inventory is held, in the aggregate, is often referred to as the "days of supply" or so many days' worth. This length of time, or float, is what determines how much must be invested in inventory. Clearly, the quicker inventory moves through the company, the lower the investment.

Another way to measure how long inventory is held is to ask how fast it turns over. This measure compares how much is spent on inventory items with the on-hand balances in total, stated in dollars. A ratio results from this comparison. For example, suppose the following:

$$\text{Annual material purchased} = \$1,000,000$$

$$\text{Value of average stock on hand} = \$100,000$$

The turn ratio is calculated simply by dividing one by the other:

$$\frac{\text{Annual purchases}}{\text{Average stock}} = \frac{\$1,000,000}{\$100,000} = \frac{10}{1} \text{ or 10 turns per year}$$

The stated goal of most inventory systems is to enable management to make this turn ratio as high as possible.

Purpose—The Essential Question

The most basic question about inventory, given that the ideal is zero investment in inventory, is to ask, why is it here? How is it serving the goals of the business to have items actually in the warehouse rather than just passing through it quickly? Why have it at all? Are there alternate ways of running the business so that one can have either no investment or, at least, a lot less?

These may seem like rhetorical questions to many readers, but are dead serious. Many very successful manufacturing and distribution firms manage businesses where either the customer owns the inventory, supplies it with orders, or where items are not bought until firm sales orders are received. Further, there are many variations on this theme, such as:

- Annual contracts, with shorter procurement lead times
- Performing receiving inspection at the vendor's
- Getting the vendor to stock the items in a finished-goods inventory
- More frequent deliveries, balancing transportation charges with carrying costs
- Flexible contracts, with short-range changes in items, dates, and quantities

A key point here is that many of the factors that can most dramatically reduce inventory investment are in the management policy area rather than under the control of the inventory planning department or system. Of course, once management has decided to conduct the business in a certain way, the effective management of inventory and a good system can control and keep the level of investment to a minimum.

The intent here is to point out that all too often there are many factors that affect the level of capital invested in inventory that result from how the management of the company elects to operate the business. These are usually simply unstated assumptions and, as a result, often go completely unexamined.

A management decision to plan the business around detailed forecasting can of itself dramatically reduce inventory investment. Similar moves in other areas can have a similar effect. Accounting for forecast error is done somewhere in the business, even if only by default. The greater the error, the more stock levels must be increased to maintain a given level of customer service. In the past, it was often cheaper to hold a lot of inventory than it was to do detailed planning. As the twin pressures on inventory increase and the cost of detailed forecasting and planning decrease, this becomes less and less true.

To summarize, then, inventory is a financial investment that a company makes for these general reasons:

- Allow for forecast error
- Allow for mistakes in planning
- Allow for record inaccuracies
- Allow for optimum buying and/or economic production quantities
- Maintain high customer service
- Smooth production and sales cycles
- Allow for unpredictable scrap during production

Classification Methods

Without some method of grouping similar items, an inventory manager would be forced to manage each inventory item individually. Assigning codes of various types to each part number allows us to use the information pyramid concept to manage the inventory investment.

Rather than assign codes randomly, one must consider the purpose, the task to be facilitated by the code. These tasks can be grouped into five major areas here. Not all will necessarily occur in every business. A given area may use more than one code to accomplish its purposes. Some examples are shown in the sample inventory record in Figure 6-1.

Control codes: Codes assigned to part numbers in the inventory records to control the use or status of the item can have several purposes. Each says something about the item, like any other piece of secondary data. Frequently, system designers assign one or two fields for denoting the engineering status of the part, whether it is still experimental, in an R&D status, or whether an upcoming engineering change will phase it out.

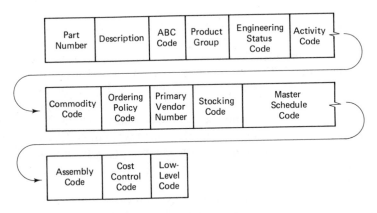

FIGURE 6-1   Sample inventory record.

These types of codes may indicate that it is subject to a certain rule or policy for ordering. Material requirements planning systems may have as many as 40 or 50 different ordering methods, each assignable to a specific part number. The part may be only an alternate use item, or it may not be used on any final assembly or subassembly. Depending on the particular system, this information will be carried in two or more separate fields.

There are also codes for assigning responsibility for tasks such as planning and buying to a particular individual. These codes enable lists to be generated by the computer containing only those part numbers for which the person is responsible.

Purchasing codes: Special codes are frequently set aside for purchasing purposes. Assigning each part number a commodity code will enable convenient reporting of parts that are purchased from the same or similar vendors, facilitating more aggressive procurement action, annual contracts, and the like. Other fields may be designated by system designers for the primary and secondary vendors from which the item is purchased. These types of codes allow special-purpose reports to be generated grouping parts for efficient purchasing action, review, and control.

Many companies use reports that allow the review of all items purchased from the same vendor at the same time, regardless of whether a current requirement actually exists to buy it or not, further facilitating the relationship with the vendor. A part may not be purchased per se from a vendor, but merely have some process performed on it, such as plating, anodizing, heat treating, or other operation. This information may be carried in either a purchasing-related code or in the status coding for the part number.

Scheduling and stocking codes: Additional fields are frequently included in the design of the inventory record that permit classifying the part according to whether it is a finished good (end item or final assembly in some industries), subassembly, manufactured component, or purchased item. These codes allow grouping for control purposes, establishing appropriate ordering rules, and to allow the planning system to select the appropriate action for the part.

Other uses for product classifications or categories are for planning and forecasting sales and finished-goods inventory policies. If a company has a large number of products it sells, it may be more convenient to forecast sales by product groupings than by specific part number. Assigning appropriate codes also allows the information pyramid concept to be used to generate higher-level management sales and profitability reports. These types of classifications systems may become quite elaborate in large companies, with several levels of subclassifications.

Costing codes: Since it is often desirable to summarize and review parts by their cost method than by other codes, special codes are sometimes assigned to facilitate the purposes of cost accounting. Most companies use one system of costing throughout the business, but there is no reason why this has to be the case. Certain parts could be costed using an actual or moving average technique, whereas others could use an annually set standard cost.

Most of the basis for current cost accounting systems are historical, in terms of what could be accomplished as a practical matter. As computer power becomes cheaper, it becomes progressively feasible to have the system use different or parallel methods for each part number uniquely.

Special codes: Some systems allow the designation of parts as nonstocked items, phantom parts in a bill of material structure (these were discussed in more detail in Chapter 4), maintenance items used on plant equipment, or as supplies that are used in small quantities (lubricating oil, for example) in the production process. These codes allow the system to distinguish them from other more normal types of items involved in the inventory planning and control process.

Every system varies somewhat from other systems in how its coding is designed, reflecting in part the uses the system designers had in mind. How the purposes discussed above are accomplished will involve varying numbers of special-purpose classification fields in the master inventory record, each containing one or more numbers or letters, each of which in turn have specific meanings.

Generally, the larger the company the system is intended for, the greater the complexity of its classification capabilities. Simple systems may have only a simple product class field, whereas really advanced systems may have 10 or more separate classification fields, each containing a set of special codes.

The key point to remember about classification systems is that their power lies in the use of the computer to rearrange into groupings for special purposes and tasks. They all use the information pyramid concept to enable summaries to be developed. Accomplishing these kinds of tasks manually is generally pretty hopeless. These codes also enable the system to make many decisions in the course of its operation, at computer speeds, that would otherwise have to be made by a human being, and everyone knows how fast that is.

Inventory Behavior—ABC Analysis

One of the frequently observed facts of inventory behavior is the law of the vital few and trivial many, otherwise known as *Pareto's law,* or the *80/20 rule.* In inventory management, this means that 20% of the parts consume 80% of the inventory investment. Figure 6-2 illustrates this distribution of inventory value. The curve is also termed a *Lorenz curve.*

To generate this kind of information, a special program multiplies the unit cost times the average monthly or annual usage figure to obtain an extended usage value. The extended usage values are then ranked in descending order (highest to lowest). The resulting list illustrates Pareto's law, in that the top few items involve the most investment, with a long list of small-volume, relatively inexpensive items at the end.

To implement an ABC inventory management policy, management will establish the cutoff figure for each of three (or sometimes four) categories: highest (A), medium (B), and lowest (C). These codes are then assigned to each part number in the inventory record for generating various lists for control purposes. More inventory control effort, such as more frequent physical countings, different ordering rules, and closer monitoring is applied to the "A" parts than the "C" items.

Behavior—Demand Types

A given part in an inventory system is subjected to one or more types of demand. The total demand for the part will be the sum of all types from all sources. Each source of demand has different factors associated with it and is handled somewhat differently.

Independent demand is that which either comes from outside the com-

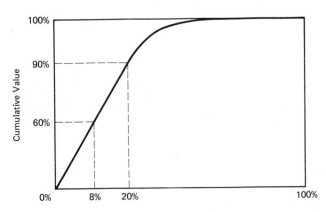

FIGURE 6-2
Inventory value
distribution.

pany through sales or warranty replacements, or from inside the company but from a source not related to how the product is actually made. An ongoing loss through employee theft would be an independent demand from inside the company, for instance.

Dependent demand comes from a calculation of independent demand on a finished or end item through the product structure. Figure 6-3 shows examples of how demand sources and types affect different parts of a typical product structure.

Since all dependent demand ultimately depends on how we manage the information about independent demand, it is obvious that the latter is the critical item to understand. Although a few companies can operate their business entirely from firm sales orders, most do or can use a mixture of forecasted demand plus actual sales orders received. Since a forecast runs essentially from today out to the end of our planning horizon, actual sales orders must be subtracted from the quantity forecasted for each period. For example:

		Week Number			
Part 436	1	2	3	4	5
Quantity forecasted	10	15	13	14	12
Actual sales orders	9	7	6	4	1
Net forecast quantity	1	8	7	10	11

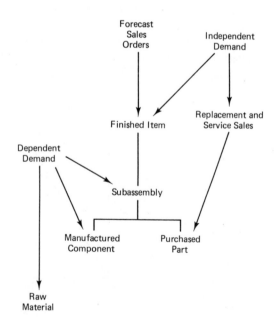

FIGURE 6-3 Demand and product structure levels.

If this step is not performed, one may inadvertently add sales orders to the forecasted quantity, a definite error. The forecast, after all, is what was estimated to be received in sales orders, whereas the actual orders are just that—actual events.

The difference between actual versus planned sales is a separate piece of information used to manage the planning cycle. So one works to the forecast quantities in order to keep the overall forecast on track.

This is particularly true if the business is a stocked finished-good type of business. Here, one makes money by using the statistical base of the forecast; it is true (assuming that it is properly done) in the long run, and in the aggregate even though large deviations are experienced at the detail part number and planning period level.

Some companies have a product line that consists of end items assembled from a large variety of possible configurations. Forecasting and planning at the end item level for these companies is an impossibility, and the use of higher-level product groups may be similarly impractical. In this case, the best method is to forecast and schedule by subassemblies that make up the different configurations or use the planning bill of material concept discussed in Chapter 3.

The final note on independent demand is to point out that some parts that are lower-level subassemblies or even purchased parts may be used to support finished items in the field. This source of independent demand must be captured and managed just like that for the end item itself. Thus the service part will be subject to two sources of demand: that from the production of the end item (dependent) and that from the service usage sales (independent).

Planning Levels of Customer Service

The easiest way to cut through some of the fog surrounding this subject is to recognize that in a sense, the company's desires regarding service are exactly opposite that of a customer. The minimum-risk, easiest way to manage a manufacturing business would be to have firm orders in hand before any money is spent. The customer, on the other hand, would rather not plan ahead at all, but just call the day before he needs something and have it delivered with 100% reliability. This would allow him to maintain his level of risk and expense at a minimum.

If the production of products were instantaneous, this might be feasible. However, since it is not, every business must compromise somewhere between these opposing points. Exactly where has to do with how much demand there is for a product, and even more, how much competition exists, either in the form of other companies offering a very similar product or one that substitutes for it. If there is no competition, the manufacturer tends to have things his way. If there is a lot, the customer gets his way.

Key factors in this equation are first, the lead time required to replace stock after it has been sold, or to meet the demand of a sales order—the production lead time, in other words. The other key factor is the cost of carrying the finished-goods inventory. The Boeing Airplane Company could, if it chose, carry a finished inventory of completed B-747s in various models. On the other extreme, if only one company had a complete monopoly on dog food, dog owners might find themselves placing orders and then waiting for eight weeks while it was produced and shipped to the store.

These are somewhat absurd examples, but they do illustrate the point that in the final analysis all customer service decisions are based on these two factors. Statements to the effect that the product is too complex, has too many options, and so on, to carry a finished-goods inventory for are just roundabout ways of saying: "We don't have to carry a finished-goods inventory to be successful; investing money in finished-goods inventory would be a poor investment, returning nothing to profit."

In effect, then, the decision not to have a finished-goods inventory is equivalent to deciding to have a permanent stockout situation. The key here is how long it takes to respond to customer's orders, compared to the competition. Once the decision is made to carry some level of finished-goods inventory for a product, the next question is how often will a stockout be allowed to occur, with its attendant risk of not fulfilling a customer's order. Figure 6–4 illustrates the interrelated nature of these two key factors with competition.

Since more and more businesses seem to be operating without a finished-goods inventory, some observations at this point are relevant. For these businesses, being competitive means being able to respond quickly. Other things being equal, the company that has a shorter internal or production lead time will tend to have the edge competitively. Similarly, companies that now carry a finished-goods inventory simply because their internal production time is so long may find that much less of it is required if a dramatic reduction in lead time is achieved through different management techniques. Since work in process is inventory also, cutting internal lead time is synonomous with reducing investment in work in process.

Whatever the reasons may be for choosing to manage customer service around a finished-goods inventory, the key is what rate of stockouts will be allowed in order to plan the level of customer service. Since the purpose of the

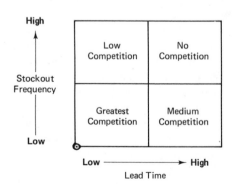

FIGURE 6-4   Competition versus customer
service.

finished-goods inventory is to shorten the response to the customer's orders, this question translates into:

- How often will a lost sale (or possibly a lost customer) result from taking too long to fulfill an order?
- How much does it cost to do business at various levels of customer service; what does it cost to make sure that the company never or very rarely fails to have the item on hand the day it is requested?

To answer this last question, one can develop the cost of preventing stockouts with finished-goods inventory. Costing the actual stockout itself is difficult because it is hard to tell if a sale is really lost, since many times customers will just wait. Even harder is to determine if a customer has been lost by taking too long to fulfill an order.

To cost stockouts, the probability of a stockout occurring is calculated, then the level of safety stock that would be required to prevent a stockout at that level of probability is determined. This probability is a function of two factors:

- Sales per day and the size of the variations
- Number of days to replenish the inventory and the size of variations

Combining these two distributions usually produces what statisticians refer to as a normal distribution, or a Poisson curve. An example is shown in Figure 6-5. The mean (peak) of the curve represents a 50% chance of a stockout. As the reorder point is raised (enlarge safety stock) the chance of a stockout occurring is decreased. However, past a certain point, increasing safety stock in progressively larger increments brings a smaller and smaller reduction in the risk of the stockout. Stated in money terms, larger and larger investments in safety stock inventory brings diminishing returns.

To summarize, decisions about customer service levels revolve around trade-offs between how quick a response time to customer demand is needed in order to be sufficiently competitive in the marketplace and how much different levels of customer service require in invested capital.

While Chapter 8 will discuss this concept in greater detail, it is apparent that significant reductions in in-plant lead time have a dramatic effect on the investment required to provide a given level of customer service. Costing customer service levels is easiest to do in terms of preventing stockouts and depends on sales per day and how quickly response to inventory stockouts can be made inside the business.

Controlling Customer Service

Decisions such as the paragraphs above describe are more useful if they are compared with actual results. Actual information can be obtained about how often customers request items that are out of stock, their actions (cancel the

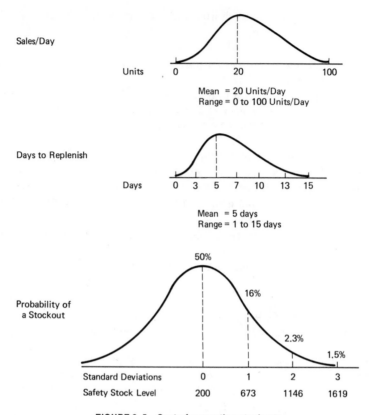

FIGURE 6-5   Cost of preventing stockouts.

order, place on back order), sales per day and variations, and how long it really takes to replenish a stockout situation. These data are critical in controlling the actual level of customer service being experienced.

With state-of-the-art systems, these data can be accumulated and provided for management evaluation in the ordinary course of business. Simply accumulating demand (how many units were requested by customers) separately from sales (how many units were actually shipped) is very helpful, as can be seen from the above in setting safety stock levels or deciding whether to stock finished goods at all.

Manufactured Parts—Dependent and Lumpy Demand

A manufactured part is any item that has had some operation performed on it to make it different from its state when first acquired. In other words, it is the state that various items are in while in between what is purchased and what is sold. The finished item is simply the last stage in a sequence of manufactured parts. Normally, an identifying part number will be assigned only if a particular stage of manufacturing needs to be identified for quality control, stocking, or other purposes. Because of imbalances in the production rate capabilities of various work centers, stocking of components, subassemblies, or solutions may be necessary.

Components are defined as being those items that are usually made in a single manufacturing step, such as molding or stamping. Two or more components may be put together to form an assembly. If the resulting assembly is not a complete product in itself, it is usually referred to as a subassembly. Two or more subassemblies may be assembled to form a final assembly, also referred to as an end item or finished good.

The same logic of successive operations can be applied to solutions, which are always mixtures of one or more raw material solutions, which in turn may have various processes performed on them, such as heating, aging, or straining. Even though solutions *look* different from discrete parts, from an information standpoint they are not. The same rules of identification, product structure relationships, stocking costing, and so on, apply as with discrete parts manufacturing. After all, what is the difference, from this viewpoint, between a box of 563 little plastic parts and a drum of 32 gallons of a solution? Each has an identifying number, quantity, and a list of what went into it.

All these different kinds of parts constitute work-in-process inventory of various types. The ideal for work-in-process inventory is that it is all continuously in process; that is, no item between the purchased part level and the finished-good level is stocked in holding tanks, a warehouse, or on the production floor. They go directly from one manufacturing process to the next.

Excluding for the moment independent demand for lower parts used in support of maintenance of finished goods, essentially all demand for manufacturing items is dependent; it is a known factor. Once the demand for the end item is stated, the demand for the end item lower-level part is a function of its product structure, scrap rates, and has a time component that is dependent completely on when the next higher assembly is made.

The assumption underlying the concept of independent demand (its date) is not precisely known. This forces the assumption that it is more or less continuous, or smooth. Since the demand for manufactured parts is dependent on *when* the next higher assembly is going to be made (and how many), this aspect of dependent demand is described as *lumpy*. For part of the time period there is no demand for the part at all, then it comes all at once, when the assembly is being made. In between the time that the item is being made, there is no demand at all for the component items, so there is no reason whatever to have them in stock at those times.

Figure 6–6 illustrates lumpy demand as it appears under an order point system (order point concepts are discussed in Chapters 3 and 7). The many small demands of individual customer orders deplete on-hand inventory until an order point is reached. At that time a replenishing manufacturing work

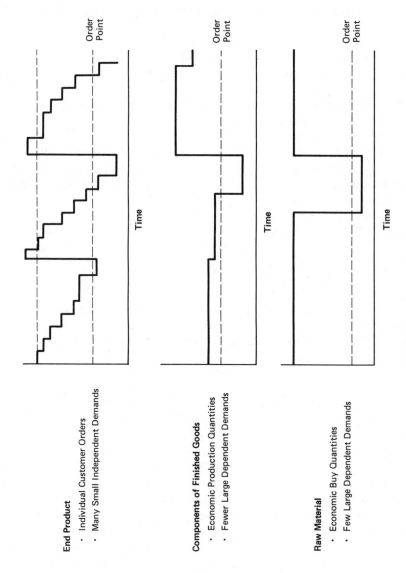

FIGURE 6-6 Lumpy demand.

order to assemble some more of the product is triggered. The component parts of that product experience no demand prior to that time, which has, in effect, been accumulating. Going further down the product structure, this effect is even more pronounced. Since raw materials (or purchased parts) usually have many higher-level usages, demands for these items must also be accumulated, in effect triggering an even larger, more infrequent order.

This process becomes even more exaggerated when many product structure levels are involved and when the raw material or component has many higher-level usages. Under an order point system, these cascading effects produce a feast or famine situation, where either there is no inventory on hand to meet requirements, or far too much, which sits around for long periods of time before being used. Material requirements planning systems were developed to deal with this situation and are explored in detail in Chapter 7.

One final point about the use of independent demand concepts (order point) in the management of manufacturing inventories; if each part or bill of material list has an order point/service level (probability of a stockout) set at some level, the probability that all of the parts will be available at the same time is substantially lower than that of any one part.

Combined probabilities are obtained by multiplying the individual probabilities of each event together. For example, if the service level of two items is set at 90% each, the combined probability that both will be available simultaneously is only 81%. Even raising the service level to 95% does little to help. If an assembly is composed of 14 or more constituent parts, each of which must be available at the same time to make it, the combined probability that they will all be available at the same time is less than 50%.

Consider the implications of this point. It means that if a manufactured item has at least 14 components, and the external world performs perfectly, there is less than an even chance of being able to make any item at the time it is scheduled, regardless of what is done with safety stocks (within reason). Thus the system itself makes it virtually impossible to schedule work with anything better than a random chance likelihood that the schedule will be carried out as planned.

By the time the disruptive effects of unforeseen events in the real world are added in, there is little hope of reliable scheduling at all, except under conditions of heavy expediting of short components (harder and harder with longer and longer purchasing lead times) *and* very high safety stocks (also more difficult under conditions of expensive capital).

Purchased Parts and Raw Materials

Most of the preceding comments about dependent demand and manufactured parts also applies to purchased items. There are some important differences. There is usually less control over the lead time than with most in-house items, which can "bump" other production items in the priority sequences of production. The vendor may have various quantity minimums. Costs may become prohibitive for transportation of small quantities if items have to be expedited. For these reasons, a great deal of safety stock is often carried for purchased items.

If a raw material is used in a wide variety of products, demand for it may be relatively smooth. Conversely, if it is used in only one or two, demand may be completely lumpy, being dependent on the production schedule for those one or two items, especially if the items are not made frequently.

One of the main benefits of a material requirements planning system is in the purchased item area. Since dates, quantities, and identities of all items needed to be purchased for production can be calculated from the product structure, production times, and master production schedule, there is no need to buy anything that does not fulfill a known, identified requirement. Probabilistic guessing at this level simply has no place.

A special case of purchased items is that of outside processing, where a partly completed item is sent to a vendor who plates or heat treats the item and returns it. This type of purchasing action is really a service, even though the part numbers will change before and after the process.

Outside processing and its costs are controlled by identifying the untreated part with one part number, shipping it to the vendor, and by identifying the processed version with a different part number and receiving it back as though it was purchased from the vendor. This sound practice for control of the item and for receiving dock purposes should not be confused with planning the purchase of parts and raw materials.

Outside processing is really part of a sequence of events within the work order cycle, normally involving a short turnaround time for shipping and the vendor's internal processing time. Another way to look at outside processing is to regard the vendor as just another work center, with an operation performed there as part of a part's operation routing sequence.

Physical Control

As the different items of inventory flow through the plant, from receiving dock to warehouse, to assembly, and out through the shipping dock, several aspects of control are critical. Bearing in mind the general principle that the information system uses data to create a picture of reality and then manipulated the data in place of the reality, it becomes clear that the system must have accurate data to work properly. So one very important aspect of physical control is to ensure that this record accuracy takes place and is maintained continuously.

Another aspect of control is more straightforward: to ensure that parts are not stolen, mislabeled, or used incorrectly in a manufacturing process. There are also some considerations of efficient material handling, storage, and access to parts when needed.

Receiving and Inspection Control

The first step in the flow of material is when it arrives at the receiving dock of the company. In order for effective control to be exercised over this activity, it is essential that no item be received unless a valid, open purchase order for that item exists. There are two reasons for this.

Financially, a purchase order is a contract binding the company to buy the item from the vendor. Payment must be geared to the purchasing function's management responsibility to control what gets bought and at what price and quantity. Further, the information system has no hope of continuously reflecting reality if items that it does not know about are allowed to appear on the receiving dock and enter the system. Requiring that an open purchase order exist for every item received and for that item's quantity and delivery date effectively forces people to keep the system accurate.

From the planning system's viewpoint, purchase orders are its means of planning and controlling all purchased items. Allowing items to enter the system without being part of the planning cycle significantly degrades the effectiveness of the planning system and will tend to hamper the system's ability to aid management in achieving optimum return on investment of resources. With a state-of-the-art system, buyers can create a purchase order in the computer system, which is available immediately for use by the receiving function to control receipts.

When an item is received, the next step is to ensure that it is properly labeled in the terms that the information system uses, that is, by being physically stamped or labeled with the part number used internally by the company to manage the item. If a lot control system is in effect, purchased material is identified as being part of one production batch run by the supplier or another. For example, with dyed textile products, two rolls of material may have the same identifying number and be called the same part number, but were made in two different batches of dye solution, which may differ slightly.

Another reason for lot control identification is for purposes of product recall, as with medical products. Proper identification attached to the actual parts or their container also ensures that material handling and production people will get the correct item as shown on a picking list. This in turn aids in keeping the information system in synch with reality.

It is often tempting to use a supplier's identification on the product as the identification for items inside one's own company. After all, it saves all that marking and labeling, which may in fact be time consuming and tedious. However, when the item is purchased from a second source, confusion is the inevitable result. The information system, of course, includes a cross-reference from the company's part number to the vendor's.

After an item is properly received and identified, it is inspected, to ensure that it meets all applicable quality standards, either by a sampling process, destructive testing of a few parts, or other inspection process. If the item is acceptable, it is moved to the warehouse. If not, it is either returned to the vendor or held for engineering and/or management evaluation as to whether it can be used as is and accepted as a deviation from normal quality standards. The outcome of this evaluation will be either a return to the vendor or moving the items to the warehouse.

It is vital that this cycle be continuously and accurately reflected in the information system, so the system will always know the actual status of all purchased items. In most manufacturing companies, the receiving cycle involves the use of a special area, where parts awaiting completion of inspection are held, since the process normally takes several days to complete. Finally, the system does not authorize payment by accounting of the vendor's invoice until the items are inspected and accepted.

The quality standards for each item must also allow that once accepted for use and moved into the warehouse, all items with the same part number will be interchangeable. The information system cannot, of course, tell the difference between one item that is marginal and the rest that are good. If this is the case and management chooses to accept what are, in effect, two different parts, they must be identified separately, with one being an alternate usage item for the good ones. In most cases, the added complexity of segregating, identifying, and keeping track of these items is not worth the trouble.

Work-in-Process Inventory Control

Movement of inventory items in and out of work in process is an area of critical importance as far as record accuracy is concerned. Ensuring that part numbers and quantities are correct is important as far as inventory balances are concerned, but for parts issued to and returned from work orders it is doubly so.

The material planning system uses the component parts required for each work order as the basis for calculating quantities and dates required for each part number. If parts are not reported as being issued to a work order, the planning system will still show these parts as being required. Similarly, if a greater quantity is issued to a work order than is required for it, requirements may be understated. Any excess must be promptly returned to the warehouse or transferred to another work order if these calculations of requirements are to be accurate.

For completed production (i.e., the parent part number of a work order), reporting errors will also cause planning errors to occur. Most systems contain logic for closing work orders automatically as the quantity completed approaches the order quantity of the work order. Reporting errors will, as a result, cause a variety of erroneous actions in the system. Unreported completed parts will leave the order open, causing scheduling and requirements errors. Completing substantially more than the planned quantity for the work order, if the reporting is accurate, will cause inventory to appear in stock that was not planned for at that time. If the reported completions were in error, the inventory balance will be overstated and the system will underplan future production.

Overall, errors in reporting material transfers in and out of the work in process can cause a wide variety of errors besides over- or understating inventory balances in the warehouse. Any error in reporting component part issues to and from a work order will cause errors in the planning system, and in the costing of the work order as well. Many companies using planning systems do not fully understand the importance of physical control and record accuracy for work in process inventory as shown on work order records. Periodic audits of work orders, or cycle counting procedures similar to warehouse inventory counts, can go a long way toward eliminating errors and detecting procedural problems associated with this type of physical control and record accuracy.

Shipping

The shipping dock is the point of sale for most companies, as far as when the end of physical control over the item ends. For control to be achieved and theft to be avoided, the authorizing document or record must originate outside the shipping department. The principle that the information system must know the status of all items to work effectively applies here as well. The key connection between shipping and the customer must be such that a sale is recorded and payment liability established at the time of shipment. For this to happen, the system must have records of the customer, a sales order, and an accounts receivable record for all sales.

With a state-of-the-art system, the sales order is entered into the system by the customer service or sales department. The system then prints the shipping documents and picking list. With very large or complex products there may also be various supporting documentation accompanying the shipment, but this method of handling shipments ensures that all related records are updated at the appropriate time, and that effective control is achieved. These documents are the basis for withdrawing items from the warehouse. In an automated warehouse system, the picking/shipping list may actually drive the mechanical stock picking system to assemble the order.

In a manufacturing environment, shipments other than for sales purposes are frequently made, such as for outside processing of parts. These shipments are made against a manufacturing or work order, with a related purchase order set up to authorize their return and payment. The same principle of accurate status of each item and order is maintained so that the system may use the data in place of the actual physical reality to plan and control the company. This means that nothing that pertains to the manufacturing process or inventory can be shipped without being on an order, so that the system can properly control it and know about the event. Merely decreasing inventory balances for shipments is insufficient; the system must know why the item was shipped, and the order is the means for that.

In many manufacturing environments, shipments are critical because they are the events that relieve or fulfill the production schedule. It follows that errors in controlling and reporting shipments will produce errors in the entire planning and production scheduling system, because the master production schedule drives the rest of the detailed internal planning system. Even in a company that ships from finished-goods inventories, errors in shipments will have a similar effect, simply because the finished-goods inventory is really only a buffer between production and sales fluctuations.

Warehouse Control and Layout

A detailed discussion of the physical arrangement of warehouse space for efficiency of material handling and optimal use of storage space is beyond the scope of this book. Some comments are pertinent, however. Since the operating principle is that the information system uses its data in place of reality, the system must have continuously accurate information about what is actually in the warehouse and where it is. In order to achieve maximum use of warehouse space, a stocking system referred to as *random stocking* is frequently used. This method requires that a stock location subsystem be used that maintains records for each batch of parts, containing part number, quantity at that location, and a code for the actual location in the warehouse.

Under a random location stock system, parts are placed in any free space when received and the location recorded. As a result, the same part number may be stored in several locations in the warehouse, reflecting different dates of receipt. In order to avoid literally losing the parts in the warehouse, the location information must be continually accurate.

Retrieval of the parts for picking is done by the system, which instructs the stock picker to get either the smallest quantity or oldest receipt date first, to free up space, avoid many locations having small quantities of parts, and rotate stock. Figure 6–7 contains an example of records used in a stock location system.

If parts are small, or for some other reason stock locations can be permanently assigned, the location code identifying where the parts are can simply be made a part of the part number record. In either case, the system can print picking documents in location sequence, assuming that the location coding reflects a logical sequence within the warehouse area. The system most commonly used is to assign sequential letters or numbers to each aisle, each bin location along the aisle, and each vertical shelf. Sequencing items to be picked in ascending se-

Part Number	Warehouse Location	Quantity	Date Located
123	23-12-C	350	2/12
123	18-9-A	200	1/20
123	13-6-B	175	1/12
	Total in Warehouse:	725	

FIGURE 6–7
Stock location
records.

quence (A, then B, etc.) means that the stock picker can always start at the "beginning" (aisle A) and go through the warehouse picking the items without having to double back.

Probably the single most important element of warehouse control and information system accuracy is that access to the warehouse must be limited to as few people as possible. This seemingly obvious fact is frequently overlooked by many companies, usually in the name of expediting convenience. It is difficult enough to make sure that people moving material in and out of the warehouse create the appropriate records without allowing anyone who feels like it to get items from the warehouse.

Limiting access to items means that the company has a better chance to ensure that only trained people receive, move, or issue stock and are held responsible for creating the appropriate transaction records to keep the system correctly informed as to item status. Figure 6–8 summarizes some of the results of various common control errors.

Documentation

The term *documentation* acquires a somewhat different meaning in a fully computerized environment. In the mostly manual days of inventory management it was learned that in order to have control of inventory it was necessary to get people to write down a record of all transactions on an appropriate form, then forward the form to the record-keeping function for posting to the permanent records. When computers were brought in, this cycle remained largely unchanged, together with its associated problems.

The problem with this method is that the permanent record always trails reality, often by several days. The actual material movement occurs, is documented, and a batch of documents is collected, sent to the data entry function, and entered into the computer system. The assumption here is that the paper form is the "real" document, with the information being entered into the computer system mainly to aid the planning system, if one was in use, or to communicate with the many potential users of inventory information.

Error	Result
Receipt not recorded	• Parts lost • System reorders • Production erroneously delayed • Inventory dollar value understated
Issue not recorded	• Production/sale prevented • Reorder fails to occur • Inventory value overstated
Location incorrect	• Parts lost • Production/sale prevented • Reorder fails to occur

FIGURE 6-8
Results of
warehouse
control errors.

In a state-of-the-art system, terminals or other data collection devices are used in the warehouse itself to enter the information directly into the system, which in turn creates any hard copies required. Thus the computer record becomes the real document, with a written or printed copy merely accompanying the parts during the move to identify them and their destination or source.

It is important to note that regardless of the medium of documentation, the principle of correctly documenting all changes in the status of an item and posting it to the permanent record remains the same, since the purpose of the record is so either people or the information system can use it in place of the item itself to make decisions.

Cycle Counting versus Physical Inventories

One of the most commonly misunderstood areas of inventory control is that of counting parts and reconciling the result to the permanent record. The physical inventory, meaning a wall-to-wall count of everything in the warehouse at one time, originated in the accounting requirement for accurate financial statements, inventory being an asset. Since these statements usually only needed to be accurate in their total dollar value, and only once or twice a year, counting errors were assumed to offset each other and were not considered a major problem.

As the need for a much higher degree of accuracy, at the part number level, grew with the development of computerized planning systems, other methods were sought. For a planning system to work, it must have continuously accurate inventory records, not just semiannually. Experience taught managers that although the total dollar amount was accurate, often the wall-to-wall method of counting produced sizable errors at the individual part number level.

As if this were not bad enough in itself, the accuracy produced by a well-run inventory documentation and control system is destroyed in the process. Worse still, since the planning system uses inventory balances as its starting point, the entire material plan is thrown into a state of serious disarray, drastically reducing its usefulness.

Individuals not intimately familiar with inventory control problems often have difficulty believing that a wall-to-wall physical count made by people who do not work in the warehouse can produce so many incorrect data. Counting parts and correctly recording the count is one of those activities that looks much harder than it appears. Delaying recognition of this fact will only serve to postpone the financial and management benefits from a material planning system.

These and other factors led to the development of the cyclic method of counting parts. A small team of well-trained individuals counts and reconciles a small number of part numbers every day. If a discrepancy between the count and the permanent record is found, serious efforts are made to determine what procedural gap allowed the error to occur in the first place. It is this activity that brings a shift in emphasis of the counting activity from one of correcting the records to developing methods for preventing them in the first place. If proper records are kept, and a random sampling of parts are counted and prove correct, CPA firms will accept the computer-calculated value of the inventory as being the true value, thereby completely dispensing the need for a wall-to-wall inventory.

This shift is more important than it may seem at first glance, since it underscores the corresponding shift from relying on the direct use of physical reality (going out to the warehouse and looking at the items) to dependence on the records maintained by the computer system. Experience has shown that without a properly managed cycle counting program, no inventory system can be maintained in an accurate, reliable state.

Another important aspect of a cycle counting program is that of counting the high-value, very significant (in terms of overall business) parts more often than the lower-value, insignificant items. The ABC method of classifying items, discussed earlier, coupled with a method of identifying the real production stoppers, will significantly enhance a cycle counting program.

Cycle counting still accomplishes the basic purpose of physical inventories, in that the permanent record gets corrected or verified that it is correct. The difference is that when all the procedural gaps are plugged, a cycle counting system merely confirms that the records are accurate. However, no system is totally perfect, and occasional errors will always creep into the records. Cycle counting, through its use of a trained individual rather than someone unfamiliar with the parts, records, and procedures, will produce far more accurate results than the shotgun approach of the wall-to-wall physical inventory.

Inventory and Other System Elements

In a business that is centered around inventory activity, whether a distribution or manufacturing business or both, the primary piece of information is the part number and all information related to it. The secondary data connected with a part number may contain a wide variety of descriptive, historical, statistical, and summary data. In order to maintain records of event-oriented activities, order records are used to connect a part number and a set of data describing the event, such as due date, customer, vendor, costs, prices, and operations to be performed.

Figure 6–9 illustrates some of the interrelationships between the primary piece of information of part number (the inventory record) and other types of secondary data that directly relate to it. These include the information used to manage the bulk of the business. In the illustration, each of the types of information feeding into the inventory record in fact represents an entire subsystem in itself. Each of these is explored in more detail in subsequent chapters.

Further, each item of secondary data in the inventory record may actually be accumulated in considerable detail. For example, quantity sold, provided by the sales order processing system from shipments, might be accumulated in

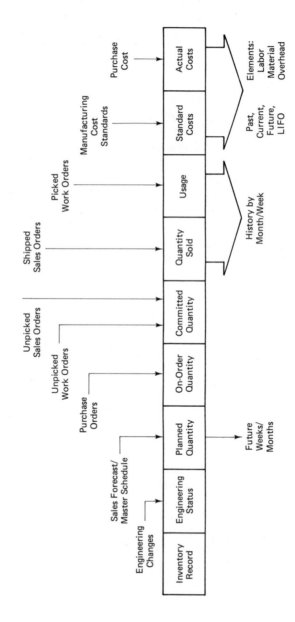

FIGURE 6-9 The inventory foundation.

monthly or weekly periods for trend analysis, or for comparisons with forecasted quantities. Similarly, cost information is frequently accumulated and carried in considerable detail by element, past, future costs, and so on.

Record Accuracy—Other Data

In keeping with the principle that the purpose of the computer system is to maintain a continuously accurate picture of reality so that the picture may be used in place of the physical reality itself to make decisions, it becomes clear that record accuracy applies to all other types of information as well. For instance, if cost figures are incorrect, calculations of profit margin, manufacturing performance, purchasing variations, and other important management information also become incorrect. Or, if work orders are released and never actually picked and moved into production, this will show erroneous committed quantities, causing inventory to increase unnecessarily.

The cycle counting concept of maintaining accurate on-hand and warehouse information in the inventory records must also be applied to all other types of records. Large-scale accounting systems, such as in banks, use the technique of reconciling two independently developed dollar totals to ensure accuracy on an ongoing basis. In the past, these concepts have seldom been applied in the manufacturing and distribution business.

As the development of more formal systems continues and more and more information resides in the computer system, this kind of reconciliation becomes practical. For example, the technique of balancing cash for a cashier can be applied to inventory. The dollar value of inventory received at cost, less the cost value of the amount shipped, should equal actual on-hand inventory value. Any variation is due to unreported loss, scrap, damage, theft, and so on. Management that is interested in real control of the inventory asset will use this information to detect these variations and develop procedures for ensuring that the events that cause them are discovered and reported so that they may be controlled.

The manual methods for developing inventory value in the past usually did not afford much in the way of real control, since the inventory valuation was "backed into" from calculations using accounts payable and sales data. The annual physical inventory usually caused a single large adjustment to be made to this month-end figure. The single, aggregate adjustment simply averages inventory variations from all causes, leaving management with little information it can use to control these variations. Information must be event oriented and specific to be of any real use to management. For example, a report that says only that inventory "shrinkage" was a certain dollar amount is not nearly as useful as one which shows that the shrinkage was associated with certain specific part numbers when they were issued to certain specific work orders.

The first report would probably lead one to hire a gun-toting guard and post him at the warehouse door, whereas the second might lead management to investigate unreported scrap rates associated with the manufacture of certain items. If the scrap is legitimate (i.e., not theft on the production line), the actual profit margin in the production of these items is less than was assumed.

To reiterate, then, record accuracy concepts applies to all records and information used to run the business, recognizing that some data are more critical than others. If information is accurate and current, the system can be relied on to make large numbers of decisions involved in the operation of the business at a rate far exceeding that of human beings and at a much higher level of accuracy. If the computer-maintained picture of reality slips out of focus drastically, the system will simply lead management toward the ditch of bankruptcy and failure in a more interesting manner than in the past.

CHAPTER 6 QUESTIONS

1. Why is inventory a type of capital investment for a company?

2. Given that inventory is purchased stock (perhaps with some value added) that the company is *holding,* what are some reasons for investing the company's capital in inventory? Why invest in inventory instead of alternative investments?

3. What are the purposes of using multiple classification methods?

4. Give several examples of Pareto's Law besides inventory behavior. What does the law really mean?

5. What are the chief purposes of applying Pareto's Law to inventory items to produce an "ABC List"?

6. What is the effect of a single part having both dependent and independent demand?

7. Why is it necessary to subtract actual sales orders from forecasted quantities (netting)?

8. What are the reasons for carrying or not carrying finished goods inventory?

9. If in-plant lead times were drastically reduced, what effect might this have on a company's finished goods inventory policy?

10. Why is it desirable to plan, measure, and control customer service levels?

11. When is it desirable to have some stockouts? Why?

12. Describe the relationship between a company's ability to respond to changing customer demand quickly and inventory levels.

13. What causes lumpy demand?

14. Why do order-point systems fail with dependent demand items?

15. Why is information and data accuracy for inventory items critical?

16. Why should shipping authorization originate outside of the shipping department?

17. Restricting access to the warehouse and stores area aids what goal?

18. In a totally computerized environment, documentation acquires a new meaning. Explain.

19. Describe the advantages of cycle-counting programs over physical inventories.

20. What are the elements of a good cycle-counting program?
21. Inventory data is related to the other activities in the company. Describe these relationships in terms of information.
22. Record inaccuracy has a ripple effect through the entire planning system. Cite some examples.

7

Executing
the Business Plan—
Material

THE MASTER SCHEDULE—THE SYSTEM DRIVER

The heart of the detail planning system is the order generation cycle, or explosion process. During this cycle, each master scheduled end item is exploded all the way down through its product structure to obtain a fully detailed plan for scheduling subassembly and component production, and ultimately for determining requirements for purchased items. Partly for historical reasons, this process is called *material requirements planning.* Since the same set of planned order records that are generated by this process are used by the Capacity Planning process and other systems also, it is referred to here as simply the *planned order generation process.*

Master scheduling, as discussed in Chapter 3, can use a number of grouping techniques to make it manageable. Regardless of which such technique is used, when the master schedule becomes input for the planned orders, it must be part number specific. For the detail planning system, then, the master schedule is the detailed definition of the quantities, timing, what the independent demand is, and how it is to be met.

The Concept of an Order

The concept of an order is probably the most central notion after that of a part number to manufacturing planning systems. Although there are many types of orders, and the number varies depending on the particular system design, all share several basic features. Put simply, an order is a way of defining an event in time. The minimum data elements for an order are:

- Its unique, identifying order number
- The part number that identifies what the order is concerned with
- The quantity of that part number, further defining what the order is for
- At least one date, to define the when of the order

In actuality, an order will always have more data than this, but just which elements depends on the type of order and the system design. A state-of-the-art system will use at least three basic types. These are:

- *Sales order:* to define customer demand on the company
- *Purchase order:* to define company demand on a vendor
- *Work order:* to define internal production needs

Of these order types, the work order is the only one of concern to the planned order generation process. Sales orders are by definition manually created, as are purchase orders. Both these types of orders reflect an agreement between two parties, in addition to the basic facts of the order itself.

Work orders are the center piece of the planning logic. There are three types. Figure 7-1 illustrates the three types of work orders and the properties associated with each. The key difference is that the planned order and the firm

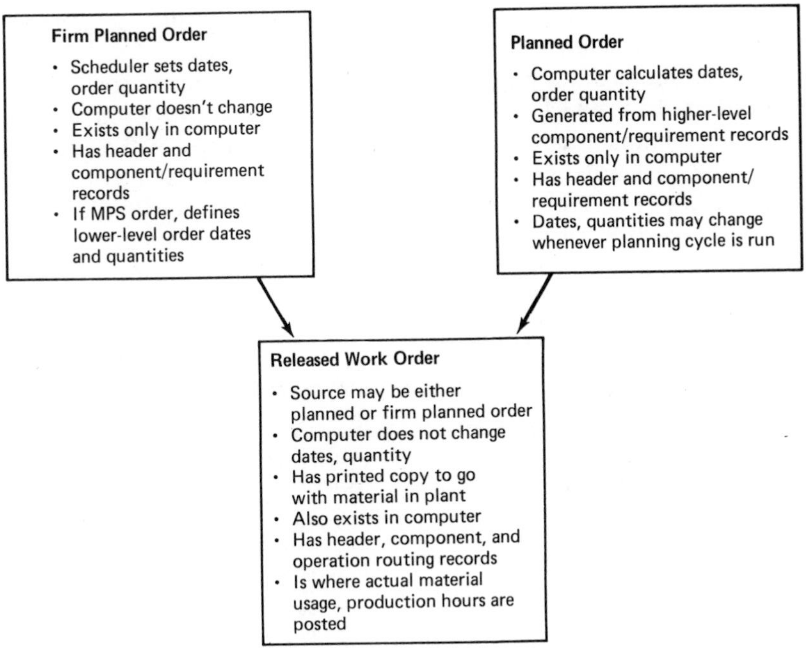

Firm Planned Order

- Scheduler sets dates, order quantity
- Computer doesn't change
- Exists only in computer
- Has header and component/requirement records
- If MPS order, defines lower-level order dates and quantities

Planned Order

- Computer calculates dates, order quantity
- Generated from higher-level component/requirement records
- Exists only in computer
- Has header and component/requirement records
- Dates, quantities may change whenever planning cycle is run

Released Work Order

- Source may be either planned or firm planned order
- Computer does not change dates, quantity
- Has printed copy to go with material in plant
- Also exists in computer
- Has header, component, and operation routing records
- Is where actual material usage, production hours are posted

FIGURE 7-1 Work order types.

planned order exist only in the computer system. These two are quite similar as far as the computer data are concerned, except that regardless of where a firm planned order occurs in the product structure, the computer may not change its dates or quantities: hence the name *firm order*. Because of this difference, however, these two types of orders have important differences in how they are used. The firm planned order forms the "anchors" of the detailed plan. Master production schedule (MPS) orders will normally be firm planned, or fixed. If the system is of the type where the sales forecast of requirements interfaces with the master schedule orders, having fixed orders at this juncture allows uncoupling the forecast from the master schedule.

As with any computer record, one of the purposes of the order record is to relate a number of pieces of information. Some of this information is very basic in nature, whereas some varies from company to company, part number to part number, or system to system. In most manufacturing systems, fixed-length records are used. Additional secondary records are added to handle related information. Figure 7–2 shows the basic elements of each of the three record types that comprise the minimum for a work order.

The work order header contains data of general applicability to the entire work order; it defines the work order. The minimum defining data would include the part number which the work order is for (i.e., that which is to be produced), how many of that part are to be made, when it is to be completed and started, and a work order number to make it unique, since there may be more than one work order with the same combination of dates and part numbers in existence at the same time.

The definition of the product is set by the product structure records. Since the records in the Product Structure file define the product without any dates, and for the minimum build quantity, usually one, a copy of these records is made by the work order generation process, but with several important pieces of data added. First, the quantity required has been extended times the order quantity of the work order header record to obtain the amount of each compo-

Work Order Header Record
- Work order number
- Parent part number
- Start and completion dates
- Order quantity (including planned scrap)

Component/Requirements Records

For each component in a single level of the product structure; one record with:
- Work order number
- Component part number
- Quantity of that part required to make parent part number's order quantity
- Date part is required

Operation Routing Records

One record for each operation required to make order quantity of parent part number with:
- Work order number
- Operation sequence number
- Operation description
- Planned production hours
- Start and complete date/time (for each operation)
- Work center (for the operation)

FIGURE 7-2   Work order elements.

nent part required to make the order quantity. Second, the individual lead times for each component part are subtracted from the start date of the order to obtain the time each component must be ordered from a vendor, or a work order to make it must be started. Finally, each parent–component record for the work order has the work order number attached to it to identify it as belonging specifically to that work order.

The material planning processing cycle normally generates only the records described thus far, that is, the work order header records and the component–requirements records. When these exist only in the computer files, they are referred to as planned orders. A firm planned order is simply a planned order that has a flag that, when set, causes the planning system to not change the order's dates, quantities, or existence (not delete it, in other words).

Order Generation Logic

The actual logic by which a set of product structure records are expanded and copied into a set of work order records is fairly simple. Figure 7–3 illustrates the process. Part Z, the product to be made, is composed of component parts A, B, C, and D. It takes 1 part A, 4 part D's, and so on to make one part Z. To create a work order for 12 part Z's, the quantities required of each component are simply multiplied by the order quantity. The process is the same regardless of how many components are needed to make the end product. The element of timing (i.e., calculation of lead times for each component record) is neglected in these examples and will be discussed shortly.

Since a full production plan hardly consists of one work order, when looked at in the aggregate, the different elements of the system interact, as shown in Figure 7–4. The master production schedule orders define and anchor the rest of the planning process by fixing the topmost level of the planning process. The inventory records are accessed to obtain current stock available, lead

Product Structure for Part Z

Component P/N's	Quantity Required
A	1
B	1
C	2
D	4

X (Order Quantity = 12)

=

Work Order Header Record
P/N = Z
Order Quantity = 12

Requirements Records

P/N	Quantity Required
A	12
B	12
C	24
D	48

FIGURE 7-3
Exploding a
single-level
product structure.

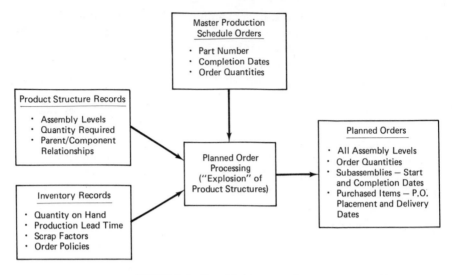

FIGURE 7-4   Planned order generation.

time for the part, scrap rates, and ordering rules. Product structure records are accessed to create planned orders using the logic defined in Figure 7-3.

Assumptions of Order Planning

This approach to creating a detailed material and production plan contains several important assumptions. If these assumptions are not reflected by real-world events, the planning process itself will contain errors to the degree that the assumptions are in error. These assumptions are:

- Order independence.
- Inventory status is known.
- All parts move in and out of inventory.
- The master production schedule exists and is realistic.
- All products to be made are accurately defined in product structure records.

Since these assumptions are both important and basic to the entire order planning process, they bear some discussion. To some extent they are interrelated. Not only must these records exist in the system, they must be accurate. Also, there must not be additional work going on that is not included in the system; that is, the planning process assumes that it is planning all the work in the plant, not just some of it.

Order independence: This means that each order stands as an entity on its own. If all components are available, the parent part number of the order can be completed. There is no direct relationship to other orders, other than in the sense that preceding ones may provide component parts for higher assembly orders.

Inventory status is known: The record for each part in the system must include not only the current on-hand balance (which obviously must reflect what is actually in the warehouse or stores area), but also the quantity that is already spoken for, or allocated to orders that are released, and whose component requirements simply have not yet been removed from stock. A second aspect of inventory status is that issues of component parts must be made to specific work orders, so the specific requirement for the component on that work order is relieved. Related is the reporting of scrap of the parent part number or of components used in the production process. Finally, completions of the parent part number on the work order must be reported not only to the work order, but to stores.

All parts move in and out of inventory: Closely related to the inventory status assumption is that completions of parent part numbers on work orders move into warehouse inventory. Essentially, these systems satisfy all demand (requirements) by issues from warehouse stock, not directly from completions of work orders at a lower product structure level. Many systems do have hybrid transactions that, in effect, move the parts into the warehouse and directly issue them to the new work order, but these are still a two-part transaction. There is a simple reason for this. Work orders are how all work in process is tracked. Completions of parent parts on work orders are assumed to still be in work in process until moved off the floor. To allow otherwise would require the use of a separate floor stock inventory subsystem that is not actually part of work in process.

The master production schedule is realistic: Since the MPS is the driver of the entire order generation process, and therefore the whole detail production plan, it follows that inaccuracies and unrealistic MPS plans would be a direct cause of inappropriate detail plans. Common problems in this area are performing work that was never part of the MPS, changing the schedule within the minimum lead time for responding to changes in the MPS, and including work in the MPS that will not actually be performed, such as in the case of insufficient production capacity. Many companies, in their understandable desire to please customers, will commit to order delivery dates that are beyond their productive capacity.

It is one thing to tell the customer something false and another to tell the lie to the planning system. If the planning system is lied to, it will dutifully calculate an overabundance of component and subassembly requirements, lead to excessive inventory, making the wrong parts at the wrong time, and other unfortunate outcomes. So the MPS must tell the system what it really expects to see produced.

All products are defined in the product structure records: Since the order generation process uses the product structure records as its basis for creating all lower-level requirements and orders, it stands to reason that all parts that are actually part of the product must be reflected in the product structure records at order generation time. Common problems in this area include leaving certain parts out, which end up not being planned, obsolete parent–component relationships, and having structure records that do not reflect how the product is actually built. This last problem can be the result of many things, usually an unwillingness to communicate between the various company functions, engineering (which may draw the product from a design standpoint), accounting (which may use a different version to cost out the product), and material planning (which may arrange parts in a different manner to make planning more convenient). There may not even be an agreement on where a set of component parts becomes a new part number. These differences are assumed to have been resolved in a state-of-the-art manufacturing planning system. To the degree that they are not, the system will produce distorted, incorrect information.

Multilevel order generation: The discussion thus far has described how a single order is created from the known variables of product structure and order quantity. The order generation process proceeds in a level-by-level process until all levels are completely planned. A software device called a *low-level code* is used to permit the system to plan each part number only once. The code identifies the lowest product structure level where the part number is used.

Figure 7–5 shows in diagram form how the different records created by the order generation process are related. Note in particular the relationships between order header records and the component–requirement records. The product structure for each part to be produced is reflected in its requirement records, which are a copy of the product structure file records. Thus part A has a top-level product structure composed of parts 12, 13, and 14. Part 12 is a purchased item, whereas the other two are made from still another set of component part numbers. The reader should bear in mind that this diagram shows only the record relationships, product structures, required quantities, and the order quantities for each order. The order policies are not explicitly called out to simplify the diagram. Lead times are not shown either. The products have been kept simple, both in number of components and number of levels.

To describe fully the precise logic followed by an order generation program in the computer is beyond the scope of this book. However, the fundamental concepts are not complex. The basic steps (using the example):

1. Starting at parts A and B, which are end items and Master Production Schedule orders, "explode" the Product Structure records by multiplying the quantities required times the order quantity.

2. For each component in the product structure, create a requirement record reflecting the total quantity required of that part to make the order quantity. Continue until all product structure level zero orders are exploded.

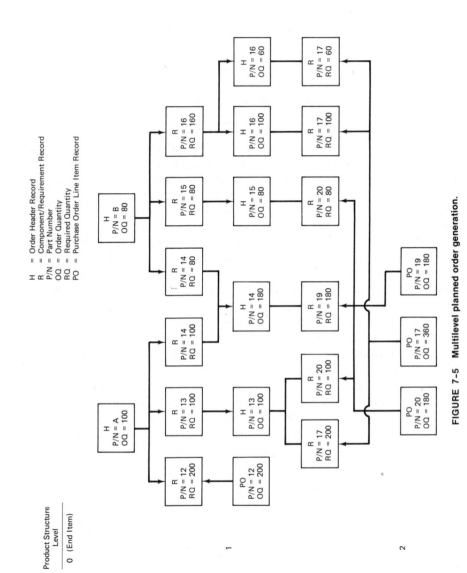

Product Structure
Level
0 (End Item)

H   = Order Header Record
R   = Component/Requirement Record
P/N = Part Number
OQ = Order Quantity
RQ = Required Quantity
PO = Purchase Order Line Item Record

FIGURE 7-5 Multilevel planned order generation.

127

3. Starting at the next product structure level, summarize all requirement records for each part number.

4. Examine the ordering policy for each part number and create one or more order header records to satisfy the total quantity required.

5. Explode the next level of order header records after all higher-level requirements are created, creating the next level of requirements records, and continue in this manner until all product structure levels are processed and orders are created to cover requirements for all manufactured parts and requirements are created for all purchased parts.

Several aspects of the example are illustrative of this processing logic. The two requirement records for part 14 were combined to produce a single order header record for the part, with an order quantity of 180. Even though part of the total requirement of 180 comes from part A's usage, and some from part B, a single order for the total will satisfy both requirements. Similarly, parts 13 and 16 both are made from part 17. A single Purchase Order for 160 meets the total required for all next-higher-level parts.

The exception to the order per requirements order policy is part 16, which in the example is assumed to have a maximum order quantity of 100. As a result, two orders are created, one for 100 and one for the balance of 60 needed. Remembering that each order header record has a unique order number, separate requirements records for each of these orders will be created. However, due to the summarizing of requirement records step, these two records, together with the one from part 13, have their requirements covered by the single Purchase Order, as discussed above. Order policies, or lot sizing, will be discussed in more detail later.

This process can, of course, be continued for any reasonable number of levels (over 100 is considered "unreasonable" here). In every case, regardless of the order policies used, the process at each level is identical. Two additional aspects of the planned order generation process, time phasing and netting against available stock on hand, are discussed below.

In a full-scale system, involving thousands of part numbers, and perhaps 30,000 product structure records, the planned order records may number upward of 100,000 records or more. The basic process by which they are produced is the same, perhaps with some refinements to speed processing by the computer. In each case, a requirement record defines a demand, and an order header record defines a supply.

Time Phasing

In addition to the records created during the planned order generation process for quantities, there is also the factor of when the demands occur and when supply actions are planned to meet the demands. To manage these data, each order header record and each requirement record has a start and completion date. For purchasing actions, the analogous dates are purchase order placement date and delivery date. The lead time for the part is the time planned to elapse between these two events.

The time-phasing logic assumes that the start date of an order is the same date that all required parts for the order must be available. So the date calculation logic always starts with the required completion date of the highest-level part, calculates the start date for the order from the lead time for the part, then sets this date as the completion (or delivery) date for all component/requirement records related to that order.

This process is illustrated in Figure 7–6. The example is an end item Z, which has a total long lead time of 23 days to complete all actions, from initial placement of the purchase order for part D on day 0, through completion of subassemblies and final production of end item Z. The product structure for Z is shown in the upper left corner, and the schedules for purchasing and production that derive from the time-phasing logic are at the lower left. The lead time data are kept in the inventory records for each part. Other chapters will discuss various methods for obtaining these lead times.

Each of the lead times may in turn be broken down into separate segments, such as delivery and receiving inspection time for purchased parts, or move, queue, and run time for made parts. For purposes of obtaining these dates for the time-phasing logic, a total planned lead time is usually employed.

Several important points are illustrated in the example. Assuming that the schedulers have told the system the truth about the planned lead times, if part D is not placed on order by day 0, there is no way that end item Z can be produced by day 23. *This fact is knowable on day 1, in plenty of time to take action.* The power of a planning system to notify the scheduler this far in advance when a delivery date is in trouble is one of the more remarkable features of these systems. All too often, schedulers, in fear of not having enough time to react to problems, build in so many cushions in the lead times that the system becomes useless as a warning device.

Looking at the example of end item Z, the result is really a critical path chart. All actions that can be completed in parallel with each other are planned that way. All that depend on a preceding action's completion before it can be started are arranged in this manner. For example, part D must be delivered before part C can be started, even if parts E and F are available. And if part B is not ordered on day 8, all the work that is already started to make part F, and to have parts D and E delivered on day 10, will be a waste.

Part C could be started on day 10, but when it is completed on day 17, it would just sit, waiting part A's completion. Part A, of course, is delayed by the failure to order part B in time. Suppose that part B is going to be 30 days late, and will not be delivered until day 42. If action is taken to reschedule end item Z out to be completed on day 53, no inventory buildup will occur. If this is not done, production people will have the joy of producing a subassembly that truly is not needed, because it will just sit for 30 days before it can be used. Unfortunately, no one is fooled by this action. Production people frequently know what is needed and what is not.

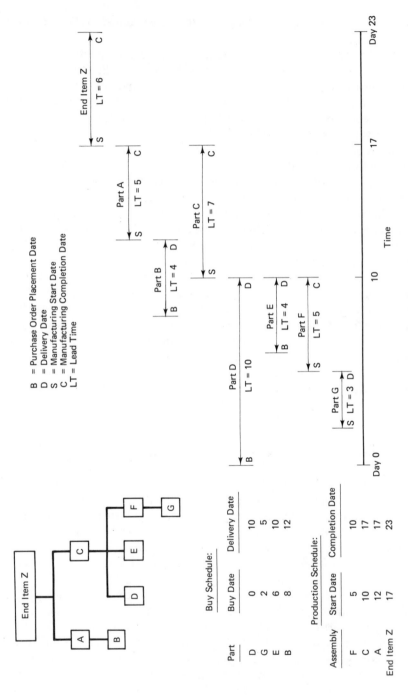

FIGURE 7-6 Time-phasing requirements.

B = Purchase Order Placement Date
D = Delivery Date
S = Manufacturing Start Date
C = Manufacturing Completion Date
LT = Lead Time

End Item Z   S   LT = 6   C

Part A   S   LT = 5   C
Part B   B   LT = 4   D
Part C   S   LT = 7   C
Part D   B   LT = 10   D
Part E   B   LT = 4   D
Part F   S   LT = 5   C
Part G   S   LT = 3   D

Day 0   10   17   Day 23
                Time

End Item Z

A   C
B   D   E   F
              G

Buy Schedule:

Part	Buy Date	Delivery Date
D	0	10
G	2	5
E	6	10
B	8	12

Production Schedule:

Assembly	Start Date	Completion Date
F	5	10
C	10	17
A	12	17
End Item Z	17	23

Netting against On-hand Stock

In the previous example of planned order generation, the process has been assumed to have ignored any on-hand balances of parts that might have been available. For a brand new product, with all new components, the planned order generation process would closely resemble the preceding logic. In the normal case, however, there is usually some stock available to satisfy at least part of the total requirement for a part, regardless of the product structure level.

Figure 7-7 illustrates the netting process for two different parts, part A and part B. There is no safety stock for part A, whereas part B has a safety stock of 25 units. In this case the planning logic will regard 25 as being the minimum, instead of zero, leaving at least 25 units untouched all the time. Each part also has a different order method. The part with the smaller minimum order quantity is ordered more frequently.

This example also illustrates the powerful effect on inventory investment from the selection of different order policies. Note that the requirements for parts A and B are identical over the planning horizon shown. Although there is a difference in the beginning on-hand quantity, in both cases an order is needed in the first few weeks. With a small minimum order quantity and no safety stock, part A is planned very closely to the quantities and time period required. The average on-hand inventory is only 2.5 units, reflecting small remainders.

Part B, on the other hand, has a safety stock level equal to approximately two weeks' average usage and a larger minimum order quantity. One might hypothesize that part B has a large setup cost. But look at the difference in average on-hand stock this creates. Even if safety stock were eliminated, the

		Period										
P/N: A		1	2	3	4	5	6	7	8	9	10	Average
On Hand: 30	Requirements	20	10	15	20	25	5	0	5	20	15	13.5
Minimum Order Quantity: 10	On Order			15	20	25	10		10	15	15	11.0
Safety Stock: 0	Projected O/H	10	0	0	0	0	5	5	5	0	0	2.5

		Period										
P/N: B		1	2	3	4	5	6	7	8	9	10	Average
On Hand: 75	Requirements	20	10	15	20	25	5	0	5	20	15	13.5
Minimum Order Quantity: 60	On Order				60					60		12.0
Safety Stock: 25	Projected O/H	55	45	30	70	45	40	40	35	75	60	45.5

FIGURE 7-7   Effect of on-hand stock on order planning.

average on-hand would still equal about 20 units, over eight times the inventory investment for part A. Assuming that the order method reflects real-world factors, a little work to make part B's setup costs smaller would clearly produce big savings.

This example also illustrates how the order header and requirement records are typically displayed. The records themselves actually have specific dates start and completion dates in them, as illustrated in previous examples. For purposes of creating a manageable display of a lot of data, the format shown in Figure 7–7 is a common method of summarizing all the requirement and order header records for a given part number. The periods may be either weeks or months. State-of-the-art systems allow retrieval of all records that were used to create a given stock status display.

The effect of on-hand stock in the order planning process is simple. If there is sufficient actual or projected on-hand stock to satisfy requirements, no order is planned. If there is not, an order is planned according to the order policy stipulated for the part. The basic formulas used to describe the relationships in the order planning process can be stated as follows:

Gross requirements	= Sum of independent and dependent demands
Net requirements	= Gross requirements less available stock on hand less on order quantity
Available stock on hand	= Stock on hand less safety stock less quantity allocated
On order	= Sum of: unreleased (planned) order quantities released, uncompleted order quantities placed, undelivered purchase order quantities

Planning Horizons and Lead Time

One of the most critical factors in the effectiveness of a detailed planning system is that of lead times. Previous examples have mentioned examples of the use of lead times. As George Plossl says: "Lead time is whatever you say it is. Plus a little." Although this certainly describes the lead time situation in an overall way, such as ordering lead times quoted to customers, the discussion here attempts to be somewhat more specific.

Put bluntly, the lead time for a part is the time required to make it, that is, the actual number of hours it takes to perform all operations required to complete one unit. Strictly speaking, lead times should be extended through the operation routing records just as order quantities are extended through product structure records. The next best compromise is the time required to complete the typical order quantity, or lot size. Add an allowance for moving the material, and the result is what may be termed the *zero-queue lead time.*

All other time is time the material spends just sitting, taking up space and company cash. In a well-run, state-of-the-art-managed company, this wait time is virtually nil. In most plants, however, there is at least some justification for keeping small amounts of work ahead of each work center to smooth out the minor fluctuations in work flow. This is termed the *queue,* or *queue size,* stated in hours, hopefully, or days, if there is a lot.

In all too many companies, not only is queue time 80 to 90% of total lead times, the situation is compounded further by including these phony lead times in the planning system. Figure 7-6 illustrated the total lead time calculation process for an end item Z. Condensing this example to show only the production parts and schedule, Figure 7-8 compares the original assumptions of lead times with the true lead times for each component and subassembly comprising end item Z.

In this example, the same product which with standard lead times takes 19 days to make, actually takes only 7 if true lead times are used for each part. The remaining 12 days represents time that either the raw material or some of the partly completed subassemblies just sat. Or worse still, the system creates order placement and start dates that everyone ignores, including vendors, because past performance has demonstrated that they were not the true requirement dates.

The purpose of this example is to illustrate two points. First, the planning horizon clearly must be far enough out into the future to cover the lead time of the longest total procurement and build time critical path. In the example in Figure 7-6, this would be 23 days, assuming that Z is the only product. Obviously, altering the end item's stated completion dates or quantities will cause disruptions in the lower product structure levels of the plan.

The second point is that how the lead times are actually stated in the system is seldom the truth, and this form of lying to the system merely causes trouble. What everyone knows informally is that the true long lead time for end item Z is only 7 days once the raw materials are in plant. This means that if true lead times are used in the system, the maximum planning horizon is a great deal shorter than if "standard" or phony lead times are used. The rule that the total longest lead time determines the planning horizon still holds, of course. It is just much shorter.

The final point about planning horizons and time fences is closely related to the master scheduling discussion in Chapter 3 of varying degrees of "firmness" in the schedule depending on how far out the schedule is. The closer to the present, the more firm. Accordingly, the most common method in state-of-the-art systems is two or more time "fences" to denote degrees of "frozenness" of the schedule. Once the near term is breached, the master schedule must be frozen, or nearly so. These fences may be indicated on stock status displays and reports, especially at the master schedule level.

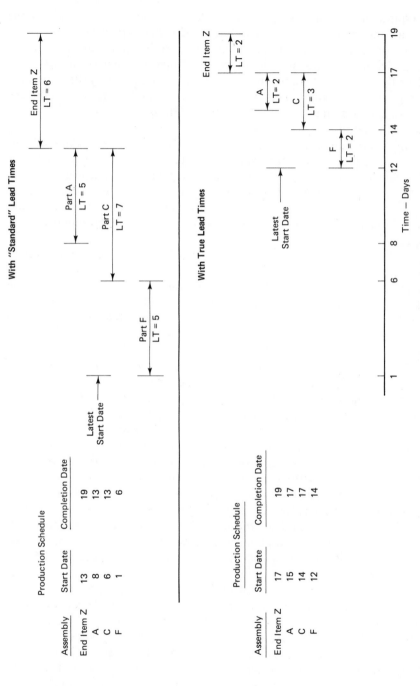

FIGURE 7-8 Effect of true lead times on planning horizons.

134

Subassembly Levels and Purchasing Requirements

Preceding sections discussed how the planned order generation process causes the creation of orders and requirements all the way down through the product structure. The process is identical regardless of the number of levels, because it is a single level at a time process. Whenever a given product structure "tree" reaches the level of a purchased part, the explosion process is completed. The same part may be used in numerous other products at many different product structure levels. Figure 7–9 shows an example of numerous requirements for a purchased item, Part A, coming from many different next-higher assembly work orders.

Since all requirements are for the same part, all have the same lead time, two weeks. This illustration shows only how the requirements fall; there are no orders defined. It can be seen that each requirement record has a delivery date by which the required quantity is needed to satisfy a start date for a next-higher assembly planned order. Whether these next-higher assembly orders are for the same or different part numbers is of no concern here.

Since the required delivery dates and quantities are known, and the lead time is the same for all, a latest purchasing action schedule is also calculated, shown on the second line. Thus the quantity of 70 that is due in the third period must be ordered during the first period if it is to be delivered on time. These seven requirement dates can actually be met by a variety of ordering methods, which will be discussed shortly.

The best method, of course, would be seven separate deliveries, each at the required times, resulting in no inventory on hand at all. Of course, all quantities could actually be placed on order with a vendor well in advance of the required delivery date. In the case of purchased items, the lead time refers more to a latest action date than the actual specific order placement date. For example, an order for part A could be placed in period 1 with seven delivery dates, for each of the requirements shown. If there are substantial fixed delivery costs, making numerous small deliveries excessively costly, a compromise order method would be used, resulting in perhaps two or three deliveries.

Even in this simple example, it is possible to see how inventory comes to be stocked, even though it really serves no purpose. There really is no justification for safety stock at the purchased part level, other than an occasionally unreliable vendor. Material handling costs at the ordering company are most often fairly linear; that is, they vary in direct proportion to the quantity handled.

Other costs associated with having the parts in stock also tend to be linear. Only transportation and the vendor's minimum ordering quantities serve as justifications for having fewer, larger orders. Of course, in all too many cases, the real truth is that a single large order is placed just because it is easier for the person preparing the requisition or purchase order.

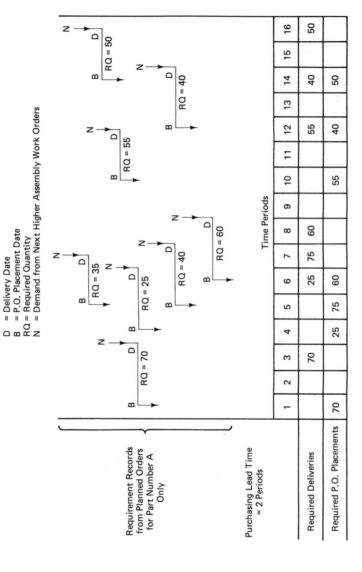

FIGURE 7-9 Purchased item requirements.

Lot Sizing and Order Policies

As was demonstrated in Figure 7-7, inappropriate order methods can be one of the biggest causes of excessive inventory. If all order policies were strictly per requirements and parts were delivered on the day required, there would be no raw material or subassembly inventory at all. Since a vast array of management problems literally disappear when a company is run with virtually no inventory, this is a worthwhile goal to pursue. Chapter 13 discusses how far some companies have gotten, and how they have done it.

The subject of safety stock, or safety time, as it is sometimes called, is discussed separately. Here the discussion will be confined to variables other than forecast error, the normal justification for safety stock. The variables that are usually involved in calculating optimum lot sizes (order quantities) include the following factors:

- Quantity price breaks (i.e., more for less)
- Bulk shipping savings
- Ordering cost, including processing of the order; setup costs, if applicable; certain handling costs
- Carrying charges for stock on hand
- Unit cost of the item

From the viewpoint of the discussion thus far, it is clear that there are two general ways to develop order quantities. Order exactly what is needed and no more, or some compromise method that produces order quantities larger than what is actually needed. This method is termed ordering *lot for lot* and assumes that ordering or setup costs are negligible. Part A in Figure 7-7 is ordered with this method. Ordering lot for lot results in the minimum possible carrying costs, investment, and risk of capital, and the least possible business overhead in the material control area.

All other methods use an optimizing formula of one sort or another. Any of these methods will result in some stock on hand in between requirement dates. The point of view of this book is that management is better advised to expend efforts to minimize the cost variables that justify more inventory, rather than simply measure them and crank them into a lot-sizing equation. The commonly used optimizing formula type of order method is discussed briefly below.

Economic order quantity: The economic order quantity (EOQ) equation has been around since material control's earliest days. Like any formula, it relates certain variables according to how each behaves. Figure 7-10 illustrates in graph form the variables involved in the EOQ equation. Annual carrying cost, for example, is assumed to be linear, to vary in direct proportion to the amount of stock on hand. Within reasonable limits, this is probably sufficiently ac-

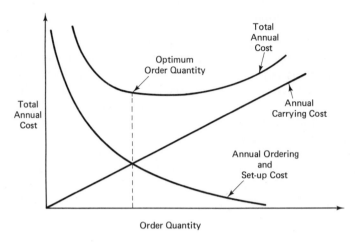

FIGURE 7-10 Economic order quantity.

curate for most situations. Since carrying cost and ordering costs are the two primary variables in the EOQ equation, and the use of this equation is so pervasive, some closer examination of its assumptions is warranted.

The notion of carrying cost itself contains several assumptions. The most significant is that the only relevant variables are measurable costs. In every business operation there are many costs that are influenced only indirectly by others. These are usually referred to as *intangible cost relationships*. Figuring out the connection is difficult, in other words. Difficult or not, however, the relationships are still there.

For example, when a company substitutes automated equipment for production labor, it gains more than just the labor savings. The company becomes easier to manage, because there are fewer supervisors, a simpler management structure, and less communicating to do. The same kind of simplification occurs when dramatic reductions in inventory take place. The business just gets easier to run.

As far as tangible costs go, few companies ever do any kind of study to determine what their carrying costs really are. When such studies are done, the resulting number is invariably higher than everyone had thought. Some studies have produced numbers such as 40% or higher. Finally, the most likely relationship for carrying costs would be a U-shaped curve, high for small quantities (some space has to be assigned to the parts) and high for very large quantities since special warehousing equipment or facilities might be required.

Ordering cost, including setup and transaction costs, is the other EOQ variable. Except for setup costs, ordering is mostly the result of creating a new order, placing the purchase order, or creating accompanying drawings and similar support tasks. Other than the transaction costs, setup is the main cost of interest to planners.

Figure 7-11 illustrates the relationship between the number of orders per

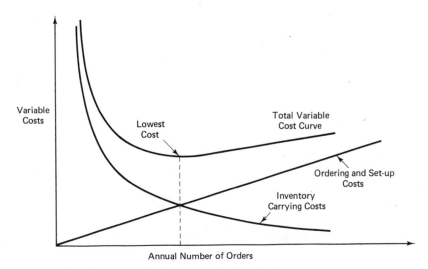

FIGURE 7-11   Ordering cost relationships. (Source: Powel, H.W., and
Weeks, T.G., *Production and Inventory Control Handbook*, ed. James H.
Green, New York: McGraw-Hill, 1970, pp. 6-11.)

year and the variable costs of ordering and carrying inventory. Note that the
resulting total variable cost curve is relatively flat. This means that for the
number of orders above the optimum, or lowest-cost point, large increases in
the number of orders bring only a small increase in the total variable cost. This
means that the equation is really somewhat insensitive to the number of orders.
Put another way, if one decided arbitrarily to increase the number of orders
(i.e., more smaller orders), the only penalty according to the assumptions of the
EOQ formula would be a slight increase in total variable costs.

If the EOQ formula is solved for a number of setup cost values, holding
all other variables constant, the result is the curve shown in Figure 7-12, plotting setup costs against the order quantity that resulted from plugging that
value into the equation. Clearly, the result is a rather flat curve. This means that
very large increases in setup cost must occur before significant changes in order
quantity result from the equation.

Results from exercises such as the preceding tend to support the conclusion that the EOQ formula and its relatives really should be assumed to cover a
wide range of order quantities, to establish minimum and maximum order
quantities, for example. Further, in many companies setup time, methods, and
the resulting cost is treated like a given. Even though it takes substantial reductions in setup cost to cause the EOQ formula to produce a substantially smaller
order quantity, substantial reductions in setups can often be obtained.

Period order quantity: A popular variation of EOQ, used for ordering dependent demand items is *period order quantity* (POQ). This technique involves

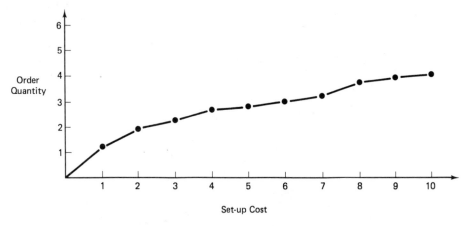

FIGURE 7-12   Setup cost and order quantity.

calculating the ordering interval after solving the EOQ formula to obtain the order quantity. The major objective here is to avoid carrying stock during periods of no demand, similar to the time period coverage method. The ordering interval is obtained as follows:

$$\frac{\text{Annual demand}}{\text{EOQ}} = \text{Orders per year}$$

$$\frac{\text{Periods per year}}{\text{Orders per year}} = \text{Ordering interval}$$

Like other EOQ-related formulas, POQ proves ineffective when the demand is discontinuous or nonuniform.

Other formula methods: There are four other methods used to balance or otherwise relate setup / ordering costs and carrying costs. Each assumes that inventory is consumed at the beginning of each period. So carrying cost is not accurately reflected. Each approaches the problem of arriving at the best order quantity and interval with a different method. Whatever advantages each has tends to be diluted because they require continuous replanning (frequent recalculations of net requirements). All of these methods assume a certain stability of demand over the ordering interval or planning horizon.

A set of orders calculated with one of these methods will minimize the sum of ordering and carrying costs when the plan is static. However, when constant adjustments to a changing demand are factored into the analysis, the apparent savings from these optimizing approaches diminishes. And as demand becomes lumpy, more discontinuous, and changes more frequent, the savings are reduced proportionately. In other words, when real-world situations are examined, it becomes increasingly difficult to justify ordering anything more than what is required, or as close to it as possible. Only in production environments where a high degree of stability of demand is experienced do these optimizing approaches show significant savings.

In spite of these arguments against the effectiveness of EOQ-based lot-sizing formulas, it is true that there are a significant number of cases where one or the other may be useful. A brief discussion of each follows.

Least unit cost: This method considers one or more period's net requirements and determines the appropriate order quantity that produces the minimum per unit cost, including unit setup and unit carrying costs. Only one lot at a time is considered, so actual unit costs may vary quite a lot from one lot to the next. The technique, in effect, moves one period's requirements into one order quantity or another, depending on which would produce the lowest unit (average) cost. Its usefulness is limited to situations where orders are few, and demand stable, and even then, another technique may work better.

Least total cost: This method attempts to overcome the one-lot-at-a-time problem with the least unit cost sizing method. It uses a calculated economic part-period factor to attempt to equalize costs for all lots in the planning horizon. It is calculated as follows:

$$\text{Economic part-period factor} = \text{EPP}$$

$$\text{Setup cost} = S$$

$$\text{Inventory carrying cost per unit per period} = I$$

$$\frac{S}{I} = \text{EPP}$$

The *economic part-period factor,* put simply, is the cost of one unit for one period, similar to a term such as man-month. Order quantities are selected under this method where the part-period cost is closest to the EPP, as calculated above. This technique seems preferable to least unit cost in that it is more direct and overcomes some of its disadvantages.

Part-period balancing: This is another variation of the effort to achieve minimum inventory cost by calculating an optimum order quantity and interval. PPB uses the same basic technique as least total cost, except that it adds an adjusting routing called look-ahead/look-back. Since this adjustment depends on the existence of net requirement conditions that trigger it, it will frequently produce the same results as least total cost.

The balancing routine's purpose is to consider additional demands outside the period normally covered by the LTC calculation of optimum lot size.

This is to prevent keying an order to a period of low requirements, or including the peak requirements from one period that would be held for a long period, increasing average stock levels. At first examination, PPB seems to be an improvement over least total cost.

Put briefly, the limitations of PPB are similar to those of the other two methods. None of them look sufficiently far ahead. Orders farther out in the planning horizon will inevitably be recalculated as those periods move closer in time. Under some circumstances, the look-back feature will force more and smaller orders, contrary to the intention of the whole exercise.

Wagner–Whitin algorithm: This technique is the most complete of all the formula-based lot-sizing techniques. It is also understandable only to the very technically inclined user. Since it uses a dynamic programming model as its basis, it virtually requires a computer to use at all. In the rare inventory planning case where the planning horizon is stationary, where demand is both firm and known, the Wagner–Whitin algorithm will work well. However, in most cases of material planning, these factors just do not hold, so when the plan subsequently is modified, the Wagner–Whitin algorithm may actually produce less desirable results than other, simpler methods.

Fixed order quantity: This method is used to a surprising extent, in spite of its obvious drawbacks. Sometimes there are quite sound reasons for fixing the order quantity at a set amount, regardless of the level or intervals of demand. A piece of productive equipment may have a batch size to it, and must run only a one type of part at a time. Sterilized products may have to fit into a small sterilizer. Under normal circumstances, however, most of these "reasons" turn out to be poor justifications for a sloppy ordering technique.

State-of-the-art systems can produce order quantities in any reasonable multiples of a unit of measure, so the order can be tailored to handling or packaging size requirements, and still size the order according to the time and size of the demand.

Time period order coverage: This method is similar to the fixed order quantity method in that a major part of how the order is sized is due to some arbitrary decision which may or may not have basis in the real world. It consists of simply specifying that any order produced by the system will include the requirements of the period in which the order is to be completed; however, many periods out into the future are to be included. This has the effect of specifying the ordering interval; that is, an order will be created every three periods if the time period to be covered is three periods, except in periods of zero demand. All variation in the level of demand within that time period is covered by the varying order quantity.

Figure 7-13 illustrates an example of this widely used ordering method. In this case, the stock on hand of 30 is sufficient to cover net requirements through

Period

P/N: A

On Hand: 30

Safety Stock: 0

Order Policy: 3 Periods

	1	2	3	4	5	6	7	8	9	10	11	Period Average
Requirements	20	10	15	20	25	5	0	5	20	15	10	13.1
On Order			} 60			} 10			} 45			10.5
Projected O/H	10	0	45	25	0	5	5	0	25	10	0	11.4

FIGURE 7-13 Fixed time period ordering.

143

the first two periods. Since the projected on hand goes negative in the third period, an order is planned for completion during that period, and the order quantity is enough to cover requirements through the end of the fifth period. Note that the average resulting projected on-hand balance is 11.4 units. This means that stock on hand will, in effect, be greater than period requirements for almost half of the periods. The excess stock is not needed to satisfy any requirement; demand is known, calculated, and periods of minimal or no requirements are clearly identified. If there is an unusually high setup cost involved in justifying this order method, clearly some effort to reduce the setup cost would enable the elimination of some extra inventory.

Probably the chief attraction of the time period order method is that it is convenient. It means that only so many purchase orders must be placed for the part, or that the part must be scheduled only every so often in production. This alone may be enough justification in some cases, although once again, some intelligent management action to simplify the ordering or changeovers to a wider variety of parts within a time period will produce significant reductions of inventory.

Modifying factors: Besides the facts of the demand size and intervals, there may also be other factors impinging on the calculation of an appropriate order quantity. Limitations of productive equipment may require a maximum or a minimum order quantity, or both. There may be lot traceability rules in effect, meaning that a given order may be regarded as a production batch for product recall purposes. The production process itself may be a batch process, with practical limits on its size. Whenever any of these kinds of considerations apply, it is appropriate that a maximum or minimum order quantity be established and used in the order sizing method. These limits act in conjunction with another order sizing method, such as any of those previously discussed.

Planned, or expected scrap from production process may be another modification factor. In this context, scrap refers to scrap of the parent part number as a completed product. Planned component scrap is included in the quantity required calculation when the product structure is identified. The effect of parent part number planned scrap is to inflate the order quantity by the scrap rate, or percent. Thus, if an order quantity calculation resulted in a planned order quantity of 100 units, and the scrap rate for the part was 3%, the resulting net order quantity would be 103. The quantity of 103 units would be ordered, 103 sets of component parts pulled and issued from stock, and during the production process, it could be expected that three completed parts would be found too defective to accept or rework acceptably. These three parts could be scrapped (discarded) and still result in a sufficient quantity to satisfy the calculated demand.

Many production processes are such that various sizing parameters must be included in the order-sizing calculation. Molds may be made so that they produce matched sets of 17 parts per mold cycle, or some other number. Frequently, packaging or palletizing considerations may apply. A liquid process may take place in tanks of a certain size. State-of-the-art planning systems include these multiple factors in the ordering calculations.

Order method selection: The preceding discussion of lot-sizing methods has clearly been oriented toward attempting to have the reader understand the inherent advantages of lot-for-lot ordering. Ordering only what is needed—no more, no less—will produce a carrying cost of zero, since parts are supplied just in time to meet their demands. When there is no demand, there is no on-hand stock.

As has been said repeatedly throughout parts of this book, the simplifying effect on the entire business that the elimination of component and subassembly inventory has can be remarkable. This alone is one of the major benefits. The potential alone is sufficient to make it a major company goal; to modify operating procedures in the plant so that virtually all intermediate inventory is eliminated, including the purchasing of production equipment that facilitates rapid setups and changeovers to different products. Careful scheduling of vendor deliveries and master schedules that are firm for a reasonable period out into the future all facilitate this elimination of inventory. Note that these concepts are not inventory reducing methods, but inventory *elimination* methods.

One of the fundamental assumptions of this book has been to always start with the technique of assuming that no inventory at all is a desirable and possible state of affairs, and to require careful justification in every case where it is decided to have stock on hand for other than very brief periods.

In the author's experience, most efforts to reduce inventory have been only symptomatic and superficial. Even early planning systems were usually seen as reduction techniques. In fact, the question is one that is fundamental to how the business is operated, to an extent that the question of inventory planning technique becomes almost secondary. Certainly, attempting to solve what are in truth fundamental problems in how the business is managed with selecting an improved lot-sizing algorithm merely diverts management attention from intelligent action. Of course, managers are human beings, too, and it is only too human to hope that a computer system, with its "magical" abilities will resolve all the problems that seem beyond one's immediate abilities.

Planned Order Management

Since the subject of planned orders involves product structure levels below the master schedule level, in most cases these will be managed internally in the system by the computer. In some cases this may include purchasing actions if the vendor is planning on a blanket purchase contract method.

This means that most changes in the system will not be readily perceivable by the user, simply because they are so numerous and frequent. State-of-the-art systems notify the user manager when action is required via a variety of exception reporting mechanisms. Some examples would be in the case of late vendor deliveries, noncompletion of production due to machine breakdown, or when the system has been forced to schedule an order with a start date in the past.

In each case, the method of developing an exception report is basically the same. A program is designed which reads all the records in a certain file, comparing values held in the program, such as a certain date, with values contained in the relevant data fields in each record. Those records that meet the criteria are printed on a report, while those that do not are simply passed up.

It is important to understand the fundamental flexibility of this process. Virtually any criteria can be specified in this type of program. Furthermore, several levels of tests can be applied, with the resulting records being categorized, such as by degree of lateness. An example of this process would be creating a list of past due purchase order deliveries. The program would be specified to read each open purchase order record and compare the record's due date with the current (or another) date. Once all those records that were selected by this step are identified, they could also be broken down into those that are 5 days late, 10 days late, and so on.

State-of-the-art systems contain report-generating software to allow managers to create special-purpose, one-time reports for each unique circumstance. Since a full manufacturing system creates and maintains a very large number of records in its data base, it is seldom practical to attempt any form of management of the system by dealing with individual records. In fact, even displaying the order and requirement record data in categorized form such as is shown in Figure 7–14 may be too much detail to be handled conveniently.

Previous example displays of orders and requirements in the preceding text have been simplified to aid understanding. In the example in Figure 7–14, both requirements and orders are broken down into categories according to their class or status. Even in this display, the numbers in each box, such as the released orders in the past due column, may represent more than one record (i.e., more than one order with completion dates falling in the same time period). Since the number of part numbers in a system may run into the thousands, to use a fully detailed display such as this would involve creating enormous reports that no human being could be expected to absorb.

As a result, a detailed understanding of how the system functions internally is very important for management in order to use and design effectively the exception reports needed to keep things flowing smoothly. If the overall operation is correctly managed, exception reports will be brief and involve relatively straightforward corrective action. The essential concept here, to reiterate earlier statements, is that virtually all management action really concerns the plan itself (i.e., future events). Corrective action in the immediate time period for unplanned events should be relatively minimal. Some examples of exception reports would be the following:

- Past due purchase order deliveries
- Purchase orders placed with insufficient lead time

Part Number: C
Safety Stock: 20

Stock On Hand: 47

Allocated: 10

Net Available: 37

Order Policy: 2 Periods

Periods

	Past Due	Current Period	1	2	3	4	5
MPS Requirements			10		15		
NHA Requirements	40	30	20	15	25	30	10
Planned Orders				45		40	
Firm Planned Orders			40				
Released Orders	53						
Projected On Hand	50	20	30	60	20	30	20

FIGURE 7-14   Detailed stock status display.

- Work centers with overload conditions
- Work orders with past due start dates
- Work orders with material usage variances over 10%
- Work centers with queues exceeding two days

These reports are only a small sample of reports that are possible from a state-of-the-art manufacturing system. The reader can easily supplement this list from his experience and imagination. In actual practice, a company may find it practical to develop dozens of special-purpose exception reports. Various filtering devices may be employed to screen out small variations from plan to increase further the usefulness of these reports.

Net Change Processing Assumed

Early material requirements planning systems were regenerative; that is, the previous file of planned orders was dumped and a new one generated from the master schedule data. This cyclic mode of planning contains several assumptions about the way a company is managed that inevitably lead to difficulties.

The most important point is that the original plan will soon come to have so much wrong information in it that it simply has to be discarded. A corollary is that the original plan will have changed so much (within the planning lead time) that creating a completely new plan is preferable to revising the previous one. A second corollary is that the plan can be allowed to become somewhat out of date between planning cycles without harm.

In many individual cases, these assumptions may cause no harm, especially in simpler companies. However, the primary assumption of this book is that it is desirable and practical to have all information used to manage the company maintained by the computer system on an up-to-the-minute, interactive basis, as is the case with a state-of-the-art system. Closely connected with this key assumption is that an integral part of good business management are procedures to keep the company's information base accurate at all times. In other words, errors are simply not allowed to creep into the system.

The net change processing logic itself is straightforward. The planned orders and requirements records are updated with changes in independent and dependent demand and with changes in product structure or routings as these changes actually occur. For instance, if a product's engineering design is changed somewhat, such as by substituting or adding a new part number to its product structure, the system merely deletes the new obsolete requirement records and/or adds new ones. Any changes that logically follow in lower-level planned orders are also made. Only those records affected by the product structure change are modified, with others being left alone.

For changes in demand, net change processing modifies only those order and requirement records affected by the new demand. Order dates and quantities may be changed, new orders created, or previously planned ones deleted, depending on the exact nature of the change. Thus if a master schedule item at the finished-goods level (a firm planned order) is rescheduled out into the future two weeks, net change processing logic also reschedules the lower-level orders and requirements for all subassemblies and purchased parts belonging to that finished item's product structure. Since the rest of the plan is unaffected by this rescheduling action, net changes are made to it.

Managing Planned Orders with the MPS

One of the most common occurrences in manufacturing is incompletely handling the consequences of production and vendor delays. In most cases, the part is simply late, while work proceeds on all related subassemblies and other purchased parts are received. However, since the late part is in fact a required part of the final assembly, work on the related assemblies can proceed only so far. After this point is reached, the partly completed product just sits as part of work in process.

Some of the consequences of this old habit include the following:

- Work on the uncompletable product consumed productive resources that could have been used to complete other items that are now behind schedule.
- Work-in-process investment has been inflated, with no measurable benefit to the company.
- Components and raw materials are now tied up in the uncompletable product that may now be preventing other items from completion, causing them to fall behind schedule.
- The total time required to build the product has, in effect, been lengthened, not shortened, as is the goal.

Preventing this situation is not difficult with a state-of-the-art system. Exception reports identify the tardy lower-level part or purchased item. Through pegging (to be discussed shortly), the master production schedule items in which the part is used can be identified. One or more of these MPS items can be rescheduled out into the future so that the items can be produced in the normal fashion.

Figure 7–15 illustrates an example of this process. The original MPS completion date for end item Z was day 30. Through exception reporting, part D has been identified as not being available until day 32. Unless end item Z is rescheduled, the planning system will cause part B to be received and consumed in the production of part A which will sit until day 39, when end item Z can actually be started. Even if part A is used in a number of end items, which may not be dependent on part D's availability, A's requirement is still overstated for day 24.

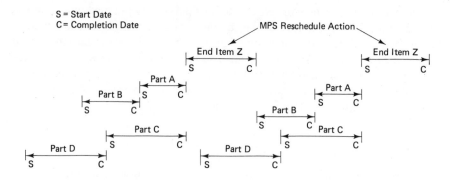

Problem: Part D not available as scheduled on Day 17; now available on Day 32

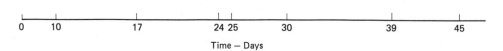

Time — Days

FIGURE 7-15   MPS relieving lower levels.

If end item Z is rescheduled to be completed on day 45, as shown, this action will cause the scheduled production and purchased part delivery requirements to be moved out by the same amount, thereby relieving requirements for all related subassemblies and purchased parts used in end item Z. This action eliminates the undesirable conditions mentioned above and illustrates clearly how the MPS controls the schedules for all lower-level items.

It is important to understand that this situation can also be created by increasing MPS quantities inside the total lead time for the end item. Adding a new quantity to the previously planned level for end item Z to be completed in less than 20 days will cause an immediate past due requirement for part D. If the lead times shown are in fact the true lead times, and they should be, there is no way that this new requirement for end item Z can be met. The only intelligent action is to reschedule it into a period when it can be met.

In real-life situations, this logic is often obscured by product structures with hundreds of parts, many product levels, and multiple next-higher assembly usages. Nevertheless, failure to reschedule at the MPS level to relieve related component demand still has the same consequences. Also, there is usually some leeway, such that small shortages or degrees of lateness will make little difference. Clearly, defining how much shortage or lateness should lead to MPS adjustments is the subject for design of appropriate exception reporting logic. This will vary from company to company, and even from one product line to another.

Engineering Changes

Another important area of potential schedule disruption is modifications to requirements due to changes in the product structure. If new components are added within the required lead time, the situation described above will be created. Components deleted from a product structure cause somewhat less of a problem, although obsolete stock on hand may result.

If engineering changes are introduced within the total planning horizon, but outside the minimum total lead time for the end item, only changes to planned orders will result, shifting requirement quantities and dates around in time to respond to them. It is changes within this minimum total lead time that cause disruptions. If it proves, in fact, possible to introduce additional or new requirements within the total lead time, and not simply to cause a shortage in another product using the same part, the lead times in the system are overstated and are what were referred to earlier as phony lead times.

Schedule disruptions resulting from this kind of action are preventable by enforcing time fence policies for introducing changes to the schedule and product structure, and by using true lead times for planning.

Use of Firm Planned Orders

In every production environment there are a variety of situations that require modifications to the normal planning logic even in the most complete system. Remember that a firm planned order, in effect, freezes the schedule for all lower-level items "under" that order. Normally, this is done at the MPS level and to define independent demand for lower-level subassemblies and components. Firm planned orders can also be used to "plan around" various production process disruptions, such as planned equipment shutdowns or to use up perishable raw material stock. Normally, however, firm planned orders used at product structure levels, other than for MPS purposes, will tend to subvert the effectiveness of the planning logic and so should be avoided. A state-of-the-art system provides so many different ordering methods that it is seldom desirable to use what are in effect manual orders to modify the normal ordering logic and interrelationships between component structures.

The Order Releasing Cycle

One of the most critical steps in the production planning and execution logic is that of work order release, that is, the conditions that must be met before a planned order can be actually released to the plant for picking of material and production. Figure 7–16 shows the basic logic used by an "automatic" releasing cycle and the relationships between the records.

Several important points apply to order releasing. Since releasing an order implies that it will shift from a planned state to being in actual production, it is critical that the order not be released until it will actually be started. Further,

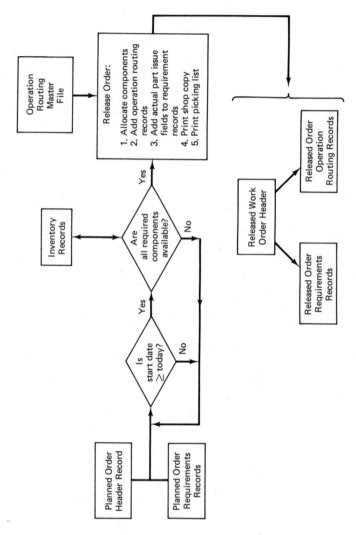

FIGURE 7-16 Order release cycle.

the release action is where required components are reserved for a specific work order. To summarize, then, work order release should not occur until the last possible start time, all components are available in the required quantities, and work center capacity is adequate.

Other steps included in the releasing cycle include the printing of a hard copy to accompany the material through the production cycle, and printing of a material picking list for warehouse action. The use of a material picking list, however, may be highly modified in state-of-the-art management, where many items are delivered directly to the assembly or production process area, bypassing the warehouse. Or, materials required to be issued from the warehouse may be organized on a picking and work center delivery schedule instead of a work order-by-work order picking list.

Released Orders and Work-in-Process Tracking

Another important part of the release cycle that takes place internally in the computer system is the creation of additional records and expanded versions of planning records so that actual material usage and production hours may be recorded for the work order. Figure 7–17 shows in symbolic form how the data fields for an open work order are related in a state-of-the-art system. There may, in fact, be a great many more fields than are shown, but these are commonly used.

The work-in-process records include a separate record for each component part used and a separate record for each operating routing step. Thus a complete set of records for a single released work order may number in the dozens or even hundreds for complex products. In addition, there may be other records for special purposes, such as tracking other cost, engineering, or tooling factors. Taken together, all these records constitute the work order record set.

Each component for the work order is posted to the requirement record for that component part number and is accumulated in the quantity issued field. Other actions, such as scrap and returns to the warehouse, may also be posted to these records. Additional fields may be calculated for display or report purposes, or calculated and actually maintained in the record itself.

This logic permits a really detailed picture of material usage for a specific work order. From this detailed picture, the information pyramid concept can be employed to produce accurate reports of material usage variances, planned versus actual scrap usage, product costing, as well as schedule adherence and other performance measurements. In a state-of-the-art system these performance measurements are part of the management techniques used to operate the business. Since a great deal of the basis of the entire planning process is carried forward to these work-in-process records, the resulting comparison of

Header

Work Order Number	Parent Part Number	Order Quantity	Start Date	Completion Date	Release Date	Quantity Completed	Quantity Scrapped
Quantity Rejected	Actual Start Date	Actual Completion Date	Date Order Created	Related Sales Order Number	etc.		

Requirement

Work Order Number	Parent Part Number	Component Part Number	Quantity Required	Date Required	Quantity Issued	Balance To Be Issued
Quantity Scrapped	Quantity Returned	Date of Last Issue	Planned Component Cost	Actual Component Cost	etc.	

Operation Routing

Work Order Number	Operation Sequence Number	Operation Description	Work Center	Dept No.	Labor Type	Tool Number	Crew Size
Planned Production Rate	Planned Move Time	Planned Queue Time	Planned Set-up Time	Actual Quantity Produced	Actual Move Time	Actual Queue Time	
Planned Hours	Actual Hours	Actual Set-up Hours	Quantity Scrapped	Quantity Rejected	Date Operation Completed	etc.	

FIGURE 7-17 Typical released work-order record data fields.

154

planned versus actual data gives rise to a whole set of closable loops that can be used by management to control the business in a way that was simply not practical until recently.

A related argument about product costing is what may be termed the traditional accounting versus the systems point of view. Traditional accounting has usually attempted to develop management information concerning product costing from the standpoint of the general ledger. Under this approach, various subledgers are maintained to which dollars costs are posted. The month-end closing process produces dollar figures which are, in effect, the difference between two or more ledgers, or account balances.

The point of view here is that while information produced this way may be useful to some extent, it is not nearly as useful as information developed using the approach described above, using the work order record set to create a picture of the entire production process for a given product. By tracking the actual events themselves, data are trapped at the lowest possible level. When good procedures and systems techniques are employed to keep this data stream current and accurate, it follows that all summary reports developed using these data will be accurate as well, possibly even more accurate due to the averaging process that takes place when numerous similar events are summarized. This entire process is discussed in greater detail in several other chapters.

One important point about tracking work in process should be emphasized. A key assumption of this method is that all completed quantities reported to a work header are assumed to move into the warehouse (i.e., nonfloor stock). This means that work in process, from a material tracking point of view, consists entirely of component parts which retain their identities until becoming a completed parent part number on the work order, at which time their movement out of the work center is to stock and out of work in process.

If parent part numbers in one subassembly work order are in fact moved directly to another work center, where they are component parts on a higher assembly work order, a double transaction is used to report the event, one moving the parts into the warehouse, and the other moving it back out as an issue to the next-higher assembly work order. Whether two separate transactions are used or not, the effect is the same; there is a losing work order reflecting the quantity moved as a completion, and a gaining work order showing it as a component requirement issue.

Chapter 8 discusses the function of the operating routing records in detail. For purposes of understanding the order release cycle, it is here that the routing records are actually copied, expanded to include data fields for actual performance, and attached to a specific work order in the system. At this point each operation in the set is scheduled onto the work center in which that operation is to be performed. It is from these records that detailed capacity management, work center scheduling, and prioritizing of work order operations is performed.

Pegging of Demand

To understand pegging, the reader should refer back to Figure 7–5, which illustrates the relationships between product structure levels, work order header records, and component requirement records. Chapter 4 discussed the concept of where-used lists, or looking "upward" through the product structure.

Pegging uses a similar logic, but it develops the equivalent of a where-used list through both the released and planned order header and requirements records. The actual execution logic of pegging is somewhat complex and will not be discussed here. The basic technique is that of using record pointers to develop a chain of records that may be entered at any point and traced upward, either all the way to the top (the end item level) or through some predetermined number of levels.

The resulting report is detailed and shows exactly where all the demand for a given component part is coming from, that is, which parts and order numbers are causing the (dependent) demand for that part. Although not a part of normal management activities in a system, pegging is essential for making the kind of MPS reschedule actions described under "Planned Order Management." In many companies, a single raw material or component part may be used by a great many higher-level items. If only a given amount of the raw material is available for a time period, some of this excess demand must be unloaded. Without being able to identify which orders are creating the demand, such action is impractical or impossible.

Even though the entire where-used chain may be followed up the product structure to the master schedule level, only the last, or MPS, level need be displayed. This list provides a set of alternatives for reschedule action. Other information may be sought, such as finished-goods stock levels, customer requirements of relative importance, cost of the products, or other supplemental information to aid in the decision as to which MPS order(s) to reschedule. Although previous examples of this type of action used material nonavailability, the same action should occur in cases of significant work center overload conditions (i.e., where the work center or plant load exceeds available capacity).

Safety Stock

There is a very simple rule to remember when discussing safety stock in a state-of-the-art planning system: do not have any. The only two possible justifications for safety stock are to allow for forecast error in finished-goods inventories and to allow for vendor unreliability at the raw material level. Even in the latter case, improved purchasing action with the troublesome vendor can often improve reliability, as will be discussed shortly. A possible third case could be in the case of certain production processes having a very high degree of unpredictability of scrap rate.

The purpose of safety stock is to allow for unpredictability. Since a properly managed state-of-the-art system eliminates virtually all uncertainty within the company itself, and provides extensive tools for reducing hard-to-predict factors outside the company, most historical uses of safety stock are simply not justified. The largest single source of uncertainty is at the master production schedule or finished item level (i.e., in the form in which the product is sold).

To understand this point of view fully, consider several examples. Figure 7-14 contains a sample material plan using safety stock. Since the ordering logic is triggered whenever the projected on-hand balance is less than or equal to the safety stock level, the safety stock never gets used. If plant performance to plan is the source of uncertainty, management action to correct this situation is far more useful than simply carrying safety stock. In addition, the safety stock level in combination with the order method employed may cause entire order quantities to be carried through long periods of no demand, further inflating inventory levels with no benefit to the company.

Another variation of safety stock that is sometimes employed is *safety time.* This is the policy of deliberately scheduling vendor deliveries or work order completions some time ahead of their actual required date. The net effect is virtually indistinguishable from that of carrying safety stock. Inventory levels are inflated. Safety time has the additional disadvantage of increasing lead times, especially if it is included in the planned lead times used by the system to calculate requirement dates. This, in turn, may lead to false exception reports of late deliveries which clutter up the system and make it less credible. Finally, as in any other case where false dates are used, the company loses credibility with either the vendor if a purchased item is concerned, or with plant personnel if a manufactured part is involved. The message that a company's requirement dates may be ignored seems to be the one message that everyone always hears loud and clear.

PURCHASING UNDER MRP

The use of a well-managed detail material requirements planning subsystem provides an excellent base for a wide variety of purchasing actions and policies. In the past, many purchasing agents were charged with getting the best price or terms for parts, often at the expense of inventory levels. Vendors often have minimum order quantities or practical shipment quantities. Although a state-of-the-art system will not itself eliminate these factors, it does provide an information base that can greatly strengthen the negotiating position of the buyer.

In many companies, material is purchased by having a material planner complete purchase requisitions close to the minimum order date for the part and vendor. This is the date on which the vendor has said he must have an order in order to meet the buying company's required delivery dates. This process ignores any future requirement, and proceeds largely on an order at a time basis. The purchasing agent may, of course, realize that the company will need more of the part, and so will agree to a larger order quantity. Other actions may be more desirable.

Referring to Figure 7-9, one can see that a potentially large amount of information is available to assist the purchasing function. Included is a completely time-phased picture of exactly when each part is needed, the quantities, and the dates on which orders must be placed. The following paragraphs explore several methods of making fully effective use of this information.

The Goal of Purchasing

Besides the normal purchasing goals of obtaining the best possible price, terms, and quality for purchased parts, under the concept of state-of-the-art management, an additional, very important goal is to have parts of satisfactory quality delivered to the company the day they are to be used, or as close to this date as possible.

The existence of a solid basis of information concerning future purchasing actions (i.e., the detailed material plan) allows the virtual extension of the planning process into the vendor's operations. Instead of just responding to orders placed, vendors can now be included in the entire planning cycle.

A variety of special reports can be created from the planning data base to facilitate this process of interfacing with the vendor. A report grouping material requirements by commodity or by vendor can be used to negotiate a master contract for all. Various performance and costing summaries can be developed, together with dollarized projections of purchasing volume with the vendor. The planned purchases from the vendor can even be stated in terms of his capacity requirements. In highly engineered products, sophisticated costing techniques can be used to improve the buyer's negotiating strength. Historically, relationships between buyer and seller, even in a manufacturing context, have often been those of adversaries. Fortunately, this approach is becoming obsolete as companies realize their interdependence.

Extending the System into Vendors

With the detailed planning information available from the system, natural extensions can include various information both to and from the vendor. A state-of-the-art system includes summarized stock status information from the vendor, to facilitate the material planning process. In exchange, the company can furnish the vendor with its requirements as they are calculated within the planning horizon, thereby facilitating the vendor's own production planning.

A key step is improving relations with the vendor to include quality control conducted at the vendor's facilities, so parts are delivered already inspected and approved. Although this step is generally not practical for all vendors used by a manufacturing company, it certainly is for the key items, including the A-level inventory items and those with long lead times.

Since long vendor lead times are often a company's Achilles' heel in the planning area, special efforts to obtain arrangements with these vendors can pay handsome benefits in simplifying the planning and management of the business. Often, greatly improved responsiveness can be obtained by contractually agreeing to certain levels of business. Information in the planning data base can often greatly facilitate this process.

If the vendor is also operating under something resembling a state-of-the-art system, furnishing information directly to and from each company's computer data base is not difficult to do, and the information can be easily incorporated into each company's planning process. A variation of this for vendors that are physically close to the manufacturing facility is to bypass completely the entire requirements–purchase order–delivery–stocking–issue cycle. If quality assurance is either acceptable without receiving inspection of each shipment, or is performed at the vendor's facility, shipment can occur at order release time, with the delivery schedule consisting of components used on specific work orders.

For parts managed under this concept, the assumptions required include finished-goods inventory at the vendor's, acceptable quality of stocked items, computer communication of the data, and next-day deliveries of parts directly to the production area. The benefits in terms of reduction of inventory are clearly substantial—virtually none at all.

"Paperless" Purchasing

Building on the concepts above, it is entirely practical to use computer data links to connect the company's information system with that of a vendor. With proper system controls and contractual provision protecting both sides, the company's purchasing requirements can be fed directly into the vendor's order entry system, completely bypassing the entire cycle of printed purchase orders. Even invoicing can be simplified in this fashion, especially where large volumes of parts are concerned.

There is conceptually no reason why both the purchase order document and the vendor's invoice paperwork cannot be eliminated by a properly constructed contractual agreement governing shipments and payment schedules. A purchasing technique as described above can also feed an accounts payable system directly, creating an appropriate invoice record internally. It is the author's belief that both companies in fact can experience a greater level of control over their material and financial status operating under this kind of interlinked mode than is normally experienced with the usual paperwork jungle of written purchase orders and mailed, printed invoices.

Instead of having each company's computer system read its files, print a document, and mail the document, only to have someone at the other company reenter the same information into their computer, it is far more reliable simply to transmit the information over data communication lines directly.

In fact, many companies now order material totally over the telephone, never sending a written "confirmation" hard copy, even without any kind of overall contractual agreement. The basis is simple. If the receiving company accepts the parts, verifiable from shipping records, it is liable for either returning the parts or paying for them. There is little risk to the vendor, especially if an informal customer relationship already exists.

The Flexible Purchasing Agreement

The preceding concepts lead directly into the method of arranging purchasing agreements to cover an entire plan, with "orders" simply becoming shipping data instead of a specific contractual agreement. Figure 7-18 illustrates the time frames of an example flexible purchasing agreement. This kind of approach matches the degree of precision of the production plan itself. The further out in the future the plan is, the more uncertain as to details it becomes. Sharing this information with a vendor helps him to plan better, thereby improving his ability to meet one's own company's requirements.

In exchange for agreements about shipment reliability and quality assurance, the buying company agrees to extend its range of commitment beyond the single-purchase-order approach. In return for its agreement to purchase a definite dollar volume, it receives much greater flexibility as to specific parts needed and exact shipping dates. Using this approach, both companies can reduce their inventory investment substantially. The buying company can

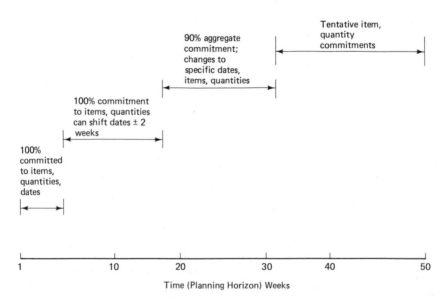

FIGURE 7-18   The flexible purchasing agreement—example.

schedule deliveries with a high level of precision, since the action takes place close to the actual date of need. The selling company can avoid making the item until shortly before it is to be shipped.

The only negative aspect of this approach is the slight risk that the buying company could wind up having to accept delivery of some items that it no longer needed. However, if the planning process is reasonably well managed, this risk is slight. Also, the selling company, by agreeing to shorten its lead times, could conceivably wind up with excess raw material stock if demand suddenly evaporated. In spite of these minor disadvantages, the numerous and substantial advantages to both parties clearly outweigh the drawbacks.

Limited-Capacity Vendors

Many raw material suppliers have production processes that are extremely capital intensive and inflexible as to production rates. Refiners and foundries are some examples. The result, from the buyer's point of view is that the supplier's customers just get in line, and the line is often quite long, particularly in times of business growth. The planning system can convert its purchasing requirements into capacity units used by the vendor, such as pounds, tons, gallons, or production hours. These data can in turn be used to negotiate and manage a flexible agreement such as that described above.

In the case of a foundry or plastic molding supplier, the specific part to be molded need be specified only shortly before the production run actually begins. All the rest of the vendor's lead time is just waiting in the queue to get to the production step. The same logic holds for many other raw material suppliers, including chemicals and a variety of metal products. The reason for this phenomenon has been discussed earlier: Very few products really take long to actually make. So production activity is only a part of total ordering lead time.

The net effect of these and similar approaches is to shorten the buying company's ordering lead time with the vendor by obtaining "head of the line" status in exchange for guaranteeing the vendor a certain amount of sales, and thus profit.

Returning briefly to the concepts discussed in Chapter 3, the effect of substantial reductions of purchasing lead times can be stunning in their simplification of the operation of the entire business. Instead of having to plan in detail for six months into the future, a planning horizon filled with uncertainty as to specifics, even though the aggregate may be fairly certain, the company need plan in detail only a few weeks in advance. Also recalling the number of records involved in creating and managing a complete production plan, it is easy to see how many fewer of these records there are to manage, run exception reports against, and so forth if the entire planning horizon is substantially reduced. This in itself is a reflection of the overall simplification of the business.

Inventory Turnover and Purchase Order Management

As of the writing of this book, American businesses are still patting themselves on the back when they achieve inventory turn ratios of over five times per year for most manufacturing companies. Many still have turn ratios lower than this. A few well-managed plants, relatively speaking, have turn ratios of 10 times or more, with a few approaching 15 or 20 times.

Meanwhile, Japanese companies, including large, very capital intensive ones, often achieve inventory turn ratios of 50 to 60 turns per year. These are really an illusion, in the traditional sense of inventory management. These companies have largely eliminated inventory from the internal operation of their businesses, which is why the numbers are so high. This kind of operating performance is achieved using the central concepts repeatedly emphasized in this book of eliminating waiting times from production processes, eliminating safety stock, freezing production schedules within lead times, and by cultivating very close relationships with their suppliers. Production is frequently scheduled by the hour, and material deliveries may occur more than once a day, a far cry from the weekly production schedules and huge, infrequent deliveries experienced by most American firms.

Although it is not suggested that American firms can or should emulate those management techniques that are peculiarly Japanese, many of these concepts are simply good management, and are not culturally related. Viewed from the standpoint of using purchasing information to improve inventory turnover, a number of techniques discussed here can and often have been used by American firms to achieve substantial improvements in inventory turnover. These include the following:

- The planning system can compare short-run requirements to control and recommend shifts in delivery dates of purchased parts.
- Receiving data can be accumulated and used to provide performance information on a vendor, such as on-time deliveries, quality levels, early/late shipments, over/under shipments, and the like.
- The system information can be used to create a closer, less adversarial relationship with the vendor.
- Quality and deliveries can be organized to permit delivery directly to the production area, eliminating a great deal of material handling and inventory float that benefits neither company.
- Two companies' computer systems can exchange information, greatly shortening the reaction time for both companies, and eliminating a great deal of paperwork.
- Perform receiving inspection functions at vendor's, in cases where inspection is necessary; "pre-receive" parts.
- Trade off inventory carrying costs with shipping costs to obtain a series of dates and quantities that can be managed to improve turnover.

- Shorten in-plant lead times to reduce the need for firm, specific purchasing commitments far out into the future.
- Consider helping problem vendors with their own internal production lead time problems in order to improve the company's ability to rely on the vendor.

These and other related concepts assist in the improvement of inventory turnover by keeping inventory out of the plant and in a state where it can be managed without having to own it.

DISTRIBUTION REQUIREMENTS PLANNING

For those companies that have a single manufacturing facility producing items that are shipped to multiple selling points (i.e., regional warehouses), a special problem exists in the accumulating and netting of independent demand. Normally, each warehouse will serve a sales region, each of which has its own sales forecast and differing demand cycles. Sales in one area may be higher than normal for a product, while in the same time period, another region may be experiencing slow sales.

Distribution requirements planning (DRP) offers a set of tools for avoiding the feast or famine cycle and large safety stocks frequently encountered in efforts to manage inventory effectively under this environment. There are a variety of good business reasons for having multiple warehouses stocking the same items, such as the need to provide quick response to customer orders, economies of shipping, and a relationship to overall customer service, to name a few.

Some companies have attempted to deal with this situation in the past by having a single sales forecast that is used to plan production at the plant. Each warehouse, however, carries a certain amount of safety stock, and orders from the plant using an order point/order quantity technique. This situation will normally lead to substantially more inventory in total than under the DRP approach. Additionally, the extra inventory still does not provide the desired minimum level of stockouts at the warehouses because the plant's production suffers from peaks and valleys and the inability to plan inventory in the aggregate.

Figure 7-19 illustrates an example of distribution requirements planning under a three-warehouse, one-plant situation. Each warehouse/sales region has its own forecast of independent demand. The illustration employs a safety stock level of approximately two periods average demand, although in many cases it could be much less. The receipts line for each warehouse shows when shipments are expected from the plant, in the form of planned orders.

These planned shipment orders are netted to obtain a projected on-hand inventory for each location, then summed into a total warehouse demand at the plant. The plant's planning system uses these data to plan shipments/orders,

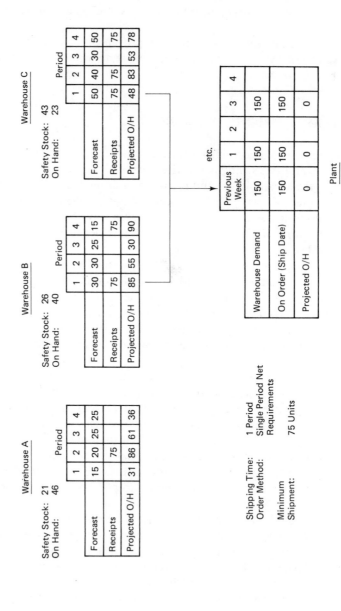

Warehouse A

Safety Stock: 21
On Hand: 46

	1	2	3	4
			Period	
Forecast	15	20	25	25
Receipts		75		
Projected O/H	31	86	61	36

Warehouse B

Safety Stock: 26
On Hand: 40

	1	2	3	4
			Period	
Forecast	30	30	25	15
Receipts	75			75
Projected O/H	85	55	30	90

Warehouse C

Safety Stock: 43
On Hand: 23

	1	2	3	4
			Period	
Forecast	50	40	30	50
Receipts	75	75		75
Projected O/H	48	83	53	78

etc.

Plant

	Previous Week	1	2	3	4
Warehouse Demand	150	150		150	
On Order (Ship Date)	150	150		150	
Projected O/H	0	0	0	0	

Shipping Time: 1 Period
Order Method: Single Period Net Requirements

Minimum Shipment: 75 Units

FIGURE 7–19 Distribution requirements planning.

164

which are also netted to obtain a projected on-hand balance. In the example, no safety stock is used at the plant, although in some situations plant safety stock may be justifiable. Economies of shipping are reflected in the minimum shipment quantity of 75 units. If the shipment minimum quantity were less, more frequent shipments could be made, reducing safety stock in all locations.

Not shown in the example, but often used in DRP systems, is the tracking of quantities in transit, especially if shipment times are long. The interface between the summed warehouse demand and the production plan is, of course, the master production schedule. By bringing all factors involved in the real-world independent demand together, substantial improvements both in inventory turns and customer service level are possible over the alternative method of treating the plant as the location where independent demand is experienced. Independent demand, in fact, occurs at the warehouses. Thus the DRP system logic mirrors the real world and hooks the physical distribution process into the "front end" of the detailed production planning system.

Closely coupled with the effective use of DRP is market research and planning coupled to each sales region, so independent demand is identified closer to its actual source, the customer, thereby making the sales forecast itself more accurate. A more accurate forecast will in turn aid the master scheduling process.

In a state-of-the-art system, a distribution resources planning subsystem will also be in use. This system uses the planned shipments generated by the DRP planning logic to develop and plan shipments by weight and volume of the planned shipments or loads and personnel required to load and handle the shipments, and to calculate required warehouse space to store the shipment when received at each warehouse location, the capital investment required by the inventory tied up in each shipment, and the expenses involved in the shipments themselves.

It can readily be seen that the DRP process in many ways mirrors the material and capacity planning logic used to plan and manage the actual plant operation itself. This illustrates how flexible and powerful these concepts are, that they can be applied to a wide range of physical events in the manufacturing arena, and finally, that the more closely a system mirrors actual reality, the more useful it becomes in successfully managing a manufacturing and distribution business.

CHAPTER 7 QUESTIONS

1. Describe the types of orders and their data elements.
2. How is an order "exploded"?
3. What are the five assumptions of order planning?
4. What does time phasing assume and how does it work?
5. List several examples where the ability of a planning system to predict problems would be useful.
6. Why are requirements netted against on-hand stock?

7. Describe several important ways in which phony lead times will cause a planning system to fail to reach its potential.

8. List the five factors used in calculations for optimum lot size.

9. Describe the result of substantial reductions in setup cost on order quantity under the different lot sizing techniques.

10. How are the two different types of scrap (parent and component parts) handled?

11. What is the primary objective of the order-method selection process?

12. Describe how exception reporting works. Why must the reader of an exception report understand how it is produced? Give some examples.

13. What are the consequences of beginning production of a part before all of the components are available? What are the correct actions with a state-of-the-art system?

14. How does the introduction of engineering changes within minimum total lead time affect the schedule?

15. Define a firm planned order.

16. What are the steps in the order releasing cycle, whether automatic or manual?

17. What is the released work order record set? How is it used to track work in process?

18. Contrast product costing under the traditional accounting viewpoint with that available with the work-order record set.

19. Give some examples of reports developed from released work-order records using the information pyramid technique.

20. What is pegging of demand? Under what circumstances would a company want to require its system to maintain this data?

21. What are the three possible justifications for safety stock? What is the central purpose of safety stock?

22. What should a company that uses a state-of-the-art system do with its material purchase requisition forms?

23. Describe the goals of purchasing under MRP, and describe how a system might be extended into key vendors. What would be the benefits of extending the system in this way?

24. How do "paperless" purchasing and flexible purchasing agreements work?

25. What actions should the purchasing manager take facing the following situation table?
    • Total lead time is very long
    • Most of the lead time is due to one supplier, who has limited capacity
    • Competitors are quoting very short lead times and are taking sales away

26. List some of the techniques that are often used to achieve substantial improvements in inventory turnover through the purchasing activity.

27. What effect does the implementation of a distribution requirements planning system have on the forecasting of independent demand?

28. Describe how distribution requirements planning nets demand between final sales points and the plant master production schedule.

29. When should in-transit inventory be explicitly tracked?

8

Executing
the Business Plan
in the Plant

The chapters thus far have described various techniques using state-of-the-art systems and management methods for running the business up to the point of actually bringing the work into the plant for production. Some discussion has been made of the information structure of the plant, work centers, operation routings, and the identification of subassembly levels.

The key factor in the plant is *actual* capacity. The APICS dictionary defines capacity as "the highest sustainable output rate which can be achieved with current production specifications, product mix, worker effort, plant and equipment." Note that this makes no reference to machine rates, work standards, or any other more theoretical definitions of how much work *might* be produced.

It should also be emphasized that there really is little meaning to the concept of plant capacity, as a whole. True capacity of a plant is, in fact, limited to its slowest key work center. Imbalances occur mostly through failure to realize this simple fact. It does the company little good if the plant simply produces what it can rather than what is needed.

This chapter is devoted to a discussion of the techniques used in state-of-the-art systems by enlightened management to plan and manage the capacity of the productive resources of the company, to manage the work in process to achieve minimum work-in-process investment, minimum in-plant time for work, and the simplest possible structure for the business.

It is the author's opinion that the primary reason for the many failures experienced by manufacturing firms in using these tools is that attention to the basic tenets of good manufacturing management was lacking. The system, as is too often the case, was an effort to overcome the problems created by this lack of good management, which, of course, it can never do. Good business results, after all, are invariably achieved by excelling at the basics rather than by elaborate sophistication.

The reader should bear in mind that each of the areas discussed here, as elsewhere in this book, comprise considerable bodies of knowledge in themselves. There are entire books written on areas such as shop floor control and master scheduling that are treated as subtopics here.

RELATIONSHIP TO OTHER
PLANNING ACTIVITIES

Capacity planning techniques fall into two broad categories, based on the techniques and data bases used and the planning horizon to be covered. These two categories include the following:

- *Long-range techniques.* These methods are involved with the development of business and production plans, and use a variety of simulation techniques to develop estimates of productive resources required to meet various possible product mixes and sales levels.
- *Short-range techniques.* This area of planning essentially starts with the master production schedule as its outer limit in time, using the detailed planned and released order data base. Although results may be summarized for management use, they are developed with a fully detailed plant profile (work centers) and by using full operation routings.

Both of these techniques are substantially overlapped with the steps required for developing input to the MPS, as discussed in Chapters 3 and 7. Capacity management is also intimately tied to the planned order generation process and the order release cycle discussed in Chapter 7. As in any subject matter consisting of highly integrated concepts, some redundancy and use of terms that are not fully explained is inevitable.

Figure 8-1 illustrates in symbolic form the general problem of capacity. In the short run, output, the bottom of the funnel, is essentially fixed within narrow limits. The order generation process produces a detailed plant load that precedes both order release and completed production. Long-range capacity management attempts to define the size of funnel needed. Short-range planning attempts to make smaller adjustments in capacity and to achieve optimum output through intelligent sequencing of work in the plant.

In a broad sense, all capacity management activities fall into one of five categories, even though only two sets of basic techniques may be used. The

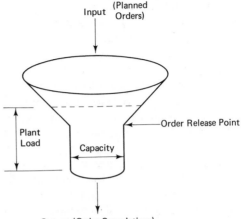

FIGURE 8-1   The production funnel.

chief differences between each are the degree of detail needed and the time horizon covered. Figure 8–2 shows these differences in chart form. As with any other planning technique, the further out in the future one is attempting to plan, the more the plan should be based on aggregates of data and averages. Conversely, attempting to use average-based methods to manage situations requiring detailed information and specific actions will produce less than desirable results. These five categories may be defined as follows.

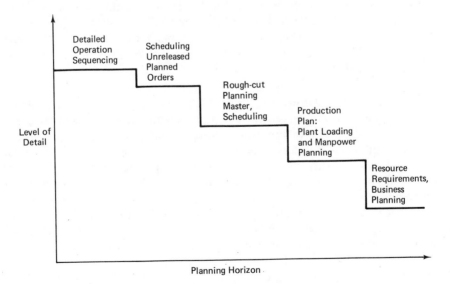

FIGURE 8-2   Different levels of capacity management.

Resource requirements planning: This type of plan covers the longest range, three to five years into the future. Repeated simulations may be run, using economic simulation modeling tools, and/or summary bills of labor or routings and a summary work center structure.

The major objective of resource requirements planning is to identify large changes needed in capacity within the lead time required to acquire them. Examples would be construction of new or additional plant space, procurement of equipment, design of special machinery, and determination of capital investment required to support the proposed level of business activity.

Production planning: Developing a summary-level production plan, covering the period of one to three years out, is desirable to refine further the resource plan and identify more specifically factors that must be resolved within a shorter lead time. Examples include the labor force, tooling needed, and the product mix that makes best use of productive resources. Other objectives of this level of production planning are to aid in developing marketing plans, anticipate work force expansion and contraction, and in negotiating very long term procurement contracts.

Rough-cut planning: This technique has a specific objective; to develop input for the master production schedule that will actually fit current plant, equipment, and work force limitations. As has been reiterated repeatedly, the MPS must be realistic, and rough-cut capacity planning helps confirm that it will be.

Depending on material availability factors, rough-cut capacity planning will be used in conjunction with confirming gross material availability. Normally, planning bills of material and planning bills of labor or routing, or similar tools, are used. This stage of capacity planning marks the first point where actual capacity limitations are considered. These may or may not include considering work already in the shop (normally not).

Scheduling unreleased orders: Once the MPS is prepared, it is used to generate planned orders. Within the general constraints identified by the rough-cut planning process, this step uses infinite loading techniques, since the MPS-produced schedule for planned orders reflects an "ideal" or most desirable schedule. Although work already in process is considered, specific work center capacity limitations are not, so that needed adjustments may be identified and planned for in advance.

The purpose of this activity is to identify over/under loads on individual work centers and to spot potential production bottlenecks. Actions connected with scheduling unreleased orders include minor MPS changes (dates, quantities), relatively small changes to work center capacities (overtime, shifting labor force around), and rescheduling subassemblies with firm planned orders. At this stage, all priorities are by order due date, using standard order lead times.

Detailed operation scheduling: This activity in most cases uses released orders that comprise work in process. Priorities here are determined by operation due dates, a lower level of detail than order due dates. It is the lowest level of scheduling detail, in that specific operations are sequenced into specific work centers at assigned times. Although normal scheduling is backward from the due date, forward scheduling may be used, together with compression of operation lead time to calculate new operation start and completion dates, if a past due start date condition results.

Capacity Management Interfaces

All five types of capacity planning essentially use two kinds of tools, simulation techniques at the gross level, or detailed calculations involving planned or released work orders. Figure 8-3 shows the various places in the overall manufacturing management process where these techniques are interfaced,

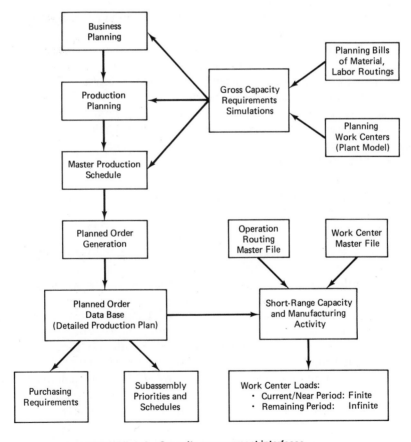

FIGURE 8-3 Capacity management interfaces.

realizing that the level of detail of their outputs may vary considerably from one situation to another.

Factors that determine the degree to which a company should engage in a great deal or only a small amount of each of these types of planning activities include the lead time required to procure resources, product complexity, production lead times (build time), whether the market is a volatile, finished inventory market or build to order, and the amount of capital investment required for production, to name a few.

For example, company A may be engaged in the production of a simple product from an engineering and production standpoint, which requires a large amount of fixed capacity resources that take a very long time to plan for and to bring on-stream. In this case, the long-range planning should be rigorous and well founded as to probable market size and the amount of plant and equipment that will be needed to serve this market. Short-range capacity management can be simple and straightforward, since production levels are relatively fixed, and the product mix stable.

Company B, on the other hand, is engaged in the production of a wide variety of items from a single plant, each of which serves somewhat separate markets. Production facilities are general purpose and may be used to produce a wide variety of products. Lead times for raw materials are short and the work force can be expanded or contracted to a substantial degree.

In this case, company B's management should perform long-range planning only at the most summary level, to estimate gross production hours in the key areas, but should do a rigorous, detailed job of managing plant resources in the current period and immediate future, emphasizing short-range capacity management techniques.

Long-Range Capacity Planning Techniques

There are a variety of statistically oriented modeling or simulation methods that do not involve the use of a product-oriented data base, but which are primarily financial in nature. The following discussion will not center on these, but it is focused on the technique of using a summarized or aggregated version of the company's product and facility information.

Chapter 4 discussed various ways to develop modular or summarized product structures that may represent an entire group of products. A similar logic may be employed to develop planning oriented operation routings. To use the actual detailed routings for each part made may involve many thousands of records and complicated computer runs. By using these summarized versions, this entire collection of records can be summarized into a small number of records, reflecting an average of what is the case for a whole product group.

Figure 8–4 illustrates in brief form how a planning routing is constructed

Actual Product Routings

Product Group	Part Number	Operation Number	Production Rate	Crew Size
A	1	010	50	1
		020	40	0.5
		030	75	3
		040	100	2
		050		
	2	010		
		020		
		030		
		040		
		050		
	15, etc.	etc.		
B	16	010		
		020		
		030		
		040		
		050		
	17, etc.	010		
		etc.		

etc.

Planning Routing

Product Group	Resource Type	Labor Hours Required	Machine Hours Required
A	Molding	5	7.6
B	Boring	2	8.0
C	Milling	9	4.5
	etc.		

Averages

Planning Routings are developed from averaging actual product routings.

FIGURE 8-4 Planning routing—example.

173

from the routings of many products in several product groups. Many repetitive data that are redundant for this purpose are eliminated. Unneeded precision is thereby not included in calculations using the records. Some detail in each group of records is omitted for clarity. The key points are that the five or more routing steps in each individual part number are reduced to one or two for each product group, reflecting key productive resources that have long lead times for changing. Those steps, such as inspection or finishing that have short lead times for change, are omitted. Production hours (labor and machine) are averages of those experienced for the whole group.

The result of this process is a small number of records which are simple to modify, reflecting different assumptions, quick to process in a computer, and produce reports that are easy to understand and use.

These summarized routings can be extended against a variety of proposed production levels and product mixes to produce annual, quarterly, or monthly plans. Variations in the degree of categorizing and grouping of products and routings can also vary the degree of detail in the planning process. By including modularized or summarized product structures in the planning process, a complete, well-based, long-range requirements plan with all important factors included can be produced quickly and easily.

Resource Requirements Planning

Figure 8–5 shows the relationships between the various parts of the resource

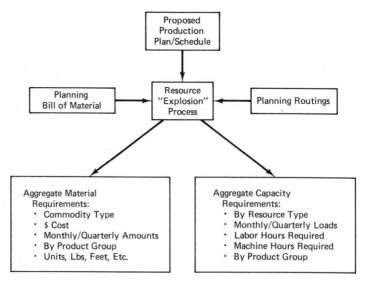

FIGURE 8-5   Resource planning cycle.

planning process. Notice that the basic logic is the same as for the detailed planning cycle in that it includes "exploding" material requirements using product structure records and similarly exploding routings to obtain what are, in effect, summarized work center loads.

Since the base of the process is summarized, so are the outputs. Results of this process are data of interest to top management. Both material and capacity requirements for meeting a given proposed level of production and mix can be dollarized, or otherwise converted into easy-to-manage, yet still accurately based terms. This type of process, using data as its starting point corresponding to a company's expected and/or known products and production methods, forms a solid base for planning.

The results of this process can be as detailed as needed. For a given level of production of a specific product group, the system can calculate the required amounts of each resource needed. Applying a dollarization process should occur only after these calculations are made, and can be modified according to various assumptions about inflation. This may be done independently of the other calculations, which, after all, simply represent physical events and are essentially unrelated to the units of cost themselves.

Using this kind of logic, a complete resource plan can be developed, such as the example in Figure 8-6. The planned quantity for the period (year) is simply multiplied times the pounds of each required commodity type, and by the labor and machine hours required for each resource type. In the example, unit costs for each commodity type, labor, and machine hours were applied to obtain a dollar cost.

It is important at this point to grasp that commodity type W, for instance, could represent an entire group of plastic or metal components or solutions that have as their common element a single type of material. Similarly, resource type F-1 might represent many different actual machining centers, heat-treating furnaces, mixing tanks, or assembly processes. Instead of losing accuracy by the averaging process, it is actually gained, as was discussed in Chapter 3. Precision is removed from the process because it is meaningless this far in the future, thereby simplifing its use and increasing its useful accuracy. The information in this example resource requirements plan can become the basis for decisions such as the securing of credit lines with financial institutions, the public offering of stock, or construction of a new plant.

It is these decisions that need to be identified so far in advance. Once the lead time for making them has passed, little can be done but to run a fire drill in an overloaded plant or, even worse, to continue operation of a plant at a small fraction of its capacity. All parts of the resource plan are important. A new plant may be indicated, for instance, but if the labor component is not included, it may be located in an area where insufficient labor of the skills needed is available.

(000 Omitted)

Planned Quantity	Product Group	Commodity Type	Material Lbs.	Material $ Cost	Resource Type	Production Labor Hours Required	Production Labor $	Production Machine Hours Required	Production Machine $
30	A	X	110	770	M-1	150	3,000	228	3,420
		Y	20	320	F-1	60	1,200	240	2,880
		Z	5	153					
Totals:			135	1,243		210	4,200	468	6,300
20	B	W	75	340	M-1	110	2,200	167	2,006
		X	15	105	F-2	35	700	136	1,632
		Y	2	32					
Totals:			92	477		145	2,900	303	3,638
Total All Groups:			227	1,720		355	7,100	771	9,938

FIGURE 8-6 Example of annual resource requirements plan.

WORK CENTER LOADING LOGIC

Since both long- and short-range planning processes use some type of work center loading logic, a full understanding of how it is performed is required. The conceptual key is the basic work order record set. Demand time, quantity, and identification are stated in the header record. Material and production resources required for a base unit quantity of what is identified is stated in the material and routing records.

Although the logic is slightly modified when planning product structures and routings are used, it is basically the same whether demand is stated in an order header record or uses another technique. For all capacity requirements planning processes, following the processing of the master production schedule, either planned or released work orders are used and the logic uses the following steps in its execution:

1. Read each order header and get the routing for that item from either the routing master file or released order records.
2. Explode the run times in each routing for the order quantity to obtain processing time for each routing step for the order.
3. For each operation, calculate the start time by subtracting the times required for processing, setup, and queue time from the required completion time, giving a backwards scheduling process.
4. Accumulate the setup and processing hours for each work center, as stated in each operation routing record.
5. Display the resulting work center load according to hours required for each time period in the display format: shifts, days, weeks, months, quarters, or years.

This process is illustrated graphically in Figure 8–7. In the example, the records for operations for four work orders that are to be performed in a single work center are represented. The different heights of each operation record represent the load imposed simultaneously on the work center; that is, work order 23 might require a crew of five to perform, or require splitting onto several identical machines in the work center, whereas work order 61 might require only a crew of two, or one machine, to perform.

The horizontal axis for each operation record represents the duration of the load in time (i.e., its start and completion time). If the load imposed by each operation used the same crew size or machines, the height of each operation record would be the same. The sequence in which each operation is "dropped" onto the work center's time frame is determined by their relative priority: normally the operation due dates. The result is a picture of the total work load planned for the work center for each time period. These data can be presented either in table form, with numbers, or graphically, as in the example.

A numeric presentation of the maximum load levels illustrated in the figure might be as follows:

Planning Period

W/O	1	2	3	4	5	6
12	5					
23		10	10			
42			8	8		
61				5	5	5
Total	5	10	18	13	5	5

The alert reader will notice that the example contains some simplifications. The periods represented are larger units than those used in the calculation of start and completion times in the routing records. The table above merely shows maximum load levels, not total loads, which would be the load level times its duration, or the area under the line. In other words, the area contained in the block for each operation record represents the actual total work load imposed by that operation. The actual resulting picture, then, is somewhat complex.

In real-world situations, these complex data are normally presented in a variety of simplified ways. Only the load for a given day or shift may be shown. The work center usually has a more linear production rate than represented here; that is, it can actually work on only one work order's operation at a time. Or, the total hours required may be listed by work order. The complexity of this

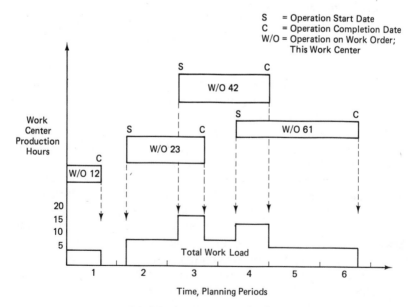

FIGURE 8-7 Work center loading.

simple example should illustrate to the reader why it is so difficult to manage this kind of information using manual methods. This is especially true if there is any degree of complexity in the production mix performed in the work center, or if a great many work centers are involved in the scheduling of an order and many orders are in work in process at the same time.

Thus far, any capacity limitation in the work center has not been considered. Figure 8-8 shows a work center load, graphically, where a capacity limitation exists. Some periods are overloaded and some do not have enough work. This is termed an *infinite load* and is produced by using standard queue times in the operation records, and by using order due dates to determine priorities (not operation due dates). The result is an *ideal schedule,* that is, the schedule that is produced by the planned order generation process, in which each order is exploded independently.

Clearly, this gives rise to potential contention for resources where capacity limitations exist, as they normally do in every factory. How this contention is resolved is the subject of finite loading, or operation sequencing, to be discussed later. A key point here is that in a great many situations it is desirable to identify the capacity required to meet the ideal schedule, since it is most closely linked to the master production schedule, which may include contractual delivery dates for products.

Planning Horizons and Time Fences

Time fences are a management technique for allowing a time frame for certain events to occur. At some point, a production schedule must be "frozen" (i.e., no further changes are allowed). This will normally be when the time until pro-

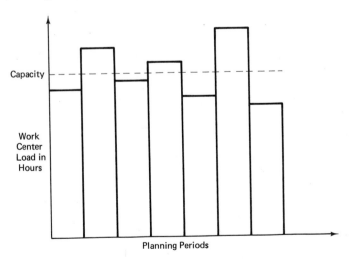

FIGURE 8-8   Infinite capacity loading.

duction equals the minimum required for responding to changes. As was discussed in previous chapters, making schedule changes, especially increases, within the lead time for responding to the change only brings about confusion. Increasing the demand for one product within the lead time for procuring additional required materials will simply cause another to come up short.

Similarly, if there is a capacity limitation somewhere in the production sequence of a group of products, increasing the work load for one will only cause a bottleneck for another, which will simply fall into a past due state. This rob-Peter-to-pay-Paul syndrome is all too common. It is a form of self-delusion.

There is an ongoing debate among practitioners as to which kind of fence policy works best. Usually, a fence policy will work acceptably as long as only small changes are allowed as exceptions, but even here, the point is that if the change can be handled, then the lead times in the system are false.

Since only one or two materials used in production may have long lead times, a variable time fence for demand changes affecting the requirements for these items may be used. Changes not affecting these key materials may be acceptable, as long as the lead times for the items concerned are not violated. The MPS will normally have a total planning horizon somewhat further out in the future than the longest lead time, so tentative purchasing requirements can be furnished to key suppliers, and gross capacity planning can proceed using infinite loading.

In Figure 8-9, the MPS horizon on the right end would represent this limit. On material planning reports, an additional time fence representing the demand change time fence may be used, that is, the time within which changes to the existing MPS will be accepted.

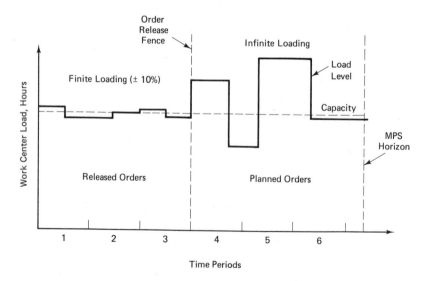

FIGURE 8-9 Capacity planning time fences.

For capacity management purposes, the important time fence is that for order releases. This management policy, implemented in the system, will reflect the earliest possible time an order can be released for production. Properly done, this policy recognizes that the latest possible release for orders is the most desirable, and simplifies ensuring that required materials are available for commitment to the order, and that adequate capacity in each required work center is available.

For purposes of input/output control, order release is input to the starting, or what is sometimes called the *gateway work center*. To manage work center queues, this input must be balanced with output actually experienced at work centers. Order release also marks the beginning of the more detailed planning/scheduling method of operation sequencing. Within the order release time fence, capacity is assumed to be relatively inflexible at each work center, or adjustable only within small limits (i.e., finite).

Plant throughput is maximized by scheduling techniques using queue time compression, and backward and forward scheduling in combination, with operation due dates being the priority setting method, instead of order due dates, as is the case on the future side of the order release time fence.

LEAD TIMES

Few concepts are more central to understanding manufacturing planning and management than that of lead time. Failure to understand and properly manage lead times is the cause for a vast list of management problems. Purchasing lead times were discussed in Chapter 7. In the plant, lead times fall into two broad categories—those for orders and those for operations—reflecting the two basic levels of detail of information used in managing the plant.

The only part of lead time that is directly affected by worker or machine productivity (production rates) is the time required to perform a given task. All other aspects of lead time are controllable by management.

The lead time for an order is calculable from the sum of the network formed by the operations required to produce the quantity on the order. Figure 8–10 illustrates this network. In the simplest case, one operation is performed sequentially after another, giving a simple sum. In many instances, however, various material handling techniques, accompanied by appropriate information control systems, can shorten this lead time by overlapping or splitting an order.

In the illustration, an order requiring four operations to be performed is illustrated. Using backward scheduling logic, the start and complete times for each operation are calculated. The order due time is hour 24. The time required to complete operation 040 is five hours, yielding its start time of hour 19, which in turn becomes the completion time for the preceding operation, 030. The process is continued.

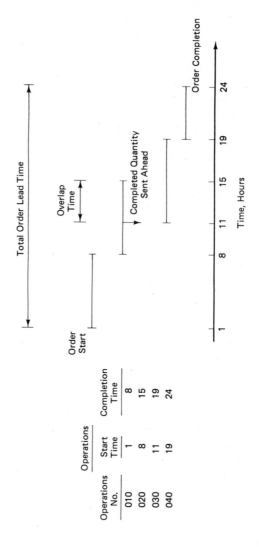

Operations No.	Operations		
	Start Time	Completion Time	
010	1	8	
020	8	15	
030	11	19	
040	19	24	

FIGURE 8-10 Lead time for an order.

The scheduling logic in this case has been instructed that operation 030 may begin after three hours of production on operation 020 has been completed, generating an overlap. This means that after a certain minimum quantity has been completed in operation 020, it can be sent ahead to the work center where operation 030 is to be performed, so that it can be started. In an assembly line, all operations are, in effect, overlapped in this manner.

Working back to the first operation, its start time is hour 1 which becomes the start time for the order. The total order lead time, then, is 24 hours. This information may be passed to the planned order generation processing and used to calculate order start dates, or a standard lead time may be used for each part number. The use of standard lead times for parts is less desirable because it usually builds in excessive amounts of queue time. The selection of lead times for order generation purposes is a conceptually difficult one, since it must be used to create the order in the first place. Normally, the standard or master routing for the part can be used to calculate a representative lead time.

Operation Lead Time

Since order lead time is really just the sum of operation lead times, and queue time occurs at the operation level, a detailed understanding of operation lead time factors is helpful. If all operations for an order included no queue time at all, scheduling of the operations becomes completely inflexible and rigid, since each operation is linked to the preceding and subsequent ones.

If a plant's operations consist of general-purpose work centers each capable of performing a variety of tasks, such as molding machines, mixing tanks, or machining centers, sequencing operations for optimum work flow becomes more difficult. Therefore, some buffering is needed in the scheduling process to allow for some resequencing of operations, and so every minor blip in the production flow does not cause a work center to run out of work.

Figure 8–11 illustrates how the lead time factors are used in scheduling an operation. The amount of time required to perform operation setup and run tasks are fixed by the production rate for the part. Before and after these tasks, however, there is some wait, or queue time, during which the material just sits.

During backward scheduling, no queue time compression is assumed, giving an earliest start time for the operation, the completion time being a given from either the order due time, or the earliest start time of the subsequent operation. The fields in the operation records used by the system to calculate schedules contain this information: setup, run, before processing queue, after processing queue time, and an allowable amount each may be compressed. Alternatively, this information may be carried in work center records in some cases.

Maximum compression of lead time gives the latest start time, as illustrated. The result is a range of start times that the operation can actually be begun without jeopardizing the required completion time, thus buffering the

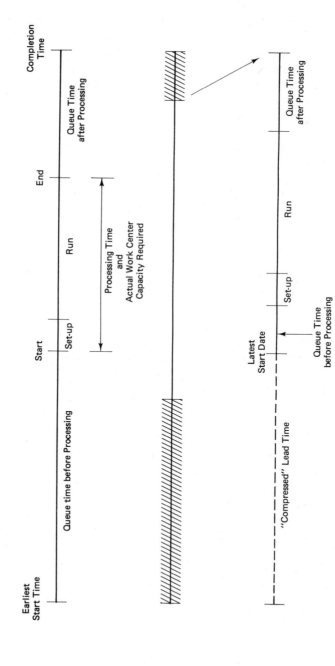

FIGURE 8-11   Operation lead time and queue reduction.

184

scheduling process as it is actually to be executed. Considering that this buffering process is continued throughout all operation records for an order, and that a given order may have dozens or even hundreds of operations required for its completion, one can readily see that a considerable total buffer may exist in the scheduling of an entire order's operations.

In most American manufacturing firms that do not utilize highly specialized (part-specific) machinery in their production process, queue time comprises more than 80 or even 90% of total order lead time. Queue time, then, is the major determinant of the level of work-in-process inventory (capital investment) required to operate the plant. In many companies, well-conceived management programs to reduce this queue time substantially have therefore brought about large reductions in work-in-process inventory.

MANUFACTURING ACTIVITY PLANNING— SHORT-RANGE PLANNING

The preceding sections in this chapter have largely concerned themselves with the kinds of information and logic used in the various planning and scheduling techniques. Manufacturing activity planning is concerned with the actual use of these techniques, in a logically related fashion, to manage the production side of the business on a day-to-day basis. Included are pre-release planning, sequencing of operations in work in process, and dispatching of work to work centers. Also related is the management structure required to execute these tasks properly.

Pre-release Planning

The MPS produces an infinite work center load as far as the plant is concerned even though rough-cut smoothing is done. Since it is usually impractical to schedule the work centers this way, the planned orders in the detailed planning data base need to be rescheduled to some extent. This process is termed *load leveling*. Coupled with it may be some changes in capacity, such as adding a second shift in heavily overloaded work centers, or shifting of work force if significant underloading occurs.

In some cases this rescheduling will need to be done at the MPS level, causing all related subassembly schedules to be shifted. In some cases, the judicious use of firm planned orders will enable work load "humps" to be managed at the subassembly level.

Prior to actual release of an order, the system will check that all required materials are available. Using a finite scheduling technique for released orders will help ensure that ample capacity is available for that order before it is physically released. Input/output analysis can be used to aid in this process. Although most computerized manufacturing systems now in use do not perform any capacity checking as part of their release logic, there is no inherent reason why they cannot, although the logic is somewhat more complex than that for checking material availability.

The essential truth of manufacturing that is most often avoided by management is that short-run scheduling is finite. The belief that somehow "pressure" can make things get through the plant faster will die a slow death. To be sure, something like iron discipline is required in any formal system, but discipline is one thing and pressure from the unplanned, "holler and bellow" school of management is another. If there is insufficient capacity—actual capacity—the only thing that can be done is to increase it to get more work out.

At the heart of manufacturing activity planning and management is a continuous flow of accurate, promptly reported information from the factory floor. Since the work order record set is the information base of work in process, most information goes to it. Figure 8–12 illustrates this flow of information from its sources. Each type of data has its own place and importance, and brings different consequences if not accurate or prompt. Since early computer systems were mostly batch oriented, promptness in the sense needed by manufacturing was not possible. Simple overnight updating of records, fine for accounts payable, is far too late for shop floor control purposes. Only on-line, right-now reporting of events as they are occurring seems to work.

Of particular importance for scheduling purposes is completed order quantities, since it is these that, when converted to standard hours (planned hours), establish earned hours, or work accomplished, by each work center. Actual hours do not determine how much work was completed, only what it took in productive resources to obtain it. Capacity, then, is used up by actual

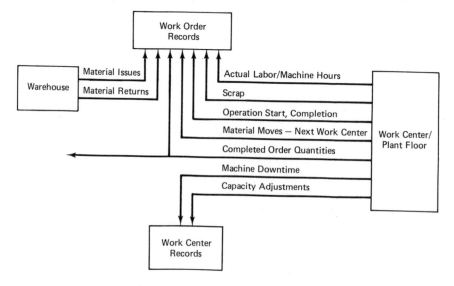

FIGURE 8-12 Actual work order data.

hours, but the plan is consumed by standard hours. Clearly, measuring both is of vital importance.

Operation starts, completions, and interoperation moves feed the scheduling logic, to queue work up at succeeding work centers properly, and provide information for dispatching purposes. Work center data, used by scheduling, have lower inaccuracy or lateness effects, but can cause disruptions and the creation of invalid or unworkable schedules nontheless.

In summary, pre-release planning manages the boundary between the planned orders in the system and the infinite work center load they produce, and readies orders for passing the order release time fence into work in process in an orderly, effective manner.

Operation Sequencing—After Release

All activities preceding order release are planning in nature. Once released, the order begins to be actually worked. All actual production in manufacturing really occurs at this level of detail. Techniques that fail to recognize this distinction will always fall short of their goals.

In arranging operations in a runable sequence, detailed scheduling logic must emulate what actually occurs in the plant. Moving from a statement of what the scheduler would like to happen to what really happens involves several methods: backward scheduling, queue time compression, and forward scheduling. The original schedule, as previously discussed, is normally developed with backward scheduling logic. Since this sometimes creates operation start dates that are in the past, something else is required.

Attempting to schedule using dates in the past creates a whole set of problems, mostly because this kind of date is information garbage of the purest form. It merely diverts attention from intelligent action. Although to some extent the degree of "past due-ness" may be said to reflect a priority of some sort, it fails to reflect priorities on a basis relative to all other work in the plant. The scheduling system must assume remaining operations to be runable on their calculated dates. Since this cannot usually be done at the same time, significant numbers of past due operations exist. The net result is that the whole plant ends up running itself in a past due state, making all dates in the system unreliable.

The something else required begins with compressing the queue time for operations that otherwise would fall into a past due start date state. The system will attempt to schedule them using a later start date, until the latest start date is reached. Once this date is reached, the only logical, realistic thing to do is to schedule forward, calculating a new completion date for the operation. In the past, even though this is what actually happens on the shop floor, people seldom bothered to write down the new, actual completion date, just leaving all dates in a meaningless state and shifting to some other method of deciding priorities.

Priority determination of work in a shop floor has been the subject of many production control papers. Even though the tools exist in state-of-the-art systems for calculating and assigning all priorities using dates or times only, discussion persists. It is not really practical to run a double-blind experiment such as those used for drugs, for example, but detailed, carefully constructed analytical studies have clearly demonstrated that the use of operation due dates as a method for establishing all work priorities will result in less work in process and faster throughput of work in the plant.

The simple reason for this is that all other methods of choosing priority assume that as a matter of course there will be considerable amounts of queue time for all work, relatively large amounts of work in process from which to select, and that the problem is one of choosing from this pile of partly completed work. These methods only divert management attention from the real problem, which is that all this extra work in process is unnecessary and its existence only compounds all other problems.

In a state-of-the-art system, the bulk of the logic described here is executed in the computer by scheduling software, with exception reports being used by management to spot problem areas in time to take corrective action. The job of management is to ensure that the input to the planning process is realistic, that policies concerning time fences are adhered to, and that data coming from the plant reflect a high degree of accuracy and are completely current at all times.

To accomplish these scheduling chores, additional fields are used in the operation records besides those already mentioned. There may be various optional or required splits of an operation onto multiple identical machines within one work center. Alternate work centers may be defined, which may include outside vendors to handle overloaded work centers. These can be scheduled just like any other work center, with the advantage that sufficient lead time for shipping is allowed by identifying the need in advance, rather than after the work center falls into a past due condition from overload.

Dispatching

In large, complex operations where there is a great deal of work in process at any one time, detailed operation sequencing chores have been historically handled by centralized or decentralized dispatchers. The function was, and often still is, performed by shop foremen, who in effect become the real schedulers of work in the plant. This is a mistake, since the foreman is as far as can be from knowing all the relative priorities of work in the plant and/or to customers.

This function, as traditionally performed, is largely obsolete in a state-of-the-art system, since the bulk of the decisions are the result of calculations performed by the scheduling system, creating centralized dispatching, in effect. There is a tendency, inherent in the manually performed version of the task, to again assume large queues of work, little sending ahead of completed quantities, and long, long lead times for work in the plant. The usual final result is hot lists and expediting of severely past due work that customers are screaming for.

If one were to deliberately plan for failure, or at least large difficulties in running the business, the checklist for such a plan would include the following out-of-control situations in the production area:

- Not ensuring that required materials were committed for production prior to releasing work to the plant
- Overloading the schedule with more work than could actually be accomplished
- Allowing large amounts of work in process to clutter and confuse operations on the shop floor, resulting in cannibalized assemblies, and stolen and lost material
- Failing to adjust capacity of resources in sufficient time to enable production to stay on schedule
- Allowing all priorities within even a large plant to be governed by a completely informal system run largely by word of mouth, political connections, and personal favorites
- Creating an information system that functions in name only, since it is continually sabotaged and not reinforced by even top management themselves

It is a sad commentary on the state of management affairs in many of the major businesses in the United States that this list is an accurate description of how the vast majority of manufacturing companies are actually run. At the time this book is being written, awareness is just beginning in the manufacturing community that it is mostly better management that has enabled Japanese and German companies to achieve production efficiencies and business effectiveness that leave the average American manager gasping in disbelief. And it is precisely at the juncture where work hits the shop floor that things fall apart the most. The factory has become the stepchild of American business, and its management has been seen as a less than honorable profession by a great many ambitious managers.

Even though its mechanism changes dramatically in companies using a state-of-the-art system, the dispatching function as a point of management responsibility remains quite workable. Its job is best carried out by releasing work to the plant at the last possible moment, by scheduling work in the smallest possible increments, and by continually monitoring actual capacity closely, making prompt, effective changes to adjust capacity to meeting the day-to-day work flow in the plant.

Of special interest are the units of scheduling. If a work order can be completed in a four-hour time span, it makes no sense at all to schedule its start for just somewhere in a ten-day span, meanwhile tying up all materials and inflating inventory that much more. State-of-the-art scheduling systems allow hourly scheduling for short-run jobs. Managing setup techniques so that they are quick and simple allows frequent changeovers from one part to another, making shorter production runs possible. The dispatching function, then, is the key to keeping the entire plant on schedule, by working effectively at the lowest possible level of detail to control and fix small problems before they become big ones and cause major disruptions in the work flow of the plant.

Management Structure

If the truth be known, at many companies much of the production management structure consists mostly of people just passing the buck to someone else. In these firms, marketing often takes no responsibility for developing any kind of sales forecast, preferring to just pressure manufacturing into responding to crisis situations with key customers. The financial function, just as often, "controls" inventory by setting arbitrary limits on total inventory, shutting off all purchasing when the level gets too high. Or, alternatively, throwing up their hands and allowing a serious cash crunch to develop.

In this scenario, design engineering has no communication with manufacturing engineering because they are elite specialists with clean hands. Consequently, products that are impossible to produce get designed, then redesigned in manufacturing. Production control in these companies often consists of a staff that prepares shop documentation, puts orders "on the schedule," and simply gives the whole mess to the shop foreman.

So where does the buck stop? In the shop, the end of the line. Often a great deal of time is spent in the shop trying to locate material and expedite seriously past due orders through the mass of work in process, interrupting other work as a consequence.

As in any other business situation, proper communication of the right information to the right people at the right time involves clearly assigning responsibilities to specific people and structuring their reporting relationships to facilitate smooth communication. In the manufacturing activity planning and control area, this is best facilitated by a structure that separates establishment of priorities from production, planning from execution. In this scheme of things, a brief list of responsibilities for production planning and plant operations management would resemble the following:

1. *Production and inventory management* are responsible for:
   - Setting all priorities, and schedules, from MPS down to the lowest level, so that all remain in relative balance and consistent with the independent demand defined in the MPS.
   - Ensuring that required material is available for production, since they are between production and procurement, and establish all material requirements via the master schedule.
   - Providing a steady flow of work to all work centers, or an alternative use of labor resources when imbalances/underloads occur.
2. *Production supervisors/foremen* are responsible for:
   - Actual production, production efficiencies, employee training, and supervision.

- Ensuring that production resources are maintained in the proper state, machine care, and timely repairs so that disruptions to the schedule will not result.
- Performance to the schedule, not just total output, including maintaining fixed, minimum work queues at work centers.
- Providing accurate, prompt input of actual performance data to the plant information system, so that accurate schedules can be developed, accurate product costing can be performed, and material usage and production efficiencies can be tracked effectively.

By assigning responsibilities in this fashion, it separates the two important functions, performing the work and setting priorities. Inevitably, priorities end up being changed whenever any line supervisor must decide between the productivity that he is being measured on and the priority that someone else said he wanted, but is not held clearly responsible for. By including job measurements that include more than just simple, raw output (e.g., schedule adherence, data accuracy, work center queues), management can ensure that the foreman is more integrated into the company as a whole.

Of course, coupled with assigning all priority decisions to the production and inventory management function is planning the work for the foreman so that his staff does not run out of work simply due to a planner's whim. And since the setting of priorities, sequence of work, and planning of material availability are so closely interlocked, it is entirely appropriate that they be assigned to the same management function.

RELEASED WORK ORDER MANAGEMENT

Computerized systems, as the preceding sections have described, can greatly aid in performing the planning process. The planning process, done correctly, continues right up to the moment of work order release and beyond, merely shifting its level of detail and focus somewhat. Once in the plant, a released work order becomes part of work in process. The planning system essentially assumes that if an order is released, it is so that it can be worked. Therefore, releasing orders that cannot be actually worked violates this basic assumption, and cannot help but cause confusion and disruption.

Once released, the emphasis of the system shifts toward comparing the planned activity with what is actually happening. Thus, extremely prompt, accurate input of all data elements concerning plant activity becomes the key to effective management of work in process. Refer again to Figure 8–12. Each of the lines represents a class of information flowing from the plant's work centers into the system, where it is used to perform material allocation decisions, all costing, and most important, detailed operation sequencing. Since the latter activity's output is the daily, or shift dispatch list, errors at this point clearly lead to schedules with already completed work, or with work that cannot be performed.

Two key parts of this data flow are information concerning material movement from one work center to the next, which involves informing the detailed scheduling system that the order is now part of the next work center's queue, and completed order quantities, which, when converted to standard hours, is the basis for relieving the work load imposed on the work center by the work center loading process. It is of particular importance to notice that the schedule is relieved by *standard* hours, not actual hours.

If this distinction is not made, the result is that planned hours are relieved with actual hours worked. In this case, all the planned hours may have been expended, but the job not completed. It is in the comparison with planned versus actual hours to perform a task that standards have any meaning and allow the tracking of efficiency and detecting inadequate standards and planning assumptions.

If a plant produces a uniform product, measuring output in terms of units is meaningful. Otherwise, the most effective measure is to convert units produced into standard hours. The detailed scheduling process (finite loading) starts with the available capacity in each work center, and loads amounts of work into each up to its available capacity.

Chapter 7 emphasized the importance of accurate data concerning material issues and receipts at the warehouse, and the consequences in the planning system of failure to ensure this accuracy. The situation is quite similar regarding the plant and the detailed operation sequencing function. It is the actual output of each work center that counts, the actual hours required, actual scrap, and material movement that is needed by the detailed scheduling system if it is to create shift schedules for each work center that are useful.

With timely, accurate data concerning events in the plant, problem areas can be spotted and acted on before they become larger ones, which is the key to work order management. Ed Folse, past president of the Los Angeles chapter of the American Production and Control Society (APICS), describes this as staying out of trouble, as opposed to getting out of trouble. Exception reports using a variety of logic can pinpoint troublesome orders, operations, work centers, and parts surprisingly fast if an accurate flow of data from the plant is maintained.

There have been many attempts to manage work in process using information that is gathered during the day and processed in batch mode during the night. To the author's knowledge, virtually none of these efforts has met with success, simply because things happen far too fast on the factory floor to permit this kind of delay. Errors in preparing input cause errors in the next day's schedule, and themselves tend to be hard to correct, because the associated documentation (the work order) and its material may no longer even be in the work center. A few hours in a work center can be a relatively long time, during which a lot of things can change. As a result, only on-line, immediate updating of work order files using data input devices on the plant floor in or near work centers seems to work very well.

Cycle Counting of Work-in-Process Information

Cyclic counting techniques have long been in use in warehouses to purge inaccurate information and detect system loopholes. A similar program should be used for work in process, with the primary objective of identifying problems with the procedures used to prepare and input data, and the secondary objective of purging incorrect information from the files. Certain types of errors tend to remain in the system, whereas others show incorrect quantities and hours for records still in the system. Exception reports can help with the first type, but cycle counting of work actually in the work center will definitely improve the quality of information used by the scheduling system.

Closely related to cycle counting techniques are reconciliation techniques, long used in banks and other financial institutions as control mechanisms. Given the existence of a detailed data base concerning work in process, accurate data concerning material in and out of work centers, scrap data, and accurate data concerning actual hours worked, there is no reason reports cannot be prepared (and are in some companies) showing total dollars into and out of each work center for a time period.

This technique can flush out reporting errors, and illuminate unreported scrap, unscheduled or unreported work, as well as other discrepancies. It also helps support management efforts to communicate the message to plant people that information accuracy is a vital part of their jobs. As an ex-banker himself, the author has been appalled many times in his career in manufacturing with the casualness with which manufacturing people treat material worth hundreds of thousands of dollars. It is even worse when the consequences to material and capacity planning efforts are considered.

Work Load Balancing

Balancing of assembly lines is a concept quite familiar to operations research people. It involves selecting equipment production rates, personnel staffing levels, and an overall assembly line movement rate that enables each operation not to overrun its successors, or to cause too much waiting time at preceding steps: keeping everyone in step, in other words. The same logical concept can be applied in companies using multipurpose work centers, with a more random flow of work through the plant. The detailed operation sequencing process is an effort to perform this kind of balancing of work between work centers with varying capacities.

This "logical" or nonphysical assembly line concept is achieved with detailed operating sequencing scheduling using operation due dates/hours under conditions where the following occur:

- The operation sequences produced for each work center by the scheduling system are enforced (i.e., performing work in a different sequence is not permitted).

- Completed quantities at each work center are sent ahead as soon as economic movement quantities are finished, producing considerable overlap of operations within each work order; timely, accurate data reporting is assumed.
- Frequent, small adjustments to work center capacities are made to allow for unforeseen problems, minor planning errors, and other changes, to keep each work center on schedule.
- An absolute minimum of work center queue is allowed, permitting received material to be worked on almost immediately in each work center.
- Plant equipment, machinery, and work force is of high quality and maintained in a reliable, predictable state where machine downtime is planned and absenteeism is either scheduled or covered by cross training.

Plants that are scheduled and operated under these rules experience the absolute minimum possible work in process, the quickest possible flow of work through the shop, and the least number of problems managing work in process (simply because there is so much less of it to manage). Every manufacturer understands the economies of scale that come with an assembly line. In the past, this form of production was suitable only for really high volume manufacturing, and until the advent of really effective computerized scheduling systems, could not be emulated in a random work center plant environment.

With a state-of-the-art, computerized scheduling system that is properly managed, many of the economies of the assembly line can be achieved in a random work center environment. With closely coupled scheduling, all work centers involved in the production of a specific part set up to produce that part close to the same time. The result is that the parts move rapidly through the shop.from raw material/components to a finished state and off the plant floor virtually as quickly as they would with an actual, physical assembly line. Only the material movement time may add a significant difference compared to a physical assembly line.

Input/Output Control

Input/output control is a set of techniques for controlling levels of work in process that originated prior to the development of state-of-the-art systems and the management techniques that have been discussed in this chapter. It was felt that one effective way to prevent total work in process from building to unacceptable levels was to release only as much work to the plant as the plant put out, thereby holding the total work in process at a relatively constant level.

Some of the drawbacks to this approach are obvious from the discussion thus far. Most important, it obscures bottlenecks that are occurring at specific work centers. It is the sum of total work center backlogs that determines actual total plant backlog. Not releasing work that does not use a backlogged or overloaded work center will simply cause those items to become past due and an underload condition to develop in other work centers. For these and related reasons, it may safely be concluded that gross plant input/output is, in itself, a marginally effective tool in a state-of-the-art system environment. The tools exist to manage work at a much lower level of detail.

It is at this lower level of detail that input/output control methods have some effectiveness. It can also be useful to help manage key, critical, or "gateway" work centers in the overall flow of work through the plant.

There are four basic kinds of information that comprise input/output control data. They are:

- *Planned input:* work awaiting its start at a work center, either from work order release, or by movement from a previous work center, during a specified time period
- *Actual input:* work actually started or released to a specific work center during the specified time period
- *Planned output:* work that was previously released or moved to a work center that was expected to have been completed during the time period
- *Actual output:* work that was actually completed during the time period

In each of these cases, the work is stated in a common term, such as standard hours, that is, the time assumed by the run quantity and the production rate specified in the routing master for the part and operation and/or work center. The difference between planned input and planned output is the planned deviation, or number of hours of work expected to be added to or subtracted from the queue at the work center.

Similarly, the difference between the actual input and actual output is the *actual deviation,* or actual change to the queue of work at the work center. This information enables one to examine the queue input and output at a summary level for a number of work centers without having to review mountains of data. When presented in summary form, using the planned and released operation records as a source, one can also view the factors influencing queue size for several recent periods as well as what is planned for the immediate future. Figure 8–13 illustrates an example of input/output information.

In the illustration, the desired queue size is stated as 150 hours of work, approximately equal to half of one time period's planned output. In period 9, it is 240 hours. To reduce the queue size, more work is planned to be completed (output) than is planned for input to the work center through period 13. At the beginning of period 13, the queue size is 155 hours, slightly over target. Also, although actual output is less than planned, actual input was also less than planned, so the planned change in queue size occurred anyway.

In a real work situation, of course, some inquiry would be made in order to understand why both sets of actual events were less than planned, and what the consequences will be in the immediate future. If a bottleneck in production at a work center preceding this one is preventing material movement into the work center, the reduced queue size is a temporary event, and the planned reduction in work center capacity in period 13 (from 300 hours per period to 270) would be a mistake. The cumulative deviation of -55 indicates that there

				Period			
Input	9	10	11	12	13	14	15
Planned	270	270	270	270	270	270	270
Actual	275	265	230	255			
Cumulative Deviation	+5	0	−40	−55			
Output							
Planned	300	300	300	300	270	270	270
Actual	305	260	280	295			
Cumulative Deviation	+5	−35	−55	−60			
Queue							
Planned (150)	240	210	180	150	150	150	150
Actual (270)	240	245	195	155			

FIGURE 8-13   Input/output control. (Source: Lankford, R., "Input/ Output Control: Making It Work," APICS 23rd Annual Proceedings, 1980, p. 419.)

is some scheduled work ahead of this work center that is not moving as planned; the 55 hours of work will presumably show up some time in the future, bloating the queue unless it is now reduced to a lower than target level.

Enlightened management will use the information presented in this and related reports to take steps to adjust capacity in this work center, such as in period 13, or in the preceding work center that appears to be experiencing bottlenecking. At this stage, the degree of "past due-ness" is minimal and can be compensated by small capacity changes. If these changes cannot be accommodated, the intelligent thing to do is relieve the schedule at the MPS level to equal the capacity that is available, and avoid clogging up the shop with work that cannot be completed.

One of the key steps in enabling small capacity adjustments without disrupting the work force is an extensive, ongoing, cross-training program. Closely related in many firms is identifying alternate work centers in advance of problems, and/or outside vendors who can perform overloaded work.

This little example illustrates how the detailed data base of operation routing records can be summarized for management review and action, using the information pyramid concept. It could be further revised to display only those work centers that have cumulative deviations greater than, say, 10%, enabling management to focus even more directly on the areas requiring immediate action. Chapter 9 examines the use of system-maintained information in comparing planned versus actual information in more detail.

Information from Work Order Management

The flow of planned information developed by the planned order generation process, the order release cycle, and the detailed operation scheduling system merges with a substantial, detailed flow of information from the plant floor in the work order management system. From this mass of data, numerous reports can be prepared, using exception reporting logic, enabling management to direct its actions toward keeping the business plan on track in the plant.

The key to this process is ensuring that not only is the planning information accurate, but that the flow of data from the plant is accurate and very prompt. When this is the case, a great many reports can be constructed to fit specific operating realities, enabling management to control effectively activities such as the following:

- *Schedule control:* order releases and material movement
- *Queue control:* such as illustrated above, both for individual work centers and the plant as a whole
- *Actual versus planned costs:* continuously during production of a part, after completion, or with an average of many similar work orders
- *Variance reporting:* such as material usage, labor and machine efficiency, and scrap
- *Identifying specific problem areas:* such as chronic problem work centers, difficult-to-make parts, consistent above- or below-standard production rates, specific capacity limitations, and many others
- *Detecting planning and reporting errors:* such as incorrect material issues, or labor reporting

Lot Control and Serial Number Traceability Considerations

Although a full discussion of these two areas is beyond the scope of this book, since they apply only to certain industries, a brief explanation of what is involved will be helpful. An example of a company using lot control traceability is a medical device manufacturer. In this case, the company must keep track of where each lot of purchased raw materials/components went during the production cycle, and in which lots of end item production the supplier-furnished raw materials ended up. The chief purpose is to minimize the impact of possible product recall for safety reasons.

For example, the production of disposable syringes uses a small part called a plunger cap, which seals the syringe on the inside, giving it its pumping action. Companies making these and similar products must be able to recall only those already-shipped lots of syringes containing a certain, specific lot of rubber plunger caps that are suspected of having some chemical flaw. The only alternative would be to recall every syringe produced, clearly a disastrous action to the company.

Another variation of this theme is in highly engineered products where extremely high reliability is required, such as in many aerospace companies. Serial number traceability, when extended to the full production cycle, means the same as lot control traceability, except that each individual part has a unique identity provided by a serial number. It, too, may have to be traced through the production cycle so that the specific end item can be identified that contains the specific purchased item with a specific serial number. The purpose is somewhat similar in that product safety and reliability are involved. Also, improvements in engineering design are a major factor in these cases.

In both lot control and serial number traceability, the net effect on the information system is that each component part number used in the product structure acquires an extension, either the lot number or the serial number, to identify it from other items with the same part number. Thus, if a specific part number that otherwise is used once on a product is actually produced from components made during three different production batches from a vendor (or lower-level subassembly work orders), three records must be kept in the work-in-process system, one for each lot used of that part number, and the quantity of each that was used from each lot.

Clearly, this introduces a considerable level of complexity and volume to the data base. However, given the requirement that such information must be maintained, it is clearly easier to maintain it in a computer system, where the process can be largely automatic, assuming that the system has been designed for this kind of tracking.

Looking at this problem from the standpoint of work order management, it means that data accuracy is even more important, since possible product recall/safety may be involved, and that there may be some change in how orders are generated and managed on the plant floor. Techniques such as long production runs may be less practical, since physical control of components becomes more important; that is, they must be physically kept together and not mixed with other similar parts. Maintaining all information in the computer system may be more difficult, and making a complete break from written documentation similarly difficult. This in turn may make it more difficult to make the computer system data base more reliable, since people always tend to rely on the written documentation first.

Since the major premise of this book is that virtually all information concerning the entire production process is maintained in the computer, especially work in process and factors involved in planning material and capacity requirements, it is of critical importance that efforts to maintain duplicate hard copies of computer-maintained data not be assumed.

Summarizing Work Order Management

Having discussed the major aspects of managing released work orders in the plant, a brief review of this complex area is in order. The activity of managing released work orders in the plant begins shortly before order release, where checking to ensure adequate capacity at required work centers is performed, in connection with the load-leveling process of finite work center loading. These functions can and should be performed by the computer system. They are built on a solid base of accurate, timely data input from the plant floor concerning actual work being performed in each work center and fed into the operation routing records for each released work order being worked.

Thus the key management task here is to take effective steps to ensure that this flow of data is timely and accurate on a continuing basis, so that the computer programs can perform as desired and produce meaningful, optimized schedules of operation sequences for each work center on a daily or shift basis.

Closely tied to this process is continuous monitoring of input and output at each key work center, that is, those where a potential capacity constraint exists. Frequent, regular action to adjust capacity up and down in each work center, in small increments as the work load fluctuates, ensures smooth work flows and reliable production and allows the company to stay out of trouble rather than getting out once in. Effective use of employee cross-training programs and alternate work centers (and/or outside vendors) significantly aid in this process.

Finally, in a management and systems environment that uses these tools to control its work in process, it becomes possible to control work center queues in a way that was possible in the past only in nonrandom work center production environments. The use of overlapping operations and send-ahead quantities, coupled with computer-maintained work order records, allows a company to bring its in-plant lead times very close to those experienced by an assembly line, or at least close to the actual time required to produce the product by creating a logical, nonphysical assembly line in the computer system. In this environment, work in process is at a minimum, and therefore becomes much easier to manage—a major advance in itself.

MANAGEMENT OF WORK CENTER QUEUES

The topic of queue control is a recurring thread throughout this book. It is mentioned frequently, perhaps even tiresomely, because experience has lead the author consistently to the conclusion that it is one of the least understood areas in manufacturing management, and in any case, the one where a state-of-the-art computer system can have the most impact in achieving dramatic simplifications of the business.

Work center queues may be defined for purposes of this discussion as inventory that is waiting for an operation to be performed on it at a work center. This is distinguished from inventory still in a warehouse, awaiting issue to work in process. The APICS Dictionary defines a queue as being simply a waiting line of jobs awaiting being worked at a work center.

It is important to understand that a queue is definitely an inventory investment, and as such should be considered in the same light as any other inventory investment, not simply taken for granted. Many companies have exerted great effort to control and minimize warehouse inventory, while devoting little or no attention to queue inventory.

Chapter 6 took the viewpoint that the essential starting point for justifying any inventory investment made by a company is to determine how it serves the company's objectives. This analysis should be performed in as much detail as any other capital investment of similar size should be. With inventory, especially work-in-process inventory, there is the disadvantage, peculiar to inventory investments, that the more of it there is, the harder the business gets to manage. Presumably, most other capital investments in a manufacturing firm benefit the business by increasing productivity or providing some competitive advantage, and not necessarily to complicate operating the business. So there is an additional, difficult-to-quantify effect of increasing investment in work-in-process inventory.

Some work in process clearly is necessary because the production process itself is not instantaneous. Although productivity clearly affects this level of inventory, it is the subject of the additional inventory that forms work awaiting processing that is the focus of this section, not that required by the time required to make the products.

It is important to grasp the effect that reducing queues can have on work in process investment. Hewlett-Packard's printed circuit board plant, which otherwise was well run, with a relatively current material requirements planning system and enlightened management, experienced reported reductions of work in process exceeding 60% simply by reducing queues at each work center. If current work-in-process inventories at a hypothetical similar company were $3 million, this means that nearly $2 million of this inventory investment could be eliminated as a capital requirement for operating the business, with the additional benefit that plant lead time would shrink by an even greater percentage. This Hewlett-Packard plant reported that it was able to reduce its plant or ordering lead time from four months to slightly less than four weeks.

No great magic was involved in achieving these gains, other than a reasonably good operation scheduling system, good management practices in dealing with its people, and a well-planned program of cross-training and assignment of responsibilities to the correct departments. The organization structure discussed previously serves as a model.

Figure 8–14 illustrates a comparison of identical work flows at a hypothetical three-work-center factory. In the illustration each small horizontal line represents a separate work order awaiting work at the work center. The queue is represented by a "stack" of work orders, with each being run on a first-come, first-run basis. The top example represents a situation one commonly finds in multiple-work-center manufacturing. Each work center has a number of orders ahead of the current job being worked. If one assumes that each little line represents one job, each of which takes an average of one day to complete, each work center has about seven days work ahead of it (i.e., each job waits an average of seven days at each work center before it gets worked

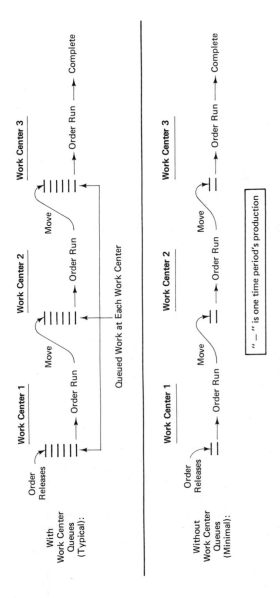

FIGURE 8-14   Effect of work center queues on work-in-process.

on). Thus, in the top example, it takes about 21 days for one order to complete the production cycle, even though it needs only three days of actual work. This situation is *not* an exaggeration of situations actually experienced at many companies; often the queues are actually larger.

In the bottom example, work center queues have not been eliminated completely, but were reduced to two days, with only two orders awaiting work at each work center, besides the one actually being worked. The result is that total production time is now only nine days, a reduction of 12 days. Inventory investment required to operate the plant has been reduced by a similar proportion.

Since the value of material increases as more work is performed on it, as it moves through the production process, and as more components are added to it, the effect of queue reduction is greater at work center 3 than at work center 1, in terms of inventory value. However, the effect on reduction of in-process lead time is the same regardless of where the reduction is made. It just gets shorter, simply because it spends less time waiting and a greater proportion actually getting worked on.

The example can be further enhanced by imagining a reduction to zero queue at each work center, achievable with operation overlapping. Even if each operation were overlapped only slightly, the amount of time a single work order would take to get completely through the three-work-center production cycle would shrink to three days, its actual run time, eliminating 18 time periods' worth of inventory from work-in-process investment, an 85% reduction. In addition, the company gets the additional benefits already mentioned of a more competitive, responsive market position, a reduced necessity for firm purchasing commitments so far out into the future, plus the obvious simplification of the entire scheduling process and operation of the business.

Justifying Work Center Queue Investment

Having examined the effect of different queue sizes on work-in-process investment, some attention needs to be devoted to the circumstances under which a work center queue represents a good business policy decision, not just an accident attributable to oversight. Normally, there is only one fully justifiable reason for allowing work center queues, and that is to act as a buffer to smooth out work load fluctuations in cases where a reasonably tight capacity constraint exists at the work center. Since capacity is time perishable (it must be used now or be lost forever), keeping a work center busy all the time can be important in staying on an overall production schedule. What this means in everyday terms is that if the total work that must be performed by a work center over a longer time period requires that it be in relatively continuous operation, if it is idle for part of that time period an inevitable behind-schedule condition will develop that will be difficult to overcome.

Besides this principal reason for allowing work center queues, there are a number of reasons that may be termed "pseudo" reasons. Since these are commonly used as justifications, they deserve some examination. The common ones are:

- *The staff must be kept fully occupied.* This situation can only work in the short run, because either there is enough total work in the long run to occupy the staff fully, and fit the justification discussed above, or there is not. Eventually, it will run out of work if it is not, and a queue can only serve to encourage the staff to work slower so that they can keep busy. A variation of this is found in highly specialized work centers. It may be believed by management that these can perform only one set of functions, or that other workers in other work centers would resent a cross-training program.

- *A good-sized backlog of partly completed work is needed to enable the quick satisfaction of back-order or other behind-schedule situations.* This is an open admission that work in process is not being really scheduled but is just created to allow expediting of "hot" items. If scheduling is done, with minimal queues, it becomes almost impossible to expedite, since all work flows through the shop in close to its minimum time anyway.

- *A very expensive piece of capital equipment must be kept fully occupied at all times to justify its investment.* This is similar to the first reason; either there is enough work in the long run or there is not. A large queue of work before and after such a work center will result in long periods of idleness if there is not, accompanied in the meantime by excessive inventory investment and distortion of related production schedule requirements. More frequent, shorter periods of idleness would be preferable, expensive or not.

- *The work load fluctuates so much that a large buffer is needed to even things out.* If this logic is applied throughout a multiple-work-center manufacturing business, much of the fluctuation experienced at individual work centers is due to the telescoping and contraction of slack in the work flow through the shop being exaggerated greatly by all the total queue in the shop. Properly scheduled and controlled, it is usually found that the work load can be leveled without having large queues. This situation is analogous to the stop-and-go traffic experienced in a freeway jam; it is caused entirely by the increase and decrease of the space between each car surging back and forth. Viewed from the air, such a freeway is clearly having a steady flow at its "output" end even though each driver experiences a substantial fluctuation in his speed.

There are a number of other undesirable situations that can occur in the presence of large work center queues. One of the most pernicious is the end-of-the-month shipping crunch. At the first of each month, the plant spends all its time starting work orders, so nothing is completed to be shipped. As the end of the month approaches, all hands turn to and the large pile of work in process is scavenged for every item that can be rushed through to completion in order to meet the monthly production goals.

This situation is often accompanied by such distortions as pressure to keep the accounting month open many days into the following month so that all shipments which hit the dock on the last day and could not be physically shipped can be recorded in the previous accounting month. When production goals are stated in weekly or daily instead of monthly terms, this distortion will often disappear, since work must be started at the same rate as it is completed in order to meet each day's or week's production objective.

Getting Control of Queues

There are several aspects to a good queue management program that are needed to be effective. First, queues must be measured on a continuing basis, not just occasionally. A state-of-the-art system provides these data from its operation completion and material movement data, reflected in the change in the current operation awaiting work.

Next, a study of each work center's capacity, flexibility of capacity adjustment, and long-run work load should be used to establish a minimum, planned, or standard level of queue. Maintaining this level of queue becomes the responsibility of the work center supervisor or foreman. It is his job to ensure that it is not exceeded on the average. It is production control's job to schedule the work in as smooth a fashion as possible, consistent with the levels and priorities stated in the master production schedule.

If an initial study discloses that actual queues are substantially greater than the desired planned queue levels, a plan of action to reduce them must be developed and implemented. Total work input to the plant usually must be decreased for a time, while the excess work-in-process inventory is worked off. Careful releases of work orders is also often needed to keep the plant balanced, as each work center gets down to its desired queue level.

Once desired levels of work center queue are achieved, they are maintained by the technique of frequent, small capacity adjustments, coupled with detailed operation sequencing as discussed earlier. The key to maintaining these levels of queue is regular management review of actual versus planned queues at each work center, coupling performance to work center supervisors' performance reviews, and by an ongoing program of cross-training of the labor force. Sending a few members of the labor force home an hour or two early from time to time with pay is not a terrible disaster, should no other alternative be available.

It is vital to any queue control program that everyone in the production labor force, from managers to low-skilled helpers, understand in at least basic terms why queues are being reduced, if that is the case, and/or why they are maintained at a low level. Similarly, something resembling the management structure described earlier must exist so that day-to-day activities are tied to the right individuals' job performance reward/punishment system.

Results from Effective Queue Management

Companies that have implemented queue controls such as described here consistently report a number of desirable results. Some of these are:

- *Increased productivity.* The lack of work ahead of a work center tends to cause supervisors to "pull" work from preceding work centers in order to keep busy. With less time spent handling changing priorities, work flow is smoother within each work center. With the proper reward environment, running out of work is not a bad thing; low productivity is.

- *Reduced work-in-process inventory.* Reductions of more than 50% are common, with many achieving much greater reductions.

- *Shorter lead times.* In many companies, this also results in fewer engineering changes to work in process, quicker ability to respond to short-term customer needs and other competitive advantages, in addition to drastically shrinking the entire planning and forecasting horizon.

- *Simplified scheduling.* With fewer orders to schedule and reschedule, the entire problem of setting priorities and managing work in process becomes much easier. There are just fewer decisions to be made.

To summarize, an effective program of queue managing, using state-of-the-art information systems coupled with an appropriate management structure, results in a substantial simplification of the business operation itself. Whole classes of problems that are otherwise intractable either disappear altogether or become relatively insignificant. The company is better able to focus on the essential problems of actual productivity, equipment reliability, control, employee morale, and efficiency of the business, rather than struggling with a huge mass of partly completed work, constantly juggling priorities, expediting, and drastically over- and underloading work centers.

MANAGING TOOLING

Tooling may be defined as reusable items which are attached to, or used in conjunction with, a more general-purpose piece of production equipment to enable it to produce a specific part. Included are various types of fixtures, jigs, cutting devices, and fitting gauges that, in effect, specialize the machine and/or work center for producing a specific part or for performing a specific operation on a specific part. Although reusable, tooling normally has a finite life span (i.e., it wears out and must be replaced).

Not all manufacturing companies use tooling. Production equipment may be very specialized. Tooling may be a permanent part of the machine, or may never leave the work center. Some types of tooling are consumed by the production process and function in effect, as a component part that is issued like any other part, but just disappears during processing. Tools of these types can be handled either by considering them to be a part of the product structure or part of the work center's equipment. They are not scheduling constraints.

The kind of tooling environment to be discussed here are those tools which can become a schedule constraint in that their nonavailability prevents the part from being produced. Nonavailability can result from several conditions. There may be a limited number, such as only one. Or contention for their use may occur if they are used in more than one work center. They may be out being repaired, such as occurs in a molding operation. The current location of the tool may be unknown, due to poor record keeping. In any of these cases, not having the tooling available will prevent the part from being produced, even if all required components are available and there is sufficient capacity in the work center.

For these reasons, in a production environment where tooling is a production factor, tooling must be scheduled and planned in the same fashion as material and capacity. In addition, tooling may form a major investment for the company, and therefore should be managed like any other productive asset. A state-of-the-art system contains a full tool management subsystem, including:

- Tracking of each tool's current location
- Expected remaining life of the tool
- Tool structure, where a tooling kit is involved
- Tool requirements planning, similar to MRP
- Complete usage history
- Last and next planned calibration dates
- Tool cost and purchasing information
- All where-used relationships, including new products
- Engineering change information for the tool

If tooling quantities are limited and have multiple uses, availability of tooling usually cannot be fully assured at time of order release. In these cases, contention for use of tools is resolved during detailed operating sequencing, so that two operations using the same tool are not scheduled for running at the same time.

Physical control of tooling is similar to that for inventory items. They are kept in a locked, controlled-access area and their issues and receipts are documented and controlled in the same manner as inventory items. In some cases, especially with periodic calibration, each tool may have a serial number, to distinguish it from others. The system may not schedule its use past a required calibration date or number of uses.

The design and development of tooling, which may be a specially designed item, is closely coupled with manufacturing engineering planning, and in some cases with design engineering as well. Quality assurance tolerances and production reliability is intimately connected with tooling design in many cases.

In companies where tooling is complex and issued in kits, or sets of related tools that are used in the production of a specific part or a group of related parts, the tooling subsystem logic will resemble that of the material requirements planning system. The kit structure will be reflected in a tooling product structure, with parent–component and where-used relationships within the kit being identified. Each kit is "exploded" using the same logic as for planned order generation for material. This logic will not be reviewed here, as it is already familiar to the reader.

Tooling, then, comprises an area of critical importance for many manufacturing firms, although not all. Where it is a factor, it must be planned and controlled to the same degree of accuracy and reliability as material and capacity. A state-of-the-art system will maintain all information concerning the tool's nature, cost, usage, structure, and location. Its issuance is planned for and scheduled as a normal part of the production planning process. The operation sequencing performed by the computer can schedule tooling as well. Failure to ensure that these activities occur and are in coordination with other production planning processes will invite disruptions of schedules, increases in work in process, and behind-schedule conditions.

MANAGING VENDOR-PERFORMED PROCESSING

At numerous points in the preceding discussions references have been made to the various factors involved in planning and controlling work which involves sending partly completed material outside the plant to a vendor's facility, where additional processing is performed before returning to the plant for subsequent processing.This is a complex procedure and one that is often poorly performed as a result. It is further complicated by the use of vendors as alternate work centers to offload a capacity overload. The following paragraphs are intended to bring these various factors together; to summarize and bring into focus how this important activity can best be planned and managed using state-of-the-art systems.

The most basic aspect is identification of the material. A part number is the normal identification method, with a unique part number being assigned to each stage of the part as it changes during the production process. Thus a raw casting will have a unique number, a partly machined casting one that is different, and the finished item still a different part number. Since a number of operations may be involved, using many work centers in between these part number changes, identification of the part at these stages is complicated, and can be performed only by associating the part number with its last completed operation if it is in one of these "in-between" states.

If the vendor-performed processing is a permanent part of the processing cycle (i.e., it is always sent out), the best approach is to have the part completed on a work order (or issued directly from stock) prior to its being shipped. This gives the shipped item a unique part number identifier. When returned after vendor processing, it should have a different part number, reflecting its changed state. It can then become a component and be issued to a next-higher assembly work order for subsequent processing. This approach also has the advantage of simplifying operation sequencing of released work orders. The part is shipped on a vendor processing work/purchase order and is distinct from work-in-process scheduling. Its handling at the receiving dock upon its return is like that of any other purchased item.

The more complex case is that of variable use of a vendor's facilities. In this case, the vendor is identified as a "pseudo" work center that is used as an alternate work center by the detailed operation sequencing/work center loading system's logic. If an overload occurs at the work center that is normally used, the system schedules the operation to be performed at the vendor's facilities and adjusts the operation lead time accordingly. The work order must still be linked to a purchase order so that the receiving operation can operate normally and the required interface with accounts payable can be logically managed by the system.

When shipped, the part is identified with its starting part number and the operation number last completed. After the vendor's operations are completed, the parts are received under the same part number, but with a subsequent operation shown as completed. The amount of the purchase order cost is the vendor's charge for performing that operation. It is charged to the work order for product costing purposes.

If the vendor in either of the cases above has a capacity constraint, or if a contractual arrangement has been made whereby a certain volume of capacity has been purchased, the vendor should be identified as a work center in the capacity planning system and loaded using finite scheduling logic. In this manner, a shipping schedule can be derived from the system's operation records together with the expected time the parts will be returned and available for subsequent processing. Required shipping documents can also be generated from these data to identify the parts, their destination, and planned shipping and return dates.

Vendor-performed processing is often one of the most heavily expedited areas in a manufacturing plant. It is often believed that the vendor can be pressured into performing work instantaneously. Since this is often not the case, a behind-schedule condition may be blamed on the vendor. Neither of these actions help achieve a really effective working relationship with the vendor, who after all is needed by the company in order to complete its products.

Use of state-of-the-art computer systems to plan, schedule, and control vendor processing can aid significantly in improving this relationship, getting better turnaround times and lower costs by using the system to aid the vendor in planning his work flow.

Much of the confusion in this area is exaggerated by failure to identify parts clearly as described above, little or no advance scheduling of vendor-performed work, failure to use work orders to plan and control the work, failure to use purchase orders to control receiving of the parts and payment, not including the vendor's capacity in overall capacity planning, and by not adjusting operation or part lead times to allow for shipping times and the vendor's own work-in-process queue times. Managing the work flow to and from vendor processing facilities requires the same level of production control effort—perhaps a dedicated scheduler—as any significant work center or group of work centers belonging to internal work in process. The same techniques for ensuring quality control as with other purchased material apply here as well, including such techniques as certification of the vendor's process control and on-site inspection of parts.

In terms of the records used by the system, the chief modifications for vendor processing are that a normal work order is flagged in its header record as scheduled for vendor processing and a link created to a purchase order, planned by the system and handled similar to other purchase orders. Special work center records may also be used for scheduling and capacity planning purposes, with periodic updates obtained from the vendor.

Properly performed, using state-of-the-art systems, the outside processing vendor can be brought into the mainstream of the planning system, scheduled and controlled to the same degree of precision and accuracy as other work performed within the plant. The overall result is smoother flow of work, reliable vendor performance and cost, and improved performance of the business.

FACILITIES MANAGEMENT

Although only a brief examination of this area falls within the scope of this book, several important issues impinge heavily on the ability of a state-of-the-art manufacturing system to accurately plan and control production. Of course, the whole subject of production equipment is a vast field in itself. Any planning system involving production equipment and machinery assumes that the equipment will actually be available and operating at the time it is scheduled. Thus reliability, or predictability of production rates and availability, is paramount to achieving a reliable plan.

Decisions involving the exact equipment to be employed are intimately linked to long-range planning, the strategic plan of the business, and the capacity planning. Of concern to the planning cycle are several areas which are discussed below.

Maintenance of Equipment

Of critical importance here is preventive maintenance, which allows the company to plan when and how long each piece of equipment will be unavailable to the system for scheduling production. Clearly, the preventive maintenance program must have its own schedule, based on the design of the equipment and the reliability of its component parts.

In a state-of-the-art system, maintenance activity is planned and scheduled using maintenance work orders, triggered by scheduled maintenance dates maintained in the work center records. Cumulative maintenance costs, performance history, and reliability data are also maintained in these records. By including scheduled downtime data in the work center records, the production scheduling programs can determine when the work center will be unavailable for production and schedule work around that time period. There may also be some impact on the master production schedule.

Parts used in the maintenance activity can be managed with the same inventory management tools as for production material, including usage history, cost, ordering policies, and other elements. Although the author is not personally aware of such an application, there is no reason a work center whereused set of relationships for maintenance parts cannot be used to manage maintenance parts using records similar to product structures. In this area, effective management of maintenance inventories, relationships with suppliers, and forward planning can yield significant benefits to both the company and the vendor.

Many companies ignore the value of effective preventive maintenance programs, fail to plan and budget for them, and in general wait until equipment fails to devote maintenance effort to it. Much of this is due to a misguided effort to increase production in the short run, only to lose in the long run due to unreliable equipment that is no longer capable of reliably producing high-quality parts. Just as often, companies attempt to plan for their equipment unreliability by introducing buffers in the plant lead times, increasing work center queues, and similar hedges. As previous discussion has established, this kind of action brings problems that are greater than the cost of a good preventive maintenance program.

Plant Layout

As a company moves farther into state-of-the-art scheduling of its work in process, interwork center movement of material becomes more of a visible factor in production lead times. It has always been there in these cases, but has become more obvious as lead times shrink. Machinery is often arranged by similarity of function rather than by similarity of product produced. Thus milling machines of different sizes may be grouped together even though no product flow uses more than one of them. If machinery is arranged according to the flow of operations performed on the parts belonging to a common product group, material movement time will be reduced (as will material handling cost). It becomes more practical to use conveyors and other types of automated equipment.

In general, the more closely a plant layout can be made to resemble an assembly line, the more efficient the production processes will flow, and the more effective detailed operation scheduling can become. The benefits are reduced work in process, simplification of management of the work flow, and shorter in-plant lead times.

Production Balancing

Operations research includes among its arsenal of efficiency techniques the concept of production line balancing. This technique involves determining the appropriate production rates for all elements of a production process so that work moves through each work center at a steady rate. In view of the basic fact that the overall production rate for a product is limited by the slowest work center involved, this concept has applicability to non-assembly-line businesses as well. This becomes even more relevant when one considers that a state-of-the-art detailed operation scheduling system creates a "logical" or nonphysical assembly line through a random work center plant.

The capacity management system can provide information regarding comparative production rates actually achieved at each work center, and at all work centers involved in a given work flow. Enlightened management uses this information to plan equipment changes, identify bottlenecks, and avoid the purchase of high-capacity equipment that will remain idle because of a limiting work center elsewhere in the work flow.

Overloading and Underloading of Machines

Many American companies purchase production equipment and then attempt to run it at its fastest possible production rate. The outcome is predictable. Like any mechanical device that is run too hard, premature wear, unpredictable failure times and modes, and poorer-quality products result. Some of this is due to confusing a machine's theoretical production rate, or its cyclic production rate, with the effective rate expectable in the long run. In the long run, the machine's resultant unreliability will bring its overall production capacity below what it would have produced had it been run consistently below its rated capacity, reducing wear on its components, and allowing it to function more in line with the designer's intentions.

The impact of policies on the ability of a state-of-the-art planning system is obvious. As equipment becomes unreliable, so does the plan. The resultant disruptions to the work flow clearly increase the total cost of producing the part and running the business in general. The additional complications to management of work in process, capacity management, and material planning add a layer of chaos to the business's operation that can only serve to defeat efforts to meet the company's growth and profitability goals.

Special-Purpose versus General-Purpose Equipment

In an effort to hedge large capital investments against future uncertainty of product mix, many companies purchase production equipment that is very general purpose, requiring complex setups in order to produce each particular part. Since one machine can produce so many different items, many may actually require the use of the same fast machine.

Viewed from the production planning viewpoint, special-purpose machines greatly simplify the scheduling and capacity management process. Contention from different parts needing the same piece of equipment at the same time is reduced. Production flow for a given product involves machines that are more or less dedicated to it, enabling production line balancing activities to be effective, reducing or eliminating setup time, cost, and problems. The effect from eliminating contention for machines means that the work load for each product line can vary independently, with a minimum of interference from each other.

Besides the advantages accruing to the ability to plan and schedule production, special-purpose machines may often cost less than their general-purpose counterparts. Training of production staff may be less, since setups are easier or nonexistent. Often, such machines can be made to be almost completely automatic, further simplifying the staffing problem.

At this writing, American manufacturing companies are beginning to examine seriously the differences between American manufacturing methods and those used by Japanese companies. One of the differences often noted is that the Japanese companies make heavy use of special-purpose, highly automatic production machinery. Often machines are capable of producing only a single part. The Japanese report that this approach greatly simplifies the operation of their plants—the planning of the work flow—increasing its reliability and level of quality achievable, since each machine can be fine-tuned for that specific item. This kind of fine tuning is almost impossible with general-purpose machinery, since it is heavily dependent on tooling, and sometimes a setup person's skill and that of the operator, to produce a consistently high-quality product.

CHAPTER 8 QUESTIONS

1. The key factor in the plant is *actual* capacity. Define capacity and explain why it is so important.

2. What really limits total plant capacity?

3. Explain the differences between long- and short-term capacity planning in terms of purposes, techniques used, and data involved.

4. Contrast resource requirements planning with rough-cut planning.

5. Describe how the different types of capacity management are interfaced to other activities in the manufacturing management process.

6. Why use planning routings to perform long-range capacity planning?

7. Where in the process should a production plan be dollarized?

8. Describe the steps involved in work center loading logic.

9. Explain the difference between the results of work center loading as reflected in work order operation records and how it is displayed on a screen or report.

10. What is an infinite load or schedule? How does it differ from a finite load?

11. What are the purposes of using a time-fence policy?

12. When should each type of loading (infinite and finite) be used? What physical events correspond to the time fence?

13. What is a gateway work center?

14. How is the lead time for an order calculated?

15. Describe the steps used in backward scheduling the operations of an order?

16. Distinguish between operation and order lead time.

17. What is the purpose of queue time?

18. Explain what occurs when queue times are compressed, and how earliest and latest start times are calculated.

19. Why does queue time reduction bring such drastic reductions in work-in-process inventory investment and in-plant lead times?

20. What are some techniques for load leveling work centers?

21. Why is short-run scheduling almost always finite? Why does the "pressure" method of attempting to increase production seldom work?

22. What are the kinds of information needed from the plant floor to control short-run schedules? Why is promptness so crucial?

23. Once an order is released to the plant floor, what does the system assume?

24. What must be done when backward scheduling produces start dates that are in the past?

25. In the forward scheduling process, how are earliest and latest completion dates calculated?

26. What is the best method for establishing work priorities in the plant? Why?

27. Under what circumstances can operation splits be used? Alternate work centers? Routings?

28. List at least four situations on the out-of-control checklist.

29. What is the objective of the dispatching function in the well-run plant?

30. List the responsibilities for:
    a. production and inventory management;
    b. production supervisor/foreman.

31. Why is the schedule relieved by standard instead of actual hours?

32. Why should work-in-process information be cycle counted?

33. Under what conditions can the scheduling system create a "logical" or non-physical assembly line?

34. What is the objective of input/output control?

35. Identify the four basic kinds of data that comprise input/output control data.

36. Assume management has embarked on a major queue time reduction program. Using input/output information, what is the first action to be taken by production control?

37. List five activities that can be controlled effectively with work order management information.

38. What are the objectives of lot and serial number traceability? Describe briefly how it is achieved.

39. What is the effect of adding traceability requirements on component part number records?

40. Assuming that work center queues exist to smooth work loads, how can management keep from having idle workers if reduced queues result in no work at a work center?

41. Explain how operation overlapping has the effect of eliminating work center queues.

42. What is the only justification for having a queue of work at a work center?

43. There are four common "pseudo" reasons for allowing work center queues in the text. List and explain each.

44. Describe the steps involved in developing and maintaining an effective queue management program.

45. What are four of the consistently reported results from effective queue management programs?

46. Define tooling, and its relationship to production equipment, operation routing records, and to work centers.

47. In production environments where tooling is a production factor, what are the elements of a complete tool management subsystem?

48. Why can tooling be a serious schedule disrupter if not effectively managed?

49. What is the most basic aspect of vendor-performed processing?

50. How can regularly performed vendor processing be included as a normal part of the planning process?

51. Why is a special type of purchase order required for vendor-performed processing?

52. Where does the vendor's charge for work performed get charged for product costing purposes? For invoice control purposes?

53. Why is vendor-performed processing often one of the most heavily expedited areas in a manufacturing plant?

54. Why must preventive maintenance be scheduled?

55. What are the consequences of failing to plan, budget, and effectively manage preventive maintenance programs in a manufacturing plant?

56. What is the most important single objective of plant layout?

57. Briefly explain what is involved in production balancing, and why it is important even in a random work center plant.

58. What is the impact on the schedule and productivity of overloading production machinery (i.e., running it faster than it is designed to run)?

59. A company can acquire special purpose or general purpose production equipment. Explain the advantages and disadvantages of each.

9

Measuring Performance— Closing All the Loops

The preceding chapters have covered the nature and function of the data base used by a computer-based information system to manage a manufacturing company. Chapters 7 and 8 discussed in detail the techniques used to develop and maintain detailed plans for all resources used in the manufacturing process. In keeping with the thrust of this book, heavy emphasis was placed on the computer functions, since these constitute the most important aspect of a highly automated management environment.

In this chapter the discussion will be centered on using this active data base to develop a variety of control techniques to be used by management in measuring the performance of the company, as compared to its plans, to identify problem areas for special attention, and to evaluate the effectiveness of actions by key managerial functions. Since the entire concept of the systems described thus far is to develop a detailed plan covering all significant activity in the plant, control emphasis is placed on comparing the planned activity with the actual events as reported to the system. These comparisons of planned versus actual events can be made at many levels of detail throughout the system and can form an extremely effective method of controlling what actually goes on in the company to a degree not even conceivable in the past. It is perhaps here that the power of a computer system becomes most apparent.

THE PERFORMANCE MEASUREMENT PROCESS

In the past, management was forced to rely more or less on reports prepared by managers themselves, or by their staff. People largely reported their own activities, with only a modicum of cross-checking of results really possible.

Month-end accounting reports formed the most common company-wide reporting technique that was independent of individual managers. As was discussed in Chapter 2, these are characteristics of an informal system environment.

A fully developed manufacturing resources planning and control system is definitely a formal system. As a result, it provides a more objective, standardized method of reporting than is possible under an informal system. Under an informal system, personal trust of key managers is a vital ingredient, and where absent, is often a source of serious problems. Although trust is certainly an important ingredient under a formal system and to the effective management of any company, the reporting of results becomes less dependent on the reliability of any one individual. Consequently, as a company evolves into a more formal system environment, a pronounced shift of management emphasis is required for the system to become a full success.

A closed-loop system is one in which constant comparisons between planned and actual events are made. Figure 9-1 graphically illustrates this process. Causes for deviations between planned and actual results invariably lie either in the execution of the plan, or with a problem in the plan itself. Without this comparison process, or without accurate actual data, the planning system is just an order-launching system, a statement of what management would like to have happen.

This is one part of the system that must actually be performed by people. The computer system itself can only compensate to a degree by adjusting its planned quantities, dates, and so on, when actual events do not correspond to its original plan. The computer cannot get people to do things except in the presence of clear direction from management. It cannot ensure that people feed it accurate, timely data, that they follow the plan instead of some personal agenda, that they perform their jobs competently, or similar factors critical to the success of a manufacturing company.

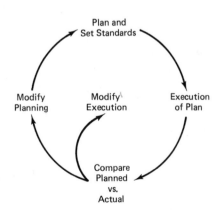

FIGURE 9-1   Closed-loop performance
measurement.

Management emphasis shifts, under a formal system, toward a number of specific areas, each of which is discussed briefly in the following paragraphs. Each of these areas is related to the others, and they can have a common goal of ensuring that the system functions to maximum effectiveness as a powerful communications tool containing numerous automatic features, such as planned order generation and detail operation sequencing of work in the plant.

Ensuring Ongoing Planning

Since the system is a dynamic, responsive one, keyed to the day-to-day flux of actual events, it is critical that planning in detail be an ongoing activity. The annual, quarterly, or monthly production planning of the past, when applied to a state-of-the-art manufacturing system, will yield mediocre results and be found to make producing to plan a difficult process at best. As one moves from the general to the detail level of the system, that this activity be ongoing becomes progressively more critical.

Even at the level of sales forecasting, it is important that the forecast be revised and updated frequently. The old annual or semiannual forecasts of the past, which become progressively more useless during the year, simply will not work in a state-of-the-art system environment. Management's top priority then, is ensuring that the planning activity be done continuously, be of a consistently high quality, and be carefully performed. Only then can the system perform its automatic functions to assist in this process.

Ensuring Accurate, Timely Data

Closely coupled with the importance of the planning activity is ensuring that management's overall plans are correctly translated into data input into the system, especially at the master scheduling level. Similarly, the entire performance measurement process depends totally on the presence of a detailed, highly accurate, and up-to-the-minute flow of information about actual events.

In this area, it is vital that management establish effective policies and procedures to ensure that this flow of data is correct. These policies must also be reflected in the evaluation of a specific individual's job performance, be coupled to the reward system used by the company, and where it falls short, be a cause for reprimand or other disciplinary action just as much as stealing material or goofing off on the job is. Failure of a given department supervisor, work center foreman, or planner to manage data in their area will invariably have sizable consequences elsewhere in the company. This sensitivity and interrelatedness of company functions under a formal system environment needs to be appropriately recognized by company-wide policies if optimum results are to be achieved.

Understanding Automatic Functions

There is an inherent tendency in a highly computerized environment for people to end up with little understanding of how or why the system performs the way it does. This is an abdication of management responsibility. Since the computer cannot itself decide whether it is right or wrong, people must. This process of abdication has often been aided by data processing personnel who wish to serve their own interests, to preserve their strength of position in the company, so that they can become the "witch doctor" of management, to name a few motives.

Since managers must understand what it is that they are being held responsible for, they must understand equally those functions over which they have direct, right-now control, and those which are performed more or less automatically. To accept anything less is a cop-out, an abdication of responsibility. It will merely provide a convenient excuse for failure.

This understanding of system functions falls into two areas: a detailed understanding of system functions in the areas directly affecting a manager's area, and a more general understanding of all other related system functions. These functions can be clearly documented in noncomputer terms, as this book illustrates. For full system effectiveness, managers must not only be responsible for understanding how the system works, but for specifying new functions, changes to logic, and how the data are to be used. Data processing is simply the handmaiden in this management process, and cannot be responsible for specifying how the system is to work.

Controlling System Interfaces

Even though a state-of-the-art system is highly integrated, there are functional areas that are more or less independent, corresponding to the different managerial areas of responsibility within the company. It is important that each of these areas be clearly identified with a specific management function, such as purchasing. Each function, then, becomes responsible for certain data fields in the records maintained by that function. The points of interface with other functional elements of the overall system require management coordination as with any other interdepartmental interface. Each must understand the effects of its actions on the other areas.

A more specific part of controlling system interfaces is the issue of system security. In an on-line environment, many people have instant access to the data base and may perform a wide variety of functions. Clearly, a state-of-the-art system includes a sophisticated security system allowing management to designate who may access which files and programs. Since unauthorized access to the data base is a potential problem of significant consequence, management must ensure that the area of system security is controlled properly.

Communicating via System Data

Another tendency left over from less formal system days is that of ignoring data in the system, using an informal technique, the telephone, face-to-face conversations, memos, and so on, to communicate matters that really involve data in the system, due dates, order quantities, part number effectivities, and the like.

It is important that management cause the system to be a central tool for the operation of the business by requiring that reports be generated from the data base, and that all actions involving system data be communicated by entry into the records maintained by the system.

In early batch systems, this was often impractical to do. The results were that the production plans tended to become out of date, costs became wrong, and other disturbing results ensued. In an on-line environment, accuracy becomes much simpler. In fact, some versions of state-of-the-art system emphasize communicating within the system by adding action files, message handling, and electronic "in-baskets" to the system's design. Thus, if a scheduler simply logs on to the system, he automatically gets all his messages, and the system remains up to date at the same time.

Management by Limits, Tolerances, and Exceptions

Management by exception is hardly a new management technique. However, it acquires special significance in a state-of-the-art system environment. Since the information pyramid concept allows reporting at the summary level from a large base of detailed information, for the first time management can operate by specifying quantitative limits to operational data, then use computer-generated reporting mechanisms to signal out-of-tolerance conditions.

If this concept of managing is to reach its full effectiveness, clearly management must have a detailed understanding of how the system works, the data that are maintained, and what different data mean when they are reviewed by a program that generates an exception or out-of-tolerance condition report. Since the amount of information that is really involved in running a sizable manufacturing facility of any complexity is truly enormous, there really is no other feasible means to ensure good management control. The importance of this technique thus becomes truly central. The discussion that follows in this chapter will detail how this process is performed and include several examples.

Use of Cross-Checks and Reconciliations

Since the state-of-the-art system is highly integrated, it becomes possible to develop auditing mechanisms whereby the total of one activity, such as material received, can be meaningfully compared to material paid for through accounts payable. Other examples include reconciling material moved to and from the production floor with actual stock still in work centers and reconciling hours reported as direct-to-work orders to amounts paid to production employees. In the past, differences in the way the same information was handled from one department to another made this kind of reconciliation process cumbersome and therefore was seldom performed. As any banker will testify, however, the use of cross-checks and reconciliation techniques is a potent tool in gaining control of the business's information, especially in the financial area.

Continuous System Improvements

Even though much of the information presented in this book and elsewhere is often interpreted as being the last word in how advanced systems tools can be used to improve the management of the business, the truth is that there is no such thing as a state-of-the-art system in the sense that it is ever completed.

Enlightened management includes, together with its ongoing program of other business improvements, continuing efforts, budgets, and personnel devoted to improving the system's design, revamping critical functions, and making the logic used internally by the system more consistent with the current day-to-day reality experienced by the business.

This sort of ongoing effort to improve continually the operation of the system is really no different from other programs that are intended to increase the productivity, competitive posture, and overall effectiveness of the business.

The goal of performance measurement, then, is to ensure consistent, high-quality planning by measuring the effectiveness of the company's performance to the plan, the effectiveness of the plan itself, and by clearly identifying areas in the company where there is a significant divergence between planned and actual events.

THE INFORMATION BASIS OF A CLOSED LOOP

Most often, performance measurements are presented at a very general level, such as planned versus actual gross sales. This level of information is useful, but only as a general confirmation or denial that the activity being compared is at an acceptable level of performance. It cannot do more than merely point management's attention in a particular direction, nor can it serve as the basis for any serious corrective action.

The general form of what will be referred to here as the performance measurement formula is as follows:

$$\frac{\text{Gross actual activity}}{\text{Planned level}} \times 100 = \text{performance } \%$$

A commonly acceptable tolerance level for this type of general performance measurement is ±5%. In many cases, however, a much finer tolerance may be required. In measuring the accuracy of inventory on-hand balances, a goal of 98% accuracy and a tolerance level of 5% could lead to the conclusion that a 93% accuracy level would be perfectly acceptable, which is definitely not the case. This would be tantamount to saying that it is perfectly all right that 7% of the part numbers in the system can be erroneously planned, an event that would be guaranteed to hobble the planning system seriously.

When the totals used in the general performance measurement formula above are derived from the results of a record-by-record comparison at a much lower level of detail, the purposes of the general measurements are served, and the basis for any corrective action or changes to planning methodology is well founded.

Developing a Detailed Performance Measurement

Illustrated in Figure 9-2 is an hypothetical example of a performance measurement performed in detail at the record level. The record could be a part record, with inventory or scrap data, an order, or an operation record. The quantity information could be quantity completed, scrap, shipments, or other data. The logic of the comparison is similar in each case. The information shown in the first three columns would be resident in the record, while the two variance columns would be calculated for purposes of the performance report.

The first variance calculation is simply the actual quantity less the planned. The calculation is set up to produce a positive variance when actual is greater than planned. In some cases, such as where the goal is to achieve a minimum level, it may be desirable to reverse this calculation to show that an excess of actual over planned is a negative result. Notice that since the absolute size of the data in both the planned and actual columns varies widely from one record to the next, the result is a wide difference between the sizes of the variances. By converting each to a percentage, these differences are reduced to a more standard form that can be used to select only those records that exceed the allowed tolerance figure.

At the bottom is a statistical summary of the results of the analysis. The

Detailed	Part Number, Order, or Operation Record	Planned Quantity	Actual Quantity	Variance Quantity Actual − Planned	Variance % $\frac{\text{Var. Qty}}{\text{Pl. Qty}} \times 100$
	1	140	145	+5	+3%
	2	230	250	+20	+8%
	3	75	53	−22	−29%
	4	60	60	0	0
	5	210	270	+60	+29%
	6	180	195	+15	+8%
	N				
Totals		895	973		

Summary		
	Mean Variation %	= 3.2%
	One Standard Deviation	= 18.7%
	Range: −29% to +29%	
	Total Variation	= +78
	Total Variation %	= 9%

FIGURE 9-2   Developing a measurement summary.

sample size (number of records included) is too small in this example to yield really meaningful statistical data, but will serve to illustrate several points about the process:

- A mean average, which includes an allowance for the size of the variation between records, is used instead of the simple arithmetical average, which does not. The mean calculation formula's results are not changed as much as a simple average is by the presence of a single very large value in the data.

- Although the range of the variance percentages is from -29% to $+29\%$, a single standard deviation of 18.7% reveals that two-thirds of them fell within a range of $\pm 18.7\%$. Given the small population size, as the statisticians call it, this information does not reveal much here, but with large numbers of records in the analysis, it definitely would.

- Even though the mean variance percentage is relatively small, 3.2%, the range is quite large. If the range were not included in the analysis, some important problems might be obscured. An inquisitive manager probably would want to know why these extremes coexist with more well-controlled results.

- If the entire analysis was performed in a manner that is commonly used, at the gross total level, completely different results are obtained. Adding the total planned quantities and total actual quantities and calculating the variance at this point yields a 9% total variance percent. This result is misleading, as an examination of each record discloses. It is a by-product completely of the absolute sizes of the quantities, and as such is quite affected by these differences. Thus a single record with a numerically large difference, although a small percentage, will cause this figure to be distorted.

    Given the type of data used in the analysis, and the range of different quantities in the planned quantity column, a total variation quantity of $+78$ is a meaningless number; it tells nothing of value about the data it summarizes. The point here is not that the 9% figure is worse than the 3.2% figure. It could just as easily have been the reverse. The point is that it does not convey the correct information about the behavior of the data included in the analysis. It is just a number, nothing more.

- The analysis is actually performed at the record level. Each record's comparison stands on its own and can be selected individually if its variance percent falls outside a specified tolerance limit. In the example, a tolerance percent of 10% might be selected, which would yield a list of records 3 and 5 and the same totals for the entire set of records. It is at this level that investigation of problem areas must actually occur. The analysis may be said to be item specific; it yields totals, but can specifically identify records (and the corresponding physical reality) that caused the totals to be the way they are.

Although it is not the purpose of this chapter to get into a detailed discussion of statistical theory (and none is needed) it is important to grasp the basic fact that a range of physical event values do tend to be grouped around a mean. The result, when plotted, is the familiar (to statisticians, anyway) normal distribution curve, illustrated in Figure 9-3. One may ask why one should use this ap-

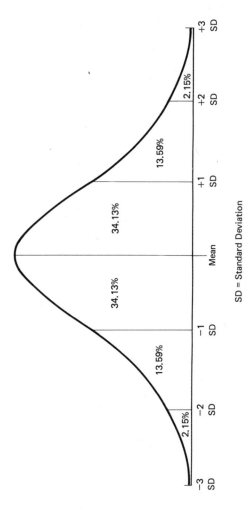

SD = Standard Deviation

FIGURE 9-3   The normal distribution curve.

proach in a business management context. The answer is simple: so that managers can focus their attention and priorities on the real problems, as revealed by a performance measurement, instead of chasing pseudoproblems or ignoring significant ones.

This important point needs some emphasis. Suppose that the numbers in the example were sizes of parts, all produced by the same machine, with the variances being the actual physical differences between the design dimensions and what the machine actually produced. It is entirely possible that if only averages were used, neglecting the range and deviation information, an acceptable average tolerance would result, even if not one of the parts were actually within its individual tolerances. In this case, it is absolutely critical to perform the analysis on an item-by-item basis, converting each to a standard unit such as percent, to highlight that a real problem exists with this machine. The point here is that this analogy holds for virtually all information that would normally be used for a performance measurement in a company; it is just a fact of physical reality.

Sources of Data

There are two primary sources of data that are used in a performance measurement. In the first, both the planned and actual information are maintained internally, such as from the planned order generation process and actual work order completions. In this case the performance measurement is simply a computer program that reads all the records and performs its analysis. In other cases, a specific effort is required to gather the actual data, such as with a cycle counting program. These data may or may not be input to the system where it is maintained for periodic analysis. If it is, then once entered, the analysis is simply the same type of computer program as in the first case; it reads each record and performs its analysis.

Performance Measurement Results

In countless small ways everyone makes value judgments concerning events in their environment. Business management is no exception. In each case the observation of actual events is matched, often unconsciously, with a belief about how things should have been. If there is no such belief, a judgment is not possible.

In the past, and still in many businesses, operations are evaluated with this same semiconscious approach. The planned part of the judgment action, the belief about how it should have been, is often a poorly arrived at piece of the equation, often being based on hunch, past events, "experience," or other nonobjective information. Or simple totals of an actual activity may be reviewed with little explicit comparison to any original plan of action. If sales are up a lot, then everything must be okay, right? Not necessarily, as the company may in fact be out of control and headed for a serious cash or capacity shortage.

The outcome of the kind of logical, objectively based performance measurement approach presented here are as rational judgments concerning the operation of the business. As such they are freer than the results of other approaches from the personal, subjective, or politically based judgments that creep in with subjective techniques. By using the large data base maintained by a state-of-the-art system as the starting point, a sizable number of performance measurements become possible. In each case, an important area of the business is examined according to clear rules, matched to goals, and the outcome is an indicator of how well things are going in that area. The result is greatly reduced finger-pointing, blaming of others, and disagreements over how good or bad things really are.

Since the goal of a planning-oriented system is to make virtually all decisions concerning the business during the construction of the plan rather than in the physical reality of the warehouse and plant floor, it follows that the adequacy of the plan itself is a point of major concern. It is the focus of performance measurement, the starting point. All the specific kinds of performance measurements discussed in the following paragraphs are designed to disclose first, that a problem may or may not exist in that area of the company. The cause of the variance, if significantly different from goals, will either be an error in the planning process or difficulties in executing the plan.

If the performance measurement is carried out using the approach described above, it will also yield clear, specific information concerning exactly where the problem is, what its nature is, and with some investigation at times, what needs to be done to improve the result.

The actions driven by the outcome of the performance measurement process include the following:

- Modify planning logic or data used in the plan.
- Make policy or procedural changes to the execution side of the business, improve controls, reassign responsibilities, change job responsibilities or personnel.
- Decide that no changes are needed; the results are good, within acceptable limits, and further improvements would be impractical or have a low priority for the business.
- Even though results are within targeted tolerances, try to improve performance by narrowing the target tolerance or range of acceptable performance.

Finally, even though a state-of-the-art system using effective, well-thought-out performance measurement techniques to analyze system data is in place, nothing will improve unless management *acts* on the information available. Only management that is committed to long-term improvement of the business's performance will find performance measurement to be a powerful tool in this process. For the less committed, interested only in short-term results, performance measurement will be less useful.

The Traditional Accounting Viewpoint

Before proceeding to examine specific areas for performance measurement, some of the methods used by traditional accounting in many companies should be addressed. Many of these accounting-oriented control systems have served their companies well, but it is just as often that one finds accounting data riddled with inaccurate information, identifying a problem area but failing to provide guidance for fixing it, or just plain too late to be useful.

Because accounting historically has revolved around a transaction-oriented set of general ledger accounts, many types of information were developed by dollarizing the transactions themselves for a given period of activity, such as a month. At month-end, the transactions are totaled up, journal entries created, and closed to cost of goods sold or another account.

Figure 9-4 illustrates an example of two different ways to develop a material usage variance dollar amount. On the left side is the traditional accounting approach, where each material issue and production completion transaction is extended individually. By using only the material standard cost for the completed parts, the assumed value added by production is separated, focusing on the material content of the finished item, which theoretically should equal the sum of all the material issued and used in its production.

In an actual accounting system, each of these two types of transactions would be posted as opposite entries to the variance account. The balance remaining in the account would be either a debit or credit balance and would thus reflect a total positive or negative variance.

On the other side of the illustration is an example of how material usage data are obtained from closed work order records, using the component/requirement record data. The planned order explosion process creates the planned quantities of each component part, while actual quantities of each part are posted by the system to the component records together with the inventory records' on-hand balance. To keep the example simple, it is assumed that the planned order quantity and the actual quantity completed are equal. If they were not, a simple adjustment would be required for each of the issue quantities, a "reexplosion," in effect.

Both methods yield a material usage variance dollar amount that can be posted to the ledger accounts and closed to cost of goods sold. The accounting method used the raw transactions, whereas the systems management method, if it may be so named, develops the variance in specific terms that mirror actual reality on the production floor. Consistent variances associated with specific components on a certain assembly would indicate either a product structure error, or unplanned scrap in the production process. This information would be much more difficult to obtain, if it could be obtained at all, from the accounting viewpoint example.

Material Issue Transactions
(Quantity × Standard Cost)

Each Closed Work Order's
Component Records:

P/N	Quantity Required	Quantity Issued	Unit Standard Cost	Usage Variance Quantity	Variance Cost
A	10	12	$10	2	$20
B	8	9	$ 6	1	$ 6
C	12	12	$15	0	0
D	10	9	$ 7	−7	$−7
					$19

Less:

Production Completion Transactions
(Quantity × Material Standard Cost)

Material Usage Variance $ Amount

= Material Usage Variance
$ Amount

FIGURE 9-4   The accounting versus systems management viewpoints.

Additionally, the information obtained from the work order component records is available more or less continuously rather than only at the end of an accounting period. Corrective action is a more natural part of the day-to-day flow of the business. In the example here, what is actually going on is that the system, since it is a mirror of reality, traps information in terms of that reality, part numbers, orders, and specific quantities. The accounting approach, on the other hand, works only with dollars, and there are no dollars in the plant, only parts and orders.

In addition, the accounting approach may build in an assumption that the product structure information is correct and that it is a report of unplanned scrap or poor control in the plant, when in fact this might not be the case at all.

In a state-of-the-art system environment, then, the work order records would be used to develop the material usage variance information in detail, part number by part number, presenting only those parts that exceeded a certain, specified tolerance, with the resulting totals being dollarized for posting to the general ledger as part of the closing process to develop cost of goods sold for the profit and loss statement.

IMPROVING PRIMARY DATA BASE ACCURACY

There are a variety of performance measurement and closed-loop comparison techniques available in a state-of-the-art system to measure the accuracy of the primary production data base, which is the foundation of the entire planning and control system. Figure 9–5 illustrates in symbolic form the relationships

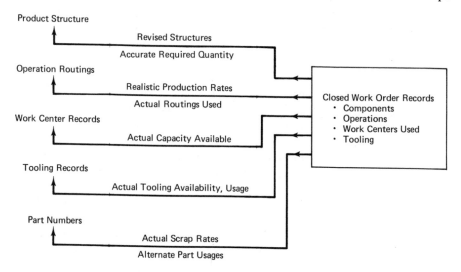

FIGURE 9-5   Improving the primary data base.

between the closed work order records and the kinds of feedback information that can be developed to purge the primary data base of errors and inaccuracies. Some of these analyses are somewhat involved, as far as a computer program is concerned, but are not difficult to understand. Although there is some overlap, each of the five areas will be considered separately.

Product Structures

One common demand source "leak" is alternate component usage, that is, the use of a part number that is not specified in the product structure in place of one that is; or, even worse, a part number that is actually used, but should not be, in the product structure. Some companies have gotten control of the situation by simply not authorizing the warehouse to issue any part that is not on a system-prepared picking list without the approval of the manufacturing engineer responsible for that product structure. This results in "forcing" either the product structure to become corrected or the correct part to be used in production.

A comparison of actual versus planned part numbers and quantities used in the component records of closed work orders will disclose a variety of product structure errors and/or production problems. These include planned versus actual scrap, quantities required errors, some types of quality problems, alternate part usage, and obsolete product structures (that never get used in the planning process and should be purged from the files). Also possible is a measurement of how quickly engineering changes are introduced and whether work in process is being disrupted by engineering changes.

The primary objective of these comparisons is to provide information used to make the product structure records become more in line with actual plant events, so that the planning process will be more reflective of what is actually going on in production.

Operation Routings

The operation routing records associated with closed work orders can be analyzed for differences between planned and actual production rates by part number and work center. Although there is always room for debate in this area, it is important that the planning system use production rates that are actually experienced, so that the detailed operation sequencing and work center loading will be accurate. Fixing a productivity problem in one or more work centers may also be appropriate action for parts experiencing significant deviations in production rate, but in the meantime it is important that the planning be realistic.

Work center activity is also available from this source, and can be used to compare planned versus actual work center capacity. A work center may have a standard work crew of, say, 10 men, but if only 7 show up every day on the average, then the planned capacity in hours based on the regular availability of

10 men will be in error and the work center will consistently be overloaded by the loading and scheduling functions, leading to bottlenecks and delays.

Inaccuracies in the routing files can be detected by identifying both operations that are never used in the plant (that never have any activity reported to them), or where unplanned operations are consistently required to produce the item. Consistent use of work centers other than the planned ones can be identified either in the records themselves or by comparisons with the master routing.

Information developed from work order records is one of the most valuable sources for improving the accuracy and reliability of the data base used by capacity management and the detailed operation sequencing programs. Inaccuracies in these data will produce corresponding inaccuracies in capacity plans and work schedules.

Work Centers

Actual data available from completed operation records can aid in determining work center capacity, already mentioned, identify attendance problems, and unplanned machine downtime. Also, the planned operation routings may assume that a certain labor pay grade is to be used in the production of a part within a given work center. Actual data from the completed operations can disclose that higher- or lower-paid personnel were employed in making the part, affecting labor planning and product costing.

Since unplanned machine downtime is a major cause of production disruptions, the effectiveness of a preventive maintenance program can be evaluated by comparing planned downtime rates (i.e., expected surprise failures) with the actual downtime from both scheduled and unscheduled sources.

Tooling

Another source of production delays and scheduling disruptions is unexpected nonavailability of tooling. By comparing actual tooling issues reported to operations with the planned tooling used in the routings, errors in the routings can be detected and corrected. Reported delays due to tooling nonavailability can be compared against quantities of tooling on hand and in an issued status and compared in turn against a targeted minimum rate.

Especially important is the detection of tooling that is actually required in the production of an item, but that is not shown as required in the routing and tooling reference records. If this linkage does not exist for a tool, the demand for it will be understated and its usage planning will be in error. Similarly, including tooling in the routings that never gets used will cause excess tooling to be procured, (or made) and stocked. Every unplanned tool issue is a potential source of disruptions, as some type of error exists in the primary data base.

Part Numbers

Several areas of inaccuracy associated with part number records can be identified by comparing work order records with product structure records, and/or comparing product structure records with the part master records. Of particular interest is the identification of obsolete stock. Part numbers that have no where-used linkage are not used, or at least are not being planned. If these parts are in fact being used in work orders, their planning will be in error, since they are not included in a product structure. This can be another variation of the alternate component usage problem.

Besides concerns about the accuracy of the material planning process, there may be additional concerns about the consistency of the end item's configuration, since a high rate of alternate part usage indicates that either the product is not being made as designed, or that various configurations are being shipped, with a possible serious impact on product quality. In highly engineered products, configuration control may be a vital issue.

Scrap rates really fall into two areas, individual component scrap and that of the entire completed assembly. Consistent variations in component usage in the production of a part that do not correlate with over- or under-runs of the order quantity indicate a product structure error and/or production problem. If the completed quantity on work orders consistently is more or less than the planned order quantity, and the actual components issued is approximately equal to the planned quantities, the scrap rate contained in the part master record may be in error. This rate is used to inflate the planned order quantity so that production will end up with the planned quantity of acceptable parts. If the scrap rate in the part record is wrong, the planned order quantity will be incorrectly inflated.

In summary, then, the work order record set serves as a major collection point for planned versus actual events in the planning and production process. Among the most important sets of comparisons that can be made are those that can lead to improved accuracy in the primary data base used by the planning systems.

OPERATIONS-ORIENTED PERFORMANCE MEASUREMENTS

Forecasting and the Master Production Schedule

Most of the factors relating to this important interface were discussed in Chapter 3. A performance measure of how well the forecasting information is being used, and how accurate it is, can be obtained from the following three simpler measurements:

- Forecasted quantities versus actual shipments

- Forecasted quantities versus MPS quantities
- The frequency of MPS changes within the planning lead time, as measured by the percentage of purchase orders that are placed with due dates in less than the stated lead time, and by the percentage of work orders that are scheduled into a past due condition (past due start dates at time of order generation)

Purchasing Performance

In evaluating purchasing performance it is important to remember that the key activity is purchase order line items, not the complete purchase order itself, which may cover a long list of items. Figure 9–6 illustrates some of the more important performance measurements that can be derived from purchase order records, and the data sources from which they are derived. Since the purchasing function is responsible for managing the company/vendor interface, performance of vendors should be included as well.

These measurements fall into three basic categories, the placement activity itself (i.e., how well purchasing is able to cover requirements generated by the planned order process), cost variances, and vendor performance.

In most cases with purchasing activity data, the planned part of the measurement is simply a target, or goal, and the actual part of the data is what is derived from the system itself. However, there are some planned activity assumptions implicit in several cases. The existence of requirements assumes that they will be covered with orders. Standard costs are the planned costs. Lead times for procurement action are planning targets.

One key measure of effectiveness of purchasing activity is how well it is able to cover requirements. This can be determined by taking the percentage of parts in the system with uncovered requirements that are within the procurement lead times. These are guaranteed problem cases, although they may be caused ultimately by MPS actions within lead time. If the lead times are true, there is almost no way the supplier can be on time.

Closely related to the covering of requirements is the percentage of purchase order line items that get changed, so the ratio of purchase order change

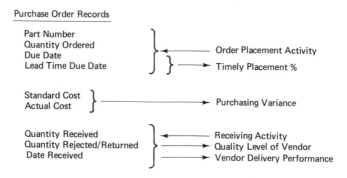

FIGURE 9-6   Purchasing-performance data.

actions to initial purchase order placements is a guide to how disruptive MPS changes are, the accuracy of the detail planning system in general, and the ability of procurement actions to keep up with the planning cycle.

Purchasing cost variances are fairly straightforward. Either the standard cost is unrealistic, or the buyer was not able to obtain favorable terms. Some review of these data is important, as its causes may lie in premium prices being paid for inside lead time purchases, unfavorable order quantities, special requirements for labeling or packaging, or other custom treatment not assumed at the time the standard cost was set.

In one case in the author's experience, a company costed and priced a special customized version of its regular catalog products at standard costs. The result was an appearance of profitability in this line of business in spite of the fact that many custom components and packaging items were bought at higher prices than standard. In reality this part of the business was a money loser.

In the receiving area information is available in the system to compare due dates versus actual delivery dates, received versus ordered quantities, and quality information, including rejections, marginal products (barely acceptable only after an in-company engineering review of the shipment), and actual returns to the vendor.

In the purchasing area it is important for management to set performance goals in those areas where direct planned versus actual comparisons are not very straightforward. It is important that ongoing efforts be made to investigate discrepancies identified by the performance measurement process and actions initiated to improve the results where problems are indicated. The benefits to the company can be substantial.

Warehouse Management

Like many other areas in a manufacturing company, operation of the warehouse can often be an Achilles' heel, in that if it is well run, no one notices, and if it is not, the ramifications can be substantial. Poor physical control of material can result in significant planning errors, lost stock, production disruptions, unplanned scrap, quality control problems, and just plain confusion in the business.

A state-of-the-art information system contains a great deal of information that can be used to evaluate the effectiveness of warehouse management. There is an additional advantage in that the nature of the information focuses the performance measurement on results achieved by warehouse management.

The warehouse is the company's material bank, often containing more dollar value than many banks actually have on deposit. It is mute testimony to the now outdated values and assumptions of management (mentioned earlier) that this value often goes unperceived, and is frequently managed in a very loose, casual manner that does not reflect either the size of the financial investment or its importance position with respect to the effective management of the company.

No bank would tolerate errors in its accounts approaching 1%, yet many sizable manufacturing companies have inventory information systems where only 50 or 60% of the on-hand balances are correct, and where large adjustments to the book value of inventory are routinely made at year-end. One of the chief physical control points for a bank is the teller operation, where elaborate procedural controls ensure a virtual 100% accuracy rate for transactions and account balances.

The warehouse operation in a manufacturing and distribution company is equivalent to the bank's teller operation. If accurate records (essential for the planning process), a low material loss rate, and efficient support of production are to be achieved, procedural controls with "tightness" approaching those used by banks are required and have a similar or greater payoff for the company.

Several key performance measurements of the warehouse operation are discussed below, including effectiveness of cycle counting, stock picking effectiveness, unplanned stockouts due to record inaccuracies, and warehouse scrap.

Cycle counting results: Chapter 6 discussed cycle counting programs, their effectiveness, and the advantages of cycle counting compared to the wall-to-wall physical count method of confirming on-hand balances. As discussed earlier, the cycle counting activity is of little value if improperly performed, so close monitoring of its effectiveness via several measurements is a legitimate upper-middle management activity.

Figure 9–7 contains an example of a cycle counting report. Each part to be counted is scheduled, using either a planned count interval, number of transactions, or some other basis. The actual date of counting is recorded, as is the on-hand balance of record on that date and the actual count quantity. From these basic data the system can produce reports of the cycle counting activity, including physical count and dollar variances, percentage of accurate records, and whether the counting activity is on schedule.

The basic performance measurement formula for cycle counting is:

$$\frac{\text{Parts correct}}{\text{Parts counted}} \times 100 = \text{Inventory accuracy}$$

This formula serves as a gross indicator of the effectiveness of the inventory record-keeping function, including transaction control (all movements correctly documented) and data entry (all transactions correctly entered and posted).

Additional focus is needed, however, to sharpen management's attention. A report showing the relative size of adjustments entered after a cycle count, using the data shown in Figure 9–7, are important. Numerous small adjustments indicate a different control problem than a few very large ones. Some will be

Part Number	Unit Cost	Planned Count Date	Actual Count Date	Record On-Hand Quantity	Quantity Counted	Count* Variance Quantity	Count Variance $ Amount
A	$12	10/7	10/15	450	375	−75	−$900
B	$23	10/7	10/7	823	823	0	0
C	$ 5	10/7	10/9	265	351	+86	+$430
					Net Total Variance		−$470

*Variance = Counted − Record On-Hand Quantity

FIGURE 9-7   Cycle counting results report—example.

part dependent, reflecting difficulties in obtaining accurate counts or in identifying the parts correctly. Both the physical quantity variation and the dollar size of the adjustment need to be reviewed, as they are independent to some extent.

Another factor bearing on record accuracy is the volume of transactions. If a part experiences a high volume of transactions, it will tend to have more errors than a part number having a low volume of transactions. High-transaction-volume parts that have a chronic accuracy problem, as identified by the performance measurement process, will be candidates for steps such as improved labeling, double counting, or other control procedures.

Since merely comparing those parts actually counted tells only part of the story, comparing counts scheduled with those actually performed is important. If the cycle counting program is to be fully effective, it must stay on schedule so that the assumptions behind the counting intervals do not become meaningless. In this area a performance measurement formula such as the following will be useful:

$$\frac{\text{Scheduled counts}}{\text{Actual counts}} \times 100 = \text{Counting schedule performance}$$

This measurement will assist in determining whether cycle counting staff is adequate, whether they are doing their work, and whether the assumption that the parts counted reflect the current accuracy of the entire inventory record population is true. Cycle counting is, after all, a sampling process even if in the long run all parts are counted.

In this same vein, a performance measurement showing parts counted compared with the total number of inventory records will indicate the degree to which management may have confidence in the inventory record data, as verified by the cycle counting program.

Finally, the entire cycle counting program is easier to run and has a higher degree of accuracy where inventory movement transactions are posted immediately in an on-line environment, since reconciliation of physical counts and unposted transactions is eliminated from the cycle counter's task.

Stock picking control: In some companies there is no clear standard for how long the warehouse should take to pick stock, stage it, and move it to the production area. Often there is much expediting of "hot" work orders. Another variation is that the order releasing cycle generates picking lists, which sit in the warehouse supervisor's desk until someone asks for the material from a production department. Either case is undesirable.

The objective of stock picking control is to ensure that a stable, minimum time elapses between order release and the start of production on a work order. This time period represents a form of inventory float which, beyond the minimum, provides little benefit to the company. A report measuring this activity might resemble Figure 9-8, where several released orders are examined.

The basis for comparison in the example is that a standard has been set of 16 hours for the picking, staging, and issuance of all material for each work order to production. Both dates and times are shown since using only dates fails to provide enough visibility and would obscure some problems. In actuality, such a standard might be substantially less than the 16 hours used in the example.

The results of the stock picking control report indicate that either the standard is optimistic or that some control problems exist, since only two of the six orders were processed within the standard. Order number 12 clearly encountered a problem, such as lost material, a temporary stockout, or something else preventing its complete staging.

The report illustrates the basic process of performance measurement. Gather data at the detail level, summarize them for review, then use specific items that exceed the measurement tolerances at the detail as the basis for investigation. The outcome of this process (especially if performed regularly) will be an improved understanding of the operation being measured, confirmation of the degree of control that actually exists as well as assumptions used

Work Order Number	Order Release Date/Time		Material Issue Date/Time		Elapsed Time, Hours	Variation from Standard
10	8/16	8:00 AM	8/16	3:00 PM	7	+ 9
11	8/16	8:00 AM	8/17	9:00 AM	17	− 1
12	8/16	3:00 PM	8/20	10:00 AM	59	−43
13	8/17	8:00 AM	8/17	1:00 PM	5	+11
14	8/17	8:00 AM	8/19	10:00 AM	18	− 2
15	8/17	1:00 PM	8/18	6:00 PM	21	− 5

Average Elapsed Time = 25.4 Hours
Average Variation   = −6.2 Hours

Assume:
- 2 shift, 16 hour days (8 a.m. to midnight)
- Standard picking time is 16 hours
- Report date/time is 8/20, 11:00 a.m.
- Variance = standard minus elapsed time

FIGURE 9-8   Stock picking control report.

elsewhere by management and the system, and continual improvement in the operation itself. The process is essentially a structured method of focusing attention where it is needed, and a communication process for improving efficiency.

Unplanned stockout rate: This measurement is more of a goal-setting process than a comparison of planned versus actual. The goal, of course, is to have zero unplanned stockouts, that is, no situations where the inventory record showed that stock was on hand when in fact there was none, or it could not be found. Since it is partly an indicator of record accuracy, it is closely related to the cycle counting performance measurement process. In addition, it may be an indicator of inaccuracies in a locator system, such that the stock is in the warehouse but cannot be found in a reasonable time period.

Since an unplanned stockout can cause a serious disruption of the planning and detail scheduling process, even a low level of unplanned stockouts should be taken seriously by management. Two forms in which this measurement can be presented include:

- The number of unplanned stockouts per month or week
- The percentage of unplanned stockouts to total part numbers issued during the period

Warehouse scrap: In many companies, damage or loss of material within the warehouse is negligible. In other cases, it is significant but a reporting mechanism to measure it does not exist. Damaged parts may be issued, only to be scrapped in production, disguising the real cause of the scrap. Finally, some companies do experience loss and damage of material during storage at a significant level due to weather, inadequate storage environment, or other factors. In all but the first instance, a reliable reporting mechanism within the system should exist and management should establish policies encouraging the correct reporting of scrap at its origin point.

From a performance measurement standpoint, warehouse scrap is similar to unplanned stockouts; zero is the goal. The same process applies. Gather information at the detail level (scrap transactions), summarize for review, and examine specific instances where a sizable amount of scrap is occurring to improve material handling techniques or equipment, storage facilities, or packaging.

Production Control Performance

It is one of the ironies of manufacturing that production control itself is often not part of any kind of performance measurement process. A state-of-the-art system, however, provides the basis for a number of individual measurements which, taken together, serve as an excellent evaluator of the efficiency of the production control staff and the effectiveness of the planning system.

Even if top management ensures that high-quality forward planning and forecasting is performed, the company has a high-quality product and production data base, and numerous other control mechanisms are in place, the production control staff may fail to use properly the tools available in a state-of-the-art system, and much of the potential benefit will be lost. Hence this vital area should be as much a part of the measurement and goal-setting process as other functions. Some examples of measurements of effectiveness in the production control area include the following:

- *Percent of on-time order releases.* Serves as a measurement of overall on-schedule condition.
- *Percent of unreleased orders with past due start dates.* A closely related measurement of schedule condition.
- *Percent of released orders with past due start dates.* Another schedule condition indicator, indicating how often orders are likely to be expedited.
- *Percent of released orders halted or not worked due to material shortages.* Indicates effectiveness of material allocation preceding order release and validity of schedules.
- *Percentage of released orders going more than a certain number of days without being worked.* Indicates some types of excessive queue and schedule imbalances, over- and underloading conditions.
- *Percentage of work center hours that are over- or underloaded.* Indicates work load smoothing effectiveness.
- *Percentage of released orders halted due to tooling nonavailability.* Another indicator of pre-release planning effectiveness and a cause of excessive work center queues.
- *Percentage or frequency of work center stoppages due to insufficient work input.* Also indicates how effectively the load smoothing/work leveling activity is performing.
- *Work center queue levels, planned versus actual:* Not solely a production control measurement, but provides a major indicator of overall lead time control, planning, and scheduling effectiveness.
- *Overall inventory levels.* When coupled with planned or target levels, especially within product or commodity groups, indicates the overall effectiveness of material planning process; also useful when compared to ratios of inventory to sales, shipments, and turnover.

In each of these areas, the system provides some or all of the data for the comparison. The comparison of actual data with a target may include either simply an objective, or desired level, and/or simply the planning generated by the system itself, such as order start dates. No single indicator can show whether an activity that is so interdependent with other areas as production control is being operated at maximum effectiveness. Intelligent management review of these data will result in improvements to staff training, changes to daily work priorities, and other efforts to improve the effectiveness of the company's planning and control system.

Manufacturing Activity Performance

A state-of-the-art system yields a large amount of precise data concerning planned versus actual events on the production floor. Figure 9–9 illustrates the relationships between a number of types of planned versus actual data available in a state-of-the-art system. In each case, a different performance measurement can be created from the large number of individual records involved. In most cases, the result of a planned versus actual comparison should be paired with a standard or goal set by management.

For example, management may set a goal that 95% of all operations will be started on or before their planned start date. A comparison of actual versus planned start dates, available from the operation records of closed work orders and/or completed operations, will produce the actual percentage currently being experienced in the plant.

A report created from these records may indicate that only 90% of operations were started on or before their planned start date, a 5% shortfall from the goal. Some investigation may disclose that many of these were caused by tooling breakages or overloads in one or two key work centers. As in other cases, the detail basis of the measurement can provide information leading to action that will result in an improvement in the situation. Since most of the information available from the manufacturing activity has been discussed in some detail elsewhere, only a brief discussion will be included here to focus on the performance measurement process.

For purposes of simplifying discussion, these measurements can be grouped into three primary areas: standards accuracy, capacity management and scheduling effectiveness, and overall efficiency and quality control. Performance measurements that are available from a state-of-the-art system that can be used in each of these areas include the following:

Standards effectiveness: The work order record set uses and collects actual data that can be used to validate standards used in planning, costing, and

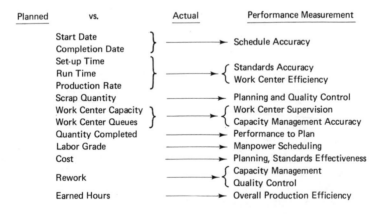

FIGURE 9–9   Manufacturing activity performance measurements.

scheduling. Each area can be paired with a management goal, and/or used to focus efforts to increase efficiency in specific ways, such as reduced setup times. Examples include:

- Setup times
- Run times
- Production cost
- Labor grades used in work center

Comparison of planned versus actual data in each of these areas can provide the basis for both a performance measurement and improved, more accurate standards for use by the planning system.

Capacity management and planning: The planning system uses several important data fields in its processing which then must be frequently, if not continually verified and updated with current information. The work order record set contains planned versus actual data that can be used for this purpose and for measuring work center performance, including the following:

- *Work center capacity:* also applicable for evaluating the effectiveness of work center supervision
- *Work center queues:* evaluates both scheduling and work center effectiveness as well as priority controls
- *Start and completion dates:* for evaluation of performance to schedule and priority control
- *Work center downtime:* in conjunction with other work center data and maintenance scheduling, to evaluate how effectively preventive maintenance is scheduled and performed, as well as how much "surprise" equipment failures or significant employee attendance problems are affecting production

Information resulting from measuring performance in these areas will assist in providing the basis for continual improvements in critical factors affecting the company's ability to plan and schedule its production at the detail level (i.e., where the work actually gets done). The best planning processes can fall apart in the plant if assumptions about work center capacity and supervision are not frequently or continually validated by comparison with actual events.

Efficiency and quality control: In a sense, quality assurance and efficiency are simply another way to view the production process control that occurs at each work center. The planned versus actual data in the work order record set provides insight and a basis for measurements and improvements here as in other areas, including the following:

- *Quantity completed:* indicates potential problems with scrap, rework, other process controls, or the lot-sizing policy used for the part

- *Rework hours:* lost capacity that may not have been included in the capacity planning process; if significant, may account for continual behind-schedule conditions that occur even when everything else is correct; also process control and quality problems with equipment, tooling, personnel, or product design
- *Earned hours:* quantity completed times standard hours for the quantity; an effective overall indicator of production efficiency, work force levels, morale, and scheduling effectiveness

In this as in other areas where manufacturing activity performance is measured, one of the most important factors is that goals be set, actual results compared to goals, and new goals and/or revised operating methods instituted. Only through this basic, good management practice can a company provide an effective mechanism for the ongoing improvements needed in a manufacturing company to keep pace with competition, new technology, and resources.

Product Costing

One of the oldest, traditional habits in manufacturing companies is that of the annual setting of standard costs, and the resulting full-year profit planning and budgeting process. In a huge majority of companies these annual rituals are just that, as little study can be devoted to the development of accurate, meaningful standard costs upon which the entire plan should really be based. In reality, it is simply not practical to attempt a realistic review and revision of three or four cost elements involved in 25,000 part records all in a short time period. Yet this is frequently what one finds.

In a state-of-the-art system, tools exist for providing a continual review of standard (planned) versus actual costs. Each time a part is purchased or produced, information is available to verify or deny the accuracy of the assumptions underlying the standard cost for a given part. To wait an additional 10 months before revising the standard is pointless and serves only to convey the message to middle and lower management that the standards really are not to be taken seriously.

Although Chapter 10 discusses the financial aspects of manufacturing as they appear in a state-of-the-art system and are used by enlightened management, a discussion of some important points in the context of performance measurement and the closed-loop system is warranted here. A major basis for verifying standard costs is variances, which is discussed in Chapter 10.

Probably the most important single aspect of a state-of-the-art system insofar as product costing is concerned is that the system provides tools for capturing detailed information regarding actual events, part numbers, quantities, costs paid, actual labor grades, and so on. That these actual data can have costs applied to them does not obscure this fact. The standard cost assumes that certain types of events will occur and will be reflected in costs experienced by the company. By trapping variances at the event level, a solid basis is provided for making realistic assumptions about the immediate future and therefore about the validity of the standard cost data.

As an example, suppose that a company finds that overall, the production rates reflected in its product routings are accurate, although large variations are experienced from one part number to the next. In this case, the overall profit plan, based on a certain volume of production and product mix, will probably be reasonably accurate. However, if the product mix shifts significantly from planned, the entire profit plan itself will tend to become unrealistic and the company will experience considerable difficulty in performing according to plan. It should be emphasized that exceeding the profit plan is just as bad as falling short, since either case proves that the planning process itself, or its data are faulty.

In summary, then, an enlightened company using a state-of-the-art system can and should continually evaluate and revise its standard costs, using planned versus actual data available in the system, to create a continually accurate costing base so that profit planning can become as integral a part of the business as sales forecasting and other planning activities.

Shipping Performance

Although not a major part of the business per se, the shipping and traffic departments can have their performance measured also. Two areas of interest are the ability of the department to respond to sales order pick list releases in a consistent, efficient manner and the area of freight costing.

The performance measurement process involved in measuring sales order picking, packing, and shipment is virtually identical to that used in measuring warehouse efficiency in processing pick lists for work orders and will not be repeated here. A standard turnaround time should be established as a working assumption and a goal and actual performance measured as the time between sales order release (pick list creation) and shipment date/time. Review of these data will clearly identify month-end crunches, shortages of trucks, packaging, traffic problems, and a host of related difficulties that are candidates for improvement.

One of the consistent fantasies indulged in many manufacturing companies, as discussed earlier, is the practice of trying to complete and ship 80% of the month's total production during the last three days, only to have the shipping and traffic department become totally overloaded. Viewed from the customer's point of view, shipping is just another work center, and as such, can be just as much of a bottleneck as a complex milling machine. Allowing these crunches to continue merely builds in a significant set of inefficiencies, increases shipping costs, raises the chance of significant error from overworked shipping personnel, and reduces the opportunity to make more optimum shipping arrangements.

Freight costs in most companies are paid for by the customer. However, they are often a very significant cost of the total delivered product, and when they turn out to be significantly higher than quoted by the sales staff, only serve to reduce the customer's confidence in the company. It really does little good to throw up one's arms and plead that "we just can't control the trucking companies" when a larger than anticipated shipping bill is received by the customer.

Although freight information, at least on the planned side, is not necessarily a part of the manufacturing system, or even in the system, the actual data do appear in the sales order entry and shipping records. It is also true that an efficient, creative, properly loaded traffic department can often find better, less costly ways to ship the company's products than one that is overloaded, poorly manned, and seldom included in the performance measurement process.

Customer Service Levels

Besides the broader measures of customer service level, a state-of-the-art system includes information for measuring the impact of scheduling and shipping performance in response to customer demand. These measures include:

- *Percent of late shipments.* Can be compared with a planned, or expected level and coupled with a goal to get more on time.
- *Current past due orders.* Measurement can include the dollar value, can be ranked by the ABC method according to selling price to focus attention, and can be summarized by number of days past due and the range of lateness (worst to least).
- *Future dated orders likely to be shipped late.* Although a little more complex, in a state-of-the-art environment, production completions are more predictable than under an informal system, and it becomes possible to predict which sales orders are going to be shipped late, and by how much. These too can be ranked by the ABC method and selectively evaluated according to causes of lateness (ordered inside lead time, production or other resource nonavailability, etc.). The goal is to reduce the rate, clearly, and if not, to notify the customer at the earliest possible time of the actual shipping date he can expect.

Overall Business Plan Effectiveness

Since the business planning process is the capstone of all other, more detailed processes, and is really the level at which top management and stockholders evaluate the company, it is only logical that performance measuring include several aspects of the business plan as well. As has been repeatedly emphasized, the performance measurement process is simply a rational series of steps involving the setting of goals, measuring of actual results, and comparisons of same to foster improved, more realistic goals and/or improved ways of achieving them. While a large number of measurements of the business plan are possible, only three key ones need to be mentioned here, including the following:

- *Return on investment.* Reflects how well the capital assets of the company were used and how well their use was planned. As with other areas, substantial differences reflect either poor planning or substandard performance to the plan.

- *Profitability and gross margin.* Reflects potential unrealistic assumptions about product costs, production efficiencies, or sales volume that were made in the business planning process.
- *Aggregate sales and production.* At a gross level, reflects whether the entire sales forecasting and long-range planning process is reasonably accurate and whether significant management problems may exist in the company. Whether, for example, the market existed, but production never got up to expected levels, even though capital was expended for resources.

A significant difference exists between the performance measurement process for the business plan and that of other areas. Measurements taken at this level do not necessarily provide the basis for improved planning and/or execution of the plans. Management must resort to other, more detailed measurement processes to provide the information required for improved operating results.

For this reason, one part of the performance measurement process needs the other. A business cannot be effectively managed at the general level only; it must be based on a solid foundation of detailed planning and execution. As was made clear at the outset of this book, there is no such thing as the big picture, only one lacking in accuracy. Although it is certainly true that meaningful summaries of information can be created, if these summaries are based on hunches, rough approximations, and out-of-date information, the summary itself will be resting on a bed of quicksand, ready to sink the best intentions of top management.

CHAPTER 9 QUESTIONS

1. The comparison of what two kinds of data represents the essence of the performance measurement process?
2. What part of the performance measurement process is specifically a human step?
3. There were eight different areas of management emphasis discussed in the text that need to shift when moving into a formal system. List and briefly explain at least five of these.
4. Describe the information basis of a closed loop and explain why it can be used with information at virtually any level of detail in the company.
5. Describe the basic steps in developing a performance measurement from a collection of records.
6. Why are statistical means and standard deviations used to analyze raw data, and why is it reduced to a standard percentage format for management use?
7. Why should a measure of the range of variation from the mean always be included in this type of analysis?
8. Why does performing an analysis at the gross total level give completely different results than if it is done at the detail level and then summarized?

9. Is the performance measurement process an example of the information pyramid concept? Why?

10. What are the two primary sources of data used in performance measurement?

11. How can a computer substantially aid in the performance measurement process?

12. What are the most important results of using the performance measurement process as an integral part of company management?

13. Identify three important outcomes of the performance measurement process.

14. What must management always do with the results of performance measurement information?

15. What is the value of regular performance measurements performed for maintaining primary data base accuracy? Identify some of the benefits of such a program.

16. Identify two simple measurements of how effectively the forecast relates to the master production schedule.

17. What are some of the reasons that measurements of the effectiveness of the purchasing activity can be so important?

18. What is the alternative performance measurement approach where the standard comparison of planned versus actual data cannot be made, or is impractical?

19. What are some of the undesirable consequences of poor warehouse management (poor physical control of stock)? How can performance measurement focus on actions for improvement in this area?

20. Describe several ways in which a warehouse's functions resemble those of a bank.

21. Besides cycle counting results, identify at least two areas within the warehouse operations that are good candidates for ongoing performance measurements.

22. Of all performance measurements, why is cycle counting particularly important?

23. Identify and briefly describe at least six examples of measurements of effectiveness in the production control area.

24. Management at a company has just reviewed its performance in the manufacturing activity area and has found that several important performance measurements have fallen significantly short of their goals. What is the next action it should take?

25. Identify at least six of the manufacturing activity performance measurements that can be obtained directly from the work order record set. (Eleven are mentioned in the text.)

26. Explain the relationship of the shipping activity to the level of customer service and to schedule performance. Identify several potential problems that can be brought to light by regular performance measurement in this area.

27. What is the objective of measuring customer service performance levels?

28. How does the process of performance measurement of the overall business plan effectiveness illustrate the principle that performance measurement cannot be effectively done at a general level only?

10

Financial Management Aspects

This chapter includes discussion of financial information that can be obtained from integrated manufacturing systems. The difference between what will be termed the traditional accounting viewpoint and the newer approach, termed the information systems approach, are also discussed. Finally, some analysis of obtaining variances and direct costing concepts will be explored.

Accounting is the original business information system. Double-entry bookkeeping has its origins in the merchants of Venice during the early Renaissance. In more modern times, companies have developed very elaborate systems to keep track of assets and liabilities and report them to the owners, the financial community (banks, stock market), and management.

Until the development of computer systems and the concepts of systems management, accounting information had little competition. One aspect that is an inherent difficulty with accounting developed information is that it is in-direct in nature. It reports all information in financial terms, not in the terms in which physical events actually occur. New, nonfinancial information systems, on the other hand, track and report actual physical events directly. In this respect, the kind of information systems discussed in this book may be said to mirror reality.

The good news about the new systems for management is that the infor-mation they produce (if the system is so designed) can direct management's at-tention to which specific kinds of events offer opportunity for improvement. In some cases, reports can be generated that are surprisingly specific, certainly when compared to the traditional month-end accounting profit and loss statements, expense schedules, and budget performance reports.

The essence of this viewpoint is that companies are not in the business of buying and selling money. It is physical events that are involved, materials converted, and value added through labor and machinery operation. That these events can be subsequently described in terms of a currency does not alter the fact that it is the physical events themselves that management must control.

Simply because no other method existed in the past that was practical, and because for centuries businessmen were interested primarily in whether they were getting richer or poorer by each transaction, accounting has been the sole source of information until now.

This should not be taken to mean that financial information is not important, because it certainly is. Further, physical events stated in terms of a currency is probably the only way they can be reduced to a common demoninator, and in so doing, make the overall activity intelligible. And whether the company is getting richer or poorer by its transactions is certainly important.

Traditional Accounting Approach

In terms of an information system, traditional accounting systems have a number of characteristics in common, such as:

- Each system has its own separate files, linked at best by journal entries to others.
- Each type of system is geared to do only one thing, such as accounts payable, payroll, or cost accounting.
- The person who manages this type of system typically operates relatively independently from the rest of the company, even in an area such as cost accounting.
- Information is transaction oriented, in that records of physical events are recorded from their "raw" state in terms of dollars. If other information is included, it is on a supplementary basis.
- The data "belong" to the accounting department. In most cases, responsibility for accuracy rests with a person in the accounting department, who is expected to check information that is received from other departments for accuracy before allowing it into the accounting system.
- Often, a unique version of data received from other departments is maintained, further removing responsibility for accuracy from nonaccounting departments.
- Information is periodic in nature, end of the month or year-end, for example. It covers events between certain dates. In between times there is normally little or no information available.

One can readily see the origins of the separate department approach to running a business. Each department keeps only the information needed to perform its function. Accounting, one way or another, brings it all together and keeps top management informed. To do this, accounting frequently "translates" information received from other departments into its own terms.

In the area of cost accounting, which is a primary concern here, cost standards are often involved. Typically, these are relatively fixed and revised periodically. Since profit planning is usually based on standard costs of one sort or another, the development of standards is often the most important cost accounting function. In order to perform the costing accounting function, the cost accountant usually must, in effect, gather his own data, pass judgment as to its accuracy, and make decisions about allocating indirect costs. These tasks are accomplished for the most part without involvement of managers outside accounting.

Information Systems Approach

An alternative to the traditional accounting approach has become available to management only in recent times. The development of systems analysis concepts during World War II, and subsequently of computer-based information systems, has enabled management to design systems that gather and report directly on specific events.

For purposes of the discussion here, it will be assumed that systems management refers to information systems that are integrated in nature; that is, the system spans department lines of authority. Company-wide systems, where the entire system is not the responsibility of a single manager, are still a novelty. Some of the same people may be involved in running these systems, but they have different responsibilities than under the more traditional approach.

Integrated information systems have some important characteristics in common, including:

- Data enter the system at its source, such as via an on-line computer VDT.
- The source point of the data is responsible for its accuracy, not someone downstream.
- Responsibility for information accuracy is much further down in the organization. There is less of an assumption that data must be "checked" by a supervisor or someone from accounting before they are considered correct.
- The flow of information is more or less continuous, so reporting it on a continuous basis is a natural result. Exception conditions are easier to spot as they occur, when something can be done about it. Period endings are just cutoff points and are not required to develop the information itself.
- Information is communicated widely throughout the company. Only one version of information is needed; others merely confuse the issue.

One may ask what the role of the accountant is under the information system environment. The accountant's role shifts markedly away from one of direct responsibility and toward one where coordination, monitoring, reconciling, and analyzing is more central.

Take inventory as an example. Traditionally, unless a company had some reason to maintain perpetual inventory records (on cards), accounting provided the only information about inventory that was available, via accounts payable (purchases) and accounts receivable (shipping). Material requisitions for issues from stock to work in process and warehouse receipts to maintain a work-in-process inventory account were often maintained. But the information was reported in dollar amounts and was primarily intended for top management.

In this example, all inventory accounts were maintained in the same fashion. The document reporting inventory movement had to have a dollar amount calculated for it (e.g., cost times quantity), with the extended total being posted to the accounts via a journal. No part-number-level, on-hand-balance type of record keeping is required to produce a financial report of inventory.

Typical accounting controls to ensure accuracy of systems such as this include making sure that all serial-numbered documents were accounted for, that they were properly signed (to ensure that the reported material movement really did take place), and that the clerk properly costed and extended the items. Thus the audit function is almost entirely within the accounting function. People within the other departments have little responsibility, directly, for information accuracy.

With a background like this, it is little wonder that many companies experienced problems with information accuracy when first installing even a simple perpetual inventory system. Sometimes they were even maintained within the accounting department, which really had little interest in part number specific accuracy. It was the dollar amount they were most interested in. Even if the card records were maintained in the warehouse area, top management regarded the accounting reports of inventory as the "real" ones, even if enormous adjustments were routinely booked after physical inventories.

One simple reason for this is that one way or the other, the company absolutely must have a financial report of inventory, even if it is not very accurate. So the records in the warehouse were considered secondary and never extended at their dollar amounts to obtain a total inventory dollar amount. Because accounting procedures require that things balance, it was always hard for people to believe that enormous errors could creep in anyway.

The New Responsibilities

Under the integrated information systems environment responsibilities shift. If management fails to make the shift open and visible, problems are inevitable. If the new responsibilities are clearly assigned and accepted, some significant benefits can accrue to the company. Three major ones are:

1. Responsibility for information accuracy is where it can be really effective, that is, where events are actually occurring, not somewhere downstream from the

event. Also, the relationship between the events themselves and the information is much clearer and immediate.

2. Duplication of effort is eliminated, together with the duplicate, conflicting sets of records. Because of this, communication is much better, since everyone "reads the same mail" and shares the same assumptions.

3. Information accuracy is much greater, benefiting both planning and operational parts of the business. Shortcuts associated with manual methods are no longer necessary to develop information needed for decisions, because the amount of data to be summarized or analyzed is less relevant.

Companies that are well along the way of the integrated, state-of-the-art information system generally report outstanding performance figures. Twin Disc, Inc., reports sales figures that rank it 351st in the second Fortune 500 lists. Its average return on equity over a 10-year period ranks it 38th on the same list. Quite a bit of effort has been spent at Twin Disc by some farsighted managers to develop a comprehensive integrated information system. The results speak for themselves.

It is important to make a distinction at this point. There are two perspectives for accounting information: one that measures the company from an investment standpoint, and one that measures internal operations. Top management's primary interest is usually in the performance of the company as a financial entity and is therefore interested primarily in the former.

Information falling into this area is of less interest to middle and lower management people simply because they have less control over it. Examples of this type of information include the typical balance sheet, profit and loss statement, and various expense and income schedules. All of these are produced via the general ledger and its subsidiary accounts.

The other type of information has to do with the internal operation of the company. It is with this group that the focus of the remainder of this chapter is concerned. This includes the traditional cost accounting area, various budgeting processes, and a variety of operational reports that may not be directly accounting in nature.

Integrated manufacturing systems can produce a much wider range of data concerning planned and actual costs, all based on actual events, or planned events, than was ever available in the past. Actual costs are tracked via the released or closed work order records. Planned costs can be developed from the planned order records. In each case, records that correspond to actual physical events are extended via system-maintained costs to obtain dollarized amounts as a result.

Financial Information from Planned Orders

In this section four types of information will be considered: material cost projections, labor cost projections, and overhead allocations, and, relating to material costs, purchasing commitments.

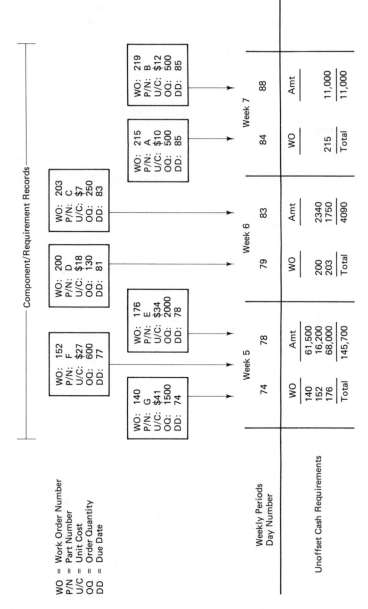

FIGURE 10-1 Costing planned orders—material.

252

Material cost planning: The planned order records contain detailed information about each part number's required quantity and dates. These records can be extended, using the standard (or another) cost amount, as is illustrated in Figure 10-1, to obtain a precise projection of cash requirements for purchases. The planned order data are in terms of required delivery dates, so the figures can easily be offset by the normal payment period for invoices.

This exercise can be extended for the full length of the planning horizon. The result is a solidly based report on how much money will be required, when, and exactly for which items and from which vendors they are likely to come. The data can be summarized by commodity type, end item, product group, vendor last purchased from, or other basis.

Besides cash requirements, this kind of information can prove to be a very effective aid to negotiating mutually favorable terms with major suppliers. Costing material requirements from planned orders can also provide a valuable input into the cash planning process, together with other reports, such as labor projections. If it appears that working capital will be in short supply, a detailed report like this could aid management in setting priorities for negotiations. For example, negotiations might be initiated to obtain better financing terms with a few key suppliers, that would aid a cash shortage, or the converse if the company's cash position is expected to be strong.

Labor cost planning: Although detailed routing records are not maintained in a planned form, as are material requirements, the orders can still be exploded through routings and work centers to obtain the planned labor, by labor grade and hourly rate required to support the production plan. This would provide added cash planning information, and may aid in planning overtime pay.

Figure 10-2 illustrates the process by which a computer program would develop this information from the planned orders, standard operation routings, and work center data. The process can at the same time accumulate expected overhead that would be absorbed, using the overhead rates in the work center records.

This process is dependent on a fairly high level of accuracy in the work center and routing data, as well as with a planned order file that is likely to resemble what will actually get produced. Depending on the system, this information could be developed during the normal capacity planning processing runs.

Projecting overhead absorption: The same process described above, which develops detailed labor hours from the planned orders, can also calculate the amount of overhead cost that would be absorbed by the planned labor hours. If the planning horizon is of sufficient length, or if the resource requirements process is of sufficient detail, assumptions made about the volume of direct labor hours can be checked in developing the overhead rates. If these rates prove to be significantly off, they can be adjusted before actually being used.

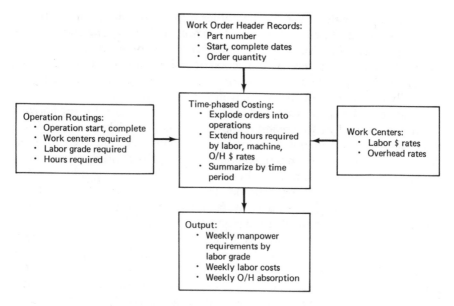

FIGURE 10-2 Costing planned orders—labor.

One significant advantage of this approach of checking the validity of overhead absorption rates is that it can interrelate labor hours, overhead to be absorbed, and product line.

Purchasing commitments: Blending into the planned cash expenditures for material are those commitments already made in the form of firm purchase orders. The process of developing a time-phased purchasing commitments report that may be broken down by a number of categories (vendor, product line, commodity type) is essentially the same as that illustrated in Figure 10-1, except that open purchase order records are used instead of the component requirements records.

In this process, open, firm orders are extended at their actual cost according to their due dates. Payment terms can be included in the logic if it is significant. At the same time, the actual prices shown on the purchase orders for material can be compared with their standard and potential purchasing variances identified in advance. (The purchasing variance does not actually get booked until the supplier's invoice enters accounts payable.) Significant errors in either standards or purchasing actions can be detected automatically and reported.

Actual Cost Data

The area of tracking actual costs of production is one of the most important to any company, because many decisions follow from the information. As shall be discussed later, many of these decisions may have a faulty base.

In the past, before fully integrated systems were available, cost account-ants took a variety of often heroic (due to the huge volumes of manually processed data) approaches in attempting to measure actual product cost in a reliable, consistent manner. Elaborate job costing systems were set up, together with various subaccounts for work in process inventory and labor, or various hybrid systems implemented.

Most of these efforts required some degree of compromise, either using averages or allocated amounts (just calculations) to obtain all or a major por-tion of the product cost. Other approaches include simply assuming that stan-dard material usages prevailed and charging cost of goods sold with the stan-dard cost amounts for material that should have been used. This is sort of a dollarized backflush method.

Some bizzare results sometimes attended these systems. In one system, material issues from stores into work in process had to pass through the manually maintained inventory records section, where the latest moving average price was added to the transaction before it was entered into the cost ac-counting system. Due to insufficient personnel in the section, it fell severely behind, over five months in processing transactions.

Besides the obvious fact that inventory records were useless, this meant that a progressively declining portion of material issues appeared as cost of goods sold. In this company, billings were based on input to work in process (progress billing). No one noticed that there was a problem until billings de-clined to the point where a cash flow shortage developed.

In another company, variations on standard catalog products were sold to government agencies at prices that were somewhat higher than those for regular items. Since costing used a standard cost backflush method, it was believed that the orders were very profitable. This situation continued for many years, until a carefully performed study disclosed that the variations required expensive, highly expedited substitute components, usually produced on overtime; that the company normally lost money on the overtime; and that the company normally lost money on the business when *all actual* costs were included, not just the standard ones.

These and similar situations become less of a problem with an integrated state-of-the-art manufacturing system. The reason is very simple. The actual events, material usage, and manufacturing hours, labor and machine, are reported directly to the work order, where clearly established standards are also on record.

Since the work order record set was discussed in detail in Chapters 7 and 8 together with the reporting mechanism used to report material issues and shop hours to the component requirements and the routing records belonging to the work order record set, these steps will not be repeated here. Regardless of whether the work order record set is used in a classical job shop environment, with a work order document issued to the plant floor, material issues reported to the order, and labor hours reported to the operation, or whether the order is used as a planning and reporting device as a flow or control order, the logic is the same.

In this logic, the relationship between the planned quantity of each part number and plan hours for each step and the actual events is clearly established. The planned side of the data is generated from the same product structure and standard routing records used to develop the standard cost and ultimately the profit plan. Actual events are reported to the system and recorded by it in exactly the same terms as were planned; the units of comparison are the same.

All that remains from this logic to obtain accurate product costing information is to apply, in an entirely separate, independent step, cost amounts for each part number and labor grade (or machine) used, as shown in the work order record data. These amounts are extended and totaled for the work order. Having the basic data present in the same physical records where the planned side of the data exists allows great flexibility to reporting costs. If historical work order records are kept, a series of work orders for the same part can be averaged, both at the summary level and with the detail needed to obtain a very clear picture of the direct cost of the product.

If the work order takes a fair amount of time to complete and/or involves many components, the accumulated postings to the work order record set can be used to report progress on the order. Problems with scrap, orders that are overrun, or underrun, errors in product structure (such as a part number shown as required, but that never gets issued to the order), and reporting problems in the plant all show up in reviews of the planned versus actual data maintained in the work order record set. As was stated above, applying dollar amounts to these data is a separate step, and in fact could use any of several alternate sets of cost data to evaluate profitability under different circumstances.

Developing Variance Information

The author has seen a number of well-intentioned accounting-oriented systems that were designed to produce variance information. Most used dollarized transactions that were posted to ledger accounts. At month-end some variances would get "closed" to others, and ultimately to cost of goods sold.

An example would be a material usage variance. In the accounting or ledger-based reporting, two sets of transactions would be dollarized and offset. One side would be the material usage dollars, for each item completed, extended at standard quantities and standard cost. The other side would be actual material issues to work in process at standard cost. The material usage variance due to quantities used that were different from planned would be the net difference.

This approach will yield a dollar amount that corresponds to unreported scrap, product structure errors, and so on. What it lacks is the right kind of information that can direct corrective action without further tedious research. It is for this reason, among others, that these variance systems seldom reach their apparent usefulness.

What is needed is part number or work center specific types of data, or better still, a relationship between a certain component, for example, and a parent part number. In this approach, a material usage variance could be reported when component part A is used in the production of parent part B, but not when used in the production of parent part C. If information is reported in this fashion, management can go straight to the heart of the problem by examining the method by which the two parts are assembled.

This kind of variance information is easily provided by the part number and work order/parent part number relationships maintained in the work order record set, plus related records, such as part master and purchase orders. Although some accountants may be not comfortable with reporting systems that do not involve the traditional double-entry bookkeeeping, most will welcome the availability of improved financial information.

Variances are one of the forms of management by exception. They are monitors, performance measurements, and signals of out-of-tolerance conditions in the company. Enlightened management uses them as discussed in Chapter 9 to set goals of performance for operating management and other employees. The difference is that most variances eventually get charged to cost of goods sold, either explicitly or by being included in another expense category.

Variances developed from the work order record set and related records may be termed event-based variances, as contrasted to ledger-based variances. Both have a dollar value, but they differ in where the dollarization process occurs.

One of the prime goals of any variance is to measure performance to a planned activity. A distinguishing feature of financial variances is that they reflect directly on the profit planning process used by the company. Several issues related directly to variances and profit planning include:

- Should standard costs be revised often?
- If so, how is profit to be forecasted?
- Does it really make a difference whether reduced profit (cost is higher than planned) is booked as a cost variance or as a "normal" cost, which it would if the standard were increased?
- Are variances really worth pursuing if the development of standard costs is just an annual rite in which 97% of the material costs are increased by an arbitrary figure, rather than being based on actual purchasing or production data?

These issues are not especially trivial, although seldom confronted directly. In some cases in the author's experience, a company's unwillingness to confront the inadequacy of the standard costs led to the unworkability of variance reporting. Sloppy standards seem inevitable when policy requires that all standard costs be revised simultaneously, usually at year-end when everything else is going on.

If standards are revised on a regular schedule, like cycle counting, a profit plan can be prepared or updated at any time and the part-oriented data become a constant, gradually changing overall, but much more precise at the detail level.

Direct Costing

No discussion of financial information in a manufacturing context is complete without examining direct costing techniques. Direct costing grew from numerous observations as to the inadequacy with which nondirect costs are handled. Traditional accounting methodology has all company costs converted, in effect to direct costs. Usually, one of several methods is used to simply increase direct cost by a percentage to reflect its "share" of the overhead costs.

Like any traditional technique, burdening direct costs to reflect overhead was more appropriate when the proportion of total costs was mostly direct. In the good old days, manufacturing consisted of a much higher percentage of labor and material costs; manufacturing was not so capital intensive or automated. A convenient method of determining the correct price to charge for products was to look at the total expenses for the year and observe that rent, selling, and administrative expenses were, say, 15% of total expenses.

The way to set a minimum price in this situation seems simple. Add up all the direct costs, then multiply times 1.25 to include a decent profit margin above overhead costs. Any distortions or poor decisions resulting from this procedure were probably not a problem.

Today, however, things are a different story. Many companies now have production environments which are highly automatic, meaning that they have largely fixed costs. Laying off the entire work force and buying no material would cut expenses by only a small percent. This means that costs that behave fundamentally differently with respect to plant volume are being grouped together. Direct costs increase in direct proportion with volume. Indirect costs, however, decrease proportionately with volume. This means that if a company is using the traditional "full"-costing approach, it will tend to increase its prices in slow times and decrease them in good times—precisely opposite the results that would appear to make sense.

Of course, the part of this dilemma that compounds the difficulties is that the methods by which these "full" costs are obtained varies considerably with the accounting decisions made relating to the "absorption" rates to be used, expected volume, and so on. A classic example is the automobile industry, for years facing declining volumes. As volume declines, prices are increased in an effort to "cover" all costs.

This step initiates and feeds a downward spiral in volume and an upward one in price. It also allows management to believe that it is dealing with the situation effectively, when the correct response may be to aggressively and promptly cut the cost of the excess capacity.

Direct costing methods view all income in excess of total direct costs for a product as "contributing" to gross profit, which includes indirect costs. The greater the contribution, the greater the probability that all indirect costs will be paid and that there will be profit. It does not mean that prices should be only a little above total direct cost. It does allow a company to price and cost its products in accordance with the logical cause-and-effect relationships actually existing between costs in the company.

In truth, if total product cost is to include all indirect costs, actual product cost really depends on:

- Product mix
- The level at which plant and equipment is utilized
- The overall level of business

All of these factors vary considerably, even over a short time in many companies. This means that actual total product cost varies considerably as well. As a result, decisions about pricing are obliged to be incorrect frequently.

By using a direct cost method of establishing costs, management's attention is more focused on what is actually occurring at that moment with respect to the three factors listed above. For instance, if business is slow, accepting work at a lower than normal price would assist in paying the fixed costs of the plant. Refusing work at a lower than normal price (based on long-term averages) because it failed to "cover" its costs would aggravate the low-volume situation.

In these situations, which typically face every business all the time, the belief that overhead costs can be accurately handled via the allocation and burdening method seems incorrect, because the method leads management to make decisions that are the opposite of what a more straightforward approach would support.

Regardless of the merits of direct-costing techniques, there are two principal reasons why they do not enjoy more popularity:

- In industries where the product is complex, has many levels of assembly, takes a very long time to build, or where a very large portion of the total cost is fixed (such as capital intensive production or high engineering content), it is very desirable to include fixed, overhead type costs in the incremental costing of the product as it proceeds through the manufacturing process. If the product is progress billed, this may make a particularly large difference on cash flow.
- The Internal Revenue Service (IRS) requires burdened inventory valuations for tax purposes. As a result, most companies have traditionally kept just one set of books (it is hard enough to do that) that conforms with IRS rules.

An integrated manufacturing system can easily produce both sets of data because it maintains information about events, which are costed in a separate process. Therefore, it is a simple matter to produce two sets of information.

Direct costing data can be used for day-to-day operations and decision making within the company, while periodic reports could be produced for tax-related or inventory valuation purposes.

This example illustrates clearly, as elsewhere in this book, the inherent advantage of being able to implement systems that plan and track actual physical events. The benefit in terms of improved business performance and information cannot help but improve all areas of financial reporting and control. In this way, advanced, integrated systems can aid the financial and accounting function to fulfill its responsibilities of accurate, timely reporting of information concerning the assets and liabilities of the company.

CHAPTER 10 QUESTIONS

1. What is the fundamental difference between the way accounting systems report events and the way newer systems do?

2. When is it appropriate to discuss events in their financial terms and when is it not?

3. Characterize information systems as they have been traditionally developed under the accounting approach.

4. Describe the information system approach, its characteristics, and contrast it with the traditional accounting approach.

5. Describe how responsibility for information accuracy shifts under the integrated information systems environment in the three major areas.

6. Describe the four types of financial planning information that can be drawn from the planned order records.

7. What are some of the consequences of using actual costing methods that do not parallel physical reality, but represent some measure of approximation?

8. Identify several examples of actual costs that are often not charged to a product, but are considered to be overhead items, simply because the company lacks a convenient mechanism for collecting the information.

9. Explain how the work order record set, when used as a basis for actual costing, allows the physical events themselves to be tracked and costed separately. Explain how alternate sets of costing data could be applied to the same work order information.

10. Explain and contrast event-based variances with ledger-based variances.

11. Identify and explain briefly at least three issues directly related to variances and profit planning.

12. Why is there no hope that standard costs can be really accurate when all costs are revised only once a year and at the same time?

13. Explain the basic difference between traditional overhead absorption accounting techniques and those of direct costing.

14. How can the use of absorption accounting lead management to make decisions that are, in fact, the opposite of those that make rational sense?

15. What are the three factors that actual product cost really depends upon?

16. Describe briefly the two reasons why direct costing techniques do not enjoy more popularity.

17. With state-of-the-art systems, is there any reason why two sets of cost techniques could not be simultaneously maintained?

11

Management in
the New Environment

As of the writing of this book, there is a rapidly growing awareness, not only among those in manufacturing businesses, but by the general public as well, that a wide variety of cultural, economic, political, and technological forces are working to make the traditional approach to business management less and less successful. Companies that have seldom examined or revised their management techniques are being literally destroyed in market after market.

Even General Motors, the one-time king of large-scale manufacturing, is experiencing severe problems, as is the rest of the automobile industry. And the automobile industry has a lot of company in many other industries. On the other hand, there are a number of companies in many industries that have achieved substantial internal growth rates for long periods of time, moving successfully into a wide variety of markets successfully dominated previously by other firms. It is to these success stories that one looks for validation of various management concepts.

In these successful manufacturing companies, a number of characteristics in their management techniques distinguish them from traditional companies experiencing problems when confronted with serious competition. Many are literally decades ahead of older, traditionally managed companies. Some of these characteristics include:

- Heavy emphasis on the human environment, with continual, extensive education and training programs, a more open, communicative style, and consideration for individual needs

- Management structures reflecting a heavy involvement at all company levels with long- and short-range planning
- A widespread assumption that not only is rapid change a fact of life, but it can be used to advantage if the initiative is taken to create the changes
- Continuous, ongoing efforts to improve the company's systems, management skills, and operations through heavy investment in all kinds of productivity equipment, leading-edge manufacturing techniques, and advanced computer system applications
- A more complex, flexible organization structure, often where a manager may have more than one reporting relationship, and where teams are often formed to accomplish specific objectives involving several work groups or departments

Viewed from a historical perspective, the original business organization structure was derived from the military, built on a basically one-way flow of communication directed toward coordinating the activities of many people acting toward a single, easy-to-understand objective. In the military model, the planning function and the information feedback functions are performed by entirely separate parts of the command organization (i.e., by upper-level staff and by military intelligence).

Business, especially manufacturing, was historically confronted with a similar problem; a great deal of work that needed to be coordinated toward a primary, understandable objective. As noted above, the assumptions of this method of business organization are becoming less valid all the time, as products and operating environments become progressively more complex. Planning and careful integration of the entire operation at all levels becomes more and more an essential ingredient for success.

This shift involves mainly a move toward a more complex, integrated, and formal method of operating the business. Chapters 1 and 2 discussed some of these issues, especially the difference between an informal and a formal organization. Big is not necessarily formal, nor is small necessarily informal. One of the ironies of this age is that as the computer moves more and more toward a position of prominence in manufacturing businesses, people skills and motivational factors become more important at the same time. The bulk of this chapter focuses on these issues.

Education and Training—A Central Issue

Companies that have created substantial successes with the manufacturing system concepts discussed in this book invariably spend significant amounts of company resources on educating and training their people. The chief distinction between education and training is that education concerns itself with creating understanding, so that "why" questions can be answered. Training, on the other hand, is task specific; it answers "how" questions and is intended to develop proficiency at a job.

An effective education program includes all levels of management, especially during a major implementation project. In this case it is vital not only that everyone be properly educated as to the whys of the system, but that training of specific people in specific tasks be based on a solid foundation of understanding developed through an effective education program. One of the primary causes of manufacturing system failures is the interrelated facets of top management understanding, commitment and involvement, and education and training of the entire company. All too often it is assumed that only production and inventory control people need to be "trained."

Goals of education: Viewed in the context of manufacturing systems (or other formal system environment), the purpose of the education activity is to facilitate the achievement of these goals:

- Alter and/or maintain the company's social culture: its values, assumptions, and specific objectives
- Improve understanding of how things really work and/or how they will work in the future (after implementation)
- Improve communication among various management areas by providing a common language and mutually agreed upon goals, purposes, and methods
- Facilitate acceptance by users of responsibility for success of the system (especially during an implementation project)

The desired outcome of effective education for managers is the much higher level of professionalism required for success with integrated manufacturing systems. A professional in this context is a person who is more knowledge oriented, is more of a planner and thinker and less of a crisis solver (and crisis creator), hustler, and expediter.

The American Production and Inventory Control Society (APICS) has developed a first-rate education and certification program. Completion of this program should be mandatory for everyone involved directly or indirectly in the P&IC function. It is a standard type of program, where those who achieve Certified or Fellow status have definitely demonstrated knowledge and proficiency in all areas of production and inventory management by passing well-designed, objectively graded examinations. There are no honorary awards; the examinations are not easy and can be passed only by someone who has studied diligently and worked hard to develop his understanding and knowledge of the field.

APICS certification should also be encouraged for those elsewhere in the company, such as data processing, production supervision, purchasing, finance, and marketing. In a company managing itself with a state-of-the-art manufacturing system, APICS certification is a prime qualifier for promotion, pay increases, and evidence of commitment to the job and company. This is because in an integrated system, it is *required* that *everyone* understand why things happen as they do, and how each part of the system affects and is affected by other parts.

As with other important company goals, top management must not merely "support" education, it must require it as a determinant of job retention, performance reviews, and advancement. When this is not done, or if it becomes a low priority after an initial successful implementation project, the system will ultimately fail. All levels of management must be involved and participate, and individual managers must be held accountable for the participation of their subordinates and for actually obtaining day-to-day results from the education and/or training.

Properly designed, an education program includes broad conceptual material that is brought into focus by the inclusion of company-specific material. It must be ongoing, a permanent part of the company's operations, and should be coupled closely with other education and people development programs.

Goals of training: Since training is job specific, it is by definition company specific. Properly done, it is relevant and keyed directly to the current environment in the company. It should also build on a solid foundation of understanding achieved through education. Merely training someone in a rote fashion will produce less than desirable results. On-the-job training is seldom sufficiently effective. Effective classroom-type training sessions should be coupled with "lab" work in an on-the-job context, similar to apprenticeship programs.

Since the content of a training program is job specific, the manager or supervisor responsible for the job's performance should review the training material and content and be at least partially responsible for its relevance and accuracy. He should also be accountable for seeing that the trained person gets positive results from the training program and that the desired proficiency is achieved.

The goals of a training program then include the following:

- To produce proficiency at certain tasks.
- To enable the person to achieve a low error rate, to produce high-quality results consistently.
- To facilitate actions based on knowledge and understanding.
- To initiate a self-learning process so that the person can continue to increase his proficiency on his own. This goal is almost impossible if only a rote training method, with little education, is used.

Education and training methods: Designers of education and training programs have a wide variety of tools to choose from. Ideally, a program consists of a mix of techniques, since each is better suited to certain types of material and/or individual learning styles than others. A typical list includes the following:

- University and college courses
- Technical courses
- Consultant's training courses and seminars
- Conferences and workshops
- Videotaped material
- Computer-assisted training programs
- Textbooks and journals
- APICS resources

APICS itself provides a substantial array of educational resources, including:

- Certification study guides
- Certification courses and exams
- Day and evening seminars and workshops on a wide variety of topics
- Various training aids
- The APICS dictionary and bibliography
- Monthly dinner meetings
- Active membership in an APICS chapter also enables one to meet other professionals with direct experience in the field and offers an unparalled opportunity for sharing information and experiences

It is the author's experience that the APICS is one of the least fully exploited resources available to manufacturing managers, who by and large still often regard production and inventory management as a largely clerical function. This is somewhat like saying that a bank loan officer is just a clerk because he just works with numbers and signs papers all day.

The production control function is the manufacturing company equivalent of the bank's investment portfolio manager; it is where major investment decisions are made and assets committed, hopefully with the goal of producing an above-average return. To relegate this important function to a person who has a low level of professionalism, poor understanding of his function, and who is poorly supported by management is a management goof of the first order. Managers in companies sharing this viewpoint should not be surprised when their inventories go out of control, deliveries slip, and work in process is a mass of red tags and expediting.

The choice of which education and training method to use depends on several factors. The company's environment and management style is important. People may be accustomed to a lot of direction or may be used to working more on their own initiative. The content of the material itself is important. Some topics simply cannot be presented effectively in the job context, or require the use of diagrams, charts, and other visual aids to be effective.

How participants learn best (their learning style) is a critical factor. Many people will ignore a videotape but pay close attention to an in-person presentation by an instructor, whereas others do better with a videotape that they can stop, rewind, and replay themselves.

The content itself may dictate the choice of method. Job specific training programs must be highly tailored to the company and may be best in a discussion-type environment where questions can be asked and resolved. Educational topics covering broader issues or a range of techniques to understand may be best absorbed via texts and other reading matter.

In summary, a company's education and training program is a critical factor in the success of its information system. This fact is recognized explicitly and given a high priority in companies using state-of-the-art manufacturing systems. The programs themselves are carefully constructed to reflect the most effective way to convey understanding to the company's staff. The program is tied to performance improvements, job descriptions, promotion qualifications, and pay raises. Its content is, where appropriate, largely subject to review by specific managers for the appropriateness of the material for his area. Finally, everyone in the company, from top manager to the lowest clerk, is involved in some form of education and training.

Information-Oriented Management Structures

As discussed earlier, the traditional organization structure for manufacturing businesses is military in origin. The objective was to make the product. Highly autonomous department heads ("commanders") ran their independent departments in military style, using an autocratic, authoritarian model of control. Decision making was from the top down, "orders from headquarters." The implicit assumption was that middle- and lower-level managers and line people really knew too little to be entrusted with any part of the decision-making process. A closely correlated function was simply the division and specialization of labor. The planning that was performed by the company took place strictly at the topmost levels.

Although some elements of this hierarchical model of organization will always be needed, companies have long since grown far too complex in many industries to permit this method of running the business to be very effective. A few people at the top simply cannot know enough, and in any case other people in the company have a great deal to offer and the company is always better off by including these people's contributions. Nevertheless, many traditionalist managers have a hard time believing that anything other than the rigid, authoritarian style of management can be cost-effective and efficient. They usually change their minds when a more progressive competitor begins to devour their share of the market.

In a progressive company using state-of-the-art management methods and information systems, all information is shared and resides in a single, integrated data base maintained by the computer. Since each department no longer has "its own information," management must ensure that each part of data in the system is clearly the responsibility of specific managers. Thus the organization structure, viewed from the standpoint of information, relates to the data base used by the company approximately as illustrated in the simplified diagram in Figure 11-1.

It is important to understand the distinction between responsibility for information in this sense, and that used in the past. Design engineering, for example, will always originate drawings and part structures. In the traditional environment, design engineering simply issued copies of drawings to manufacturing engineering, which promptly redesigned the product so that it could be produced in many cases. Copies of either document went to accounting, which again rearranged the information to suit its purposes.

In the state-of-the-art environment, design engineering not only originates design information, but must do so in a form that is usable by everyone else, namely by maintaining all design data in the data base.

Management responsibilities in the new environment are therefore much more interlinked, overlapped, and interdependent and much less autonomous. Management must function much more as a team. The reader is again referred to Chapter 2 and the distinctions between formal and informal systems, and the information flow differences in each.

It follows that in a highly integrated environment, poor performance by a

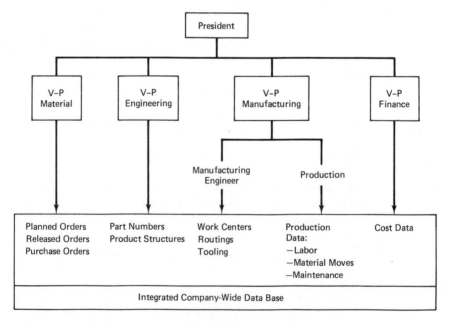

FIGURE 11-1 Management structure with integrated system.

single manager or department has a much greater impact on the business as a whole, and is much more visible to everyone. If performance is significantly below what is required, serious damage to the company's performance may even result because poor information coming from one critical area is used by everyone else. Since there is, in effect, only one copy of all information, it is much harder for other departments to compensate for poor information from a poorly managed department.

This is one of the primary reasons education, training, and top management involvement are so critical to the success of an integrated system. If seriously incorrect or untimely engineering or planning information enters the system, it will be dutifully communicated everywhere in the system. This is further compounded by the fact that computer functions replace manual methods in many areas. Various minor calculations and decisions are done mechanically, automatically. In the process, the ability to constantly apply human judgment is lost, since a computer program has only as much "judgment" as the system designers put into it.

For example, if a material planner in a manual environment constantly works with what he knows to be unrealistic, inaccurate sales forecasts, he can compensate by increasing safety stocks, overordering, or the reverse. A poor master schedule, however, will dutifully be exploded in the same manner as a good one. In the earlier years of material planning systems, companies sometimes got rude shocks when production ground to a halt in a major product line because critical components were not included in the bill of material records, and therefore were not planned and ordered.

In an integrated system environment, a much higher level of cooperation is required to obtain results. If present, the results will usually be considerably improved over anything achievable under even the best manual system. The structure of the company, including position job descriptions, the reward/punishment system, and the unwritten social value code reflected in people's day-to-day behavior, must reflect these differences. A personality type that functions fine in an autocratic environment, the drill instructor type, for instance, will have a hard time being effective in a company where participative management styles are in use. This person's behavior will alienate others and make the cooperation necessary for success difficult to come by.

A current barrier to state-of-the-art systems, and the success they can bring in many manufacturing companies in the United States is that less than 20% of company presidents came up through the manufacturing ranks. Most climbed the corporate ladder up the marketing, engineering, or finance ranks, and as a result have very little detailed experience in the production side of the business. For these people to openly attempt to deal with production management problems is to put them squarely in the area in which they are the weakest. As a result, most of these people tend to regard manufacturing operations as a "black box" not to be tampered with unless absolutely necessary.

This situation is most unfortunate, especially for companies now experiencing competitive or other market position problems as a result of poor manufacturing operations management. Unfortunate or not, it is still true that an integrated manufacturing system requires for success that the chief operating executive understand, become actively involved in, and be committed to the implementation and use of the system. There simply is no other way. The chief reasons for this, *especially* during an initial implementation, include the following factors:

- These systems are highly integrated; everyone must participate effectively. Uncooperative department managers can defeat the entire system. Often only the chief executive officer (CEO) can resolve these conflicts and/or bring the laggards into line.

- New management functions are required and must be properly fitted into the existing company management structure. Since some are at a high level in the company, only the CEO can ensure that this is properly accomplished.

- Substantial resources are required to develop and implement a system of this magnitude that affects virtually all internal company operations. Since the CEO is the ultimate arbiter of how company resources get allocated, he must understand why such large sums of capital are required for the project's success. To a lesser extent, this is also true to maintain an ongoing system. Substantial budget cuts in an already implemented system for training and data processing will eventually bring the company to its knees.

- An implementation project of this size requires a very high priority within the company. Only the CEO can ensure that this priority is maintained, via monthly management review and on a day-to-day basis. If allowed to drag out, the project will become bogged down, people will be sidetracked onto other things, and the project will fail.

- Measurable performance goals are needed, both for an implementation project and as an ongoing control device to keep the company's information system in good shape. The system will be, in fact, an integral part of the entire management process. It is how the company is run.

- A major project within the company requires a full-time, top-notch project manager. Only the CEO can ensure that such an individual is relieved of other responsibilities so that the project can be effectively managed. Few things will kill an otherwise good project faster than a project manager who is marginal or who is not highly respected throughout the company. A part-time project manager will not succeed, either.

Finally, the new organization structure, created with the full understanding and support of the CEO, must emphasize and clearly assign planning responsibilities at all levels that were probably not done at all in the past, or were done informally. Control mechanisms become much more important. Performance measurements that ensure consistent, high-quality results are a key factor in keeping the company on track. Especially if many of these factors were not strong in the past, only the CEO can ensure that they become an integral part of the company's management structure and social culture.

Constancy of Rapid Change

Many of the larger companies in the United States have been in more or less continuous production for 30 to 50 years. During this period many companies enjoyed relatively little in the way of serious competition, using economies of scale of production and marketing to achieve dominance in the market. The economy was also characterized during this period by constant growth, stable, low prices for raw materials, and a fixed exchange rate for the dollar which made exported products expensive to foreign countries. It was a safe, stable environment in which to manage a manufacturing company, at least compared with the climate of the 1980s.

During this same time period, the economy underwent a sizable shift toward a service economy. Interest in manufacturing declined. The brightest business school graduates seldom went to work in manufacturing, preferring the faster tracks of marketing and finance. Manufacturing was the black sheep of the business family. It acquired, with some justification, a reputation as a place where one's career could get stalled for years; many did, exhausted by the frustrations, pressure, and long hours.

Stated in blunt terms, the management of many manufacturing companies simply fell asleep at the wheel. Since the best and the brightest young people seldom went into manufacturing work, those that remained tended to cling to traditional patterns of behavior, with autocratic methods, attempts to manage by brute force, pressure, and threats, and a general resistance to change and innovation.

One of the important outcomes of this autocratic style of management is the assumption of an adversary relationship with the company's own employees and key suppliers. The negotiated, detailed legal contract became the way of relating, instead of developing mutual trust and acknowledgment of interdependence. In order to have continued labor peace, it became necessary to essentially give in to most union demands, creating a pattern of increasing costs without concomitant increases in productivity. Everyone forgot that the lowest-paid person's value is reflected in the value and price of the finished product. Everyone thought that buyers would just have to continue to pay ever-increasing prices.

In the production and inventory control area, many companies have continued with methods that are not particularly different from those of the 1940s, especially in those companies that have been in stable markets since that time.

The great awakening: During the late 1970s, it became clear to many observers that American manufacturing was in deep trouble. Incredibly well-organized Japanese and German companies were producing high-quality, well-designed products that were flooding the American market.

On a more subtle level, foreign companies were making serious inroads into basic manufacturing capabilities, including foundries, machine tool makers, fasteners, and others. The fundamental manufacturing capacity of the country experienced and still is experiencing considerable permanent shrinkage. Many types of technology that have been traditional American strongholds seemed to slip across the border. Some very large, well-financed companies began to have serious difficulties and enormous losses.

On the positive side has been the development of APICS and its body of knowledge. Manufacturing systems embodying the APICS knowledge have proven successful in an amazingly wide variety of industries. Not all companies are in trouble. Some have grown into formidable competitors on the world market as well as the domestic market. Every concept discussed in this book has been proven in actual use. All of these concepts were developed originally by practitioners in the field who were constantly striving to develop better ways to manage the business. There have been failures, of course, and from them has emerged a better understanding of how manufacturing really works, why various concepts work, and when they do not.

The new environment: One of the primary outcomes of the great awakening, as it is termed here, is that change has been accepted as a permanent feature of the manufacturing landscape. Manufacturing management can no longer assume a secure market share and dominance over competitors due simply to size or control of resources. Even technological leads can no longer be assumed to be anything more than a temporary state of affairs.

More and more companies, and the unions that are connected to them, are beginning to understand that not all costs can be passed on to buyers. At some point buyers begin to decide that the product is not worth having, or that it is just not worth the price. What the economists refer to as a consumer's marginal utility curve is behind the drop in many companies' sales, especially big-ticket items like automobiles. The years and years of continued price increases finally reached a level where many people simply cannot afford to buy, and/or decided that they would rather spend their money on other things of greater relative value to themselves.

Barriers to change: There are a number of common attitudes found in the social culture in many manufacturing companies that are serious barriers to change for that company. These include, but are certainly not limited to:

- *Tradition-oriented thinking.* "We've always done it this way and it has worked." This attitude is most inappropriate in a period of rapid upheaval and change in the marketplace—rather like the ostrich sticking his head in the sand when threatened.
- *Not sticking to and improving the basics of good management.* Many companies have substituted or attempted to substitute incredibly complex methods of operation rather than face dealing with the basic issues. The Japanese have amply demonstrated what continual efforts to simplify the business and become very competent at the basics can accomplish.

- *Viewing employees as a disposable commodity.* Many companies spend little or no money on training and improving their work force, preferring instead to hire and fire as business cycles ebb and flow. This often results in a residue of the most marginal employees, effectively flushing out the most innovative and energetic. Closely related is the assumption that only management is competent to decide what employees should best do with their time at work. Workers are often viewed as simply drones, to be ordered about, thereby stifling the creative energies of the very people who are often in the best position to understand problems.
- *Rigid management structures, designed mostly to protect individual executives' territorial fiefdoms.* In these companies little or no interdepartmental cooperation is found. Accommodating the company to even the smallest change in customers' needs is difficult and painful.

Springboards to flexibility: Management literature, both in academic journals and in practitioner-oriented periodicals, is filled with well-substantiated research and case histories of companies that have learned successfully to cope with continual change. A few companies have seemingly mastered the art of managing enormous internal growth and change. These companies seem to be able to harvest a bumper crop of good managers, loyal employees, and creative people in general, while others are dying on the vine. These companies have a number of things in common. The following list includes some of the more important ones:

- Continual projects to improve people, systems, and management capabilities
- Effective use of person-to-person communication skills, team building, and other techniques to develop a cooperative spirit among managers and employees, reducing the adversary climate found in traditional companies
- Clear reinforcement of creative, innovative behavior among employees, both line and management
- Acceptance of the risks involved with a changing environment and intelligent action to evaluate and manage risks
- Substantial investments in ongoing education and training programs and other forms of human development
- A mobile, highly cross-trained work force, reducing the stultification of creativity that comes with having the same task for too long, and adding to the day-to-day flexibility available to the company
- Attention to detail as a habit of management, reducing the habit of attempting to use the "big picture" approach to make major decisions
- Becoming highly planning and control oriented, with continual efforts made to compare plans with actual results and to narrow the gap by improving both planning and execution

The author often is surprised at the number of high-ranking managers who regard these things as risky and revolutionary, as being not tried and tested. There is no mystery as to why they work. That much is well established. The mystery is why so many otherwise intelligent and capable managers avoid implementing them.

The Computer Moves to Center Stage

Only the most isolated, uninformed person in business these days has escaped a strong awareness of the impact of computers. It is clear that America, and the Western world in general, is undergoing a not so subtle revolution. Computers and their varying uses are proliferating at a truly mind-boggling rate.

Chapters 1 and 2 discussed how the computer can maintain a picture of reality via its data base, then process that data base instead of reality itself to perform tasks that would be inconceivable manually. This is in addition to the sheer efficiency of maintaining records and communicating timely information. If anything, the rate of improvement in the capability of computer systems is itself increasing rapidly. Even experienced professionals in the computer business are sometimes overwhelmed by the rate of change—by the rapidity with which improved capabilities are becoming available.

These rapid changes involving computers are being driven by very powerful forces. As a result, the proliferation of computers is and will continue to be enormous. It is perhaps unfortunate that so many otherwise competent managers have so little grasp of computer concepts and are just plain uncomfortable with the machines.

Sociologists and social psychologists sometimes observe that the toys that children play with are just miniature versions of the things these little people will be concerned with, will use easily, and will value when they become adults. During the 1940s and 1950s a whole generation of people grew up playing with toy cars as children. These people grew into a life centered around cars. Operating on them, working on them, and understanding how and why they work are considered commonplace and usual. The current generation of children is playing with computer games, and growing up with terminals and personal computers. They are perfectly comfortable with bytes, disk records, and programming. These people, when they become managers, will have no trouble using computers in their work, and will be upset if they have to work without them.

The costs of computer systems, hardware and software, are still a barrier in the minds of many. That hardware costs continue to drop dramatically is well established and publicized. It is often said that software costs are rising so rapidly as to offset much of the reduction in hardware costs. Usually, the reason is attributed to rising programmer salaries. The author believes that a somewhat different position is warranted by the facts.

It is true that programmer salaries are increasing rapidly, that good programmers are scarce, and that projects are difficult to carry through. However, the primary reason that business systems are so costly to develop is that software development problems are mostly in the design area. Actual coding of programs is usually only a small part of a software development project. Software design is really a management problem, just as in precomputer days managers and supervisors designed procedures and forms. In most companies, few if any managers are conversant with computer system design. Also, the people who can talk to the computer—programmers—seldom have anything substantial in the way of business experience, so are not conversant with the business realities faced by the managers and staff. The result is an enormous communication gap.

All too often a computer system ends up being designed initially by the programming staff for the most part, with superficial involvement by managers, who can relate to the system only after it is working. The next stage is what may be termed design by rework. The original design, since it reflected the programmers' view of the situation, is inadequate and must be heavily modified, revised, and sometimes completely redone. It is this reworking stage that makes software development projects take so long, become so frustrating, and cost so much.

In the rare project that is completely designed by knowledgeable users to a high degree of detail, the actual programming simply becomes a task to be performed against a known standard, the specifications. A number of programmers can be brought to bear on the coding task simultaneously, and the system can be operational in a relatively short period of time, and at a predictable cost.

Electronic office concepts are still too new to evaluate fully as to how extensive they will become and when. It is already clear, however, that in many companies radical changes are already being wrought. Text processing is greatly speeding document production in many companies. This book is being written on a word-processing system, eliminating much of the expense and hassle associated with writing, editing, and formatting. Further, word-processing systems are becoming more integrated into what used to be thought of as traditional data processing, and with other capabilities, such as message handling, document filing, and electronic mail systems.

There is a powerful message to managers in all of these developments. In the company of the not-too-distant future, acquiring computer skills will be a make-or-break proposition. Those individuals who are able to adapt to the extensive use of computers, either by personal growth and learning, or by their childhood experiences, will have a huge advantage over their less progressive peers. In short, key managers will need to understand computers and data processing or will simply lose out. By the same token, companies whose managers as a group do not understand computers and data processing will have a less than favorable competitive position and will need to be better than their competitors at other things just to stay even. There could be tough sledding for many companies over the next 10 to 15 years.

New Management Skills

Besides the computer skills mentioned above, the manager of the manufacturing company in the near future and beyond will need a different set of skills than in the past. He must be comfortable in thinking in terms of systems, planning methods, and highly efficient control and execution techniques.

The old autocratic methods may die slowly, but die they will. Companies where the individual is respected and has dignity simply do better than those where he or she is just a number, a replaceable labor unit. So the manager of the future will be more people oriented and will use a more participative style of management. The cultural climate in these companies will encourage better communication among people than in the past, and be characterized by employees with better interpersonal skills. There will be fewer cases of management simply issuing orders. Responsibilities will be shared more often and interdependencies acknowledged. Teams and work groups will become more important as they are based more on respect for the individual person and less on the superman manager concept.

Managers in the new environment will understand that no system can work without the full consent of the people using it. This consensus must be obtained either before implementation or during it. There is no such thing as a successful implementation of a system without employee consensus, so wise managers will not move forward with implementation plans until what Oliver Wight refers to as a "critical mass" of people in the company understand and agree with the purposes and methods of the system.

Figure 11–2 summarizes a number of important differences in management styles between the traditional manufacturing manager and that of the new. Laced through the new style list are a number of characteristics that facilitate the use of formal systems. Comparing the two, a number of obsolete habits, styles, and assumptions become apparent, including:

- Willingness to tolerate (and create) crises
- Unwillingness to make long-term commitments
- Acting immediately instead of planning and analyzing
- Nonabstract thinking, belief that manufacturing can best be managed in a concrete, action-oriented fashion
- Assumption that other employees and managers, suppliers, and customers are adversaries to be manipulated, deceived, and tricked where possible
- Assumption that gain for one's self, one's department, or one's company can come at the expense of an adversary group
- Assumption that change always involves big risks, and that not changing does not involve substantial risk

These lists are not intended to be an exhaustive discussion of this subject, but are presented to stimulate the reader's thinking and to focus attention on

Traditional	New
Autocratic	Participative
Individual Responsibility	Shared Responsibility
One-Way Communication	Consensus Process
Insensitive to People	Concern for Morale
Lone Wolf/Hero	Group Leader
Fear Motivations	Systems-Oriented Controls
Informal, Personal Control	Systems-Oriented Controls
Problem Solver	Problem Preventer
Action, Crisis-Oriented	Planning-Oriented
Resists, Fears Change	Creates, Welcomes Change
Adversarial	Cooperative

FIGURE 11-2 Contrasted management styles.

critical issues that are closely related to business success with state-of-the-art production planning and control systems. No system can fully succeed in an environment that is not conducive to its operation, and that does not support the assumptions inherent in a formal planning and control system.

Cost of Traditional Orientation

One of the chief points of this book has been that the future is coming upon us at increasing speed. Making substantial improvements in how well manufacturing companies are run, the underpinning of any economy, is not only long overdue, but critical to the simple survival of a great many companies. For most companies, the lead time for such dramatic changes is quite long. Computer systems are now being used to competitive advantage by a great many companies and less successfully by many others.

Companies that fail to take full advantage of computer systems and other effective management tools will inevitably fall behind in the competitive race. Since the labor market is competitive, too, with companies competing for the best people, tradition-minded companies will lose out in the race for the best talent. Clinging to the old ways in the face of rapid change can only bring eventual stagnation throughout a company. This, in turn, will lead to a declining profit picture and reduced return on invested capital.

Marginally profitable companies have always had a harder time raising capital than the more robust, and there is increasing competition here, too. In America, the capital base has not grown as rapidly as is needed, especially with large government deficits, which compete for capital available on the open market, crowding out private borrowers. As long as this situation continues, and it seems likely that relatively high interest rates will be a feature of the economy for quite some time, the chief source of capital for many companies will be either equity issues on the open market or retained earnings. This situation places further emphasis on highly efficient operations and the most effective use of available capital.

Job-shop-type companies with 1.6 inventory turns per year, months of work in process, and poor use of capital equipment will have a very hard time surviving at all, let alone being highly profitable. Even capital-intensive companies in the repetitive manufacturing business must manage their assets well, since they are often even more capital intensive than many job shops.

Probably the worst aspect of stagnation of management in a company is that it becomes prone to sudden, overwhelming problems, from which it simply cannot recover. The lead time for most significant changes in managerial efficiency is in years, often four or more. Remember that the Japanese have been making this a very high priority in their business for over 20 years. Since the lead time required for anticipating problems of this sort, developing solutions, and implementing them is so long, reacting only after the red ink appears is almost always far too late.

During these turbulent times, the management of every American company should be conducting a penetrating, honest evaluation of past, current, and future efforts to improve the effectiveness of the company's management and its operational efficiency. These efforts will, in most cases, require a significant commitment of resources on an ongoing basis to produce long-lasting, effective results. Short-term projects and token expenditures for systems, training, education, and other items will simply not bear fruit.

Organizing for Planning and Control

Effective manufacturing management for the 1980s will usually require a number of additions to the organization chart for the company. There are new functions that perhaps were not done at all in the past, or were not assigned to a specific, higher-level manager.

Company presidents sometimes complain that they already have too many people reporting to them. This merely underscores the amount of information needed to manage a manufacturing company effectively in the new environment. One or two key people simply cannot absorb enough information to be effective. Although a dynamic, powerful leader is very important to a company, more and more decisions must be made by groups of people, pooling their information. Some of the new functions that the chief executive officer of the company will have to fit effectively into the management structure will include:

- Long-range and strategic planning.
- Management information systems or data processing, now a senior-level responsibility, not just someone who reports to the controller.
- Master scheduling.
- Material management, including production scheduling, inventory planning and control, and purchasing. These functions are not new, but making them function closely together is.
- Full-time project managers. These individuals will be in charge of key projects of major significance to the company. They cannot be relegated to a position far down the management structure if they are to be effective.

These new positions, or new arrangements of existing positions, will function better in the new environment if reporting relationships are not as rigid as has been the custom in the past. Key people must work together and share responsibility. This does not mean that they toss the hot potato back and forth and blame each other for their collective failures. It is possible to assign responsibilities clearly, an important management step, and still have them shared to a great extent by more than one person.

An important factor in the planning and control management environment is that of performance measurements. A number of closed-loop comparisons, such as those discussed in Chapter 9 should be used throughout the company to measure the effectiveness of plans and their execution and to develop a constantly improving set of results. This type of climate makes a company very goal oriented. That is, constant efforts are made to understand what is possible, set goals at the limits of what can be done, organize to achieve them, and measure the results.

In summary, managing in the new environment will require far greater efforts to stay in touch with the company's present and potential market segments. Planning for a variety of possible scenarios far in advance of the present will prove to be critical for many firms. Detailed planning in the nearer and current periods will greatly assist in achieving highly efficient operating results. Careful monitoring of ongoing operations, of performance to plan, coupled with intensive efforts to streamline operations and to make work flow quickly through the plant with a minimum of inventory, will substantially improve a company's chances for survival in a competitive, worldwide marketing and manufacturing environment of scarce critical resources.

Computer systems have provided, and will continue to provide, an enormous lever to management in all these areas. Effective development of new and improved systems, coupled with intelligent management of the company's information, will in many cases be the make-or-break factor for success in this new environment.

CHAPTER 11 QUESTIONS

1. Identify at least four management characteristics of manufacturing companies that have successfully maintained high rates of internal growth.
2. Contrast the organizational structure and flow of information in the modern, successful manufacturing business with the traditional, military-oriented model.
3. What is the primary difference between education and training activities?
4. Why are education and training a necessary part of the effective manufacturing management environment on a permanent, non-project-oriented basis?
5. Identify at least three of the goals of education programs.
6. What is top management's role in education programs?
7. Identify at least three goals of training programs.

8. Identify at least six kinds of education and training resources.

9. Why must education and training programs be tied directly to performance improvements, promotions, and pay raises, i.e., the reward system?

10. Explain what is meant by "information-oriented management structures."

11. How is responsibility for information accuracy assigned in an integrated system environment?

12. How does integrated information relate to a management culture that strongly supports cooperative teamwork instead of divisive competition and departmental autonomy?

13. What personality types are more suitable to the integrated system environment where high levels of cooperation are required? What types are not as well suited? What is the outcome if either type is "out of his element"?

14. Identify and explain at least five reasons why the company's chief executive officer must understand, become actively involved in, and be committed to the implementation and use of an integrated manufacturing system if the project is to be successful.

15. Describe several of the elements of what the text describes as the "Great Awakening."

16. What are at least three of the commonly found barriers to change in the manufacturing management context?

17. Identify at least five of the characteristics of companies that seem to do a good job of managing enormous internal growth and change.

18. Describe several reasons why computers and the usage of them will continue to rapidly proliferate.

19. Where are the "real" problems in system design efforts? Explain briefly.

20. How does knowledge of computer systems fit into the skill inventory of the future executive, especially in manufacturing?

21. Identify at least five management/personal behavior characteristics that are becoming relatively ineffective and obsolete in the new environment.

22. What are the likely outcomes for companies whose management continues in the traditional pattern of management through the next decade?

23. Identify at least four new functions that manufacturing chief executives must effectively integrate into the company management structure at a high level.

12

Key Computer Factors

This chapter is intended to provide the reader with some grasp of some of the more important factors in dealing with computer-based systems from a nontechnical viewpoint. The perspective is that of company management, not the data processing viewpoint. If the reader already has an extensive background in computer technology, so much the better. The management issues of risk and investment must still be addressed.

The technical information presented here is to give the reader who does not have a technical background in computers a grasp of the fundamental issues and some perspective. The computer field has grown so complex and varied that no one book on the subject, let alone a single chapter, can hope to provide more than the barest minimum of understanding. A large number of widely varying technical strategies have been developed and implemented by various hardware and software designers. Each has advantages and disadvantages. These must be weighed in light of what is required of the system. And it is in determining these requirements that a great many of the problems relating to computer systems reside.

HARDWARE OVERVIEW

Any computer system consists of a number of separate physical devices. Their combination into a specific configuration results in an actual computer system. The number, size, and performance capacity of each of these devices can vary substantially from a small desktop microprocessor to a very large mainframe. Nevertheless, the basic functions are the same.

Figure 12–1 illustrates in diagrammatic form the devices that form a basic computer system. The basic elements include:

- *The CPU.* At the heart is the central processing unit, or CPU. It is here that all programs are actually executed. The CPU is the actual computer. The other devices permit the CPU to store data, perform input and output, and to communicate with human users. The CPU contains both the main memory, where programs being executed are stored, and the processor, where machine-level instructions are executed. Programs to be run are input into the CPU's main memory from the disk drive storage unit, or from a tape drive (rarely), or directly from a visual display terminal (rarely). The CPU's output is directed to one of the other devices, termed peripherals.

- *Disk drive unit.* The function of the disk drive is to provide a nonvolatile place for the system to store data. In a typical business computer system, the disk drive unit also stores programs to be run, including the operating system, file management routines, and application program library. The data files stored include operating system dictionaries and working files, as well as the more visible data which appear on reports and displays. Some disk space is required for working area by some programs—sort of a scratch pad to store intermediate results.

- *Visual Display Terminal (VDT).* This is the familiar television-like unit, usually with a keyboard that a human being uses to interface with the computer system. VDTs vary in size, functional features, and may have their own small CPU internally. This aids the central CPU by offloading much of the routine

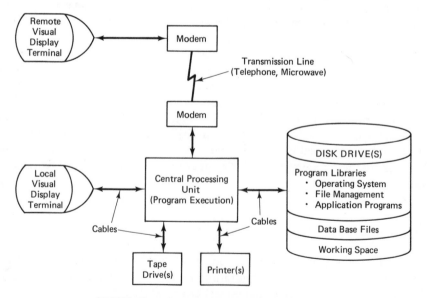

FIGURE 12-1   Computer system hardware elements.

work, such as editing and formatting data. VDTs as well as printers may be local, meaning that they are connected with a cable, or remote, meaning that they use a modulator/demodulator (MODEM) to pass data over a telephone, microwave, or other transmission line.

- *Printer(s)*. Used for creating hard copies of data, some printers may also serve similar functions as the VDT if they have keyboards. Printers vary from typewriter-like devices running at speeds of 35 characters per second all the way up to line printers that print thousands of lines per minute. Various print mechanisms are used: physical impact, dot matrix formation, thermal impression, ink jet, and laser-generated images. Naturally, costs range from a few hundred dollars to over $50,000.

- *Tape drives*. In older computer systems, before disk drive technology was very advanced, the tape drive was the primary method used to store data. Many computer systems now in use have no tape drive at all. However, tape is still very useful as an inexpensive method of storing seldom-accessed data, for transferring data from one machine to another, and for backing up files (making copies for use in the event the disk is damaged).

- *Other peripherals*. Various computer system configurations may also utilize a variety of special-purpose devices, such as card readers and punches, paper tape readers and punches (although these are generally obsolete), optical character recognition (OCR) readers, and analog-to-digital devices that are used to convert computer data to a physical response such as opening or closing a valve or switch.

In addition to the local versus remote distinction for VDTs, mentioned above, CPUs may also be linked utilizing either cables or modems. The important thing to remember about remote connections is that processing is substantially slower to almost any remote location.

However, remote processing by computer is much faster than other forms of communication. Data can be passed down a wire as though the wire is a physical extension of the CPU's circuitry, which, in effect, it is. To be transmitted over long distances, a number of other considerations come into play, related primarily to data integrity. Generally, the faster the transmission speed desired (over a remote data link), the more difficult it becomes to ensure the integrity of data (i.e., that none of it is lost or becomes changed by electrical disturbances while enroute). This difficulty quickly translates into higher cost. For most purposes, such as remote VDTs, a relatively slow line speed is acceptable. For CPU-to-CPU communication, this slowness may become a major consideration if a multiple computer network is envisioned.

Organization of CPU Memory

Although the exact organization of main memory in the CPU varies considerably from one computer to another, there are some common characteristics. In many machines, much of the operating system functions are handled in a separate, dedicated piece of memory which may be a relatively permanent part of the CPU's circuitry. In a simple, single-user computer, such as a personal or desktop computer, some functions are not needed.

Generally, as the size of the CPU increases, contention for resources increases in proportion to the number of peripherals attached. In a very large computer, the operating system, which resolves this contention, may be extremely large and complex, with elaborate scheduling routines for input/output operations and for allocating CPU time to each program being executed.

The important thing to remember is that for virtually all computers in use today, the CPU is actually working on only one program at a time, even though as many as several hundred may be in one state of execution or another. The sheer speed of a really fast computer often blurs this fact, so that it appears that many programs are running simultaneously.

Figure 12-2 illustrates in symbolic form the functional organization of a multitasking CPU running several application programs at once. The size of each function varies considerably from one computer system to another. Some types of computers seem to require very little room for overhead functions, whereas others take up a lot of main memory. It all depends on how the circuitry has been architected and how the software designer arranged the functioning of each part of software. In most cases, only the most commonly used routines belonging to the operating system are actually resident in main memory, with the others residing on the disk drive to be called in as needed to perform specific functions. The same approach is often used for other system-wide software, and sometimes even in application program design.

One of the major distinctions between types of computers is minicomputer architecture and the design of a mainframe computer. Both types have completely different technical development histories. The mainframe computer is the modern descendent of early computers, when CPU capacity was very expensive and tape and disk speeds very slow compared to those on the market today. The design goal of a mainframe is to make maximum use at all times of the CPU's capabilities, so that its designers attempt to configure the operating system and circuitry to keep programs executing at all times, with as little idle time as possible.

In this manner it is possible for mainframe computers to process a large number of jobs at the same time, and with surprising speed. Besides mere speed, the designers of mainframes include a wide range of other hardware and software architecture features to speed throughput. Input/output operations may be stacked up or routed through multiple channels to and from the disk drives. The operating system may maintain in memory various tables where active information is stored for instant use, reducing the requirement for repeated accesses to the disks for the same data.

Each of these elements that is or may be resident in the CPU's main memory has an important function. These general functions may be described very briefly as follows:

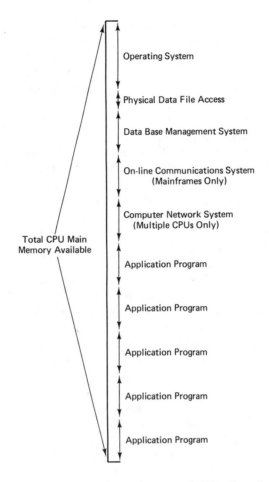

FIGURE 12-2   Typical CPU main memory functional overview.

Operating system: In its most basic form, this handles the scheduling of application programs (i.e., which ones get attention, and how much) and resolves contention for access to disk, tape drives, and printers. The operating system also handles a myriad of other more occasional chores, such as opening and closing files, rescheduling the jobs in memory, and calling in various sorting, copying, and communications subprograms to perform specific chores.

Other pieces of software (described separately here) may be included as a standard part of the operating system, such as file accesses, maintenance of indexes, or even a full dictionary to the data base. Each function that is included in the operating system eliminates a requirement that it be included in application programs.

For example, when an application program opens a file, the programmer does so by merely including a statement, such as "OPEN INVENTORY

FILE.'' This statement gets translated and ends up passing control to a subroutine that is part of the operating system, thereby relieving the programmer of writing the tedious code for opening a file every time he wishes to do so.

It should be remembered that the operating system controls all other programs in the computer system, regulates all access to the peripheral devices, and in general regulates the circuitry of the computer. It also protects the computer's logic from programs attempting to perform logically impossible functions, such as dividing by zero. The operating system detects such problems and stops the program with an abnormal end message to the user. In a very large system, the operating system may have very sophisticated scheduling and priority subroutines, and perform a startling variety of tasks to keep the huge system running at peak efficiency. In extremely large supercomputers a program can be divided up into parts and each part processed in parallel simultaneously, as opposed to one instruction at a time, the linear process used in normal business computers.

File access software: In many computer systems the file access methods comprise a separate piece of software that is logically linked into the application program and is somewhat separate from the operating system itself. Whether the file access software is more or less a part of the operating system, the results are the same—the access software is shared by all application programs.

File access software ranges from the very simple techniques required to access sequential files up to very sophisticated multiple indexes, relative record access methods, and techniques that resemble data base management systems. Whatever the capabilities offered by a given access software system, they function as tools for the programmer to use in creating the application in the minimum time and effort possible. The older hands in the computer business talk of the early days where the programmer had to code virtually every function to be performed. These tools either were not available at the time, or the computers were too limited.

Data base management systems (DBMSs): These software systems are simply complex programs that take all the file and record management chores out of individual application programs. A more detailed discussion of DBMS characteristics follows later in this chapter. For purposes of CPU organization, one needs to understand that the addition of a DBMS to the computer system adds a significant amount of overhead to the system. The DBMS functions as an addition to both the operating system and the file access software, although it may replace some of the file access software functions.

The DBMS consumes main memory, often quite a lot, and performs a number of tasks that require access to the disks (in addition to normal accesses). One should remember that an application program that uses a DBMS will normally require a bigger and much faster computer to do a task than will the same task done by a non-DBMS-based application program—that is, if the tasks are to take the same time to do. The advantage of a DBMS is the separation of records from application programs.

On-line or VDT network software (mainframes only): When VDTs are used on a batch-oriented mainframe computer, a separate piece of software is required to manage the VDTs. This software is overhead, in addition to the operating system and other software systems (such as file access or DBMS software). It queries each VDT in the network once every second or so and picks up messages (the contents of the screen) if the TRANSMIT key on the VDT is pressed.

The on-line software then reads the message to determine what program the message is to be processed with, and finds, loads, and runs the program. Then it passes the results back to the VDT that sent the message. In a minicomputer, the VDT is linked directly to an application program that stays in memory.

There are a number of important distinctions between a mainframe and minicomputer, which are discussed in some detail later in the chapter. In the context here, the reader should understand that the on-line system software refers to the additional overhead software, functioning as an extension of the operating system, that is required in a mainframe computer to manage the VDT network.

Networking software: If the CPU is part of a multiple-computer-system network, there will be additional overhead in the form of more software required to handle the interfaces with other computers. This will vary considerably with the degree of interactivity between computers. Simple batch transfer of a file from one computer to another is really not very different from transferring a file from a disk to a tape drive, for example.

However, if true interactivity is required, where VDTs from one computer can access files on another computer as though they were on the VDT's own system, the amount of overhead in the networking software increases dramatically. The concept of networking is at the center of the centralized versus distributed computer system debate, since networking software must be present to some extent in each machine in the network, thereby increasing overhead in the system as a whole. Another section in this chapter discusses this debate in more detail.

Disk Organization and Functions

In a modern computer system virtually all data files are stored on the disk drive, although tape drives are quite useful for lower-cost, long-term storage of less active data files and for backup copies of files. It is also true that access to the disk drive is the primary bottleneck in computer system throughput. As a result, most applications have to be designed with the disk drive accesses in mind, or in other words, designed around the limitations of disk accesses.

Figure 12–3 illustrates in simple form how data are stored and accessed on a disk drive's plotter. Bear in mind that a disk drive may have one platter, or it may have many, stacked one on top of another, with a read/write head for each surface. In certain disk drive designs, a fixed head resides over each disk track. This eliminates the time lag required for head movement. With the head-per-track design, the circuitry switches control from one head to another electrically rather than using a head-actuating mechanism to position a single head at the correct track. Disk drives now in use follow the same general architecture. Except for this difference, the elements and general design of most disk drives now in use follow the same general architecture. There are three basic parts to the disk drive mechanism that result in records being stored (written to) and retrieved (read) from the disk. These parts are the controller, and read/write head, and the disk surface itself. Their features and functions include:

- *Controller.* The controller receives and sends data from the CPU. It controls the movement of the read/write head and physically routes data to and from the disk surface. In order to optimize and speed up throughput, a controller will actually have its own specialized CPU internally that manages temporary storage devices called buffers. These buffers are used to accommodate the differences in speed between the CPU and the disk drive itself and to streamline actual reading and writing operations so that head travel and disk rotation are minimized.

- *Read/write head.* In floppy disk drive systems, or diskettes as they are often called, the read/write head actually contacts the surface of the diskette when reading or writing and is raised above the surface when not actually accessing the diskette. In a hard or rigid disk system, the head does not actually contact the surface, although it rides extremely close. In fact, in the Winchester type of

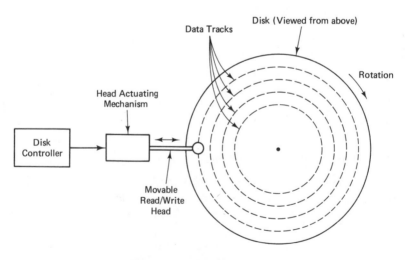

FIGURE 12-3   Disk drive elements.

hard disk drive, the distance between the head and the surface of the disk is about a quarter of the thickness of a human hair—small, in other words.

The read/write head is positioned by the controller over logical tracks that are defined on the disk surface in order to store or retrieve records that are stored on the disk's surface.

- *Disk surface.* Data are stored on a disk surface pretty much like on a magnetic tape; they are coded as a series of charges which are either present or absent, arranged in a linear fashion. The differences on a disk are that they are arranged in circular tracks with a beginning mark instead of the single long string of coded charges on a magnetic tape. They are frequently arranged in sections called blocks, which may include multiple records.

    The essential point about magnetic media is that they are a "permanent" storage medium, unlike the CPU's main memory, which is volatile. The CPU requires continuous power to retain its memory. Thus a momentary interruption of power to a computer system will cause it to lose the program and data it was executing at the moment of the interruption, but not the data on the disk.

Disk I/O Speed Limitations

Although it is true that disk speeds are surprisingly fast in some systems, at least compared to those of early data processing systems, disk access remains the critical bottleneck in most systems for all but the most computation-intensive applications. Speed of throughput with a disk system depends on several key factors, including the following:

- *The access method used.* Some require multiple accesses to the disk to actually locate the desired record.
- *Rotational speed of the disk media itself.* Floppy disk drives typically have rotational speeds of 300 to 500 rpm, while hard disk systems have rotational speeds generally in the neighborhood of 2500 to 3500 rpm. Obviously, access time in the hard disk systems will be much faster.
- *The amount of head movement required.* Some file reading methods will require the head to jump back and forth across the disk, whereas others will step smoothly from one track to the next. Density of data on the disk also is a major determinant of how much head movement is required.
- *How the file access software functions.* Including various ways of handling indexes, buffering records, and scheduling I/O operations within the CPU.

One can clearly see that simply reading a not terribly large data file consisting of 50,000 to 100,000 records will take the computer quite a while. Material and capacity planning programs are especially prone to the problem of very long run times because so many records are involved in the planned order processing cycles. As a result, a variety of special programming techniques are usually needed to keep computer run times from becoming excessive in the larger processing programs.

There are several inherent factors involved in disk drive design that limit processing speed. First, it is a rotating medium, and can be made to go only so fast before other limitations creep in, such as the extreme accuracy required for the placement of charges with high data densities. Second, the head must usually perform some movement from one track to another, or even a large jump from an outer to an inner track, where random reading is involved. There is also an impact on I/O throughput due to the way the software and/or disk drive controller handle indexes.

Although several other types of on-line storage devices have been developed which do not involve mechanical movement, (such as bubble memory) none have even approached the disk drive's universal flexibility and capacity. In a way, this is unfortunate, because disk speeds represent the primary limitation of many types of business applications that otherwise could be contemplated. These limits also add considerable complexity to the design of what otherwise might be a straightforward application, in some cases. The disk is always a factor to be considered when designing computer application systems.

The supercomputers that are currently appearing on the data processing scene are more like giant calculating machines, utilizing parallel processing of parts of a problem and extremely fast circuitry, as opposed to some new technology utilizing faster disk storage techniques.

Other Peripheral Devices

There are a number of other devices besides the central elements of CPU and disk drives that are needed to make a computer system usable. At least one visual display terminal (VDT) is used, and at least one printing device. A magnetic tape drive may also be included. The functioning of each is explained briefly below.

Visual display terminal: The VDT functions one of two ways, either as a message sender and receiver between a person and the CPU, during which times it operates relatively independently of the CPU, or as a functional window reflecting part of what is going on within a program running in the CPU. It is the most common device used to allow a person to communicate directly with a program running, or to be run, in the CPU.

There is a substantial range of capabilities and prices available with VDTs, ranging from the simplest keyboard with a screen, all the way up to highly sophisticated graphics terminals which have more power than many small computers (and cost more).

Magnetic tape drives: Tape drives store data in sequential fashion only, so are useful for making backup copies of files, since the storage medium, tape, is relatively cheap. Other common uses are to transfer data and programs. They are much slower than disk drives.

Printers: The term *printers* now really includes a wide variety of devices that create hard copies. A number of techniques are used: typewriter-like printing heads, dot matrix, laser, ink-jet, and electrostatic, to name a few. Speeds (and cost) range from typewriter speed up to 20,000 lines per minute. If a keyboard is included with the device, it can perform many of the same functions as a VDT, but must print the characters instead of just display them.

There are also a number of other devices in less common use, such as punched card readers and punches, paper tape readers and punches, badge readers, various specialized types of terminals, and an endless array of digital-to-analog and analog-to-digital devices. Computers can be made to turn switches and valves, to read measurements, and other such tasks. In each case, a special-purpose device must be used to translate something in the environment into terms that can be handled in the computer circuitry, or vice versa. In any case, all peripheral devices operate under control of a program.

SOFTWARE OVERVIEW

As discussed previously, everything the user actually experiences with a computer system is the result of software. In understanding how application systems are programmed, it is important to understand that any application language makes extensive use of system software to perform many tasks, such as physically accessing files or passing data to and from VDTs.

Application programs are where the major software investment of a company resides. System software either comes at a very low price with the computer, is included at no charge, or is purchased at a cost that is a fraction of its development cost. Although it is often true, particularly for manufacturing systems, that a purchased software package can meet most of a company's software requirements, some modifications are inevitable.

From a management point of view, this growth of investment in software is seldom handled in a business-like manner, except for major projects, although there is no reason it cannot be. The major cause for this is the "computer mystique" that this book is intended to dispel.

Virtually all application systems are programmed in what is referred to as a high-level language (i.e., one that is constructed somewhat like English). Examples include COBOL, BASIC, FORTRAN, Pascal, and many others. Each has advantages and disadvantages. All require a compiler program (or interpretation program) to convert the source code to machine language, which is what actually executes in the CPU.

Figure 12-4 illustrates the basic steps involved in producing executable programs from the source code written by a programmer. Both the compiler and link/edit programs are simply other programs. An interpreter is a program that runs concurrently with the application program and translates each line of

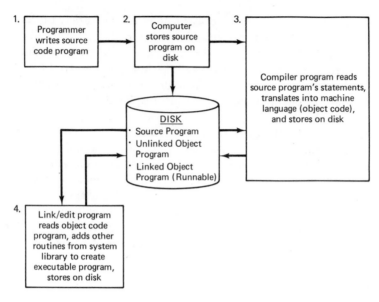

FIGURE 12-4   Compiled programming language steps.

source code into machine language as the program is executing. Interpreter systems are much slower in execution for this reason.

When one considers that a programmer must produce a runnable program, or at least what he believes to be a runnable program before compiling it, one can begin to appreciate why it takes a fair amount of time to write a single program. To design and code a complete application system consisting of dozens or hundreds of programs, the picture becomes much clearer as to why it takes so long and costs so much to develop even a simple application system. And of course, to make matters worse, to change even a single character in a program means that it must be recompiled and relinked.

File Organization Methods

Probably the most basic, most important aspect of the design of any application system is how the data are organized in the files. How long the records that are to be maintained are, how many, what data fields are included, and where they come from are the key elements of system design. It is vital that management participate intimately in this design step, and for this participation to be effective, some degree of understanding of the consequences of various design decisions needs to be present.

Although there are quite a number of file organization methods, three are the most common in business applications. These are depicted in Figure 12–5. All of these types of file organizations entail the file being created by and logically linked to the programs that use the files. The three basic types are:

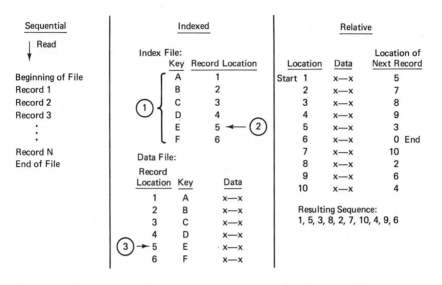

FIGURE 12-5   Common file organization methods.

- *Sequential.* These are the simplest, with records being added and read in the physical order in which they are present in the file, whether on tape or disk. Also, any disk file has its records physically sorted in a logical sequence, usually by the primary key.

- *Indexed.* This is probably the most popular file organization method. It allows retrieval of a specific record in two or three disk accesses of a file of virtually any size. The indexed method requires the maintenance of a separate file for each type of index that is stored. These indexes have their own organization, such that the file management software can read the index file and find the key to the desired record, which in turn gives the actual disk location of the physical record being accessed. The desired physical record is read on the next read operation.

  There are two important aspects to indexed file organization method. In most systems, there can be a number of indexes. One is primary, the others secondary. This use of multiple indexes allows the system designer to work with the data in the file as though it were actually organized in several different sequences, but without having to sort the file into that sequence first. This is especially useful for large files on small, slower computers, and/or where immediate on-line access is needed for records in the file. This is termed the logical sequence of the file, as opposed to the physical sequence. Adding records to an indexed file basically involves adding the record to the file's overflow area, then adding to the file index. The file is periodically reorganized to incorporate the records in the overflow area into the main file.

- *Relative access.* The relative access method is common, but less so than indexed files. The purpose is to create a chain of records through a large file, such as a bill of material component list. In this method, the location of the next record in the chain is maintained in the physical data record itself.

Retrieval of records in a relative access method chain is by reading the first record, which includes the location of the next record as a piece of data. Two basic versions of relative access use either the actual physical address on the disk of the records, or what is termed relative record number. The latter is more common, being more independent of where the file happens to be located on the disk.

Addition of records to a relative access file is another story. If a record is inserted in the middle of a chain, all subsequent records in the chain must be accessed and have their next record location addresses or numbers updated. A common variation of a relative access file is what are sometimes called ring structures, where the chain starts from and leads back to a control record that the program always reads first.

As mentioned earlier, all of these file organization methods have the file intimately tied to the programs accessing the file. This means that if 50 different programs access the same file, and one small piece of data is to be added to the record description, all 50 programs must have their record description of the file revised and the programs recompiled and relinked. This holds even if none of the 50 programs actually use the new piece of data at all.

Data Base Management Systems

The limitations of the file organization methods just discussed led to the development, starting about 15 years ago, of file access methods that separated application programs from the files. The purpose of a DBMS, put simply, is to perform all file maintenance tasks, indexes, chains, record definitions, and so on, separately from any particular program. The application program calls on the DBMS to give it a certain record with only the data fields that the program will actually use. All other fields that may be part of the record description itself (but not used) are "unknown" to the application program. Figure 12-6 briefly illustrates some aspects of DBMSs in a manufacturing system. Most important is that the actual data in the physical data files is maintained completely separately from information concerning how the data are to be accessed.

Consequently, virtually any number of different access paths can be constructed by a DBMS through the same collection of actual data. This means the entire data base can be made available on-line, and/or that the company can cease to be concerned about chasing small changes through ever-larger numbers of programs forming the application.

When one bears in mind that very common files, such as part numbers or work orders, may be accessed by perhaps hundreds of programs, the use of a DBMS can provide a major advantage. Because of their complexity, the use of a DBMS is almost mandatory in a state-of-the-art manufacturing system, because there are so many programs and constant changes to the system's design take place. The final compelling reason to use a DBMS in a manufacturing system is that the data relationships are often very complex. Accessing data

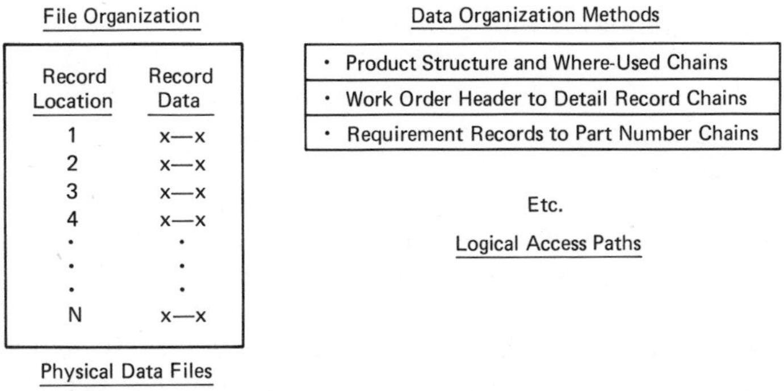

File Organization

Data Organization Methods

Record Location	Record Data
1	x—x
2	x—x
3	x—x
4	x—x
.	.
.	.
.	.
N	x—x

Physical Data Files

Data Organization Methods
• Product Structure and Where-Used Chains
• Work Order Header to Detail Record Chains
• Requirement Records to Part Number Chains

Etc.

Logical Access Paths

FIGURE 12-6 Data base management system file and data organization.

via complex pathways can be very difficult, if not impossible, using conventional file organization methods.

There are several major disadvantages to DBMSs. First, the DBMS itself is a large piece of software that must be resident in the CPU at all times to operate, even though many of its tasks are performed by routines that are called as needed. This use of memory adds, in effect, considerable overhead to the computer system. Another form of overhead is that the DBMS consumes more disk space, since it maintains more information about the physical data and uses its own files to do so.

The worse disadvantage to the use of a DBMS is that to add or read records in a physical data file, much more disk accessing must be performed. This is because all the information about where the record is located is in a larger, more complex, less quickly readable file than with simpler access methods. This requirement for much more disk accessing hits the computer system where it is slowest, through the disk I/O bottleneck.

From a management point of view, this major disadvantage does not necessarily mean that the company should avoid the use of a DBMS-based manufacturing system. To the contrary—its advantages far outweigh the drawbacks. The chief drawback boils down to the fact that a much larger, faster computer is needed to perform the same processing job that would be required without the DBMS. Of course, this translates into a larger cost for the system.

In extreme cases, a processing job may not be runnable in a reasonable time period even on the very largest, fastest computers available, simply due to the sheer amount of data if the data accesses are all through a DBMS. This may require very clever data storage techniques to speed processing of such jobs. In very large systems, a complete explosion of a master production schedule may involve processing hundreds of thousands of records.

The advantages of a DBMS are as attractive as the negative points are unattractive. Besides the separation of data files from application programs, a

DBMS allows a very wide variety of methods of accessing the same physical data. New access paths can be added without rebuilding the entire data base. Records can be chained, processed in various sequences, and grouped in a variety of ways for on-line retrieval as well as for a batch processing program to process efficiently.

In most companies, especially if there is much growth or the company is fairly large, use of a DBMS to manage the files of a full-blown manufacturing system is almost mandatory. Such systems often have a very large number of programs compared to other types of applications. Data relationships are also much more complex than with most other types of systems. In addition, there are constant changes to the data organization, addition of new fields to records, and new record types added to the data base and to the programs themselves. Without a DBMS, managing these changes through the entire system can really become a drain on programming resources.

Data Base Design

Design of a data base, or file structure, in any system is probably the most critical single task. In a manufacturing environment it is even more important because the number of records both in type and quantity is often very large. Although the discussion in this section will be brief and will not attempt to instruct the reader in how to go out and design an airline reservation system, several important factors should always be borne in mind when specifying computer applications. In present and future company management environments, knowledge of at least the basics of system design is part of the working tools of an effective manager.

Traditional computer application system design has involved, at a minimum, the following sequence of steps:

1. Design desired reports and/or screen formats (i.e., data one desires to get *out* of the system).
2. Design records and files needed to create desired reports.
3. Design the input needed to feed files.

When this approach is followed, it seems that an endless sequence of additions and modifications ensues as new pieces of information are grafted onto the system and as former problems give way to ones that were concealed by the old problems. Little thought is given to the inherent information relationships of the organization—what data might be useful in the future. Often little is done in the way of planning for future systems requirements. This approach is especially ineffective for large, complex systems.

An improved approach is the following sequence, which works well not only for complex systems, but for simpler ones as well:

1. Define overall system functions and requirements.
2. Define data structures and relationships as found in the business itself.
3. Design a data base that mirrors the company's actual data structure.
4. Modify the data base design to improve computer efficiency and run times.
5. Define detailed programs needed to perform system functions and to maintain data relationships.
6. Design input programs to gather data and update records.
7. Design specific reports and inquiries for specific situations to retrieve information from the data base.
8. Provide user-run inquiry and reporting software to enable flexible searches of the data base in response to unique situations and questions.

The intention of this approach is somewhat different from the more traditional one. The purpose of the traditional approach is to produce specific information arranged in a well-defined way to meet a certain set of conditions existing in the business. The reason this method runs into problems is that its basic assumption is that the conditions existing in the business are relatively constant. This is simply not true.

The second approach is intended to take a much broader perspective, to get a more complete grasp of the business itself, and to produce a system that will gather all relevant data in the way the information actually exists in reality. This complete data base can then be queried in response to a much broader range of questions.

Even the most complex systems also often go through a series of evolutionary steps in which the design concepts themselves become more refined. Most manufacturing system packages on the market today have gone through several complete redesigns and reprogramming as a result of this iterative learning process.

Centralized versus Distributed Data Processing

Originally, all computer systems were as centralized as possible, due simply to the enormous cost of early computers. Because the cost of hardware has come down so dramatically, and because of the increased capabilities now available on small computers, many of the early advantages to centralization no longer apply. The question of whether to utilize distributed data processing (DDP) or a centralized approach should no longer be made on financial grounds alone. It is not a hard-and-fast role that one approach is always better than the other. Each approach has its best and worst aspects, advantages and drawbacks. Some of each of these are considered briefly here.

Advantages of centralized systems: The following are some of the primary advantages of centralized computer systems:

- All data are in one place, facilitating sharing by many users on an efficient basis.
- Big computers can run complex jobs much faster than small ones.
- Better security, backup, and control of data base due to (normally) a more professional operation.
- Overall efficiency and throughput of the system may be considerably faster than DDP, depending on how a comparable DDP system is structured.
- Can have a very large number of VDTs on-line at the same time.

Disadvantages of centralized systems: Some of the disadvantages of centralized systems include:

- System failure may shut down the entire business (unless there are backup equipment facilities).
- Much of a centralized system's resources are spent resolving internal contention of machine resources, leading to very complex operating systems, data bases, and operating environment.
- If the centralized computer is a mainframe, the system software normally does not permit truly interactive processing; the screen on a typical mainframe VDT is completed without involvement of the CPU; it is transmitted as a block of data, processed, and returned. See Figure 12–7 for a comparison of the ways in which the on-line software of a typical mainframe and a minicomputer (or micro) handles VDTs.
- Mainframe on-line response is generally poor compared to interactive computers; usually not as suitable for real-time data entry as minicomputers; generally not as flexible as minis and micros in the on-line mode.

DDP advantages: Although DDP has many meanings, in this context a DDP system is considered to be a group of computers linked in a network permitting interrogation between machines. Some of the advantages include:

- The total system work load is spread throughout the system.
- The whole system never goes down; only one part of it will ever fail at a time.
- Places local files at the local site, not off in some physically remote location.
- Enables minicomputer responsiveness for many more users in a large system, since only a few users are logged onto any one machine.
- Eliminates much complexity and much of the contention for resources; each computer system in the network can have a fairly simple architecture and operating system since only a few users are working at any time.
- Since each computer in the network functions more or less independently, there is no real practical limit on the expansion of the total system, particularly if all computers do not have to be linked directly together, although some networking systems do have limits on how many machines can be in the network.

ry: The key factors in the centralized versus DDP debate center around
owing issues:

Who needs what data in the system and where is its source located?

Can local files be really local and *not* interlinked with files maintained on other CPUs? This is especially important for manufacturing systems and their highly interlinked data files.

What is the structure of the company? Is it centrally run or highly division-alized? Where is profit responsibility located? At what level is general ledger reporting maintained?

Some very large jobs just require a large computer to do at all, especially in a manufacturing system; a small computer simply cannot explode a complex master schedule involving tens of thousands of records in anything like a reasonable time period.

It should be borne in mind that these are complex issues, often clouded by managers' desire to have "their own computer" to avoid having to deal centralized, often seemingly poorly run data processing department. Un-ately, unless the DDP project is carefully thought through, the company well exchange one poorly run data processing department for several that orly run. It is well to remember that department managers know even less making a computer work than the data processing managers do.

MATED INPUT DEVICES AND
ICATIONS

computer peripherals industry has developed a vast array of special-ose devices to simplify and improve efficiency and accuracy of data entry. all, a state-of-the-art system has a requirement for a truly formidable unt of data, and serious thought must be devoted to its handling. Besides sual VDT keyboard entry method, some examples of specialized data entry es include:

- Hand-held, portable, battery-powered recording terminals.
- Optical scanning wands and readers.
- Badge-reading terminals.
- Counting scales.
- Connectors hooked to production equipment that count and feed data into a computer as a machine cycles, automatically updating inventory, for example.
- Voice input devices; these are usually rather limited in how many words and people they can "understand."
- Bar code printers that prepare labels for inventory that can be read by wands and other scanning devices.

On-Li

- On-line software ma
for messages.

- VDT is off-line (func
TRANSMIT key is p

- Polling detects TRAN
from screen, passes to

- Message handler selec
gets program from dis
it, and passes resulting

- On-line system passes
displayed.

- Entire screen is proces:

On-Line N

- User logs onto operatin

- Operating system loads
memory, connecting it

- Character-by-character a
is processed immediately

- Operating system gives e
time slices in round-robin

- All VDT activity is under

- Program for each VDT re
as long as user is logged o
swapped out if function e

- Character processing gives
processing.

FIGURE 12-7   Mainframe versus minicomputer on-line software functions.

local
with
fortu
may
are p
abou

**AUT
APP**

The
pur
Aft
am
the
dev

Disadvantages of DDP: Some aspects of a DDP network a
and some real operational limits exist in this approach. So
tages include:

- The network becomes *very* inefficient if more than a sm
must be passed between CPUs. This type of data handlir
three to four times as many I/O operations (a computer':
retrieve a single record from a remote CPU's files as withi

- Inter-CPU communication is very complex (other than
transmission of a file) and may require much overhead in e
ting some of the savings, and adding to the total system ov

- Users may bog down one computer by attempting lar
machine. A single application on one computer may n
capacity of a single machine, but the machine may already
configuration.

- Hardware and software compatibility may become a proble
fit for communications to work properly. This is particularly
system are to be added over a long period of time.

- Hardware and some software maintenance must be perforn
instead of at one place. Some remote sites may have poor phy
support, whereas others are satisfactory.

All these devices and similar ones serve to reduce data input costs, which is a major expense in a complex system. Chapter 13 discusses a complex manufacturing system developed by Yamaha that uses scanning terminals for virtually all inventory and production status information that is entered. Whenever these kinds of terminals are used, the result is usually a marked increase in data accuracy and timeliness. Since the input format is fixed in these cases, some rigidity is built into the system.

Typical applications include inventory movements, production floor data, receiving dock data, and shipping dock data. Bar-coded input must be tied to standardized container labeling which can be captured with hand-held scanning wands. Shop floor data collection systems typically use some form of badge readers, while unusual assembly line data input problems use a voice input system that hears and interprets the human voice, then displays what it "thinks" it heard for confirmation.

COMPUTER PROJECT MANAGEMENT CONSIDERATIONS

Computer projects seem to be like no other kind of business project, and therefore need some special rules for managing them. Probably the most important single one is to clearly understand that software development projects are really R&D efforts; they are virtually never underbudget and ahead of schedule, simply because it is impossible to foresee all the stumbling blocks that will occur. Only part of the task is fully identifiable at the outset, and as a result, schedules are usually poor. The bigger the software project, the bigger the risk of substantial overruns.

It is vital that the actual, ultimate users of the system actually design the system, not data processing "experts," who often have little or no actual business background. In any case, it is not the systems analysts that will make the system work on a day-to-day basis; it is the users in the departments.

The majority of the effort in a computer project is determining what the requirements are in enough detail and completing the actual detailed design. Programming is often only one-third or less of the total project effort. Efforts to shortcut the requirements definition and detailed design usually result in what may be termed "design by rework." And the more design changes are forced into a system toward the end of a project, the more difficult it gets, because the number of programs involved that probably have to be changed keeps increasing as the project nears completion.

Software packages will always speed a project considerably and save as much as 80% of the cost of development, simply because they are already written and in operation. For the same reason, project risk is easier to evaluate with a functioning system. Packages always include some features that are not needed, may run less efficiently on the computer (because of the extra features), and usually need to be modified to add features that are required.

The biggest drawback to a package approach is that it allows management the luxury of not confronting important issues of responsibility for results in detail, and skips important steps in determining the company's true requirements and completely sidesteps the whole issue of long-range systems planning. Many package systems fail during implementation simply because the company gave the project so little thought; they thought that a quick solution would solve the significant problems.

Any computer can be overwhelmed. In spite of fast CPUs and very improved disk I/O transfer rates, I/O is still relatively slow and therefore forces some compromises in design and creative programming.

Every computer project has *at least* one major disaster during implementation and/or development. Many have more.

The worst tendency in system design is to try and solve only today's problems. The company should be viewed from as broad a perspective as possible and should look as far ahead into the future as possible. Because of failure to do the latter, many systems are outgrown shortly after implementation simply because the business became more successful.

Lessons from Japan: Computer system projects do not seem to fail in Japan, at least not at the very high rate they do in the United States. There appear to be several primary reasons for this, which are consistent with the Japanese desire to excel at the basics rather than get lost in sophistication. Some reasons are:

- Include everyone in the system design process.
- Obtain complete agreement from everyone as to the system's requirements, purposes, and functions *before* starting, not during or after implementation, when they can be counted on to cause problems.
- Keep the execution part of the system simple to use. This keeps the workers' attention focused where it belongs, on manufacturing quality products, not on trying to run the system.
- Do not attempt to make the system solve fundamental management or production engineering problems that have not already been faced and resolved.

RETURN ON INVESTMENT FOR COMPUTER SYSTEMS

As with any capital investment project, management should perform a conventional return-on-investment analysis for any proposed computer project of any size. Usually, this will consist of a straightforward cost versus benefits or savings over the expected life of the hardware and software. Some other costs that should be included (that are often omitted) are implementation personnel, education, and training costs.

There are some major limitations, however, on the return-on-investment analysis process for computer projects. Attempting to compensate for these limitations can considerably complicate the analysis process. Some examples include:

- Many savings and advantages are *very* intangible, including some of the best ones.
- Some savings simply do not appear, for complex reasons.
- Unforeseen problems can cause expensive delays and large cost overruns.
- Lead time for systems projects are often so long that the requirements change substantially before the system is even implemented.
- If successful, the whole company may benefit considerably in the competitive marketplace; this may be very hard to place a dollar value on.
- Risk of failure is always present, and may result in the loss of the entire investment, with no results at all.
- Computers *always* seem to be too small and/or too slow; the chief reasons are that those "selling" the system (whether inside the company or vendors) tend to be very optimistic about the hardware performance, and that all requirements, volumes, and numbers of users are seldom included when determining the system's requirements.

None of these limitations should be taken to construe that the return-on-investment analysis should be performed, or that companies should invest their computer dollar only in sure bets with large margins of safety. Business success is not built on a no-risk foundation but on intelligent management of risks offering significant advantage.

The most valuable aspect of the return-on-investment analysis is that it forces management to identify clearly all expected savings, purposes, goals, and performance requirements for the proposed system, as well as the foreseeable costs. And if clear, achievable goals are set and pursued in a well-managed fashion, success is much more likely.

CHAPTER 12 QUESTIONS

1. Briefly explain each of the basic elements of a computer system and what its function is.
2. Why is the operating system for a large, complex computer system proportionately much larger than for a very small, simple system?
3. Distinguish between the operating systems that are typical of mainframe computers and those of minicomputers.
4. Identify several basic functions that all operating systems perform in computers.
5. Describe the features and functions of the three basic elements of a disk drive.
6. Explain in summary fashion how data is stored and accessed on disk.

7. Identify at least three factors that limit the speed of disk input/output operations.

8. Explain the difference between the program statements in a high-level programming language and machine language actually executed by the computer.

9. What are the three basic types of file access methods most commonly used?

10. What is the most important difference between the standard file access methods used and a data base management system?

11. What are the advantages and disadvantages of using a data base management system?

12. Explain and contrast the following:

    a. Traditional computer application design steps.

    b. The improved approach more typically used for complex systems.

13. Why is some degree of evolution of system design necessary, no matter how much effort is involved in the design at the outset?

14. Identify several advantages and disadvantages of centralized computer systems.

15. Assuming distributed processing to be as is defined in the text, identify at least four advantages and four disadvantages involved in its use.

16. What are the four key factors in the centralized versus DDP debate?

17. Identify four examples of specialized data entry devices.

18. Why are computer software development projects virtually never under budget and ahead of schedule?

19. Why should the ultimate users of a system be intimately involved in and responsible for the detailed design of a computer application system?

20. Where is the majority of the effort in a computer project required?

21. What are some advantages of using software packages in place of custom software development? Some disadvantages?

22. Identify at least three reasons why computer projects do not seem to fail so often in Japan as in the United States.

23. Identify at least five limitations on the return-on-investment analysis process for computer systems. Does this mean that the results of the analysis should be ignored?

13

The Present
Is the Future

This book opened with remarks to the effect that systems such as those described in the preceding chapters were developed by practical visionaries. The main purpose of this book is to stimulate those visions in others by conveying insight and encouraging further study and thought in areas particularly relevant to the reader. This approach was chosen rather than a highly detailed set of discussions because each person's business situation is somewhat different. Generally, the more specific the discussion, the fewer people who find it relevant.

In this chapter, this practical visionary theme will be carried still further. However, as is the case thus far, no concepts will be presented that are not actually in successful use in more than one industry. This is in keeping with the book's thrust and emphasis on what actually works in the real world, not some ideal setting.

At the time of this writing, Japanese companies in many industries are making their competitive presence heavily felt in the United States and major European countries. Many manufacturing people ignored these clear trends for years, ascribing their competitive advantage to largely cultural factors or to cheap labor. By now, it is quite apparent that there is much more to the Japanese industrial environment than this.

In other areas, many changes are apparent. Business is now truly international, with company after company developing international sources of raw material and actively selling in the marketplaces of many nations. Even financing has become international, with billions of dollars flowing across borders daily, and foreign companies routinely buying and selling commercial debt instruments and even equity issues in the financial markets of other countries.

Advanced technology has created new methods of production, and new methods of designing them. Computers continue their steady advance into every corner of our culture, especially in engineering and manufacturing.

All of these areas impinge on the traditional outlook of manufacturing management. Each provides opportunities for improvement in performance and, by the same token, the potential for competitive threat. It behooves the enlightened company manager to educate himself in those areas that seem more pertinent to his industry and company and to move his internal company culture in the direction of accepting and implementing as many of these ideas as seem truly useful. After all, if one's own company does not implement and profitably use state-of-the-art management techniques, sooner or later the competition will, either locally or abroad.

INSIGHTS FROM JAPAN

This section will focus on five major areas where Japanese manufacturing companies have performed especially well. These are:

- Simplifying business operations
- Quality control
- Participative management styles and a cooperative work environment
- Disciplined, formal systems
- Worldwide planning, marketing, and operations

In each of these areas, Japanese companies have excelled in ways that American and most European companies have not. Of course, there are many more factors actually involved in achieving business success in the international arena, but it is these areas that have the most impact for the topics of this book.

Simplifying the Business

Reducing the complexity of business operations is not something that Americans have generally been very good at. Since physical space and energy costs are substantially higher in Japan than in the United States, perhaps these are reasons the Japanese saw the value of simplified operations sooner than Americans. Business simplifications operate on two distinct levels: policy-type decisions, and very small, detailed techniques. An example would be a policy decision to emphasize substantial reductions of setup times, and the execution of the policy literally at the nut-and-bolt level on specific machines.

Policy-type decisions are not a problem for Americans, but becoming extremely proficient at detailed execution is. In fact, many Japanese companies have made it an integral part of their business strategy to become and remain very good at the execution side of the business. By becoming very flexible and fast in responding to changes in the marketplace, they have reduced the need to become very good at longer-range planning.

Probably 15 years or more ago, farsighted (visionary?) managers in several leading Japanese manufacturing companies began to realize that the more inventory is eliminated, the easier running the business becomes. However, to achieve this goal, the entire business would have to be modified into a tightly coupled series of interlocking functions. If the business is operated in this fashion, parts run through the business very quickly, producing inventory turn ratios in excess of 40 or 50 per year. This is the kind of performance that Toyota and other companies obtain after 10 or 15 years of working at their businesses.

The Kanban system of "just in time" inventory management is discussed later. It is a classic example of a business simplifier. Parts managed under Kanban simply have no warehouse storage at all. As a result, all inventory is out in the assembly and production areas where everyone can see it and it becomes easier to manage. Most important, since there is so much less of it, perhaps only a few *hours'* usage, it becomes a rather minor factor in plant operations.

The *Wall Street Journal* of April 8, 1982, discusses American automobile manufacturers' efforts to move in the Japanese direction. General Motors has a reported worldwide inventory of over $9 billion, with a carrying cost of over $3 billion per year. GM's automobile assembly operations require over 3000 different suppliers located all over the continent and abroad. By comparison, Toyota uses about 250 suppliers. Clearly, GM and other Detroit automobile manufacturers have locked themselves into a very complex, inventory-intensive mode of operation requiring large batch sizes, enormous storage facilities, and high transportation costs.

By allowing numerous options on cars, Detroit manufacturers have perhaps built some extra profit margin into some cars, based on labor costs, but have painted themselves into a corner from the standpoint of simplicity of business and smoothness of operation. By contrast, Japanese auto companies offer relatively few models at one time, and these have very few options that must be installed at the factory. This enables assembly operations to run far more smoothly than if every car had hundreds of options to be considered.

Another area where Japanese manufacturers have greatly increased the simplicity of their operations is by reducing setup times and eliminating work center queues through highly overlapped operations. The Kanban system operates as a "pull" system, in conjunction with very small lot sizes, to pull parts rapidly through the production system.

By simplifying the management of their manufacturing operations, many Japanese companies have been able to reduce lead times to very short periods. Toyota, for example, has a total long lead time, including time required for its suppliers to respond to significant schedule changes, of between three and four weeks. With this kind of ability to respond to the fluctuations of the marketplace, precision long-range production planning is not needed. A few critical raw materials may be long-lead-time items, and they are ordered to a long-range production plan, but these are exceptions.

To summarize, then, Japanese companies have substantially improved their ability to manage their manufacturing operations at a highly efficient level by keeping their operations, procedures, design methods, subcontracting, and production methods as simple as possible. By not requiring a single plant to make very many different products, they have kept plant sizes down and enabled each plant to reach a very high level of efficiency that comes only through specialization. Smoothness of operation brings with it substantial increases in labor and machine productivity because there are so few changes to be managed, and changes are probably the biggest trouble-causer in manufacturing.

Impact of High Quality Standards

Everyone in manufacturing has always had some degree of concern about the level of quality reflected in its products. Due to the adversarial nature of business relationships within and outside most American and European manufacturing concerns, quality has become a constantly negotiated problem. Each party seems to always be trying to get someone else to accept substandard parts. As a result, elaborate receiving inspection operations must screen not most, but all, incoming shipments at most companies. The message here is that the vendor cannot be trusted (and, in truth, he usually cannot).

Internally, for production employees, rewarded by a volume-oriented incentive system whereby someone else (in the quality assurance department) must pass judgment on his production, the same pushing match is set up. If no inspector is used, the defective parts fall into someone else's problem area farther downstream in the production process. The person who was responsible for making poor-quality parts does not see it as "his problem."

As a result, even with relatively loose quality standards, many industries consider their reject rates to be good if 90% of their parts are acceptable. What problems are caused by the remaining 10% of unacceptable parts does not even get considered (it is "someone else's problem"). Further, because reject rates often vary quite a lot, users of parts that have a typical reject or scrap rate must carry safety stock to allow for the possibility of an unusually high reject percentage in a given lot of parts. This factor further complicates the entire production process, because defective parts may not always be discovered at the time they enter the assembly process. Instead, they may turn up later at final testing, causing expensive rework.

Eliminating planning surprises: By establishing an expected, normal level of quality where virtually all parts may be considered acceptable, the Japanese have been able to eliminate virtually all receiving inspections, in-process inspections, and most rework. That this greatly reduces production costs and simplifies the planning and execution of the business goes without saying. Material planning is also simplified, since planners order only exactly as many as are needed. Planners can count on receiving the correct quantities since the expectation of quality work extends to those who count the parts (three separate counts of all parts being moved is quite common in Japanese plants); hence no safety stock to prevent unpleasant surprises is needed.

The ramifications of being able to count on virtually every part being acceptable in the production process are many. The planning process is simplified greatly: just order the exact amount required—period. This eliminates small overages that would have to be stocked (and probably lost later), or shortages that cause production problems.

The execution of a production schedule becomes simpler because if all parts can be assumed to be good, no rework planning is needed. When the product is completed, production people *know* that it will work fine. In fact, the Toyota assembly lines contain no loops for rework, as is normal for American auto manufacturing. By making *every* quality problem extremely visible, Japanese manufacturers ensure that it will be investigated thoroughly and eliminated permanently.

The benefits of very high quality standards discussed thus far are significant enough just in the inventory planning and production management areas, without even considering the benefits in the marketing areas. In industry after industry in the United States, Japanese companies have taken advantage of customer's intense dissatisfaction at products that often do not even work at delivery time, or soon need expensive, difficult-to-obtain maintenance. Whether the product is a consumer electronic item, a car, or an industrial product such as forgings or castings, no customer likes being told in effect that the seller just felt like cheating him, or that the manufacturer's inability to get the product right the first time is somehow the customer's problem.

Mostly because of this cavalier attitude about quality and customer satisfaction, even heavy industries, where shipping costs are substantial, have experienced serious competition from Japanese companies who deliver the item right the first time. Heavy castings, for example, often arrive from American foundries filled with unrepaired cracks, even sizable air bubbles (rendering the casting useless). This forces the company buying the castings to inspect carefully, repair, and possibly return almost every casting received before machining can even begin.

In contrast, Japanese companies can often deliver the same heavy castings, shipped 9000 miles, with all cracks repaired, no flaws, and even partly machined, for a lower purchase price than a local foundry.

Quality circles: After watching these kinds of events for the last 10 or 15 years, American companies are starting to wake up. One of the most popular Japanese imports has become the quality circle, or Small Group Improvement Activities, as Toyota calls them. Because their effectiveness is rooted in the cooperative aspects of Japanese culture, there is the danger that they will be misused. There are several key factors that strongly influence whether a quality circle program will be effective, including:

- Top management must understand and support the program.
- Participants must have at least basic knowledge of manufacturing engineering techniques, such as statistical analysis, data gathering, and costing techniques.
- Participation must be voluntary, not required by management.
- All feasible suggestions must be implemented as soon as possible.
- Participants must have good knowledge of the company's products, and have worked in more than one area; highly specialized participants often lack the perspective needed.
- Participants must feel committed to improvements in the company's production methods; management/supervision must not feel particularly defensive about the status quo.

A quality circle program *can* be very effective in developing many good suggestions for improvements at the detailed level needed. Honda, for instance, has what is described as an expertise program. Each worker maintains a log book containing his contributions to the company and records of his levels of expertise. The goal of every employee is to become a Honda expert. New plants are designed by low-level supervisors and foremen, not by a remote manufacturing engineering staff. The chairman of Honda (one of the company founders) describes why this approach is effective: 1000 "powers" are more effective than 100. In other words, there is a limit on how effective a few staff people can be sitting at their desks.

It is perhaps significant that Honda is the only company in the world that was not already in that business prior to World War II to enter automobile production successfully.

This is a degree of involvement in manufacturing operations that American manufacturing management can hardly imagine. Further, it blurs the distinctions between worker and manager, which today's adversary-oriented unions have trouble accepting. It seems as though the entire operation really becomes the responsibility of the workers and first-line supervisors. This is not far from the reality in Japanese companies. Production workers have full responsibility for product quality, labor efficiency, preventive and routine machine maintenance, and adherence to schedule. To the extent that other staff people, such as quality control personnel are involved, it is not in a role of primary responsibility, but advisory in nature. The staff quality assurance person advises and assists the workers in producing better parts. He does not play "let's see if I can catch you doing wrong" with the workers.

Participative Management Styles

Traditional management styles in the United States and Europe had their origins in the military. Managers were the modern versions of "natural" social leaders, and as such had prerogatives and rights not accorded to the common folk, who were expected to follow dutifully the orders of their social "betters." The repression inherent in this arrangement, of course, soon gave way to militant unionism in the United States and to socialism in Europe.

Since most of the largest companies in the United States are also the oldest, these traditions have been carried forward pretty much intact at many companies, and with only slight modifications at others. Probably the most difficult part of making a transition to a more participative mode of operation, besides developing managers with a different style, is that workers are now long accustomed to not taking any real responsibility for results. One outcome is that employees who have been at the same company for many years have often done virtually the same job, not growing or learning, but just getting paid more due to seniority "rights" garnered them by the union.

In Japanese-style management, the workers carry considerable responsibility for operational results. Each worker is, in effect, responsible for all those things that influence the results he obtains and the things he can potentially control. Since workers are not just blind servants, complete agreement as to major changes must be obtained *before* implementing any significant changes. If this approach were not followed, it would be impossible to hold the workers accountable in any kind of meaningful way for operational results.

In many Japanese companies, the quality circle/participative management effectiveness is so great that virtually all suggestions are implemented. The author recalls an experience early in his career with a company and its recently implemented suggestion program. Not only were the suggestion forms somewhat intimidating, and the boxes anonymous, but each suggestion had to be approved by not one, but two different management committees, no matter how trivial in nature. The unstated message was that management regarded employee suggestions as essentially threatening in nature, and so they would have to be carefully screened before implementation, so as to avoid upsetting management's brilliantly designed schemes. Needless to say, the company regularly lost money on major projects.

What participative management recognizes is that, at the bottom, the company consists largely of its employees. As products grow more complex and have more "intelligence content," employee motivation, skill, and knowledge become more critical as business factors. The only way to tap this resource effectively is with people's active involvement and consent. It cannot be effectively forced from people.

A high level of job security contributes a great deal to creating the kind of cooperative environment where employees can become really committed to the company and its performance. If an individual feels that his situation is tenuous, that his contribution is not especially valued by those who control his employment at the company, he will naturally withold full commitment as a matter of normal, emotional self-protection.

To obtain the full cooperation and enthusiastic motivation of employees, full employment must become a major goal for the business. This same logic holds both for individual companies and for an economy as a whole. It is probably this complete agreement on the goal of full employment by the government, business, and union sectors that makes Japanese businesses so effective; they are much less at cross-purposes than the businesses, government, and unions of other countries.

The best way to achieve full employment, whether for a company or an economy, is to always go for market share in every market that is participated in. In the short run, American companies often view this strategy as "buying" market share through giveaway, unprofitable prices. They forget that once the market is dominated, it is a lot easier to increase profitability, which of course is what the Japanese do in the long run.

Thus it appears that the strategy of participative, cooperative management styles places the needs of employees first and the demands of stockholders second. To some extent this is true. How true this may be depends on whether the stockholder's point of view is for the short- or long-term investment. In any case, at some point in its growth a company must generate sufficient profits to finance its growth, at least partially.

Considering an economy as a whole, capital in the form of savings or profits must be generated somewhere in the system. That this is the case for Japan can hardly be denied. The success of its major companies has created great wealth for the country. In the final analysis, then, a strategy consisting of going for market share first, profitability later, and making maximum use of employees' talents and energies just may be a more effective business strategy than a number of others.

Disciplined, Formal Systems

When the subject of formal systems, or high degrees of discipline, is broached to many American or European managers, the first thing that comes to mind is a fat manual full of procedures and company regulations, sort of like the post office. Employees are expected to memorize and follow an incomprehensible network of rules without deviation. If deviations do occur, "disciplinary action" or some form of punishment is to be laid on the errant employee. It is not considered important that employees understand why the rules are there, just to follow them.

Everyone knows what kind of results this approach produces in government, and few want to emulate it seriously in private business, although some try. Perhaps as a response, many companies have an undisciplined, disorganized kind of every-man-for-himself atmosphere. This is thought to be desirable because it allows the company to handle immediate changes to just about anything. In reality, the situation is often essentially out of control.

Although there are probably as many different "systems" in use in Japanese companies as there are companies, two have attracted the most attention. Kanban, already mentioned, is probably the best known. A newer system developed by Yamaha, called Synchro-MRP, is the other. Each system has its objectives, assumptions, and limitations.

KANBAN: The term "KANBAN" (pronounced more like "kunbun," with very short "a" sounds) has several meanings. In written form, "KANBAN" refers to the improvements in production brought about through the use of the kanban card system. The term "Kanban" refers to the control system itself, while "kanban" refers to the cards used in the system. As is often the case with Japanese terms, the context in which the word is used is very important.

The first thing to understand about KANBAN is that it applies largely to repetitive manufacturing environments (i.e., where discrete units are produced by methods in which the same operations are used repeatedly). A full KANBAN program requires a many-year commitment not only from top management, but at all levels of the company. As a program it includes productivity improvements, investments in different equipment, and changes in relationships between management and labor, and between the company and its customers and suppliers.

As a control system for material, Kanban is a "pull" system, in that usage of items immediately triggers upstream replenishment production. It uses two types of cards, a move card and a production card, or move kanban and production kanban. Each move card is only for a specific part number and circulates between two work centers only (the using and producing work centers). In each case, the card's quantity is one standard container's quantity. The cards, in a sense, represent the container. Thus the number of production cards in the system equal the amount of inventory authorized for the part.

Kanban card procedure: Figure 13-1 illustrates the basic move and production card flows. The key is that parts that are components for a work center are stocked in its inbound stockpoint, while those that it produces are stocked at its outbound stockpoint. The production card is, in effect, a reusable work authorization. It stays on a container of parts in the outbound stockpoint until it is picked by the using downstream work center. When the container is picked,

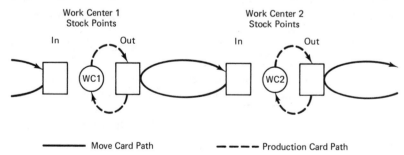

FIGURE 13-1   Kanban card procedure. (Source: Pages 22 and 23, Hall, Robert W., *Driving the Productivity Machine*, American Production & Inventory Control Society, 1981.)

the card is left behind (and placed on a production board, for example) as authorization to make another container of parts to replace the one just picked.

The move card is also attached to the container and goes with it to the inbound stockpoint at the next work center. It stays with the container until it is picked for use. At that time the move card is removed and taken back to the supplying work center (usually with an empty container) as authorization to pick another container of the part from the outbound stockpoint.

The rules for using the system are quite simple and straightforward:

- Only standard containers are to be used.
- Cards are always attached to full containers only.
- No parts may be picked without a move card.
- Using work centers must pick parts; producing work centers may not "deliver" parts.
- No production of parts without a production card.

It is vital that disciplined adherence to these rules be maintained in all cases, or the system will not work well. The amount of inventory in the system is strictly controlled by the number of cards for each part.

Requirements for Kanban effectiveness: There are several conditions that must exist for a Kanban system to work effectively, and they are peculiar to the repetitive manufacturing environment. Kanban cannot be made to work in a job shop environment. In fact, its entire effectiveness centers around its tendency to move the production of parts from a job shop mode to something resembling a process flow. These conditions are:

- The schedule must be nearly identical for each day of the schedule period, and the schedule must be absolutely frozen.
- Production must stay almost exactly on schedule every day. Even minor cumulative deviations can cause real problems and require major effort to get back on schedule.
- Not all parts can be controlled with the Kanban system, such as raw materials and large assemblies.
- A very large number of setups must be made, with lot sizes being very small, only a day's usage or so, or even less.
- As few cards as possible and the smallest containers possible should be used. The smaller the amount of inventory, the more incentive there is for streamlining production and material flow.
- Very few engineering changes, which must be hand walked through the system.
- Everything must be very visible.

Kanban, then, works well because it makes piece parts manufacturing run almost like a process plant. It encourages extensive operations overlapping, almost no queue time at all (measured as fractions of a day), and a plant layout that minimizes move time and material handling. Work centers are laid out in a logical relationship that resembles the product structure; that is, production proceeds in the same way as the parts go together, at least as much as is practical.

Figure 13-2 illustrates how work centers and suppliers are brought into a single Kanban system feeding a final assembly line. The technique for using Kanban with suppliers (or "outside makers," as the Japanese call them) is virtually identical, with numerous deliveries each day made directly to using work centers or the assembly line. There is no receiving inspection function or receiving dock.

Parts that cannot be managed with the Kanban system include large or complex assemblies; very long lead time items, such as raw materials; items with physical limitations; or items whose setup times are still inordinately long. More traditional production planning and control techniques are used with these items, such as ordering raw materials from the production plan. Items with long setup times are produced with work orders in a work center run as a job shop. Even at Toyota, which originated the system, only 60 to 70% of all parts are managed with the system.

There are several other aspects of effective KANBAN that are vital to understand. It is *not* a simple, quick project that is implemented today and shows benefits tomorrow. Actual productivity improvements come through a long series of small changes in equipment, procedures, and methods, although some inventory reduction occurs fairly early in the program. Of particular importance are dramatic reductions in setup times. These are usually difficult to come by, and often occur only after considerable analysis, experimentation, and sometimes redesign of equipment.

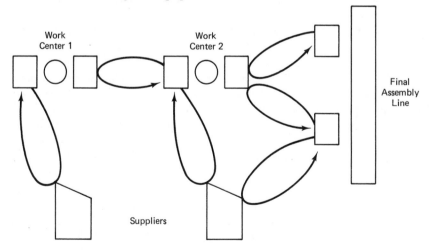

FIGURE 13-2   Kanban "pull" system linking work centers. (Source: Pages 22 and 23, Hall, Robert W., *Driving the Productivity Machine*, American Production & Inventory Control Society, 1981.)

Improvements under KANBAN come through a cyclic process of issuing the cards (prepared either manually or by computer), starting the process, and then withdrawing cards that seem not to be needed. Further card withdrawals are made that cause using work centers to experience some problems. Effort is made to develop ways to resolve these problems so that operation can continue at the lower inventory level. These changes can be of any type: setup improvements, faster production rate, or a change in equipment, for example.

Once stabilized, the cycle is restarted by withdrawing cards again. This process is repeated for all parts managed with the system, over and over again over a period of years. It leads ultimately to a substantial change in the way the entire business is operated.

Probably the most critical single aspect of KANBAN is that the schedule must be frozen and be very regular and repetitious, with every day being essentially like the previous one. The goal is to make a product mix that exactly matches the proportion in which products are selling.

In factories run under KANBAN, little or no labor efficiency reporting is done, mostly because material moves so quickly through the system that it has very little labor content; hence, labor efficiency is a minor factor in production cost.

Planning under KANBAN: KANBAN is an execution system. The production planning that drives it is relatively conventional, including long-range planning, production plans, requirements explosions (greatly simplified because every day in a schedule period is the same), and periodic negotiations with suppliers. Typically, a master schedule for three schedule periods is developed; Toyota's is three months, revised and updated once a month. The immediate future month is detailed, and once started, frozen. The other two months have less detail and are less firm.

The entire planning process, including capacity review by departments, is made much simpler because there is only one kind of schedule day in each of the three months. Department supervisors need only decide if they can produce that day's schedule. As a result, no capacity requirements planning is performed.

Material planning is similarly straightforward. Exploded requirements for the day's production yields the subassembly and component manufacturing schedule. Simply multiplying each part's daily required quantity times the number of days in the schedule period gives the total quantity of each part for the month. Finally, since every day is the same, offsetting and detailed scheduling of subassemblies is not needed.

Synchro-MRP: Companies with numerous engineering changes and a highly complex model line cannot function easily under KANBAN. The rigidity that makes it work lacks the flexibility needed to handle frequent design and model changes. Yamaha faced this situation in many of its plants. Material requirements planning can easily handle the engineering and detailed material control needed in this kind of environment, but the execution side of MRP leaves much to be desired from the Japanese point of view. Consequently, Yamaha elected to develop a system called Synchro-MRP, which combines KANBAN and MRP.

Material planning proceeds under Synchro-MRP as with any MRP system, using a master production schedule and time-phased requirements explosions. Those departments that are operated as job shops receive work orders with routings as in a typical MRP system. The difference is that departments that can be operated as repetitive manufacturing facilities use Kanban-like cards to control material movement and production. The flow between interrelated work centers is as with Kanban, as described above.

Instead of generating work orders for repetitive manufacturing departments and parts, Synchro-MRP calculates the number of Synchro cards, both move and production, needed for the schedule period. In this way, fluctuating product mixes, engineering changes, and other abrupt changes in the demand for subassemblies and components are automatically accommodated by the system.

Yamaha levels the schedule for 10-day periods. As with Kanban, each day is virtually identical. New Synchro cards are generated for each 10-day period. Two signals for additional production are used in Kanban: material available and a production card received from the downstream work center. Synchro-MRP requires in addition that a standard container(s) of the part appear on a schedule (or work order) and be shown as due on that day or time of day.

In this fashion, engineering changes can be phased in during one of the 10-day schedule periods, or at the changeovers. During a changeover, the old part number is dropped from the schedule and the new one appears. At the same time, move and production Synchro cards are generated and received in the work centers.

At a changeover the old production Synchro cards are removed from containers and new ones attached. If there are more cards than containers, the extra ones are posted on a board so that more production can be started. If there are fewer, downstream work centers must pick the cardless containers before those with cards. In this fashion, extra inventory will be used up before any further production is authorized.

The same logic applies to the move Synchro cards at a changeover. If there are not enough cards to attach to the containers at an inbound stockpoint, the work center must use up the inventory of the part before being authorized to pick another container at the supplying work center's outbound stockpoint. If there are extra cards, they are authorization to pick more containers.

Viewed in light of the functions of the Synchro cards, the MRP-produced schedule for repetitive departments acquires a different twist. In effect, it simply defines part numbers in current production. If a part number is shown as having a container due on a certain day, it will not be made unless there is at least one production Synchro card at the producing work center.

Another difference between Kanban and Synchro-MRP is that the system keeps track of the inventory balances in all the containers located at inbound and outbound stockpoints. The data-entry technique is by using scanners that read the production Synchro cards just before they are attached to containers.

At other times, material movement is tracked in and out of the plant, between plants, or during production movement by scan reading the preprinted move Synchro card. Component usage in production is relieved by backflush, or exploding the bill of material for the part just produced, then relieving the inventory balance for each component part. In this fashion, virtually all inventory movement within the Yamaha Synchro-MRP system is tracked without any keying of data at all.

For those departments operating in a job shop mode where work orders are used, operation of the system is as in a typical Class A MRP system, with bills of material, routings, dispatch lists and so on. Lot sizes, however, are always in terms of the quantity held by a standard container.

For those departments operating as repetitive centers, the Synchro card procedure just described is followed. The MRP system uses an internal flow or control order to keep track of completed production. Capacity planning is not done according to the capacity requirements planning logic described in Chapter 8, primarily since each day in a schedule is identical. Each planned 10-day schedule cycle is communicated well in advance to all departments, which are expected to protest if a proposed daily schedule is impossible.

Considered in all of its aspects, Synchro-MRP is considerably more complex than presented here. It plans and executes at a considerably more detailed level than do most American MRP systems. The power of the computer to process the enormous amount of data in this system is evident from the following. Two people prepare the master production schedule (with computer assistance) at Yamaha. When the schedule was first processed, it took over 200 hours of computer time to complete. After streamlining both the software and the system on the plant floor, this was reduced to four hours.

Common elements of Japanese systems: Both KANBAN and Synchro-MRP, as well as many other Japanese manufacturing approaches, offer several clear conclusions about how successful manufacturing operations will be managed in the future, as well as the present. All illustrate some important points, such as:

- Emphasis on reducing piece parts manufacturing to something resembling a process flow as much as possible.
- More specialization in plants and equipment.
- Highly coordinated, interlocking functioning, requiring high degrees of discipline and very accurate data.
- Very short lead times, overlapped operations, minimal setup times, and little or no queue time.

- The willingness to employ sophisticated computer systems in the management of the company as well as in the operations of automated equipment.
- Continued emphasis on keeping the plant itself and the operation as simple as possible; recognizing that complexity of operations is the enemy of efficiency.
- Continued emphasis on highly automatic production, for which labor costs are a minor factor and computers are used extensively.
- The effectiveness and virtual necessity of using very efficient operations as an integral part of the business strategy.
- A perpetual, long-term commitment to *continuous* improvements in all aspects of the business, from its systems and its employees' level of training and proficiency to the physical equipment. This is in place of the sporadic, short-term "projects" typical of many American firms.
- The necessity of gaining the active involvement and consent of employees as a necessary prerequisite of improvements in operations, whether via a better system or through changes in methods or equipment.

Many of these aspects are readily apparent in the way the Japanese have developed and implemented KANBAN, which is really a program of total improvements in quality and productivity, not just a card system, and Synchro-MRP, which has the same kind of total involvement and commitment of the whole company. Once the effectiveness of these approaches are grasped and one realizes that only a small portion of it is specifically attributable to the Japanese culture, it becomes clear that most of the outstanding results obtained by the Japanese are a consequence of good management. They were achieved by excelling at the same basics many production control people have been pushing for years (control of lead times, queues, accurate data, disciplined work force, etc.).

Worldwide Planning, Marketing, and Operations

The last insight to be gained from the Japanese success story (that will specifically be discussed here) is that of global operations. Since the domestic Japanese market is limited in size and the Japanese must import virtually every raw material they need, they were forced long ago to consider the world as their marketplace. American and European firms, by contrast, could achieve enormous growth in their domestic markets and regard exports as something to be considered when they got around to it.

As a result, Japanese firms are often very knowledgeable about the market conditions in many countries, their cultures, and what things will sell and why. The manufacturing companies of North America and Europe frequently have tailored their entire operations to a domestic market and may not have made anything that could be exported.

In a sense the remaining sections of this chapter may also be said to be about the Japanese, as they are heavily involved in the implementation and use of virtually all the concepts and approaches discussed here. However, they are not unique to Japan, and in many cases were developed first in the United States and/or Europe.

OTHER MODERN INNOVATIONS

Plant Arrangements

Laying out a plant in the form of an assembly line is a concept that probably originated with Henry Ford. There are, however, many modern twists to this old idea. Highly integrated plants such as those found in the refining and chemical industries are, in a conceptual sense, just highly integrated assembly lines.

Ford Motor Company's River Rouge plant was famous for years because it incorporates, in one enormous facility, a steel mill, manufacturing of many large assemblies, and a final assembly operation. One can only guess at the number of man-hours that went into designing its layout.

The typical manufacturing plant, however, often has job shop origins. Perhaps the owners originally were not in a single business, or were not sure where the business was going. Whatever the case, the plant layout of most companies, including some rather large ones, leaves a lot to be desired from an efficiency standpoint. Typically, machines are grouped by function, whether the company makes metal products, plastic moldings, printed circuit boards, or teddy bears. As a result, material handling time and cost account for a significant portion of total manufacturing time and cost.

In cases where a plant is built from scratch to make a specific product, plant engineers deal with this problem quite well in most cases. But few plants are built this way. Typically, there is a warehouse located separately from the manufacturing floor, sometimes at quite a distance. Work in process may often be left on the manufacturing floor, stacked up at work centers, or it may be moved off the floor into subassembly or work-in-process holding areas.

The most important outcomes from this arrangements are:

- Overlapping operations are very difficult.
- Work must be released to the floor far ahead of its due date.
- Juggling priorities of work in process is inevitable.
- Work center queues, whether physically at the work center or in a holding area, are almost unavoidable.
- There is little incentive to reduce setup times substantially; indeed, it is not even perceived as a problem.
- Material handling between operations is costly, invites problems, and delays production.
- The amount of work in process is often a substantial portion of company assets; its sheer size makes it difficult to manage well.

Warehouses usually have many of the same problems as plants laid out in the fashion described above. They are very labor intensive, with armies of fork lift trucks cruising around misplacing material and bored workers miscounting parts. If sales increase, inventory seems to go up faster, and no one ever wants to have a scrap drive to create more space in the warehouse, so it is just expanded, making the problem worse. Sometimes, a warehouse becomes so overcrowded that finding parts that everyone knows are there becomes very difficult. This situation can really sabotage the best production schedule, to say the least.

In both these areas, enlightened plant layouts and automated equipment are providing significant improvements in productivity. Developments in group technology and in automated storage and retrieval systems are discussed briefly below.

Group Technology

Strictly speaking, any time equipment used in production is arranged in the sequence in which it is actually used in the routings to make parts, so that parts flow directly from one machine to the next, it could be said to be a group technology application. However, most often people are referring to the entire activity of analyzing parts and their routings, grouping them into families of similar production flows, and then designing a machine layout for each group so that a family of items is produced in a group of machines or "cell."

The advantage of this arrangement is that piece parts production becomes repetitive, moving away from the job shop model and toward the process flow concept. In a typical group technology cell, raw material or components enter at one end and parts flow immediately and directly from one work center or machine in the cell to the next as soon as the part is completed. Usually, there is serious effort devoted to balancing the flow in the cell so that parts do not pile up or leave machines idle. The emphasis is on a fast, smooth flow of parts through the work center.

This arrangement, then, embodies the efficiency/productivity features of highly overlapped operations, zero queue time at work centers, and lends itself to automatic material handling between machines via conveyors or other devices. It will usually eliminate one or more subassembly levels in the product structure.

For example, consider a product that is made in several levels of subassembly, each of which is run in large batches, since setup times may take quite a while. This might be typical of a plastic product that is molded, assembled, and packaged. This will normally entail at least three levels of subassembly, or product structure indentures. Each level has a work order released, the machine setup, parts run, then stored for a period before being issued as components to the next higher assembly work order.

At each level there is a part number, material planning to be performed, move and queue times, and a work order to be managed. If the same part is produced in a typical group technology cell, all three machines—molding, assembling, and packaging—would be arranged in a sequence, with a material handling device between each. Setup time might be the same as when the machines were independently arranged, except that setups for all machines are made simultaneously.

Under this arrangement, once the cell is set up to produce a certain part, the raw material flows in one end of the cell and the packaged product comes out the other end. Two subassembly levels can be dispensed with, planning becomes a single-level exercise, instead of a three-level one as before, and there is only one work order instead of three. The overlapping of operations permits all production steps to occur virtually simultaneously, so that the lead time for the finished product shrinks to a matter of hours or days if the lot size is large, instead of weeks, as before.

Besides all the reduction in processing time, there is little or no material handling required between the steps. The important thing to note here is that all this can frequently be accomplished with the identical production equipment as before. It is just arranged and managed differently. Often, there may be little change in the amount of investment required to run the plant. Problems may arise in the case of highly general purpose equipment, since the assumptions of group technology do require a higher degree of dedication and specialization of production equipment than in the pure job shop model.

The discussion above is only a brief overview. A full consideration of the topic is beyond the scope of this book, and is, in any case, deeply rooted in specific products and machines. There have been some excellent techniques developed for analyzing products to develop the families of similar routings mentioned earlier. This is really the first step.

In companies where group technology has been well established for years, it has led to significant changes in the way products are designed, what kinds of options are offered, and the like, as the company's understanding of the possibilities inherent in the group technology improve. Often the first step is a radical restructuring of the product structures once the family grouping process has been completed. After the product structures are regrouped, this leads to people looking at the products' design and production differently, in turn leading to different ideas about other configurations, design improvements, simpler ways of making the product, and different production equipment.

Automated Storage/Retrieval Systems

Automated storage/retrieval (AS/R) systems are also referred to as high-rise warehouses, automatic stock picking and storage systems, and computer-managed warehouses. These systems involve specially constructed warehouse facilities in which a computer runs a system of mechanical stock storage and retrieval devices, including cranes, carts, conveyors, and other similar devices.

In a stock picking operation, for instance, the computer accepts entry of which parts are needed, keeps tracks of where it stored them, and initiates the retrieval operation automatically. The container of parts is brought to a staging area, where a person selects the correct quantity, enters the quantity, and the computer returns the container to storage. Since the system is not limited by ordinary forklift limitations, they are typically 50 to 100 feet high, making excellent use of ground space.

Incoming parts are handled similarly, with a worker entering the part number and quantity into the system as a storage container is loaded. The system moves the cart or other move device and stores the container, updating its location records for the part.

In more advanced systems, a host computer is involved in a network arrangement. The host contains the manufacturing system, with its planned order field and primary inventory records by part number. As the host system processes order releases, it internally generates a pick list. Instead of printing this pick list out on paper, then reentering it on the AS/R system computer, a linkup is established between the two computers. The host passes the pick list data to the AS/R system computer, which proceeds with the picking operation as described above. Actual parts picked data are then passed back to the host computer system, which takes any action that might be required in the manufacturing planning system, in addition to updating the master inventory records.

The processing of purchase order receipts proceeds in similar fashion, with the host system receiving and updating purchase order status information together with inventory data directly from the AS/R system computer. With this kind of arrangement, only minimal data entry is required to achieve almost complete inventory status information regarding stock in the warehouse. Since the system already knows which work orders are involved, the stock picker at the staging area need only enter the quantity picked, for example.

There are several aspects to automated warehouses that need to be considered. First, they are a major capital investment, considerably more so than a standard warehouse structure, which itself may even be a temporary building. Second, it is a highly dedicated structure that can be used for only one purpose. The company cafeteria cannot be relocated into the AS/R warehouse structure, as might be the case with a regular warehouse.

These two factors translate into the unavoidable fact that a major commitment is required by the company to construct and use one of these systems. If the market stability exists to justify it, the problem is only partly solved. This assumes, of course, that the company does not have a more advantageous use for its capital and that other methods of improving material handling productivity at a lower cost are not readily available.

The most important issue regarding automated warehouses, in the author's opinion, is whether the company is really as committed to carrying huge amounts of inventory as appears necessary. Over a period of years, a vigorous program embodying the concepts discussed throughout the book, inevitably lead to a substantial elimination of many types of inventory. Kanban-type systems essentially do away almost entirely with the need for a large, central warehouse facility.

The concern in this debate, then, is whether serious consideration of an automated warehouse may *sidetrack* management from more fundamental issues of productivity and efficiency management of the company's assets. After all, to invest heavily in equipment which permits the efficient management of another asset that, in itself, may be largely unnecessary is not the best available deployment of scarce capital.

If a Kanban-type program of productivity improvements is seriously pursued, coupled with group technology cells, and similar inventory elimination techniques, not only can the company avoid the investment and diversion of an automated warehouse, it can also eliminate the investment in inventory as well, reaping a double saving of capital, with the added benefit of higher productivity in the plant.

Returning for a moment to the opening discussion of the nature of inventory in Chapter 6, the fundamental question is still whether to have the inventory at all—if there is not some way to run the business without it. This is the goal of all inventory productivity improvements. In considering AS/R systems, every company that believes it could profitably use such a system should ask itself if it *really needs* all that inventory to run the business properly.

These deliberations should include at least the following considerations:

- Must the majority of inventory be purchased in infrequent, large lot sizes?
- Is in-plant production such that a great many parts must be made in large lot sizes with infrequent runs?
- Is there no way in which substantial improvements in productivity can be made via group technology, KANBAN concepts, MRP, or other approaches that will eliminate large amounts of inventory currently held in storage?
- In other words, is the combination of the company's production methods and supplier locations such that inventory in large amounts simply *must* be stored and handled?

If the answers to these questions are unqualified yeses, the company should consider a well-designed high-rise AS/R system. Over a period of years, there is no question that substantial savings in material handling labor, improvements in inventory accuracy, and many other benefits are available through the use of a computerized warehouse facility.

Highly Computerized Techniques

There are two major areas which specifically use very advanced computer technology: computer-aided design and computer-aided manufacturing. Each has advantages and disadvantages, costs and benefits.

Computer-aided design: Put simply, computer-aided design (CAD) systems are really automated drafting systems. They accept input via a variety of means, such as joy sticks, light pens, keyboard entry, and others to create a numeric version of a graphic display. Once the data are created on disk, they can be modified, analyzed, or manipulated in a variety of ways.

To understand what is going on in these systems, and just how computer intensive they are, it should be remembered that each point on the screen of a graphic display is a separate data item, a coordinate that is processed separately. Various programs are used to change these values as the display is processed for display, modification, or prepared for output to a printing or plotting (drawing) device.

The more complete CAD systems allow a wide range of outputs. Besides the geometric models stored as data on disk, data can also be linked to parts in the model to include materials, properties, and dimension data. Also, the part numbers assigned to each part of the assembly drawing can be output directly to a part number and/or product structure data base. Of course, the models themselves can be output by a plotter, which actually draws the model on paper, vellum, or plastic film.

One of the most important uses of these geometric models on disk are for various engineering studies which can be performed on the model data, especially if data on materials and properties are included. Sophisticated programs can perform a wide range of static and dynamic stress analysis calculations to identify potential design problems long before a prototype has ever been made. To complete processing of this sort, a stress analysis program will perform a very large number of mathematical calculations, and then turn the result into a modified graphic display and/or drawing of the original geometric model, highlighting the distortions induced by the calculated stress.

With this kind of computer assistance, the design engineer can literally see on a drawing the effect of various kinds of stress or loads. Some systems will display different stress levels in terms of different colors.

Other examples of CAD applications include interconnection analyses, interference analyses, and various types of electrical or electronic circuitry design systems. Each system has its advantages, features, and limitations. All graphic display systems that perform these kinds of functions, especially if high degrees of display resolution are required, involve equipment that is still relatively expensive and which consumes fairly large amounts of computer power. The technology advances, however, at a rapid pace, with the availability of various kinds of peripheral devices to off-load the central computer and improve resolution.

A full-blown CAD system, including software, may cost as much as $500,000 or more. Companies still need to examine their needs and the potential productivity of a system carefully before investing in these systems. As with other computer applications involving special-purpose equipment, downstream company changes or new technology may make it obsolete or of diminished utility sooner than is apparent.

For example, most CAD systems are stand-alone, in that they are not really designed to communicate data to another computer system. If a company purchases such a system, then later decides to have it output part and product structure data to a host computer's manufacturing system, there may be significant technical hurdles to overcome. Another variation on this is that software is now becoming available that can take the CAD system's geometric data and construct a numerically controlled program to make the part on a computer-operated piece of production equipment.

If these kinds of link-ups cannot be easily made due to equipment or software incompatibilities, it may severely diminish the usefulness of the original investment in the CAD and/or CAM system in that potential productivity will be lost. The solution? Plan ahead.

Computer-aided manufacturing: Early versions of computer-aided manufacturing (CAM) were usually referred to as numerical control (NC) machines. Special software is used to write programs controlling physical movements of tooling on a machine tool controlled by a small computer. This area has now grown into a highly sophisticated form of process control in some companies, where several hierarchical levels of computers may be in use to control manufacturing operations. Besides machine tools, the area now includes robotics, an entirely separate branch of CAM.

Continuous process control facilities, such as chemical plants, are run almost entirely by computers and the systems usually include various scheduling functions as well as those that turn valves and relays on and off. In these cases, the system itself is entirely tailored to the plant's physical facilities and the products that are to be produced with those facilities. This may involve an enormous amount of programming effort and software that must be essentially error-free and fail-safe in many cases.

In the case of computer-operated machine tools, the most important aspect to understand is that unless some type of interface function that develops NC programs from CAD geometric model data is available, someone must write a separate program for each part that is to be produced on the machine. This may be relatively simple or complex, depending on the part, the machine tool, and the software used to write the program. A given program can be used only to make a specific part on a specific machine controlled by a specific kind of computer.

Robotics: This area is a special case of CAM. Robots typically are used to perform manufacturing steps in which some kind of handling is required. The machines are often distinguished by their ability to reach and grasp and perform arm- and hand-like motions. Typical robot applications include welding and painting and material handling tasks in hostile environments. A robot may be so special purpose in nature that a tool is built into it, or it may be so general purpose that it has appendages that do virtually anything in the way of material handling and manipulation.

Changes in Product Design

Over the past 10 or 15 years, products typically made by manufacturing companies for worldwide markets have undergone a number of changes. Many of these affect the ability of existing companies to design, produce, and market efficiently in world markets. Some companies have become so fossilized that it is just a matter of time before they cease to function, whereas others are viable and highly dynamic organizations. Some of these changes have reduced the power or advantages that previously kept a company in the lead in its industry. Included in these changes are:

- More "intelligence" in the product; it is more likely to be clever and to require intelligence to produce and use it. Sophisticated manufacturing techniques may be required even to make it at all.
- More thought is going into designs than in the past. Advanced materials technology is coming into play, and fewer items are made out of "plain" materials such as steel or aluminum. To be competitive, designs must now be more efficient in their use of material, the space they take up, or their expected durability.
- More complexity, both in design and production, with many more parts, each of greater manufacturing complexity in the processes used to make it and the materials.
- Literally thousands of products now contain microprocessors or small "smart" chips of various sorts. Now, only the product gets used; in the future it may do things all by itself.
- There is a pronounced move away from commodity-type products and toward those in which a high level of customer service is involved. This is especially true of engineering-oriented companies, in which the use and servicing of the product may become very important to the business health of the customer. This is also stimulated by the sheer complexity of many products in that they require continual retraining of operators to be used effectively.
- The existence of worldwide markets requires companies to design a basic set of products with numerous variations and options for different world market segments.
- The cost of labor is becoming less all the time, not because people are being paid less, but because production facilities are becoming more automated. The production cost of products therefore contains more and more fixed costs, due to capital-intensive production, and less and less labor content. Labor efficiency systems become less important as management tools.
- The manufacturing cost of many products continues to drop, due primarily to automated production systems and the kind of incredibly efficient production management methods described in this book. There is just less and less room

for the kind of company that goes on with the old management methods, passing its cost increases on to buyers without much thought.

All these changes combine to require that successful companies of the future commit themselves heavily to ongoing programs of internal improvements, continuous product design innovation, and a worldwide viewpoint on operations. Engineering and intelligence of design will continue to be factors of major significance in most major markets, and will become even more important in the future.

Truly International Operations

As has been said frequently in this book, more and more of the manufacturing scene is being dominated by companies that have learned how to operate successfully in many countries and may not even be based especially in a single country. These management skills include:

- Market research for major markets, not just a big domestic market.
- The ability to manage pricing and costs in many currencies without experiencing losses.
- Financing operations using funds sources from more than one nation. It is becoming increasingly common for companies to raise debt and equity capital in countries other than those where they are based.
- Sources of supply of both raw materials and manufactured parts are increasingly international as competition intensifies for best pricing and quality.
- Knowledge of transportation systems and costs is becoming more important; air travel and shipping has become a routine fact of life almost everywhere in the world.
- Effective communication systems, both in the traditional sense (voice and text) and data communications as well. As more and more of the world's activities include or are run by computers, software and data become more significant as factors in an international company's ability to compete on a global scale.

Coupled with these international factors is improved forecasting and planning techniques, which depend on being able to gather and process very large amounts of accurate economic data using sophisticated econometric modeling techniques. One of the factors in the current business climate is that, in effect, everyone reads the same mail and watches the same television programs. When a market goes bad, everyone finds out very quickly, and when there is an upturn, the rush is on as soon as word hits the 5 o'clock news.

Managers often are able to use sophisticated decision support systems as aids in long- and intermediate-range planning. These systems help make decisions in areas that previously required only hunches and a willingness to gamble. More quantifiable data are now available for intelligent analysis in sufficient time to help the decision-making process.

As with any other set of business factors, these blend with other more typical business skills in determining which companies, and even nations, will prosper. Economic competition and financial factors, credit, manufacturing, and rights to markets are tending to replace ships, planes, and tanks as tools of international diplomacy to an extent never before imagined. Volumes of money crossing borders are now such that almost daily monitoring of national cash flow and currency balances is needed by most countries. Only time will tell whether the outcome is a more harmonious or more confrontational world.

CHAPTER 13 QUESTIONS

1. What are the five major areas where Japanese manufacturing companies have performed especially well?
2. What does "simplify the business" mean? Give some examples.
3. What improvements can occur in a manufacturing operation where acceptable part quality can be virtually assumed 100% of the time?
4. Is high quality a business simplifier? Why?
5. Describe the ripple effect of poor quality purchased items on the manufacturing operation, especially its ability to perform to schedule.
6. What are the six factors required for a quality circle program to be effective?
7. Why are these factors so important? What is the underlying thread in human behavior?
8. Describe several primary characteristics of participative management styles.
9. Why is participative management so powerful when properly handled?
10. Is a disciplined, formal system at odds with participative management goals? Explain.
11. In what manufacturing environment does KANBAN function best? What are the characteristics of this environment?
12. Distinguish between KANBAN, Kanban, and kanban.
13. Why is Kanban, termed a "pull" system?
14. What are the five rules for using a Kanban system?
15. Identify at least six conditions required for a Kanban system to be effective.
16. What are the benefits of not having a receiving inspection function or a receiving dock?
17. Identify several examples of parts that cannot be managed with the Kanban system.
18. Describe the process by which improvements are actually achieved through the use of a Kanban system.
19. What type of schedule condition is required for Kanban to work?
20. What happens to labor reporting under a Kanban system? Why?
21. Is the production planning found in companies using Kanban systems greatly different from non-Kanban companies?

22. Why is Kanban called an execution system? How does it eliminate the need for much planning?

23. Briefly describe how Synchro-MRP combined elements of both MRP and Kanban.

24. What is the role of standard containers in Kanban type systems?

25. Identify at least eight of the common elements of Japanese systems that have been directly responsible for high productivity.

26. Why are global planning, marketing, and operations important to Japanese industry, and why is it a competitive advantage in many industries?

27. What are some of the important outcomes resulting from the typical job-shop, random or functional work center plant layout? Identify at least five.

28. Briefly explain what group technology is, and how it differs from the random or functional work center plant layout.

29. How does group technology facilitate the high productivity, low inventory features of highly overlapped operations, and zero queue times?

30. Describe the arguments for and against automated storage/retrieval systems.

31. What are some of the considerations that should be included in analysis of a proposed AS/R system?

32. Why are computer-aided design systems so computer intensive?

33. What are some of the uses and advantages of a CAD system? How does one justify their cost?

34. What is computer-aided manufacturing? How does robotics relate to CAM?

35. What computer functions would be required for a factory to be run under complete computer control, i.e., the planning and scheduling system also runs automated equipment that operates under local, dedicated processors?

36. Identify and briefly discuss at least five of the important changes in product design that are increasingly part of the manufacturing environment and marketplace.

37. What are some of the management skills that are needed to operate effectively as a truly international company?

Bibliography

Chapter 3

1. *Fundamentals of Marketing,* William J. Stanton, McGraw-Hill, New York, 1964.
2. *Management,* Harold Koontz, Cyril O'Donnell, and Heinz Weihrich, McGraw-Hill, New York, 1980.
3. *Strategy and Policy,* Donald L. Bates and David L. Eldredge, William C. Brown, Dubuque, Iowa, 1980.
4. *Production and Inventory Control Handbook,* ed. James H. Greene, McGraw-Hill, New York, 1970.
5. "Marketing Myopia," Theodore Levitt, in "Business Classics," *Harvard Business Review,* 1975.
6. "Kill the Informal Forecast," Michael Webber, APICS 22nd Annual Conference Proceedings, 1979.
7. "Master Scheduling—The Bridge between Marketing and Manufacturing," Michael G. Tincher, APICS 24th Annual Conference Proceedings, 1981.
8. "Master Scheduling Requires Time Fences," John F. Proud, APICS 24th Annual Conference Proceedings, 1981.
9. "MRP to BRP, the Journey of the 80's," Terry R. Schultz, APICS 24th Annual Conference Proceedings, 1981.

Chapter 4

1. *Production and Inventory Control Handbook,* ed. James H. Greene, Mc-Graw-Hill, New York, 1970.

2. *Structuring the Bill of Material,* Joseph A. Orlicky, George W. Plossl, and Oliver W. Wight, IBM, White Plains, N.Y., 1973.

3. *Bill of Materials: The Key Building Block,* Richard W. Bourke, Bourke & Associates, Pasadena, Ca. 1975.

Chapters 5 and 6

1. *Production and Inventory Control Handbook,* ed. James H. Greene, McGraw-Hill, New York, 1970.

Chapter 7

1. *Material Requirements Planning,* Joseph A. Orlicky, McGraw-Hill, New York, 1974.

2. *Production and Inventory Control Handbook,* ed. James H. Greene, McGraw-Hill, New York, 1970.

3. "The ABC's of DRP," Cary M. Root, Andre J. Martin, and Paul N. Lomas, APICS 22nd Annual Conference Proceedings, 1979.

Chapter 8

1. *Production and Inventory Control Handbook,* ed. James H. Greene, McGraw-Hill, New York, 1970.

2. "Resource Requirements Planning," Robert E. Bechler, APICS 23rd Annual Conference Proceedings, 1980.

3. "On the Advisability of Operation Due Dates," John J. Kanet, APICS 23rd Annual Conference Proceedings, 1980.

4. "Queue Control: Utopia...or Pie in the Sky," Neville P. May, APICS 23rd Annual Conference Proceedings, 1980.

5. "Work Order Management, Key to Shop Floor Success," Edward J. Folse, APICS 23rd Annual Conference Proceedings, 1980.

6. "Input/Output Control: Making It Work," Ray Lankford, APICS 23rd Annual Conference Proceedings, 1980.

7. "Adjust Your Capacity, Do *NOT* Reschedule Your Shop Orders," Robert L. VanDeMark, APICS 24th Annual Conference Proceedings, 1981.

8. "Resource Requirements Planning and Capacity Requirements Planning—The Case for Each and Both," F. John Sari, APICS 24th Annual Conference Proceedings, 1981.

Chapter 9

1. "Performance Measurement," David W. Buker, APICS 23rd Annual Conference Proceedings, 1980.

Chapter 10

1. "The Demise of Traditional Cost Accounting," James F. Brace, APICS 23rd Annual Conference Proceedings, 1980.

2. "Shop Floor Controls: Closing the Financial Loop," David O. Nelleman, APICS 23rd Annual Conference Proceedings, 1980.

3. *Handbook of Business Formulas and Controls,* Spencer A. Tucker, McGraw-Hill, New York, 1979.

Chapter 11

1. "Materials Management Education—It Isn't Enough," Robert W. Wheatley, APICS 22nd Annual Conference Proceedings, 1979.

2. "Education: Playing the Second Fiddle," Vinnie Chopra, APICS 23rd Annual Conference Proceedings, 1980.

3. "Gaining and Retaining Management Commitment," Thomas L. Glaza, APICS 23rd Annual Conference Proceedings, 1980.

4. "Education of the People, by the People, and for the People," Carol Saunders and Steve McDonnell, APICS 24th Annual Conference Proceedings, 1981.

5. "Education—The Key to MRP Success," E. M. Barnett, APICS 24th Annual Conference Proceedings, 1981.

6. "Why Not Educate?" Mel Nelson, APICS 24th Annual Conference Proceedings, 1981.

Chapter 12

1. *Computer Data Management and Data Base Technology,* Harry Katzan, Jr., Van Nostrand Reinhold, New York, 1975.

Chapter 13

1. *Driving the Productivity Machine: Production Planning and Control in Japan,* Robert W. Hall, APICS 24th Annual Conference Proceedings, 1981.

2. "Mass Production and the One Plant Concept," Robert W. Hall and Robert B. Piepmeier, APICS International Conference Proceedings, 1978.

3. "Automated Storage and Retrieval Work-in-Process Capacity," James M. Schelle, APICS 24th Annual Conference Proceedings, 1981.

4. "Repetitive versus Discrete Manufacturing: A Middle of the Road Approach," Patrick J. Bettini, APICS 24th Annual Conference Proceedings, 1981.

5. "Closed Loop Systems in Japan: Techniques of Worldwide Applicability," Leighton F. Smith and Roy L. Harmon, APICS 24th Annual Conference Proceedings, 1981.

6. "KANBAN (Just in Time) Applications at Kawasaki, USA," Richard J. Schonberger, Doug Sutton, and Jerry Claunch, APICS 24th Annual Conference Proceedings, 1981.

Index